Selected Letters of Charlotte Brontë

Chalk drawing of Charlotte Brontë by George Richmond, 1850.

Selected Letters
of Charlotte Brontë

EDITED BY

MARGARET SMITH

OXFORD

UNIVERSITY PRESS

OXFORD

UNIVERSITY PRESS

Great Clarendon Street, Oxford ox2 6dp

Oxford University Press is a department of the University of Oxford.
It furthers the University's objective of excellence in research, scholarship,
and education by publishing worldwide in

Oxford New York

Auckland Cape Town Dar es Salaam Hong Kong Karachi
Kuala Lumpur Madrid Melbourne Mexico City Nairobi
New Delhi Shanghai Taipei Toronto

With offices in

Argentina Austria Brazil Chile Czech Republic France Greece
Guatemala Hungary Italy Japan Poland Portugal Singapore
South Korea Switzerland Thailand Turkey Ukraine Vietnam

Oxford is a registered trade mark of Oxford University Press
in the UK and in certain other countries

Published in the United States
by Oxford University Press Inc., New York

British Library Cataloguing in Publication Data

Data available

Library of Congress Cataloging in Publication Data

Data available

Typeset by Laserwords Private Limited, Chennai, India
Printed in Great Britain
on acid-free paper by
Biddles Ltd, King's Lynn, Norfolk

ISBN 978-0-19-920587-5

1 3 5 7 9 10 8 6 4 2

ACKNOWLEDGEMENTS

I am especially grateful to the Brontë Society for their permission to publish transcriptions of many of the manuscript letters in the Bonnell, Grolier, Seton-Gordon, and Brontë Society collections, and for the prompt and courteous response of the staff of the Brontë Parsonage Museum to my requests. I also thank the Society and staff for providing and allowing me to reproduce the photographs that enhance this selection. George Richmond's memorable portrait of Charlotte Brontë is reproduced by kind permission of the National Portrait Gallery, London.

I acknowledge with thanks the permission of the following libraries to reproduce my transcriptions of manuscripts in their collections: the Bodleian Library, Oxford, for Autograph b.9 no. 264; the British Library for manuscripts in Ashley MSS 161, 164,172, 2452 and in Additional MSS 38732 and 39763; the Syndics of the Fitzwilliam Museum, Cambridge, to whom rights in this publication are assigned, for six manuscript letters; and the Houghton Library, Harvard University, for five manuscript letters in the Harry Elkins Widener Collection, and three letters with the call number MS Eng. 871. I thank Richard Workman and the Harry Ransom Humanities Research Center for their acknowledgement of my notification of intent to quote from or publish manuscripts in the Research Center Collection. I am grateful to Mr Peter Henderson, Walpole Librarian, for permission to publish a letter in the Hugh Walpole Collection at the King's School, Canterbury. For permission to reproduce letters in their respective collections, I thank David S. Zeidberg, Director, and the Huntington Library, San Marino, California; Wayne Furman, the Berg Collection of English and American Literature and the Carl H. Pforzheimer Collection of Shelley and his Circle, the New York Public Library, Astor, Lenox and Tilden Foundations, Charles E. Pierce, Jr., and the Pierpont Morgan Library, New York; Margaret Sherry Rich and Princeton University Library, for letters in the Robert H. Taylor Collection and the Morris L. Parrish Collection of Victorian Novelists, Manuscripts Division, Department of Rare Books and Special Collections. The letter from Charlotte Brontë to Elizabeth Gaskell of 27 August 1850 in the Devonshire Collection, Chatsworth, is published by permission of the Duke of Devonshire. The arrangement of this volume owes much to Alan G. Hill's exemplary selected *Letters of William Wordsworth* (Oxford: Oxford University Press, 1984).

Finally, I thank Andrew McNeillie, Jacqueline Baker, and Elizabeth Robottom for their encouragement and advice, and I gratefully acknowledge Sylvie Jaffrey's meticulous copy editing, and Ruth Freestone King's proof reading.

CONTENTS

LIST OF LETTERS

LIST OF ILLUSTRATIONS

(Frontispiece) Chalk drawing of Charlotte Brontë by George Richmond, 1850. © National Portrait Gallery, London.

1. Haworth Parsonage: ambrotype photograph taken before 1861. Brontë Parsonage Museum. © The Brontë Society.

2. Watercolour portrait of Anne Brontë by Charlotte Brontë, 17 June 1834. Brontë Parsonage Museum, C21. © The Brontë Society.

3. Self-portrait in pencil by Branwell Brontë, c.1840. Brontë Parsonage Museum, Bonnell 18 verso. © The Brontë Society.

4. Pencil engraving of the 'Gun group' by Branwell Brontë, showing Anne, Charlotte, Branwell, and Emily Brontë. Brontë Parsonage Museum. © The Brontë Society.

5. Photograph of the Revd Patrick Brontë in old age. Brontë Parsonage Museum. © The Brontë Society.

6. The last page of Charlotte Brontë's letter to Ellen Nussey of 6 March 1843, including a sketch of herself waving goodbye to Ellen across the sea from Belgium. Brontë Parsonage Museum, MS B.S. 50.4. © The Brontë Society.

7. A drawing of Ellen Nussey as a young girl; artist unknown. Brontë Parsonage Museum. © The Brontë Society.

8. Photograph of Ellen Nussey in old age. Brontë Parsonage Museum. © The Brontë Society.

9. Pencil portrait of the Revd William Weightman by Charlotte Brontë, February 1840. Brontë Parsonage Museum. © The Brontë Society.

10. Portrait of George Smith as a young man. Brontë Parsonage Museum. © The Brontë Society.

11. Photograph of William Smith Williams. Brontë Parsonage Museum. © The Brontë Society.

12. Charlotte Brontë's first letter to Smith, Elder and Company, 15 July 1847, sending them the manuscript of *The Professor*. MS BPM SG 1. © The Brontë Society.

13. Carte-de-visite photograph of Charlotte Brontë, 1854, inscribed on the reverse in ink, 'within a year of CB's death'. Seton-Gordon Collection, Brontë Parsonage Museum, SG 109(a). © The Brontë Society.

14. Carte-de-visite photograph of the Revd A. B. Nicholls, taken at about the time of his marriage to Charlotte Brontë. Brontë Parsonage Museum. © The Brontë Society.

ABBREVIATIONS AND SYMBOLS

Berg	Henry W. and Albert A. Berg Collection, New York Public Library, Astor, Lenox and Tilden Foundations
BL	British Library
Bon	Bonnell Collection, Brontë Parsonage Museum, Haworth
BPM	Brontë Parsonage Museum, Haworth
BS	Brontë Society
BST	*Brontë Society Transactions*. References are to volume, part, and page(s).
CB	Charlotte Brontë
CBCircle	Clement K. Shorter, *Charlotte Brontë and her Circle* (1896)
CBL	*The Letters of Charlotte Brontë*, ed. Margaret Smith (Oxford: Clarendon Press); 3 vols., 1995, 2000, 2004
Clarendon	The Clarendon edition of the novels of the Brontës (Oxford), 1969–92
CP	*The Letters of Mrs Gaskell*, ed. J. A. V. Chapple and Arthur Pollard (Manchester, 1966)
EN	Ellen Nussey
Fitzwilliam	Fitzwilliam Museum, Cambridge
Gaskell *Life*	E. C. Gaskell, *The Life of Charlotte Brontë*, 2 vols. (1857)
Gr.	Grolier Collection, Brontë Parsonage Museum
HM	MS in Huntington Library, San Marino, California
Horsfall Turner	See *Nussey*, below
JE	*Jane Eyre*
Law-Dixon	MS formerly in the collection of Sir Alfred J. Law, at Honresfeld, Littleborough, Lancs., present location unknown
Lowell, Harvard	Amy Lowell Collection, Harvard University Library

Nussey	*The Story of the Brontës: Their Home, Haunts, Friends and Works. Part Second—Charlotte's Letters* (Printed for J. Horsfall Turner; Bingley, 1885–9) (The suppressed edition.)
Parrish Collection, Princeton	Morris L. Parrish Collection of Victorian Novelists, Manuscripts Division, Department of Rare Books and Special Collections, Princeton University Library
Pforzheimer	Pforzheimer Collection, New York Public Library
Pierpont Morgan	Pierpont Morgan Library, New York
Ray *Letters*	*The Letters and Private Papers of William Makepeace Thackeray*, ed. Gordon N. Ray; 4 vols. (1945)
Rylands	John Rylands University Library, Manchester
Rylands MS *Life*	E. C. Gaskell, manuscript of the *Life* of CB, in Rylands
SG	Seton-Gordon Collection, Brontë Parsonage Museum
Smith, 'Recollections'	George Smith, 'Recollections of a long and busy life'; typescript in the National Library of Scotland, MSS 23191–2
Taylor Collection, Princeton	Robert H. Taylor Collection, Princeton University
Tenant	Anne Brontë, *The Tenant of Wildfell Hall*
Texas	The Harry Ransom Humanities Research Center, University of Texas at Austin
WH	*Wuthering Heights*
Widener, Harvard	The Harry Elkins Widener Collection, Harvard University Library
Wise & Symington	*The Brontës: Their Lives, Friendships and Correspondence*, edited by T. J. Wise and J. A. Symington; 4 vols. (Oxford, 1932)

Symbols

< >	deleted in MS by author
[ ]	added by editor
**	placed before and after conjectural readings of phrases deleted by Ellen Nussey

INTRODUCTION

In his introduction to Charlotte Brontë's 'Emma', her never-to-be-completed last work, W. M. Thackeray wrote, 'Who that has known her books has not admired the artist's noble English, the burning love of truth, the bravery, the simplicity, the indignation at wrong, the eager sympathy, the pious love and reverence, the passionate honour, so to speak, of the woman?' Recalling his first meeting with the tiny little authoress, he remembered her 'impetuous honesty'. Many of these qualities are evident too in her letters. And there are others: her passionate truth may be leavened by an unexpected sense of humour or a lively self-mockery, her critiques of the books she read may be wittily acerbic, and her accounts of some of the key episodes in her life, such as her first meeting with her publishers, or Arthur Nicholls's proposal of marriage, are brilliantly dramatic.

At their best Charlotte's letters have the immediacy of good conversation—a quality she relished in those she received. Your letter 'is just written as I wish you to write to me—not a detail too much . . . I imagine your face—voice—presence very plainly when I read your letters', she wrote to Ellen Nussey on 19 January 1847 after sixteen years of close friendship. Most of Charlotte's surviving letters were written to Ellen, whom she had first met at Margaret Wooler's school at Roe Head, Mirfield, in 1831. Charlotte realized Ellen's limitations, but enjoyed her company: 'Just now I am enjoying the treat of my friend Ellen's society,' Charlotte wrote to her publisher's reader, W. S. Williams, on 3 January 1850, 'and she makes me indolent and negligent . . . no new friend, however lofty or profound in intellect . . . could be to me what Ellen is, yet she is no more than a conscientious, observant, calm, well-bred Yorkshire girl. She is without romance—if she attempts to read poetry—or poetic prose aloud—I am irritated and deprive her of the book . . . but she is good—she is true—she is faithful and I love her.' The two friends continued to write freely to each other for the rest of Charlotte's life, save for one serious estrangement from July 1853 until February 1854. This was caused by Ellen's jealousy of the curate Arthur Nicholls, who had usurped her privileged first place in Charlotte's affection. The rift was healed through the mediation of Margaret Wooler, Ellen was the bridesmaid at Charlotte's marriage to Arthur Nicholls on 29 June 1854, and their correspondence continued until early March 1855. After that date Charlotte, already mortally ill, had to ask Nicholls to write on her behalf.

Though we learn comparatively little of Charlotte's intellectual life from her letters to Ellen, they provide much insight into other facets of her personality and experience. In many intimate, spontaneous letters, she shares with Ellen the intense moods of adolescence: at one extreme her despair over her own spiritual crises, at the other her amusement, impatience, or excitement, often expressed with a racy disregard for ladylike reserve, or her fierce indignation at

unworthy or immoral behaviour. We hear of the joyous companionship of the
sisters at Haworth parsonage before they separated to suffer the torments of
governess-life, and before the agonizing years when first Branwell Brontë, then
Emily, then Anne fell ill and died. Ellen is told about the short-lived exhilaration
of Charlotte's early months in the Brussels pensionnat, and the later 'dreary
weight' of depressing solitude and of distrust of Mme Heger. Understandably the
strength of Charlotte's attraction to M. Heger remains concealed; but she gives
remarkably candid accounts of her reactions to some of the men who found her
attractive or proposed to her: the earnest Revd Henry Nussey in March 1839, the
lively Revd David Pryce in August the same year; and later, in 1851, James Taylor,
who seems to have drawn back from an outright proposal. From Charlotte's
letters to Ellen we learn much about contemporary provincial life: about the
difficulties of travel, the novelty of the railways, the friendly exchanges of long
visits, the financial crises in households of women; the custom of 'bride-visits',
the Whitsuntide celebrations and processions of parishioners, the lectures at
mechanics' institutes. Inevitably, we hear too of the frightening prevalence of
TB, the ravages of cholera, and the ineffectiveness of contemporary medicines
for such diseases.

The letters Charlotte wrote to her father show her constant concern for his
welfare, her understanding of his interests, and her awareness of his pride in her
achievements. Writing from London in June 1850, she describes with wonderful
vividness the animals and birds she has seen and heard in the Zoological Gardens,
and some of the pictures in the London exhibitions, such as John Martin's 'The
Last Man' 'shewing the red sun, fading out of the sky and all the foreground
made up of bones and skulls'. In other letters she tells him of her meetings with
famous writers, such as Thackeray and Mrs Gaskell, and of seeing 'great lords
and ladies'. In June 1851 she evokes for him the strange grandeur of the Crystal
Palace, where the 'living tide of people rolls on quietly—with a deep hum like
the sea heard from a distance'.

Charlotte's letters to her sister Emily show the close bond of affection between
them. From her 'house of bondage' as a governess in the service of the Sidgwicks
at Stonegappe, she writes in a brief note: 'Mine bonnie love, I was as glad of
your letter as tongue can express,' and in a letter included here, she voices her
furious resentment at the injustice of her situation, where complaints about
those 'riotous, perverse, unmanageable cubs', her pupils, bring only black looks
from their mother. Like Emily, when she is away from Haworth, she longs
for liberty and home. To Emily also she writes from Mme Heger's school in
Brussels, in one letter frankly describing the teachers who 'hate each other like
two cats' and in a second, written after her nightmarish experience of silence
and solitude during the long vacation, Charlotte describes her 'real confession'
in the church of Sainte-Gudule, as well as her determination not to return
to the priest who would try to convince her 'of the error and enormity of

being a Protestant'. A confidential letter written on 1 May 1843 from Brussels to her brother Branwell condemns 'the phlegmatic, false inhabitants' of the school—with the 'sole veritable exception' of the 'black Swan Mr Heger'. Branwell had been Charlotte's close collaborator in the endless web of their Angrian saga: their joint creation of fantastically glamorous Byronic heroes, heroines, and villains, embroiled in love and war. She did not know that her brother, now a tutor in the Robinson family at Thorp Green in Yorkshire, was entangling himself, allegedly, in an affair with his employer's wife, which would lead to his disgrace and dismissal.

Yet Charlotte herself had become infatuated with her teacher, M. Constantin Heger, who was happily married to the efficient directress of the Brussels pensionnat, Mme Claire Zoë Heger. Only four of the many letters she wrote to him after her return to England survive. Written in French, the language they had used in his lessons and conversations, they reveal her longing for his assurance of continuing friendship for her. Her last surviving letter to him, written on 18 November 1845, is one of scarcely controlled emotion: when, day after day, the long-awaited letter from her master fails to come, she is in a fever: 'je perds l'appétit et le sommeil—je dépéris'.

Certainly Madame Heger read these too-revealing letters, which were not known in their entirety to the general public until 1913. Mrs Gaskell had incorporated carefully chosen excerpts from them in her life of Charlotte Brontë in 1857, including nothing that would sully her pure image. But on 6 June 1913 the Heger family offered the letters to the British Museum, not to arouse but to quash speculation about the relationship; and the family gave permission for the letters to be published in full in The Times for 29 July 1913, with translations and an explanation by the art critic Marion H. Spielmann, who believed that English people would understand that they simply expressed Charlotte's honest admiration and gratitude.

It is fair to assume that none of Charlotte's own family read the letters to Heger during her lifetime, though her father and A. B. Nicholls were to read Mrs Gaskell's excerpts from them in the Life. But they could read Villette before her death and The Professor after it; and one wonders what they made of the master–pupil relationship in those novels—one ending in brief bliss destroyed by the dividing sea, and the other in the wish-fulfilment of perfect marriage.

Charlotte had completed her fair copy of The Professor (originally entitled 'The Master') by 27 July 1846, having incorporated in the early chapters material deriving from her juvenile tales. She and Branwell had both exploited the dramatic potential of a complex relationship between two brothers, one violent, materialistic, and cynical, the other cloaking his determination to resist tyranny beneath a cool, taciturn exterior until he breaks out of his servitude and makes his own way in the world. Such breaking out reflected Charlotte's own longing to fulfil herself as a writer. In 1836 she had written to the poet Robert Southey,

enclosing some of her poems and acknowledging her bold ambition to be 'for
ever known' as a poetess. Warned by him to put her 'proper duties' as a woman
first, and to write 'poetry for its own sake ... not with a view to celebrity',
Charlotte was sincerely grateful for his 'kind & wise advice' and his opinion
that her poems were not without merit. In fact few of her poems exceed this
modest standard; no one remembers her primarily for her verse. But when
Hartley Coleridge, the son of S. T. Coleridge, disparaged the prose tale she sent
him in 1840, she was evidently piqued by his discouraging response. No doubt
the story she sent him was immature; but despite her acknowledgement that
she was obliged for his 'kind and candid letter', her reply, both in its draft form
and in her fair copy of 10 December 1840, is couched in a sardonic, flamboyant,
hardly respectful style. She mocks the absurdity, real or pretended, of the 'great'
novelists, as well as her own literary ambitions. Fortunately for posterity, she
and her sisters possessed a creative genius which could not be permanently
suppressed or discouraged.

Nevertheless the sisters had to pay for the printing, publication, and advertising
of their first book, *Poems* by Currer, Ellis, and Acton Bell, in 1846. Some of
Charlotte's letters to the publishers, Aylott & Jones, are included in this selection.
Writing as 'C. Brontë' on behalf of 'three persons—relatives' whose 'separate
pieces are distinguished by their respective signatures', Charlotte fulfilled the
'Bells'' ambition of 'appearing before the public'. The series of letters to Aylott
& Jones began on 28 January 1846; and the little volume stole into life on or soon
after 22 May that year. Now one of the most sought-after of collectors' volumes,
the book achieved a sale of only two copies, though discerning reviews appeared
in *The Critic* and *The Athenaeum* on 4 July and in *The Dublin University Magazine*
for October 1846; and the authors' autographs were requested by one satisfied
purchaser, the songwriter Frederick Enoch.

On 6 April 1846, about six weeks before the poems appeared, Charlotte had
written to Aylott & Jones to ask whether they would also publish 'a work
of fiction—consisting of three distinct and unconnected tales'. The Bells did
not intend 'to publish these tales on their own account', Charlotte declared.
They could hardly have afforded to do so. The three tales were Charlotte's
The Professor, Emily's *Wuthering Heights*, and Anne's *Agnes Grey*. Charlotte's later
statement in her 'Biographical Notice' of her sisters was misleading: they did not
set to work on the stories when the *Poems* failed to sell as they had hoped; it is
likely that all three novels had been at least begun before April 1846. Though
Aylott & Jones refused to publish the novels, they advised the 'Bells' to try other
publishers. None of these agreed to publish *The Professor*, but in 1847 Thomas
Cautley Newby accepted, and published, after months of delay, the other two
novels. In the event, *Jane Eyre*, which Charlotte began to write in August 1846
and completed in August 1847, was the first to be published, on 19 October 1847.
On 15 July that year Charlotte had sent *The Professor* to 'one publishing house

more', the firm of Smith, Elder & Co. Instead of 'two hard hopeless lines' of refusal, Charlotte received a courteous letter discussing its merits and demerits, and adding that 'a work in three volumes would meet with careful attention'. *Jane Eyre* was dispatched from Keighley station on 24 August. The young publisher George Smith recalled that his reader, William Smith Williams, recommended the novel to him, and he 'could not put the book down . . . before I went to bed that night I had finished the MS'.

Most of Charlotte's early letters to Smith, Elder & Co. are short, businesslike, and formal; but on 4 October 1847 she wrote directly to William Smith Williams, thanking him for his kind counsel and encouragement, and modestly warning him against 'forming too favourable an idea' of her powers. He was to become one of her most valued correspondents, especially after she and her sister Anne met him personally in London in July 1848, a 'pale, mild, stooping man', quiet and sincere in his attentions to the two shy country visitors. He proved to be knowledgeable and discriminating about art as well as literature, and he helped to choose the books that the firm sent as loans or gifts to Charlotte and her family. She responded with gratitude, and with careful critiques of the books for which he sought her opinion, and much appreciation of the loan of twenty engravings from paintings in Robert Vernon's great collection. He in turn valued her advice on the possible careers for some of his eight children, especially for his daughters Ellen and Louisa, who were to become governesses. He responded with delicate and sympathetic understanding to her anxieties about her sisters' and brother's illnesses, and to her intense grief after their deaths.

The publication of *Shirley* on 26 October 1849 was followed by a long delay in completing her next novel, *Villette*, and her friendly correspondence with Williams seems to have dwindled. Perhaps he was discouraged by Charlotte's rather dismissive attitude to some of the books he sent her at this period. In 1852 only four letters to him survive before her curt note of 26 October that year. It begins, 'In sending a return box of books to Cornhill—I take the opportunity of enclosing 2 Vols of MS [of *Villette*].' There are no thanks for the books, and the last sentence is distantly cool. Happily, there is a partial revival of the old friendly relationship in a letter of 6 November, thanking Williams for his 'kind letter with its candid and able commentary on "Villette"', and in the first half of 1853 the courteous and sympathetic friendliness is restored. Her last surviving letter to Williams was written on 6 December 1853, when she had heard that the head of the firm, George Smith, was engaged to be married. Charlotte's brief, desolate note to Williams ends: 'Do not trouble yourself to select or send any more books. These courtesies must cease some day—and I would rather give them up than wear them out. Believe me yours sincerely C. Brontë.'

Charlotte first met George Smith in July 1848 when she and Anne had travelled overnight to London to prove the separate identity of the brothers Bell; for T. C. Newby had told an American publisher that he and not Smith, Elder would be publishing 'Currer Bell's' next novel. Newby had assured George Smith that 'to the best of his belief' all three Bells were one writer. Charlotte and Anne convinced the astonished George Smith that Newby had lied. Smith's natural reaction was the wish to make a show of his best-selling author. Charlotte's resistance to this, and her excitement and exhaustion, gave her 'a thundering head-ache & harassing sickness'. Thus she did not at first like her young and handsome publisher. A better understanding and warm friendship developed after she had stayed with Smith, his mother, and his sisters in December 1849. There were to be other friendly visits, companionable outings in London, and an exhilarating stay in Edinburgh. From mid-1850 Smith became Charlotte's principal London correspondent. The brief business letters she had previously written to him gave place to their friendly correspondence of late 1850, followed by twenty-four long, candid, often affectionately teasing or cheerfully satirical letters in 1851. There were fewer letters in 1852, though the friendship continued; and then a marked falling off in their correspondence from the spring of 1853, caused in part by the long strain of overwork on Smith's part as the firm expanded its banking and export business. Charlotte could not know that Smith was also more happily preoccupied with the beautiful Elizabeth Blakeway, whom he first met in April 1853. On 10 December 1853 Charlotte wrote a curt, contorted letter of congratulation to him on his engagement to Elizabeth. She wrote more warmly to him on 25 April 1854, when she had received his congratulations on her engagement to Arthur Nicholls.

Smith, Elder's managing clerk James Taylor also became one of Charlotte's correspondents. In February 1849 he had sent a candid critique of the first volume of *Shirley*. He helped to choose books sent to her by the firm, began to lend her copies of the critical journal, *The Athenaeum*, and on 8 September 1849 collected the manuscript of *Shirley* from Haworth. In December 1849, observing that he controlled the firm's clerks with his 'iron will', she suspected him of being 'rigid, despotic and self-willed'. However, in September 1850 he regained her good opinion by sending her a copy of the *Palladium* article in which Sydney Dobell had discerned the 'stamp of genius' in *Wuthering Heights*. On his farewell visit to Haworth before he left to establish a branch of the Smith, Elder firm in India, he seemed on the point of proposing marriage, but departed with no definite avowal. Two letters from India were followed by total silence on his part; and despite her recoil from his physical presence during the visit, she suffered the pain of 'absolute uncertainty' about his intentions. In July 1852 she wrote miserably to Ellen that 'All is silent as the grave.' Twelve or possibly thirteen letters to him from Charlotte survive. Careful rather than cordial, they offer opinions on the books he sent her, and on such subjects as Harriet Martineau's 'atheism', which they both deplored. Her last letter to him, dated 15 November 1851, eloquently conveys her horrified, fascinated reaction to the French actress Rachel's performance, 'wilder and worse' than human nature, showing 'the feelings and fury of a fiend'.

Charlotte's letters to fellow-authors are of particular interest, for they often reveal either directly or by implication her own literary creed. George Henry Lewes's criticism of the melodramatic elements in *Jane Eyre* and his praise of Jane Austen provoked her to a spirited declaration that Austen might be 'sensible, real (more *real* than *true*)', but without the divine gift of poetry she could not be great. Yet Charlotte recognized Austen's exquisite adaptation of 'means to her end', and distinguished it from the 'windy wordiness' to be found in the work of Eliza Lynn or Bulwer Lytton—or indeed in Lewes's own flamboyant novel, *Rose, Blanche, and Violet*, and his pretentious play, *The Noble Heart*.

Though we have only one manuscript letter from Charlotte to Harriet Martineau, there are copies of several others, and numerous letters to other correspondents about Martineau. Together they depict a relationship which began with mutual appreciation and respect, warmed into positive liking when Charlotte stayed with the older writer for a week in December 1850, then declined with Martineau's public admission of what seemed an atheistic philosophy. The friendship came to an abrupt end on Charlotte's part when Martineau alleged in a private letter and in a *Daily News* review of *Villette*, that all the female characters were full of 'one thought—love. . . . It is not thus in real life.' Charlotte never forgave her.

Regrettably, Charlotte's letters to Thackeray have not come to light. We may guess that they mingled praise for the writer she had called the 'first social regenerator of the day' with some sharp questioning of his opinions on such writers as Fielding, whom she considered immoral. In writing about Thackeray to George Smith, she emphatically deplored his literary sins, his procrastination, and his unfair presentation of women. Thackeray admitted that he deserved some of her criticism: 'I don't care a straw for a "triumph". Pooh!—nor for my art enough,' he wrote to Mary Holmes on 25 February 1852.

Charlotte's correspondence with Elizabeth Gaskell reveals much about the personality of both writers. Some forty letters survive, the first written on 17 November 1849, before they had met each other, and the last on 30 September 1854, when the newly married Charlotte warmly invited Mrs Gaskell to visit Haworth again, and to meet her husband. There had been an immediate rapport between the two authors when they met as guests of Sir James Kay-Shuttleworth at Briery Close, near Lake Windermere in the Lake District in August 1850. Gaskell, socially accomplished and at ease, well-read, and the author of *Mary Barton*, was sensitive and sympathetic to the normally shy Charlotte, and to her tragic family circumstances. Charlotte appreciated Mrs Gaskell's talent, shared her love for Wordsworth's poetry, and praised her 'cheerful, pleasing and cordial manners and . . . kind and good heart'. Their mutual liking was strengthened by Charlotte's three visits to the Gaskells' home in Manchester. Her letters reveal their general 'concord of opinion' on contemporary events and concerns. Above all, they give a unique insight into Charlotte's relationship with her future biographer. Acutely distressed by Charlotte's death, Mrs Gaskell wrote to the Haworth stationer, John Greenwood on 12 April 1855, 'Strangers might know her by her great fame, but we loved her dearly for her goodness, truth, and kindness . . . I loved her dearly, more than I think she knew.'

Letters to others who had known and loved Charlotte for many years have been included. Margaret Wooler, her teacher at Roe Head school, had become a friend in whom she could confide. When Charlotte was feeling the weight of solitude, she wondered at Miss Wooler's endurance of a similar fate 'with a serene spirit and an unsoured disposition', and was grateful for her kind wish for a reconciliation with Ellen Nussey. The reconciliation achieved, it was to Ellen Nussey and two other trusted friends that Charlotte's last letters were written: Ellen's friend Amelia Ringrose Taylor, and Laetitia Wheelwright, whom Charlotte had first met in Brussels. The letters are infinitely touching in their affectionate concern for others even while she herself was suffering 'sickness with scarce a reprieve', and in her praise of her husband's kind companionship and tenderest nursing.

CHRONOLOGY OF CHARLOTTE BRONTË

1816	21	April	Charlotte Brontë born at Thornton, near Bradford, Yorks., third child of Revd Patrick and Maria Brontë
1817	26	June	Patrick Branwell Brontë born
1818	30	July	Emily Jane Brontë born
1820	17	January	Anne Brontë born
	20	April	The family moves to Haworth, near Keighley, Yorks.
1821	15	September	Mrs Brontë dies of cancer
1824	10	August	Charlotte is taken to the Clergy Daughters' School at Cowan Bridge, Lancs.
1825	6	May	Charlotte's eldest sister, Maria (born ?1813), dies of pulmonary tuberculosis after leaving Cowan Bridge
	1	June	Mr Brontë brings home Charlotte and Emily, who has attended Cowan Bridge for six months
	15	June	Charlotte's sister Elizabeth (born 1815) dies of pulmonary tuberculosis after leaving Cowan Bridge
1825–30			Surviving Brontë children at home, supervised by their aunt, Elizabeth Branwell
1829–41			Charlotte writes about 180 poems, 120 stories and other prose pieces, in minute script, many of them set in Angria, an imaginary kingdom invented by CB and her brother Branwell. She also sketches and copies engravings
1831	17	January–June 1832	CB at Margaret Wooler's school, Roe Head, Mirfield, Yorks., where her friends include Ellen Nussey and Mary Taylor
1835	29	July	CB returns to Roe Head as a teacher, accompanied by Emily Brontë as a pupil
		mid-October	Anne Brontë replaces Emily at Roe Head
1836	29	December	CB sends specimens of her poetry to Robert Southey and tells him of her ambition to be 'for ever known' as a poetess
1837	12	March	Southey acknowledges CB's 'faculty of Verse', but advises her that 'Literature cannot be the business of a woman's life'; she should write poetry for its own sake and not for celebrity

		December	CB quarrels with Margaret Wooler for failing to realize that Anne Brontë is seriously ill; she and Anne return to Haworth
1838		January	CB returns to Roe Head, possibly with Anne
		February/ March	School moves to Heald's House, Dewsbury Moor
		December	CB finally leaves the school and returns home
1839	5	March	She rejects a proposal of marriage from Ellen Nussey's brother Revd Henry Nussey
		May–July	CB a governess to the Sidgwicks at Stonegappe, near Skipton, and at Swarcliffe, near Harrogate
		late July	She refuses a proposal of marriage from Revd David Pryce
		September/ October	CB and Ellen Nussey stay with the Hudsons at Easton near Bridlington and in Ann Booth's lodgings at Bridlington Quay
		by December	She has completed a novella, *Caroline Vernon*
1840		?November	CB sends opening chapters of a MS novel (?'Ashworth') to Hartley Coleridge
	10	December	She writes to Hartley Coleridge acknowledging his opinion that her novel is unlikely to be accepted by a publisher
1841		?February–30 June	CB governess to family of John White, Upperwood House, Rawdon, near Leeds
		July	CB, Emily, and Anne plan to establish a school
		late July	CB returns to Upperwood House
	29	September	She writes to ask her aunt Elizabeth Branwell for a loan so that she and Emily can study abroad
	24	December	She returns home from Upperwood House
1842	8	February	Mr Brontë, CB, and Emily leave Haworth to travel to London and then, with Mary and Joe Taylor, to Brussels
	15	February	CB and Emily become pupils in Mme Zoë Heger's pensionnat in Brussels
		August	They stay on at the pensionnat, CB teaching English and Emily music in return for board and tuition
	29	October	Elizabeth Branwell dies of internal obstruction in Haworth. She leaves money to her nieces

	8	November	CB and Emily return to Haworth
	29	November	Anne Brontë returns to Thorp Green, near York, where she has been a governess to the family of Revd Edmund Robinson since ?May 1840
1843	?21	January	Branwell Brontë becomes tutor to Mr Robinson's son Edmund at Thorp Green
	29	January	CB returns alone to the pensionnat Heger as a teacher. She gives English lessons to M. Constantin Heger and his brother-in-law
		August/ September	CB lonely and homesick in Brussels during the long vacation; she goes to confession at the church of Sainte-Gudule
		October	CB distrusts Mme Heger and gives in her notice, but M. Heger countermands it
1844	1	January	CB leaves Brussels
	3	January	She arrives in Haworth to find her father's eyesight is rapidly deteriorating
		July– November	She tries but fails to get pupils for a school at Haworth Parsonage
	24	July	She writes to M. Heger, longing for an answer from him
	24	October	Joe Taylor takes another letter from CB to M. Heger; she is grieved by his six months' silence
1845	8	January	She writes to M. Heger in despair at his failure to reply
		May	Revd Arthur Bell Nicholls becomes Mr Brontë's curate
	11	June	Anne Brontë receives final payment from Mr Robinson
	?3	July	CB begins a three-week visit to Ellen Nussey at her brother Henry Nussey's vicarage in Hathersage, Derbyshire
	17	July	Branwell Brontë dismissed by Mr Robinson for 'proceedings bad beyond expression'. He drinks to drown his distress
		?September/ October	CB discovers poems by Emily; Anne offers her own poems. They plan to publish a selection by the three sisters
	18	November	Last surviving letter from CB to M. Heger. She admits she cannot master her thoughts of him
1846	28	January	CB asks publishers Aylott & Jones to publish the sisters' poems

6	April	CB asks whether Aylott & Jones would publish three tales: i.e. *The Professor*, *Wuthering Heights*, and *Agnes Grey*. They refuse, but offer advice
*c.*22	May	Aylott & Jones publish *Poems* by Currer, Ellis, and Acton Bell
26	May	Revd Edmund Robinson dies. Branwell Brontë alleges that Mrs Robinson is prevented from seeing him. He is distraught
4	July	CB offers the sisters' prose tales to Henry Colburn, and then to four more publishers before July 1847. All reject them
19	August	CB takes her father to Manchester for an eye operation
25	August	He has an operation for cataract. *The Professor* is returned, rejected, the same day, and CB begins to write *Jane Eyre*

1847

16	June	Only two copies of *Poems* have been sold. The sisters send complimentary copies to Hartley Coleridge, De Quincey, Ebenezer Elliott, John Lockhart, Tennyson, Wordsworth, and probably also to Dickens
	July	Thomas Cautley Newby agrees to publish *Wuthering Heights* and *Agnes Grey*
15	July	CB sends *The Professor* to Smith, Elder & Co.
7	August	CB acknowledges Smith, Elder's reasons for rejecting *The Professor*, but mentions that a work of 'more vivid interest' is nearly completed
24	August	CB sends MS of *Jane Eyre* to Smith, Elder by rail
19	October	Publication of *Jane Eyre: an Autobiography*, edited by Currer Bell, in three volumes
26	October	CB has received the first of many favourable reviews
17	November	Emily and Anne have received the last proof-sheets of their novels
14	December	Emily and Anne have received their six copies of *Wuthering Heights. A Novel*, by Ellis Bell, and *Agnes Grey. A Novel*, by Acton Bell, published together in three volumes by T. C. Newby
31	December	'Currer Bell' disclaims authorship of *Wuthering Heights* and *Agnes Grey*

1848

*c.*22	January	2nd edition of *Jane Eyre* published, with dedication to Thackeray

	mid-April	3rd edition of *Jane Eyre* published, with a note disclaiming authorship of other novels
	*c.*27 June	*The Tenant of Wildfell Hall* by Acton Bell published in three volumes by T. C. Newby
	7–8 July	Charlotte and Anne go to London to prove to their publishers the separate identity of the 'Bells'
	8–11 July	They meet George Smith and William Smith Williams and their families and confront Newby in London
	by 12 August	2nd edition of *The Tenant of Wildfell Hall* published
	September	CB completes and fair copies vol. i of *Shirley*
	24 September	Branwell Brontë dies of 'chronic bronchitis and marasmus' (wasting). The shock makes CB ill
	October	CB's anxiety about Emily's health makes her unable to write
	by 21 October	Smith, Elder have reissued the Bells' *Poems*
	19 December	Emily dies of 'Consumption—2 months' duration'
	22 December	Emily is buried in Haworth church
1849	*c.*7 January	Dr T. P. Teale pronounces that Anne Brontë is in an advanced state of pulmonary tuberculosis
	24 May	CB and Ellen Nussey accompany Anne to York, where they stay overnight
	25 May	They arrive in Scarborough
	28 May	Anne dies
	30 May	She is buried in St Mary's churchyard, Scarborough
	7 June	CB and Ellen Nussey travel to Filey, where they stay at Cliff House
	14 June	They travel to Easton, near Bridlington, where they stay with the Hudsons
	21 June	CB returns to Haworth
	29 August	She has completed *Shirley*
	8 September	James Taylor, Smith, Elder's managing clerk, collects the MS of *Shirley* from Haworth Parsonage
	26 October	*Shirley. A Tale* by Currer Bell published in three volumes by Smith, Elder & Co.
	29 November	CB travels to London, staying with George Smith and family as the guest of his mother
	4 December	CB meets Thackeray
	9 December	She meets Harriet Martineau
	15 December	She returns to Haworth

1850	8	March	Sir James and Lady Kay-Shuttleworth visit Haworth
	12–16	March	CB stays with the Kay-Shuttleworths at Gawthorpe Hall, Lancs.
	30	May	CB arrives in London to stay with George Smith and his family
	13	June	First of CB's three portrait sittings to George Richmond
	25	June	CB leaves London for Ellen Nussey's home, Brookroyd in Birstall, Yorks.
	3–5	July	CB with George, Alexander, and Eliza Smith, sightseeing in and near Edinburgh
	6	July	She travels to Birstall
	13 or 15	July	She returns to Haworth
	19	August	CB arrives at the Kay-Shuttleworths' holiday residence, Briery Close, near Windermere
	20	August	Elizabeth Gaskell arrives at Briery Close
	?24	August	CB returns home
	7	December	Her edition of *Wuthering Heights*, *Agnes Grey*, a selection of her sisters' poems, and her 'Biographical Notice' of their lives, published by Smith, Elder
	16–23	December	CB stays with Harriet Martineau in Ambleside
	23–31	December	CB stays with Ellen Nussey in Birstall
1851	4 or 5	April	James Taylor visits Haworth Parsonage. He hopes CB will write to him in Bombay, but it is not clear whether he proposes marriage. His departure intensifies CB's solitude
	c.20	May	James Taylor goes to Bombay to set up an Indian branch of Smith, Elder
	28	May	CB arrives in London to stay with the Smiths
	29	May	She attends Thackeray's lecture on Congreve and Addison, and will attend three more on other writers
	30	May	She makes the first of five visits to the Great Exhibition
	7 and 21	June	She is impressed by the actress Rachel
	20	June	She meets Richard Monckton Milnes
	?25	June	CB and George Smith ('Miss and Mr Fraser') visit a phrenologist, Dr J. P. Browne
	27–30	June	CB stays with the Gaskells in Manchester
	30	June	She returns to Haworth

	15	November	She replies to two letters from James Taylor, but does not hear from him again
	by 28	November	CB is making slow progress with *Villette*
	8	December	She has a 'low nervous fever' and is depressed
		late December	Medication causes CB to suffer mercury poisoning
1852		January– February	CB still suffering, but gradually recovers
	?27	January– 11 February	CB with the Nusseys in Birstall
	12	March	*Villette* does not progress
	29	March	CB begins to fair copy vol. i of *Villette*
	c.27	May–24 June	CB at Cliff House, Filey, Yorks.
		July– September	She resumes work on *Villette*
	26	October	She sends manuscript of vols i and ii of *Villette* to Smith, Elder
	20	November	2nd edition of *Shirley*, dated 1853 on title-page
	13	December	Arthur Bell Nicholls proposes marriage. Mr Brontë's apoplectic reaction makes it impossible for CB to accept
1853	5	January– 2 February	CB with the Smiths in London; she corrects proofs of *Villette*
	28	January	*Villette* by Currer Bell published in three volumes by Smith, Elder & Co.
		February/ March	CB offended by Harriet Martineau's review of *Villette*. She breaks off the friendship
	21–8	April	CB visits the Gaskells in Manchester
	28	April–?4 May	CB with the Nusseys in Birstall
	27	May	Arthur Nicholls leaves Haworth for the south of England before taking up a curacy at Kirk Smeaton, Yorks.
		May–late June	CB writes three MS fragments of a story, 'Willie Ellin'
	30	June–early July	Ellen Nussey visits Haworth Parsonage
		July 1853– February 1854	Ellen's antagonism to the idea of CB marrying Arthur Nicholls causes estrangement between her and CB
		early August	CB travels to Scotland and to Ilkley, Yorks., with Joseph Taylor and his family
	?13–16	August	CB in Ilkley
	19–?23	September	Mrs Gaskell visits Haworth Parsonage
	10	December	CB congratulates George Smith very coolly on his engagement to Elizabeth Blakeway

1854		January	Arthur Nicholls spends ten days near Haworth
	3–8	April	Arthur Nicholls near Haworth. He and CB become engaged
	1–4	May	CB with the Gaskells in Manchester
	4–8	May	CB with the Taylors at Hunsworth, Yorks.
	8–11	May	CB with the Nusseys in Birstall
	29	June	CB and Nicholls marry at Haworth and begin their honeymoon journey
	29	June–31 July	They visit Conwy and Bangor in North Wales, then travel via Holyhead to Ireland, visiting Dublin, Banagher (where Nicholls's relatives welcome them), Kilkee, Tarbert, Tralee, Killarney, Glengariff, and Cork, returning to Haworth via Dublin
	1	August	In Haworth
		November	Sir James Kay-Shuttleworth offers Nicholls the living of Padiham, Lancs. He declines the offer
1855	9–?12	January	Charlotte and Nicholls stay with the Kay-Shuttleworths at Gawthorpe, where CBN takes 'a long walk over damp ground in thin shoes'.
	c.9	January	CBN has indigestion and sickness; she grows thin
	30	January	She has been confined to her bed for some days. Two doctors think her illness 'symptomatic' (of pregnancy?)
		late February	CBN suffers 'sickness with scarce a reprieve'
	31	March	She dies, probably of excessive sickness in pregnancy
	4	April	She is buried in Haworth church

BIOGRAPHICAL NOTES

Family Members

Branwell, Elizabeth (1776–1842)

Elizabeth was the elder sister of Mrs Maria Brontë, and one of the four daughters of Thomas Branwell (1746–1808) of Penzance, Cornwall. He left £50 per annum to each of his daughters, and Elizabeth was able to save some of her income. In 1815 she stayed with the Brontës in Thornton, and in 1821 was with them again in Haworth, helping to look after the family. After Mrs Brontë's death Elizabeth returned to Haworth, and kept the household in good order. She helped to educate Charlotte, Emily, and Anne, who respected her though they occasionally resented her discipline. She responded generously to Charlotte and Emily's wish to study foreign languages by financing their stay at Mme Heger's pensionnat in Brussels in 1842. At home she made a favourite of Branwell Brontë, who witnessed with acute pain the agonizing suffering from obstruction of the bowel which caused her death on 29 October 1842. By her will she left the residue of her estate to be divided equally between the Brontë sisters and their cousin Elizabeth Jane Kingston. The sisters' investment of her legacy enabled them to pay for the publication of *Poems* in 1846, and *Agnes Grey* and *Wuthering Heights* in 1847.

Brontë, Anne (1820–49)

Anne was the youngest sister of Charlotte. Her mother died on 15 September 1821, so Anne was brought up and at first educated mainly by her aunt Elizabeth Branwell at Haworth Parsonage. She was the playmate of Emily, and with her created the exotic, imaginary land of Gondal. From October 1835 she attended Margaret Wooler's school at Roe Head, until an acute illness accompanied by a spiritual crisis in December 1836 necessitated her return to Haworth. She may have returned to school for a further year. Her tribulations as a governess to the Ingham children at Blake Hall near Mirfield are echoed in those of Agnes Grey at Wellwood. At home she met the young curate William Weightman, and was admired by him. In May 1840 she became governess to the daughters of Revd Edmund Robinson of Thorp Green, near York. A 'persecuted stranger amongst insolent people', recalled in the Horton Lodge episodes of *Agnes Grey*, she longed for home, but eventually gained the respect and affection of her pupils. Her troubles increased after her brother Branwell became the young Edmund Robinson's tutor in January 1843, and it seems that she did not contradict Branwell's later assertion that Mr Robinson dismissed him after discovering his affair with his wife Lydia Robinson. Anne's contributions to the 'Bells'' *Poems* in 1846, and her novel *Agnes Grey* in 1847, made comparatively little impact. But her second novel, *The Tenant of Wildfell Hall* (June 1848) was found offensive in its frank treatment of depravity, and Anne wrote a preface to the second edition explaining that she intended to impress her moral warning by telling the truth. Anne's health declined in late 1848, tubercular symptoms were diagnosed, and she died on 28 May 1849 at Scarborough, where Charlotte and Ellen Nussey had taken her, at her own wish, in the hope of prolonging her life.

Brontë, Emily Jane (1818–48)

Emily was Charlotte's sister. She was taken to Cowan Bridge school (the 'Lowood' of *Jane Eyre*) on 25 November 1824, but was brought home on 1 June 1825 after an outbreak of 'low fever' at the school. In Haworth she was educated by her Aunt Branwell and her father, and shared with Anne the creation of their imaginary land of Gondal. On 29 July 1835 she became a pupil at Roe Head school, but soon fell ill away from home and the freedom of her beloved moors, and returned to Haworth in October. There she took on many of the household duties, but managed to study German 'as she kneaded the dough'. From October 1838 she endured six months' drudgery as a teacher at Law Hill school near Halifax. Nevertheless the years 1836–40 were her richest creative period as a poet. On 12 February 1842 she accompanied Charlotte to Mme Heger's pensionnat in Brussels, where she worked hard, mastered more German as well as French, and wrote some highly original and forceful French essays, recognizing the existence of cruelty in the animal and human world. In autumn 1845 Charlotte discovered some of Emily's poems, and with difficulty persuaded her that they were worth publication. The *Athenaeum* reviewer of the 'Bells'' *Poems* praised those of 'Ellis Bell' for 'an evident power of wing'. Emily's *Wuthering Heights*, published by Thomas Cautley Newby in December 1847, shocked and baffled many reviewers by its savagery, but some realized its unique power. Though Emily's health rapidly declined in the autumn of 1848, she refused medical help until it was too late, and died, wasted with consumption, on 19 December 1848.

Brontë, Patrick Branwell (1817–48)

Charlotte Brontë's brother was only four years old when his mother died, and he came to regard his Aunt Branwell as a mother. Mr Brontë educated him at home. He was an avid reader, and wrote prolifically, imitating magazine reviews, composing poems and dramas, and collaborating with Charlotte in their Glasstown and Angrian sagas. From 1835 onwards he begged influential writers and the editor of *Blackwood's Edinburgh Magazine* to acknowledge his poetic talent, and he succeeded in publishing eighteen poems in reputable local newspapers between 1841 and 1847. His other ambition was to be an artist. In

1835 he studied painting with William Robinson of Leeds, and in 1838 made a vain attempt to earn his living as a portrait painter. Despite his lack of skill, he produced a rather wooden portrait of his three sisters which gives some idea of their personality and features, and a second group portrait of which only the haunting image of Emily survives. His post as tutor to the sons of Robert Postlethwaite of Broughton-in-Furness from January to June 1840 ended in his dismissal, probably in disgrace. A railway clerkship at Sowerby Bridge station, 31 August 1840–April 1841, was followed by a similar position at Luddenden Foot station near Halifax. Dismissed owing to the dishonesty of a porter for whom he was responsible, Branwell returned home depressed and ill in March 1842. In January 1843 he became the tutor of Edmund Robinson, the son of Anne Brontë's employer at Thorp Green, near York. This situation he kept until 17 July 1845, when he received a letter from Mr Robinson dismissing him for conduct 'bad beyond expression'. In a letter of October 1845 to the railway engineer Francis Grundy, Branwell alleged that Mrs Lydia Robinson had declared 'more than ordinary feeling' for him, and that he had 'daily "troubled pleasure soon chastised by fear" in the society of one whom I must, till death, call my **wife**'. After Mr Robinson's death on 26 May 1846, Branwell claimed that only a clause in her husband's will prevented her from marrying him. The clause did not exist; but Branwell lost direction in his life, spent whatever money he was given on drink or drugs, incurred debts which his family had to pay, and became physically frail. He died on 24 September 1848 of 'chronic bronchitis and marasmus'—a wasting of the flesh without apparent disease.

Brontë, Revd Patrick (1777–1861)

Charlotte Brontë's father was born in Emdale, County Down, Ireland. In about 1798 he became a tutor in the family of the evangelical rector, Revd Thomas Tighe, who helped him to study theology. He entered St John's College, Cambridge in 1802, graduated BA in 1806, and was ordained priest in 1807. During his curacy at Wethersfield, Essex, 1806–January 1809, he became engaged to Mary Mildred Burder, whose family disapproved, and the engagement was broken off in or before 1810. Curacies at Wellington, Shropshire in 1809 and Dewsbury, Yorkshire until early 1811 were succeeded by a perpetual curacy (equivalent to a vicariate) at Hartshead-cum-Clifton. On 29 December 1812 he married Maria Branwell, and with her and their two baby daughters Maria and Elizabeth, born in 1813 and 1815, moved to take up a perpetual curacy at Thornton near Bradford in May 1815. Charlotte, Branwell, Emily, and Anne Brontë were all born at Thornton. In April 1820 the family moved to Haworth, where Mrs Brontë died on 15 September 1821, probably from a uterine cancer. Mr Brontë was to be the perpetual curate there for the rest of his life. In 1824 he took his four older daughters to the Clergy Daughters' School at Cowan Bridge in Lancashire, but all were brought home in 1825. Maria died on 6 May and Elizabeth on 15 June 1825, both of them from pulmonary tuberculosis. With his sister-in-law Elizabeth Branwell Mr Brontë educated the children at home for the next five years. In 1832 he established a Sunday school in Haworth, and later worked for other local causes, taking the lead in petitioning the General Board of Health for assistance in procuring a better water supply for Haworth in August 1849. By mid-1846 he was almost completely blind. Charlotte took him to Manchester, where a successful operation for cataract was performed. He was profoundly distressed by the deaths of Branwell, Emily, and Anne, and became increasingly protective of and dependent upon Charlotte. He was fiercely opposed to the idea of her marriage with his curate, Arthur Nicholls, but was gradually brought round to a more favourable view, consenting to their engagement in April 1854. After their marriage he remained on amicable terms with Mr Nicholls, who continued to care for him after Charlotte's death. Between 1855 and 1857 he cooperated with Elizabeth Gaskell in her writing of Charlotte's life, asking only for the correction of 'a few trifling mistakes', despite her misrepresentation of him as a violent man and harsh husband. He was bedridden for a few months before his death on 7 June 1861. Though he became somewhat prejudiced with age, he was a man of integrity, with a staunch, evangelical Christian faith. His published poems, moral tales, sermons, and tracts, his encouragement of his children's reading, and his willingness for them to have lessons in art and music, all enriched their lives and contributed to their achievements.

Other Correspondents and Persons Frequently Cited

Aylott & Jones

London booksellers and publishers, established 1828; later Aylott and Son. Aylott senior retired in 1866 and died in 1872. The firm published *Poems* by Currer, Ellis, and Acton Bell in 1846. In January 1850 they published the first number of the Pre-Raphaelite magazine of poetry and thoughts on art, *The Germ*.

Bennoch, Francis (1812–90)

Merchant, minor poet, and friend and patron of writers; born in Drumcrool, Durrisden, Dumfriesshire; clerk in a merchant's office in London 1828–37, head of a firm of wholesale silk traders in London 1848–74. The writer Mary Russell Mitford thought him brilliant and a fine speaker, and praised his poems. Charlotte Brontë assured him that she and her father enjoyed his visit to Haworth

Parsonage on 19 September 1853. Though she thanked him for inviting her to visit his London home, she was never able to do so.

Brown, Martha (1828–80)

A loyal servant at Haworth Parsonage, July 1841–61, and subsequently an occasional guest and helper in the household of the Revd A. B. Nicholls and his relatives in Banagher, Ireland.

Coleridge, Hartley (1796–1849)

Essayist and poet, the precocious eldest son of Samuel Taylor Coleridge. Intemperance cost him a fellowship at Oriel College, Oxford, and he did not fulfil his early promise; but he published poems and literary criticism in *Blackwood's Edinburgh Magazine*, and was admired by Charlotte and Branwell Brontë, who sent him examples of their writing for criticism.

De Quincey, Thomas (1785–1859)

An author admired by Branwell Brontë and his sisters. His *Confessions of an English Opium Eater* were first published in the *London Magazine* in 1821, and then in volume form in 1822. On 16 June 1847 Charlotte Brontë sent a copy of *Poems* by Currer, Ellis, and Acton Bell to De Quincey.

Dixon, Mary (1809–97)

A member of the Dixon family of Birmingham, which included her brother, the educational reformer and MP, George Dixon (1820–98). She was a cousin of Charlotte Brontë's friend Mary Taylor, q.v. Charlotte met Mary Dixon in Brussels in 1842–3, and her portrait of Charlotte is now in the Brontë Parsonage Museum.

Dobell, Sydney Thompson (1824–74)

Poet and critic, once famous for his dramatic poem, *The Roman* (1850), but sharply criticized for his frenetic 'spasmodic' poem, *Balder* (1854). Charlotte was grateful for his perceptive critique of *Wuthering Heights* in the *Palladium* for September 1850.

Gaskell, Elizabeth, née Stevenson (1810–65)

Novelist and first biographer of Charlotte Brontë. She married Revd William Gaskell (1805–84), Unitarian minister at Cross Street Chapel, Manchester.

Charlotte read her novels *Mary Barton* (1848), *Ruth* (1853), and most, or perhaps all, of *North and South* (1854–January 1855). She also enjoyed *Cranford*, and some of Gaskell's other stories. Charlotte first met her in August 1850, found her congenial, corresponded and stayed with her, and welcomed her as a visitor to Haworth Parsonage in September 1853. At Mr Brontë's request, she wrote her *Life* of Charlotte (1857), after visiting many of her correspondents and requesting the loan of Charlotte's letters to them. Her personal friendship and sympathetic understanding make her biography invaluable, despite her careful removal of any traces of the 'coarseness' that critics had detected in Charlotte's novels.

Heger, Constantin Georges Romain (1809–96)

Teacher of Charlotte and Emily Brontë in Brussels in 1842, and of Charlotte also in 1843. Born in Brussels, he returned there after living in France from 1825 to 1829. In 1830 he married Marie-Josephine Noyer, who, with their child, died in September 1833 during a cholera epidemic. He married Zoë Claire Parent, the directress of a girls' boarding-school (a 'pensionnat') on 3 September 1836, and they had six children. An inspired and inspiring teacher, he was a master in the Athénée Royale, a high school for boys, and also gave lessons in the pensionnat. He could be temperamental and choleric, but he was a devout Catholic and a benefactor of the poor. He recognized the talents of Charlotte and Emily, devised specially adapted courses for them, and lent or gave them well-chosen French books. Aiming to develop their analytic skills and appreciation of a wide range of literary styles, he made detailed comments on their essays, directing their attention to the need for clarity, relevance, and effective focus. Charlotte's obsession with him during her second year in Brussels, and her resentment against Mme Heger as a devious rival, became increasingly difficult for her to control. Four letters to Heger, written in 1844–5, reveal her longing for a warmer response and more frequent letters from him. His character and her feelings are reflected most clearly in her presentation of M. Paul and Lucy Snowe in *Villette*.

Heger, Mme Zoë Claire, née Parent

Was born in Brussels to a French émigré, and took over a girls' boarding school at 32, rue d'Isabelle, Brussels, in 1830. Her marriage to Constantin Heger on 3 September 1836 was to be a happy one. Of their six children, four were born by the time Charlotte Brontë left the school on 1 January 1844, and she became fond of their second daughter, Louise. Zoë Heger ran her school efficiently; but despite her initial kindness to her English pupils, her constant surveillance was interpreted by Charlotte as spying. During Charlotte's second year in the pensionnat, Mme Heger may have been aware that Charlotte was attracted to her husband. Charlotte felt that she was too often left in solitude, and yet had no real privacy. The designing Mlle Reuter in *The Professor* and the formidable Mme Beck in *Villette* have many of Mme Heger's characteristics, as Charlotte interpreted them.

Kavanagh, Julia (1824–77)

Novelist and biographer; author of *Madeleine* (1848), which Charlotte Brontë admired, and of many other books. *Nathalie* (1850), set in France, echoes *Jane Eyre* in some respects, and it may in turn have been a 'suggestive' book for *Villette*.

Kay-Shuttleworth, Sir James (1804–77), MD Edinburgh 1827

Born James Phillips Kay in Rochdale, Lancs. He practised in Manchester 1828–35, and published a study of lung disease caused by cotton-dust in 1830 and a paper on asphyxia in 1834. From 1835 to 1839 he was the assistant Poor Law Commissioner in Norfolk and Suffolk, and in April 1839 became secretary to the Committee of the Privy Council on Education. He helped to set up the pioneering Battersea Training School for teachers, opened in 1840. In 1842 he married the heiress Janet Shuttleworth (1817–72), with whom he had five children. Nervous depression and overwork culminated in a prolonged epileptic fit and his resignation from his secretaryship in 1849. He and his wife first visited Charlotte Brontë on 8 March 1850. Soon afterwards she visited their home, Gawthorpe Hall, near Burnley, and in August that year she met Elizabeth Gaskell, her fellow-guest at their holiday residence, Briery Close, near Lake Windermere. Through their social contacts they arranged privileged visits for her to art galleries and elsewhere in London. Sir James offered a curacy to Arthur Nicholls in 1854, but Nicholls, having promised to support the ageing Mr Brontë in Haworth, refused it. Janet Kay-Shuttleworth became an obsessive, religiose invalid, and lived apart from her husband after September 1854.

Lewes, George Henry (1817–78)

Freethinker, novelist, critic, playwright, actor, student of physiology, zoology, and psychology, and biographer of Goethe. Educated in London, France, and Jersey, he began to contribute to literary magazines in 1837, thereby making the acquaintance of Dickens, Leigh Hunt, and other writers. He became an accepted authority on French literature. He had four sons by his wife Agnes, née Jervis, but their 'open' marriage meant that she went on to have four children by Leigh Hunt's son Thornton. Unable to divorce her since he had condoned her adultery, he nevertheless remained friendly with Thornton Hunt, with whom he founded a radical weekly, *The Leader*, on 30 March 1850. His liaison with George Eliot (Marian Evans) began in September 1853 and lasted until his death.

Though Charlotte Brontë appreciated his reviews of *Jane Eyre*, she questioned his advocacy of a more subdued, Jane Austen-like style. She was hurt and angered by his harsh review of *Shirley*, but he atoned for this by his perceptive appreciation of *Villette*.

Martineau, Harriet (1802–76)

Novelist and writer on political, social, and economic topics. Her *Illustrations of Political Economy* (1832–4) were simple stories intended to exemplify and advocate social reforms. In November 1849 Charlotte Brontë sent her a copy of *Shirley*, acknowledging the 'pleasure and profit' derived from her works, especially her novel, *Deerbrook* (1839). Charlotte enjoyed visits to her in London (9 December 1849) and in Ambleside in the Lake District in December 1850, but was shocked by what she considered atheism in Martineau's *Letters on the Laws of Man's Nature and Development* (1851), written with Henry George Atkinson. Martineau's critique of *Villette* in 1853, mingling praise with objections to the characters' 'obsession' with love, caused Charlotte to break off the friendship. Martineau's *Autobiography* (1855) mentions Charlotte and many other writers. Though she was not a conventional feminist, Martineau believed that women should take pride in earning their own living, as she did.

Newby, Thomas Cautley (?1798–1882)

The London publisher of *Wuthering Heights*, *Agnes Grey*, and *The Tenant of Wildfell Hall*. The first two books (both printed by Newby) were full of printing errors, and Newby's advertisements implied that they were by the same author as *Jane Eyre*. In June 1848 he informed the American publishers Harper & Brothers that he would be publishing 'Currer Bell's' next work; but Charlotte Brontë's next work, *Shirley*, had been promised to Smith, Elder, who demanded an explanation. Charlotte and Anne hurried to London to identify themselves as separate authors, and to confront Newby with his trickery. Newby published many other books, including Anthony Trollope's first novel, *The Macdermots of Ballycloran*, paying him nothing for it.

Nicholls, Arthur Bell (1819–1906)

Husband of Charlotte Brontë from 29 June 1854 until her death on 31 March 1855. He was born in Killead, County Antrim, Ireland, but from 1825 he was brought up by his uncle Dr Alan Bell at Cuba House in Banagher, King's County (now Offaly). After graduating BA from Trinity College Dublin in 1844, he was Mr Brontë's curate at Haworth from 5 June 1845 until May 1853, then curate at Kirk Smeaton near Pontefract, Yorks., until June 1854, when after his honeymoon he resumed his curacy at Haworth. When Charlotte became ill he and the parsonage servants nursed her devotedly until her death. He returned to Banagher in 1861, living with his aunt Harriette Bell and her daughter Mary Anna. On 26 August 1864 Mary Anna became his second wife. He is portrayed as the 'decent, decorous' Mr Macarthey in *Shirley*. Mrs Gaskell's biography of Charlotte hurt and angered him as an intrusion on his wife's privacy, and his concern for her reputation led him to obliterate several phrases in the manuscript of *The Professor*, which he edited for publication in 1857.

Nussey, Ellen (1817–97)

Ellen was Charlotte Brontë's closest friend for almost 24 years. She spent most of her life in Birstall or Gomersal in Yorkshire. She first met Charlotte Brontë as a fellow-pupil at Margaret Wooler's school at Roe Head, Mirfield, in 1831. More than 350 letters from Charlotte to Ellen survive, forming an invaluable source of information about Charlotte's life and personality. Ellen was not intellectual or widely read, and she was not in the secret of the Brontës' published works until after Emily Brontë's death on 19 December 1848. Charlotte's preoccupation with Arthur Nicholls and her willingness to contemplate marriage with him caused eight months of estrangement from Ellen between July 1853 and February 1854. After their reconciliation through the good offices of Margaret Wooler the friendship was renewed, and Ellen acted as Charlotte's bridesmaid on 29 June 1854. After Charlotte's death Ellen made several attempts to publish Charlotte's letters to her, but she was so concerned to protect the privacy of many people mentioned in the letters by editing out too-revealing references that she never completed an edition. She did however permit bowdlerized selections from the letters to be used in Mrs Gaskell's *Life* in 1857, the American publisher Scribner's *Hours at Home* in 1870, and Thomas Wemyss Reid's *Charlotte Brontë: A Monograph* in 1877. She was eventually persuaded in 1895 to sell almost all her letters into what she imagined was the safe-keeping of the then-respected Thomas James Wise, now notorious as a forger and unscrupulous profiteer. She understood that he would bequeath them to the 'Kensington Museum'. He denied that this had been a condition of sale, and proceeded to sell most of the letters piecemeal, at a vast profit, to collectors in Britain and America.

Nussey, Revd Henry (1812–60 BA Cantab. 1835)

Brother of Ellen Nussey, he was a curate in Dewsbury 1835–7 and in Birstall 1837–February 1838, when he became 'harassed in mind'. He was asked to resign from his third curacy (at Burton Agnes) by his vicar, C. H. Lutwidge, because of his inadequacy as a preacher; but his health improved during his curacy at Donnington and Earnley, Sussex (1838–44). On 1 March 1839, after Lutwidge's sister, Margaret Anne, refused Henry's proposal of marriage, he immediately wrote to propose marriage to Charlotte Brontë, accepting her refusal with pious resignation to the 'Will of the Lord'. In May 1845 he married the wealthy Emily Prescott. Charlotte's visit to Hathersage, Derbyshire, while Ellen Nussey helped to prepare the vicarage there for the newly married couple, made her familiar with the name 'Eyre'. From July 1847 Henry and his wife travelled on the Continent in the hope that Henry would recover his physical and mental health. He died on 8 September 1860 at Wootton Wawen, Warwickshire.

Ringrose, Amelia, later Taylor (b. 1818, d. in or after 1861)

A friend of Ellen Nussey and Charlotte Brontë. Her engagement to marry Ellen's brother George was broken off owing to his mental illness. On 2 October 1850 she married Joseph Taylor (?1816–57), brother of Charlotte's friend Mary Taylor. Amelia's daughter Emily Martha (1851–8) endeared herself to Charlotte and Mr Brontë. Though often wearied by Amelia's fretfulness, Charlotte valued her affectionate nature, accompanied the Taylors on a brief holiday in Scotland and Ilkley, and wrote to her sympathetically from her own deathbed, when Joseph Taylor was also seriously ill.

Robinsons of Thorp Green Hall, Little Ouseburn, near York

Revd Edmund Robinson (1800–46) and his wife Lydia, née Gisborne (1799–1854) employed Anne Brontë as a governess from May 1840 to June 1845 for their daughters Lydia Mary, Elizabeth Lydia, and Mary. She may also have taught their son Edmund. Her experiences are probably reflected in those of Agnes Grey at Horton Lodge. Branwell Brontë was Edmund's tutor from January 1843 to July 1845, when Mr Robinson dismissed him for conduct 'bad beyond expression'. Branwell alleged that Mrs Robinson had become 'damnably too fond' of him, and that she would have married him after her husband's death if a clause in Mr Robinson's will had not forbidden her to see Branwell again on pain of losing her husband's bequest to her. There was no such clause; and Mrs Robinson married a rich elderly relative, Sir Edward Dolman Scott, on 8 November 1848, soon after Branwell's death. In 1857 Mrs Gaskell was threatened with a libel action by solicitors acting for Lady Scott, after she had stated, in the first two editions of her *Life* of Charlotte Brontë, that Branwell had been seduced and ruined by a 'profligate woman'. Copies of the second edition had to be withdrawn, and Mr Gaskell had to direct his solicitor to retract, in a public notice in *The Times*, all statements imputing 'to a widowed lady . . . any breach of her conjugal duties' and more especially imputing to the lady in question a guilty intercourse with the late Branwell Brontë. The third edition of the *Life* was extensively revised.

Smith, Mrs Elizabeth, née Murray (1797–1878)

Mother of the publisher George Smith, q.v., and model for 'Mrs Bretton' in *Villette*. A portly, handsome woman, she loyally supported her son when the defalcation of Smith, Elder & Co.'s foreign editor, Patrick Stewart, left the firm with heavy liabilities. George wrote of her 'serene courage and clear intelligence . . . she even made fun of our perilous position'. Mrs Smith and her daughters treated Charlotte Brontë with every consideration during her visits to them, but they found her excessive shyness and habit of silent observation disconcerting. Mrs Smith may have suspected that Charlotte hoped for more than friendship from her son. For whatever reason, Charlotte was unwilling to stay with the Smiths when she planned to visit London in November 1853.

Smith, George (1824–1901)

Head of the firm of Smith, Elder & Co. at 65, Cornhill, London, which published Charlotte Brontë's novels. Energetic and efficient, he paid off the firm's liabilities, incurred by the fraudulent practices of its former head of the foreign department, Patrick Stewart. He also expanded the firm's Far Eastern branches, exporting goods and books, particularly to India. He was the model for John Graham Bretton in *Villette*. He founded the *Cornhill Magazine*, in which Charlotte's fragmentary novel, 'Emma', appeared in 1860, and after making a fortune from selling Apollinaris mineral water, founded the *Dictionary of National Biography*, edited 1882–91 by Leslie Stephen, and then by Sidney Lee. Charlotte valued his friendship, found him attractive, and was cool in her congratulations on his engagement to Elizabeth Blakeway in December 1853.

Southey, Robert (1774–1843)

Biographer and poet; Poet Laureate from 1813. An early friend of S. T. Coleridge, and later also of Wordsworth. Charlotte Brontë admired his poems, which included *Thalaba* (1801) and *The Curse of Kehama* (1810), and she advised Ellen Nussey to read his *Life of Nelson* (1813). She asked for Southey's opinion of her poetry in a letter of 29 December 1836. He considered that she had the 'faculty of verse', but warned her to write poetry for its own sake, not for the fame of being 'for ever known' as a poetess.

Taylor, James (?1817–74)

A Scotsman, despotic managing clerk of Smith, Elder & Co. He corresponded with Charlotte Brontë and collected the manuscript of *Shirley* from Haworth on 8 September 1849. During his farewell visit to Haworth in April 1851 before leaving England to establish a branch of the firm in Bombay, he may have hinted at marriage, without formally proposing. Though she was not attracted to him, she was miserable when two inconclusive letters from India proved to be the last he wrote to her. His marriage to a widow, Annie Ritter, in London on 23 October 1862 was unhappy. After his return to India in 1863 he held a succession of posts as newspaper editor, secretary of two societies, and registrar of Bombay University. He died on 29 April 1874 and was buried in Sewree cemetery, Bombay.

Taylor, Mary (1817–93)

Elder daughter of the cloth manufacturer Joshua Taylor of Gomersal, Yorks.; a close friend of Charlotte Brontë, who portrayed her as 'Rose Yorke' in *Shirley*. Charlotte first met her at Roe Head, Margaret Wooler's school at Mirfield, and later visited her and her sister Martha at the school they attended in Brussels. A clever, independent, and energetic feminist, Mary travelled and taught in Germany, 1843–4, before emigrating to New Zealand. She became an enterprising shopkeeper in Wellington, from where she wrote lively, outspoken letters to Charlotte, Ellen Nussey, and others. After her return to Yorkshire in 1860 she wrote articles on 'The First Duty of Women', arguing that women should feel neither indignity nor hardship in working for their living. She contributed to *Swiss Notes by Five Ladies* in 1875, and wrote a novel entitled *Miss Miles: A Tale of Yorkshire Life Sixty Years Ago*, first published in London in 1890.

Thackeray, William Makepeace (1811–63)

Novelist. Life as an art student and journalist in Paris, where he met his future wife Isabella Shawe (1818–93; married 1836) was followed by more journalism in France and London. His first daughter, Anne Isabella Thackeray, later Lady Ritchie (1837–1919) wrote a memorable account of Charlotte Brontë's visit to Thackeray's London home in June 1850. After the birth of his third daughter, Harriet Marian (1840–75), his wife became incurably insane. Charlotte greatly admired Thackeray's *Vanity Fair* (1847–8), and in ignorance of the family tragedy, dedicated the second edition of *Jane Eyre* to him. This led to rumours that it had been written by a former governess in his household. Charlotte read his second major novel, *Pendennis* (1848–50), and in 1851 attended four of his six lectures on the English Humourists of the eighteenth century. She also had the privilege of reading (and criticizing) the manuscript of the first two volumes of his *Henry Esmond* (1852). Thackeray paid tribute to her in 'The Last Sketch', his introduction to the two incomplete chapters of her last work, 'Emma', in the *Cornhill Magazine* for April 1860.

Weightman, William (1814–42)

Licentiate in theology of Durham University 1839, ordained deacon 27 July 1839; a handsome young man who became Mr Brontë's curate in August 1839. He lectured on the classics at Keighley Mechanics' Institute in February and March 1840, enlivened life at Haworth Parsonage by his cheerful kindness, and may have been attracted to Anne Brontë. His conscientious visiting of the poor and sick led to his death from cholera on 6 September 1842. In his funeral sermon, Mr Brontë said he regarded him as a son.

Wheelwright, Laetitia Elizabeth (1828–1911)

A friend of Charlotte Brontë, she was the eldest of the five daughters of Dr Thomas Wheelwright (1786–1861), a London physician who took his family to Brussels for their education. All his daughters attended Mme Heger's school for several months from July 1842, and met Charlotte and Emily Brontë there. Laetitia, a competent linguist and musician, became a good though not an intimate friend of Charlotte after both had returned to England. Charlotte visited the Wheelwrights at the Hotel Cluysenaar in the Rue Royale, Brussels, and recalled it as the 'Hotel Crécy' in *Villette*. She also visited, and in June 1850 stayed briefly with the Wheelwrights in their London home.

Williams, William Smith (1800–75)

Literary adviser from 1845 to Smith, Elder & Co. He married Margaret Eliza Hills on 14 January 1826, and had eight children, most of whom Charlotte Brontë met during her visits to London. Though he rejected *The Professor* in July 1847, Charlotte was heartened by his discriminating response to it, and he warmly recommended *Jane Eyre* for publication. Loyal, diligent, and sensitive, he became a congenial correspondent of Charlotte, and offered comments on the manuscripts of *Shirley* and *Villette*. He wrote to her with delicate sympathy when she suffered the distress of her siblings' illness and death. Their informal, confidential correspondence became more infrequent in 1852 and 1853, but he was sent a card announcing her marriage to Nicholls in June 1854.

Winkworth, Catherine (1827–78)

An accomplished translator of German hymns, a pupil of William Gaskell, who gave her Greek lessons, and a friend of Elizabeth Gaskell. In April 1853 she met Charlotte Brontë in the Gaskells' house in Manchester. Like Charlotte and the Gaskells, Catherine and her sisters respected the views of the liberal theologian Frederick Denison Maurice. Charlotte found Catherine intelligent and sympathetic, and confided to her, before her marriage, that her decision to marry the unintellectual, Puseyite Arthur Nicholls had 'cost [her] a good deal'. *The Letters and Memorials of Catherine Winkworth*, edited by her sister Susanna Winkworth (1883) includes personal reminiscences of Charlotte.

Wooler, Margaret (1792–1885)

Teacher and friend of Charlotte Brontë. Well-educated, and reputedly a good linguist, she set up a small boarding school of nine or ten pupils at Roe Head, Mirfield, Yorks., in 1831. Her sisters Katherine and Susanna taught French and art respectively. As a pupil at Roe Head from 17 January 1831 to May 1832, Charlotte heard stories of the local Luddite risings of 1811–12, later recalled in *Shirley*. Charlotte was a teacher at Roe Head for more than two years from 29 July 1835, and earned Miss Wooler's affection. When the school moved to Heald's House, Dewsbury Moor, in early 1838, Charlotte taught there until Christmas that year. After closing her school at the end of 1841, Margaret Wooler sometimes lived with relatives, mainly in Dewsbury or Heckmondwike, but she also took extended holidays in various resorts, including Ilkley, Scarborough, and Hornsea. She became a valued friend of Charlotte, helped to heal her rift with Ellen Nussey in 1854, was a welcome visitor at Haworth Parsonage, and gave Charlotte away on her wedding day.

The Letters

1. *To Ellen Nussey, 21 July 1832*

Haworth

My dearest Ellen

Your kind and interesting letter gave me the sincerest pleasure   I have been expecting to hear from you almost every day since my arrival at home and I at length began to despair of receiving the wished-for letter. You ask me to give you a description of the manner in which I have passed every day since I left School:[1] this is soon done as an account of one day is an account of all. In the morning from nine o'clock till half past twelve I instruct my Sisters & draw, then we walk till dinner after dinner I sew till tea-time, and after tea I either read, write, do a little fancy-work or draw, as I please   Thus in one delightful, though somewhat monotonous course my life is passed. I have only been out to tea twice since I came home, we are expecting company this afternoon & on Tuesday next we shall have all the Female teachers of the Sunday-School to tea. A short time since I was rather surprised by the receipt of a letter from Miss L. S. Brooke[2]   it contained no news of consequence but she complained heavily "of the things which she understood had been said of her after she left school." I suppose the little prattling amiable Maria[3] had given her a full relation of all those disgraceful stories we heard respecting Miss Leah. I am extremely sorry to hear of the deaths of Mrs Wm Wooler[4] and Mr Carr[5] and I doubt not both those individuals will be a serious loss to their respective famillies. Your friend Harriette Carr's[6] account of Miss Isabella Sladen does not surprise me   You know I had formed no very high opinion of her from the traits Miss Hall related of her character. I do hope my dearest that you will return to school again for your own sake though for mine I had rather you would remain at home as we shall then have more frequent opportunities of correspondence with each other. Should your Friends[7] decide against your returning to school I know you have too much good sense and right-feeling not to strive earnestly for your own improvement. Your natural abilities are excellent and under the direction of a judicious and able friend (and I know you have many such) you might acquire a decided taste for elegant literature and even Poetry which indeed is included under that general term. I was very much dissapointed[8] by your not sending the hair. You may be sure my dearest Ellen that I would not grudge double postage to obtain it but I must offer the same excuse for not sending you any. My Aunt and Sisters desire their love to you. Remember me kindly to your Mother & Sisters[9] and accept all the fondest expressions of genuine attachment, from

Your real friend

Charlotte Brontë

P.S Remember the mutual promise we made of a regular correspondence with each other   Excuse all faults in this wretched scrawl Give my love to the Miss Taylors[10] when you see them. Farewell my <u>dear dear dear</u> Ellen.

MS HM 24403.

1. Margaret Wooler's school, Roe Head, Mirfield, Yorks.
2. Leah Sophia Brooke (1815–55), a fellow-pupil at Roe Head.
3. Leah's sister Anna Maria Brooke, b. 1818.
4. Sidney Maria, née Allbutt, wife of Margaret Wooler's brother, Dr William Moore Wooler (1795–1873).
5. The solicitor Charles Carr of Gomersal (1777–13 July 1832).
6. Harriet Carr (1816–98); Isabelle Sladen was the daughter of Thomas Sladen of Mearclough House, Yorks.; Miss Hall (a fellow-pupil) has not been identified.
7. i.e. Ellen's family.
8. Thus in MS.
9. Mrs Ellen Nussey, née Wade (?1771–1857), widow of John Nussey (1760–1826), and her daughters Ann (1795–1878) and Mercy (1801–86).
10. Mary Taylor (1817–93) and Martha Taylor (1819–42). See Biographical Notes p. xliv.

2. *To Ellen Nussey, 4 July 1834*

Haworth

Dear Ellen,

   You will be tired of paying the postage of my letters but necessity must plead my excuse for their frequent recurrence, I <u>must</u> thank you for your very handsome present, The bonnet is pretty, neat and simple, as like the Giver as possible It brought Ellen Nussey with her fair, quiet face, brown eyes, and dark hair full to my remembrance. I wish I could find some other way to thank you for your kindness than words, the load of obligation under which you lay me is positively overwhelming, and I make no return. In your last you request me to tell you of your faults and to cease flattering you. Now really Ellen how can you be so foolish? I <u>won't</u> tell you of your faults, because I don't know them, what a creature would that be who after receiving an affectionate and kind letter from a beloved friend, should sit down and write a catalogue of defects by way of answer? Imagine me doing so and then consider what epithets you would bestow on me, Conceited, Dogmatical, Hypocritical little Humbug, I should think would be mildest; Why child I've neither time nor inclination to reflect on <u>your</u> faults when you are so far from me, and when besides kind letters and presents and so forth are continually bringing forward your goodness in the most prominent light. Then too there are judicious relatives always round you who can much better discharge that unpleasant office, I have no doubt their advice is completely at your service, Why then should I intrude mine? If you will not hear <u>them</u>, it will be vain—though one should rise from the dead to instruct you. Let us have no more nonsense about flattery Ellen, if you love me.

Mr R[ichard] Nussey is going to be married is he? Well his wife-elect appeared to me to be a clever, and aimiable lady as far as I could judge from the little I saw of her and from your account.[1] Now to this <u>flattering</u> sentence must I tack a long list of her <u>faults</u> Ellen? You say it is in contemplation for you to leave Rydings,[2] I am sorry for it, Rydings is a pleasant spot, one of the old family Halls of England, surrounded by Lawn, and wood-land speaking of past times and suggesting (to me at least) happy feelings. Martha Taylor thought you grown less, did she? that's like Martha, I am not grown a bit but as short, and dumpy as ever. I wrote to Mary lately but have as yet received no answer. You ask me to recommend some books for your perusal; I will do so in as few words as I can. If you like poetry let it be first rate, Milton, Shakespeare, Thomson, Goldsmith Pope (if you will though I don't admire him) Scott, Byron, Campbell, Wordsworth and Southey   Now Ellen don't be startled at the names of Shakespeare, and Byron. Both these were great Men and their works are like themselves, You will know how to chuse the good and avoid the evil, the finest passages are always the purest, the bad are invariably revolting you will never wish to read them over twice, Omit the Comedies of Shakspeare and the Don Juan, perhaps the Cain of Byron though the latter is a magnificent Poem and read the rest fearlessly, that must indeed be a depraved mind which can gather evil from Henry the 8th from Richard 3d from Macbeth and Hamlet and Julius Cesar, Scott's sweet, wild, romantic Poetry can do you no harm nor can Wordsworth's nor Campbell's nor Southey's, the greatest part at least of his   some is certainly exceptionable, For History read Hume,[3] Rollin,[4] and the Universal History[5] if you <u>can</u> I never did. For Fiction—read Scott alone all novels after his are worthless. For Biography, read Johnson's lives of the Poets,[6] Boswell's life of Johnson,[7] Southey's life of Nelson,[8] Lockhart's life of Burns,[9] Moore's life of Sheridan,[10] Moore's life of Byron,[11] Wolfe's remains.[12] For Natural History read Bewick,[13] and Audubon,[14] and Goldsmith[15] and White of Selborne[16] For Divinity, but your brother Henry[17] will advise you there I only say adhere to standard authors and don't run after novelty. If you can read this scrawl it will be to the credit of your patience. With love to your Sisters, believe me to be

for ever Your's

Charlotte Brontë

MS HM 24408.

1. Ellen's brother Richard (1803–72) married Elizabeth Charnock of Leeds (b. 1803) in Sept. 1846.
2. A substantial battlemented house in Birstall, Yorks.; one of CB's models for Thornfield in *Jane Eyre*.
3. David Hume (1711–76) Scottish philosopher and author of a six-volume *History of England* (1754–61).

4. Charles Rollin (1661–1741), author of *Histoire ancienne* (1730–8) and *Histoire romaine*, 8 vols. (1741).

5. Either the *Universal History* of which the modern part, to which Tobias Smollett contributed, appeared in 44 vols. (1759–66), or the 25-vol. *Universal History* (1802–4) by Revd William Fordyce Mavor (1758–1837).

6. Samuel Johnson, *Lives of the Poets*, vols. i–iv (1779), vols. v–x (1781).

7. James Boswell, *The Life of Samuel Johnson* (1791).

8. Robert Southey, *The Life of Nelson* (1813).

9. John Gibson Lockhart, *The Life of Robert Burns* (1828).

10. Thomas Moore, *The Life of Sheridan* (1825).

11. Thomas Moore, *The Letters and Journals of Lord Byron* with a *Life* (1830).

12. Charles Wolfe, *Remains* (1825).

13. Thomas Bewick, *The History of British Birds* (1797, 1804).

14. John James Audubon, *Birds of America* (1827–38), *Ornithological Biography* (1831–9).

15. Oliver Goldsmith, *A History of Earth and Animated Nature* (1774).

16. Gilbert White, *The Natural History and Antiquities of Selborne* (1789).

17. Henry Nussey (1812–60). See Biographical Notes, pp. xli–xlii, and Letter 6 and notes.

3. To Ellen Nussey, ?October 1836

[?Roe Head]

Weary with a day's hard work—during which an unusual degree of Stupidity has been displayed by my promising pupils I am sitting down to write a few hurried lines to my dear Ellen.[1] Excuse me if I say nothing but nonsense, for my mind is exhausted, and dispirited. It is a Stormy evening and the wind is uttering a continual moaning sound that makes me feel very melancholy—At such times, in such moods as these Ellen it is my nature to seek repose in some calm, tranquil idea and I have now summoned up your image to give me rest   There you sit, upright and still in your black dress and white scarf—your pale, marble-like face—looking so serene and kind—just like reality—I wish you would speak to me—. If we should be separated   if it should be our lot to live at a great distance and never to see each other again   in old age how I should call up the memory of my youthful days and what a melancholy pleasure I should feel in dwelling on the recollection of my Early Friend Ellen Nussey!

If I like people it is my nature to tell them so and I am not afraid of offering incense to your vanity. It is from religion that you derive your chief charm and may its influence always preserve you as pure, as unassuming and as benevolent in thought and deed as you are now. What am I compared to you   I feel my own utter worthlessness when I make the comparison. I'm a very coarse common-place wretch!

Ellen (I have some qualities that make me very miserable   some feelings that you can have no participation in—that few very few people in the world can at all understand   I don't pride myself on these peculiarities, I strive to conceal and suppress them as much as I can.   but they burst out sometimes and then those who see the explosion despise me and I hate myself for days afterwards).   we are going to have prayers so I can write no more of this trash yet it is too true.

I must send this note for want of a better. I don't know what to say. I've just received your epistle and what accompanied it, I can't tell what should induce your Sisters to waste their kindness on such a one as me. I'm obliged to them and I hope you'll tell them so—I'm obliged to you also, more for your note than for your present the first gave me pleasure the last something very like pain. Give my love to both your Sisters and my thanks   the bonnet is too handsome for me   I dare write no more. When shall we meet again

C Brontë

MS HM 24383.

1. CB's impatience and frustration with her pupils, 'those fat-headed oafs', is a recurring theme in her private writings of this period.

4. *To Ellen Nussey, 5 and 6 December 1836*

[Roe Head]

I am sure Ellen you will conclude that I have taken a final leave of my senses, to forget to send your bag—when I had had it hanging before my eyes in the dressing-room for a whole week. I stood for ten minutes considering before I sent the boy off I felt sure I had something else to entrust to him besides the books, but I could not recollect what it was—These aberrations of Memory, warn me pretty intelligibly that I am getting past my prime.

I hope you will not be much inconvenienced by my neglect—I'll wait till to-morrow to see if George[1] will call for it on his way to Huddersfield and if he does not I'll try to get a person to go over with it to Brookroyd[2] on purpose. I am most grieved lest you should think me careless—but I assure you it was merely a temporary fit of absence which I could not avoid—I wish exceedingly that I could come to see you before Christmas, but it is impossible—however I trust ere another three weeks elapse I shall again have my Comforter beside me, under the roof of my own dear quiet home—If I could always live with you, and daily read the bible with you, if your lips and mine could at the same time, drink the same draught from the same pure fountain of Mercy—I hope, I trust, I might one day become better, far better, than my evil wandering thoughts, my corrupt heart, cold to the spirit, and warm to the flesh will now permit me to be. I often plan the pleasant life which we might lead together, strengthening each other in that power of self-denial, that hallowed and glowing devotion, which the first Saints of God often attained to—My eyes fill with tears when I contrast the bliss of such a state brightened by hopes of the future with the melancholy state I now live in, uncertain that I have ever felt true contrition, wandering in thought and deed, longing for holiness which I shall never, never obtain—smitten at times to the heart with the conviction that ?your Ghastly Calvinistic doctrines[3] are true—darkened in short by the very shadows of Spiritual Death! If Christian perfection be necessary to Salvation I shall never be saved, my heart is a real hot-bed for sinful thoughts and as to practice   when I decide on an action I scarcely remember to look to my Redeemer for direction.

I know not how to pray—I cannot bend my life to the grand end of doing good—I go on constantly seeking my own pleasure   pursuing the Gratification of my own desires, I forget God and will not God forget me? And meantime I know the Greatness of Jehovah   I acknowledge the truth   the perfection of his word, I adore the purity of the Christian faith, my theory is right, my Practice—horribly wrong.

Good-bye Ellen

C Brontë

Write to me again if you can   your notes are meat and drink to me. Remember me to the Family I hope Mercy is better

Monday Morning

Roe-Head

I wish I could come to Brookroyd for a single night but I don't like to ask Miss Wooler. She is at Dewsbury and I'm alone at this moment   eleven o'clock on Tuesday night   I wish you were here all the house in bed but myself   I'm thinking of you my dearest

Return me a scrap by the Bearer if it be only a single line to satisfy me that you have got your bag safely. I met your brother George on the road this afternoon I did not know it was he until after he was past and then Anne[4] told me—he would think me amazingly stupid in not moving[5]—can't help it

MS BPM Bon. 162.

1. Ellen's brother George Nussey (1814–85), who worked for the family firm. Ellen's father John Nussey of Birstall Smithies (1760–1826) and his sons Joseph (1797–1846), Richard (1803–72), and George were woollen manufacturers and merchants.
2. Ellen's mother and sisters had moved from Rydings to a smaller house, Brookroyd, in Birstall.
3. The extreme form of Calvinism developed by some of the followers of John Calvin (1509–64): the belief that individuals were predestined by God to be either 'Elect' (saved by grace to eternal life) or 'Reprobate' (eternally damned or outcast).
4. Anne Brontë, who had replaced her sister Emily as a pupil at Roe Head in Oct. 1835. Away from the freedom of the moors, Emily had become ill, and had returned to Haworth after less than three months in the school.
5. Bowing or nodding the head as a sign of recognition.

5. *To Robert Southey,*[1] *16 March 1837*

Sir

I cannot rest till I have answered your letter, even though by addressing you a second time I should appear a little intrusive; but I must thank you for the kind, and wise advice you have condescended to give me.[2] I had not ventured to hope for such a reply; so considerate in its tone, so noble in its spirit. I must suppress what I feel, or you will think me foolishly enthusiastic.

At the first perusal of your letter I felt only shame, and regret that I had ever ventured to trouble you with my crude rhapsody.   I felt a painful heat rise to my face when I thought of the quires of paper[3] I had covered with what once gave me so much delight, but which now was only a source of confusion; but after I had thought a little and read it again and again—the prospect seemed to clear.   You do not forbid me to write; you do not say that what I write is utterly destitute of merit; you only warn me against the folly of neglecting real duties, for the sake of imaginative pleasures—of writing for the love of fame & for the selfish excitement of emulation: you kindly allow me to write poetry for its own sake provided I leave undone nothing which I ought to do in order to pursue that single, absorbing exquisite gratification: I am afraid Sir you think me very foolish—I know the first letter I wrote to you was all senseless trash from beginning to end. But I am not altogether the idle, dreaming being it would seem to denote. My Father is a Clergyman of limited though competent income, and I am the eldest of his children—He expended quite as much in my education as he could afford in justice to the rest. I thought it therefore my duty when I left school to become a Governess[4]—In that capacity I find enough to occupy my thoughts all day long, and my head and hands too, without having a moment's time for one dream of the imagination. In the evenings I confess I do think but I never trouble any one else with my thoughts. I carefully avoid any appearance of pre-occupation and eccentricity—which might lead those I live amongst to suspect the nature of my pursuits. Following my Father's advice who from my childhood has counselled me just in the wise, and friendly tone of your letter; I have endeavoured not only attentively to observe all the duties a woman ought to fulfil, but to feel deeply interested in them—I don't always succeed, for sometimes when I'm teaching, and sewing I'd far rather be reading or writing; but I try to deny myself—and my father's approbation has hitherto amply rewarded me for the privation.

Once more allow me to thank you, with sincere gratitude. I trust I shall never more feel ambitious to see my name in print—if the wish should rise I'll look at Southey's autograph and suppress it. It is honour enough for me that I have written to him and received an answer. That letter is consecrated; no one shall ever see it but Papa and my brother and sisters—Again I thank you—this incident I suppose will be renewed no more—if I live to be an old woman I shall remember it thirty years hence as a bright dream—The signature which you suspected of being fictitious is my real name, again, therefore I must sign myself,

C. Brontë.

Haworth
March 16th.—1837
Pray Sir, excuse me for writing to you a second time; I could not help writing—partly to tell you how thankful I am for your kindness and partly to let you know that your advice shall not be wasted; however sorrowfully and reluctantly it may be at first followed. C. B—

MS BPM B.S. 40.25.

1. Robert Southey (1774–1843), poet, biographer, essayist, and editor; Poet Laureate since 1813.
2. CB had written to Southey on 29 Dec. 1836, asking his opinion of the verses she sent to him. In his reply on 12 Mar. 1837 he had written: 'You who so ardently desire "to be for ever known" as a poetess, might have had your ardour in some degree abated, by seeing a poet in the decline of life ... You evidently possess & in no inconsiderable degree what Wordsworth calls "the faculty of Verse." ... But it is not with a view to distinction that you shd. cultivate this talent, if you consult your own happiness. . . . The daydreams in wh[ich] you habitually indulge are likely to induce a distempered state of mind ... Literature cannot be the business of a woman's life: & it ought not to be. The more she is engaged in her proper duties, the less leisure will she have for it. . . . But do not suppose that I disparage the gift wh[ich] you possess ... Write poetry for its own sake, not in a spirit of emulation, & not with a view to celebrity: the less you aim at that, the more likely you will be to deserve, & finally to obtain it.'
3. Elizabeth Gaskell wrote in her *Life* of CB: 'I have had a curious packet confided to me, containing an immense amount of manuscript, in an inconceivably small space; tales, dramas, poems, romances, written principally by Charlotte.' (*Life* ch. 5.) See Christine Alexander, *The Early Writings of Charlotte Brontë* (1983), and Victor A. Neufeldt (ed.), *The Poems of Charlotte Brontë* (1985).
4. Used here to mean a teacher in a school, not a private governess.

6. *To Ellen Nussey, 12 March 1839*

Haworth—

My dearest Ellen

When your letter was put into my hands—I said "She is coming at last   I hope" but when I opened it and found what the contents were I was vexed to the heart. You need not ask me to go to Brookroyd any more—Once for all and at the hazard of being called the most stupid little Wretch that ever existed—I won't go till you've been to Haworth.—I don't blame you I believe you would come if you might   perhaps I ought not to blame others—but I'm grieved.

Anne goes to Blake-Hall[1] on the 8th. of April unless some further unseen cause of delay should occur. I've heard nothing more from Mrs. Thos Brook[2] as yet—Papa wishes me to remain at home awhile longer—but I begin to be anxious to set to work again—and yet it will be hard work after the indulgence of so many weeks to return to that dreary Gin-horse round.[3]

You ask me my dear Ellen whether I have received a letter from Henry[4]—I have about a week since—The Contents I confess did a little surprise me, but I kept them to myself, and unless you had questioned me on the subject I would never have adverted to it—Henry says he is comfortably settled in Sussex—that his health is much improved & that it is his intention to take pupils after Easter—he then intimates that in due time he shall want a Wife to take care of his pupils and frankly asks me to be that Wife. Altogether the letter is written without cant or flattery—& in a common-sense style which does credit to his judgment—Now my dear Ellen there were in this proposal some things that might have proved a strong temptation—I thought if I were to marry so, Ellen could live with me and how happy I should be, but again I asked myself two questions—"Do I love Henry Nussey as much as a woman ought to love her husband? Am I the person best qualified to make him happy—?—Alas Ellen my Conscience answered "<u>no</u>" to both these questions. I felt that though I esteemed Henry—though I had a kindly leaning towards him because he is an aimiable—well-disposed man—Yet I had not, and never could have that intense attachment which would make me willing to die for him—and if ever I marry it must be in that light of adoration that I will regard my Husband   Ten to one I shall never have the chance again but n'importe.[5] Moreover I was aware that Henry knew so little of me he could hardly be conscious to whom he was writing—why it would startle him to see me in my natural home-character he would think I was a wild, romantic enthusiast indeed—I could not sit all day long making a grave face before my husband—I would laugh and satirize and say whatever came into my head first—and if he were a clever man & loved me the whole world weighed in the balance against his smallest wish should be light as air—

Could I—knowing my mind to be such as that could I conscientiously say that I would take a grave quiet young man like Henry? No it would have been deceiving him—and deception of that sort is beneath me. So I wrote a long letter back in which I expressed my refusal as gently as I could and also candidly avowed my reasons for that refusal. I described to him too the sort of Character I thought would suit him for a wife—Good-bye my dear Ellen—write to me soon and say whether you are angry with me or not—

C Brontë

MS BPM Gr. E 2.

1. Blake Hall, Mirfield, Yorks., was the home of Joshua Ingham (1802–66) and his wife Mary, née Cunliffe Lister (1812–99). Five of their thirteen children had been born by the time Anne Brontë became a governess at Blake Hall on 8 Apr. 1839, the eldest being Joshua Cunliffe (1832–77) and the youngest Harriet (1838–9). Anne left the Hall in December 1839. The Bloomfields in *Agnes Grey* are said to be based on the Ingham family.
2. The wife of Thomas Brooke, a member of a prosperous family of manufacturers in Honley, three miles south of Huddersfield.

3. A 'gin-horse' was used in mines and elsewhere to work a drum or windlass for hoisting or pumping. The animal moved in a circular 'gin-race' or 'gin-ring'.
4. See letter 2 n. 17, and Biographical Notes, pp. xli–xlii. Ellen's brother Revd Henry Nussey was the curate-in-charge at Earnley with Almodington, Sussex, from Dec. 1838 until Apr. 1844. He also preached at Donnington, near which there was a school which he thought CB might run. His letter to her contained a proposal of marriage, written almost immediately after a refusal from Margaret Anne Lutwidge (1809–69), the sister of his former vicar at Burton Agnes. On Friday 1 Mar. 1839 Henry wrote in his diary, 'On Tuesday last received a decisive reply fm. M.A.L.'s papa. A loss, but I trust a providential one . . . Wrote to a York[shir]e friend, C.B.' On 5 Mar. 1839, Charlotte replied with a 'decided negative', on the ground that she lacked the mild and cheerful temperament which would make her a suitable wife for him, and that she lacked the capital to make a success of the school. See her letter to him in *CBL* i. 185–6.
5. Never mind, no matter.

7. To Emily Jane Brontë, 8 June 1839

Stonegappe

Dearest Lavinia,[1]

I am most exceedingly obliged to you for the trouble you have taken in seeking up my things and sending them all right. The box and its contents were most acceptable. I only wish I had asked you to send me some letter-paper. This is my last sheet but two. When you can send the other articles of raiment now manufacturing, I shall be right down glad of them.

I have striven hard to be pleased with my new situation.[2] The country, the house, and the grounds are, as I have said, divine. But, alack-a-day! there is such a thing as seeing all beautiful around you—pleasant woods, winding white paths, green lawns, and blue sunshiny sky—and not having a free moment or a free thought left to enjoy them in. The children are constantly with me, and more riotous, perverse, unmanageable cubs never grew. As for correcting them, I soon quickly found that was entirely out of the question: they are to do as they like. A complaint to Mrs. Sidgwick brings only black looks upon oneself, and unjust, partial excuses to screen the children. I have tried that plan once. It succeeded so notably that I shall try it no more. I said in my last letter that Mrs. Sidgwick did not know me. I now begin to find that she does not intend to know me, that she cares nothing in the world about me except to contrive how the greatest possible quantity of labour may be squeezed out of me, and to that end she overwhelms me with oceans of needlework, yards of cambric to hem, muslin nightcaps to make, and, above all things, dolls to dress. I do not think she likes me at all, because I can't help being shy in such an entirely novel scene, surrounded as I have hitherto been by strange and constantly changing faces. [I used to think I should like to be in the stir of grand folks' society but I have had enough of it—it is dreary work to look on and listen.][3] I see now more clearly than I have ever done before that a private governess has no existence, is not considered as a living and rational being except as connected with the wearisome duties she has to fulfil. While she is teaching the children, working for them, amusing them, it is all right. If she steals a moment for herself she is a nuisance. Nevertheless, Mrs. Sidgwick is universally considered an amiable woman. Her manners are fussily affable. She talks a great deal, but as it seems to me not much to the purpose. Perhaps I may like her better after a while. At present I have no call to her. Mr. Sidgwick is in my opinion a hundred times better—less profession, less bustling condescension, but a far kinder heart. It is very seldom that he speaks to me, but when he does I always feel happier and more settled for some minutes after. He never asks me to wipe the children's smutty noses or tie their shoes or fetch their pinafores or set them a chair. One of the pleasantest afternoons I have spent here—indeed, the only one at all pleasant—was when Mr. Sidgwick walked out with his children, and I had orders to follow a little behind. As he strolled on through his fields with his magnificent Newfoundland dog at his side, he looked very like what a frank, wealthy, Conservative gentleman ought to be.[4] He spoke freely and unaffectedly to the people he met, and though he indulged his children and allowed them to tease himself far too much, he would not suffer them grossly to insult others.

I am getting quite to have a regard for the Carter family.[5] At home I should not care for them, but here they are friends. Mr. Carter was at Mirfield yesterday and saw Anne.[6] He says she was looking uncommonly well. Poor girl, she must indeed wish to be at home. As to Mrs Collins'[7] report that Mrs. Sidgwick intended to keep me permanently, I do not think that such was ever her design. Moreover, I would not stay without some alterations. For instance, this burden of sewing would have to be removed. It is too bad for anything. I never in my whole life had my time so fully taken up. Next week we are going to Swarcliffe, Mr. Greenwood's place near Harrogate,[8] to stay three weeks or a month. After that time I hope Miss Hoby will return. Don't show this letter to papa or aunt, only to Branwell. They will think I am never satisfied wherever I am. I complain to you because it is a relief, and really I have had some unexpected mortifications to put up with. However, things may mend, but Mrs. Sidgwick expects me to do things that I cannot do—to love her children and be entirely devoted to them. I am really very well. I am so sleepy that I can write no more. I must leave off. Love to all.—Good-bye.

Direct your next dispatch—J. Greenwood, Esq., Swarcliffe, near Harrogate.

C. Brontë

MS untraced. Text CBCircle 80–2 and Gaskell Life ch. 8.

1. This name is not used elsewhere for Emily Brontë, but there is no doubt that the letter is to her. Cf. the 'lovely young Lavinia' 'Recluse amid the close-embowering woods' in James Thomson's The Seasons (1726–30; 'Autumn', l. 208).
2. CB had taken a temporary post as a governess in the family of John Benson Sidgwick (1800–73) and his wife Sarah Hannah, née Greenwood (1803–87) at Stonegappe, Lothersdale, near Skipton, Yorks.

3. Sentence omitted in *CBCircle*; text from Gaskell *Life*, ch. 8.
4. Zamorna, the hero of CB's early story 'Caroline Vernon', leans against the trunk of a fine tree, with his Newfoundland dog at his feet, watching his haymakers at work. The story includes a letter dated 'June 29th 1839'. See *Five Novelettes*, ed. Winifred Gérin (1971), 282, 285.
5. Margaret Wooler's sister Susanna (1800–72), her husband Revd Edward Nicholl Carter (1800–72), vicar of the newly built Christ Church, Lothersdale, and their children.
6. Anne Brontë's post as a governess was at Blake Hall, near Mirfield, where she had to cope with the unruly children of Joshua Ingham (1802–66) and his wife.
7. Probably the wife of Revd John Collins, assistant from Mar. 1839 to Revd Theodore Dury of Keighley, whose wife Anne was Mrs Sidgwick's sister.
8. Swarcliffe House in the Nidd valley had been bought by Mrs Sidgwick's father John Greenwood (1763–1846) in 1805.

8. *To Ellen Nussey, 4 August 1839*

[Haworth]

My dearest Ellen

I have been a long time in answering your last—but the fact was I really could not give you any definite reply till now and I thought it better to wait till I could say something decided.

The Liverpool[1] journey is yet a matter of talk   a sort of castle in the air—but between you and I, I fancy it is very doubtful whether it will ever assume a more solid shape—Aunt—like many other elderly people—likes to <u>talk</u> of such things but when it comes to putting them into actual practise she rather falls off. Such being the case I think you and I had better adhere to our first plan—of going somewhere together independently of other people—

I have got leave to accompany you for a week at the utmost stretch a fortnight but no more   where do you wish to go?—Burlington[2] I should think from what Mary Taylor says would be as eligible a place as any—when do you wish to set off?—arrange all these things according to your own convenience—I shall start no objections—the idea of seeing the SEA—of being near it—watching its changes by sunrise Sunset—moonlight—& noonday—in calm—perhaps in storm—fills & satisfies my mind I shall be dis-contented at nothing—& then I am not to be with a set of people with whom I have nothing in common—who would be nuisances & bores—but with you Ellen Nussey whom I like and know & who knows me—

I have an odd circumstance to relate to you—prepare for a hearty laugh—the other day—Mr Hodgson[3]—Papa's former Curate—now a Vicar—came over to spend the day—with us—bringing with him his own Curate. The latter Gentleman by name Mr Price[4] is a young Irish Clergyman—fresh from Dublin University—it was the first time we had any of us seen him, but however after the manner of his Countrymen he soon made himself at home   his character quickly appeared in his conversation—witty—lively, ardent—clever too—but deficient in the dignity & discretion of an Englishman   at home you know Ellen I talk with ease and am never shy—never weighed down & oppressed by that miserable mauvaise honte[5] which torments & constrains me elsewhere—so I conversed with this Irishman & laughed at his jests—& though I saw faults in his character excused them because of the amusement his originality afforded—I cooled a little indeed & drew in towards the latter part of the evening—because he began to season his conversation with something of Hibernian flattery which I did not quite relish. however they went away and no more was thought about them.

A few days after I got a letter the direction of which puzzled me it being in a hand I was not accustomed to see—evidently it was neither from you nor Mary Taylor, my only Correspondents—having opened & read it it proved to be a declaration of attachment—& proposal of Matrimony—expressed in the ardent language of the sapient young Irishman!

Well thought I—I've heard of love at first sight but this beats all. I leave you to guess what my answer would be—convinced that you will not do me the injustice of guessing wrong

When we meet I'll shew you the letter. I hope you are laughing heartily. This is not like one of my adventures is it? It more nearly resembles Martha Taylor's—I'm certainly doomed to be an old maid Ellen—I can't expect another chance—never mind I made up my mind to that fate ever since I was twelve years old. I need not tell you to consider that this little adventure is told in confidence—write soon

C Brontë

I had almost forgotten to settle about how we are to join if I take the coach from Keighley to Bradford and from thence to Leeds—I think I could arrive in the latter Town by 10 or at the latest 11 o'clock in the morning—will that be soon enough for your plans? & will it suit your convenience to meet me at the Inn where the coach stops?

If this project should be deemed in any way inconvenient I must contrive some other—on some accounts it would be far better to get to Brookroyd the day before—do you know whether there is any daily coach from Bradford runs anywhere within a mile of you? After all I have not yet ascertained whether my limited time for staying at the sea-side will interfere with what is necessary for your health   if it would I throw the whole scheme up at once—write very soon.

What luggage will you take? much or little?

MS HM 24418.

1. Liverpool had for many years been a great seaport and commercial town, but it also attracted visitors for sea-bathing. Possibly CB's father and her aunt Elizabeth Branwell recalled journeys via Liverpool from Ireland and Cornwall respectively.
2. An alternative name for Bridlington on the east coast of Yorks. The old town, with a fine priory church and some handsome houses, was a mile inland from the seaside resort of Bridlington Quay.

3. Revd William Hodgson (?1809–74), Mr Brontë's curate from Dec. 1835 to May 1837, then perpetual curate (equivalent to a vicar) of Christ Church, Colne, Lancs., until his death.
4. Revd David Pryce, BA Trinity College Dublin (1811–40); he died after a period of delicate health from the rupture of a blood vessel.
5. Painful self-consciousness or diffidence.

9. *To Ellen Nussey, 24 October 1839*

Haworth

My dear Ellen

You will have concluded by this time that I never got home at all[1]—but evaporated by the way—however I did get home and very well too by the aid of the Dewsbury Coachman—though if I had not contrived to make friends with him I don't know how I should have managed. He shewed me the way to the Inn where the Keighley Coach stopped—carried my box—took my place—saw my luggage put in—and helped me to mount on to the top—I assure you I felt exceedingly obliged to him.

I had a long letter from your brother Henry the other day—giving an account of his bride-elect[2]—if she be what he describes her—He is amply justified in the step he proposes to take—but Love they say blinds the eyes—so I don't know. I have not answered it yet but I mean to soon

Have you forgot the Sea by this time Ellen? is it grown dim in your mind? or you can still see it dark blue and green and foam-white and hear it—roaring roughly when the wind is high or rushing softly when it is calm? How is your health   have good effects resulted from the change? I am as well as need be, and very fat.

I think of Easton very often and of worthy Mr Hudson and his kind-hearted help-mate and of our pleasant walks to Harlequin-Wood—to Boynton[3]—our Merry evenings—our romps with little Fanchon[4]—&c. &c. if we both live this period of our lives will long be a theme of pleasant recollection. Did you chance in your letter to Mrs Hudson to mention my spectacles? I am sadly inconvenienced by the want of them—I can neither read, write nor draw with comfort in their absence. I hope Madame Booth won't refuse to give them up

I wonder when we shall meet again—have you yet managed to get any definite period fixed for your visit to us?

Excuse the brevity of this letter my dear Ellen for the truth is I have been drawing all day and my eyes are so tired it is quite a labour to write. Give my best love to your Mother & Sister and to Sarah[5] & believe me

Your old friend
C Brontë.

MS HM 24419.

1. CB had returned home after a five-week holiday with Ellen on the east coast of Yorks., staying for four weeks with Mr and Mrs John Hudson in the hamlet of Easton, one mile inland from Bridlington, and for a final week at Ann Booth's lodging-house in Bridlington Quay.
2. Not identified, but presumably not the wealthy Emily Prescott (1811–1907) whom Henry married in 1845.
3. A picturesque village about a mile from Easton.
4. Mrs Hudson's niece, Fanny Whipp, about 7 years old.
5. Ann Nussey and the invalid Sarah Walker Nussey (1809–43). Mercy Nussey was housekeeping for her brother Henry at Earnley.

10. *To Ellen Nussey, 17 March 1840*

[Haworth]

My dear Mrs. Eleanor

I wish to scold you with a forty horse power for having told Martha Taylor that I had requested you "not to tell <u>her</u> everything" which piece of information of course has thrown Martha into a tremendous ill-humour besides setting the teeth of her curiosity on edge with the notion, that there is something very important in the wind which you and I are especially desirous to conceal from her

Such being the state of matters I desire to take off any embargo I may have laid on your tongue which I plainly see will not be restrained and to enjoin you to walk up to Gomersal[1] and tell her forthwith every individual occurrence you can recollect, including Valentines,[2] "Fair Ellen, Fair Ellen"—"Away fond Love" "Soul divine" and all—likewise if you please the painting of Miss Celia Amelia Weightman's portrait[3] and that young lady's frequent and agreeable visits—By the bye I inquired into the opinion of that intelligent and interesting young person respecting you—it was a favourable one—She thought you a fine-looking girl and a very good girl into the bargain—Have you received the newspaper which has been despatched containing a notice of her lecture at Keighley?[4] Mr Morgan[5] came, stayed three days and went [—] by Miss Weightman's aid we got on pretty well—it was amazing to see with what patience and good temper the innocent creature endured that fat Welchman's prosing—though she confessed afterwards that she was almost done up by his long stories.

We feel very dull without you, I wish those three weeks were to come over again. Aunt has been at times precious cross since you went, however she is rather better now   I had a bad cold on Sunday and stayed at home most of the day—Anne's cold is better—but I don't consider her strong yet   What did your Sister Anne say about my omitting to send a drawing for the Jew-basket?[6] I hope she was too much occupied with the thoughts of going to Earnley[7] to think of it—

I am obliged to cut short my letter—every-body in the house unites in sending their love to you—Miss Celia Amelia—Weightman also desires to be remembered to you—Write soon again, and believe me yours unutterably—

Charivari[8]

To your hands and Martha Taylor's do I resign myself in a spirit worthy of a
Martyr that is to say with much the same feeling that I should experience if I
were sitting down on the plat[9] to have a tooth drawn you have a peculiar fashion
of your own of reporting a saying or a doing and Martha has a still more peculiar
fashion of re-reporting it.

MS HM 24421.

1. Martha (1819–42) and Mary Taylor (1817–93), daughters of the cloth manufacturer Joshua Taylor
   (1766–1840) and his wife Anne, née Tickell (d. 1856), lived at the Red House, Gomersal, Yorks.
2. Poems sent to Ellen Nussey and the Brontë sisters by Mr Brontë's handsome young curate
   William Weightman, for whom see Biographical Notes, p. xlv. He had discovered that none of
   the girls had ever received a Valentine.
3. 'Celia Amelia' was evidently the curate's nickname. CB's drawing of a young man in an academic
   gown, reproduced in BST (1987), 19. 4. 175, is probably a portrait of Weightman.
4. Weightman had insisted that the 'young ladies at the Parsonage must hear his lecture on the
   classics at Keighley', and they had all walked home in high spirits after it.
5. Mr Brontë's friend Revd William Morgan (1782–1858), perpetual curate at Christ Church,
   Bradford, 1815–51, rector of Hulcott, Bucks., 1851–8. CB may have used some of his traits for
   Dr Boultby in Shirley.
6. A fund-raising device for the London Society for Promoting Christianity Amongst the Jews,
   founded 1809. The ladies of a parish made and contributed drawings, fancy work, baby-clothes
   and the like to the basket, and sold them 'perforce to the heathenish gentlemen thereof, at prices
   unblushingly exorbitant'. See Shirley, ch. 7.
7. Ann Nussey was to replace Mercy as Henry Nussey's housekeeper.
8. Perhaps derived from 'Charlotte', as 'Eleanor' from Ellen. A 'charivari' was the 'rough music'
   made with kettles, pans, tea-trays, etc., in public derision of an unpopular person.
9. The grass 'plot' in front of the parsonage.

11. To Ellen Nussey, [?7 April 1840]

[Haworth]

My dear Mrs Menelaus[1]

I think I'm exceedingly good to write to you so soon—indeed I am quite afraid
you will begin to consider me intrusive with my frequent letters—I ought by
rights to let an interval of a quarter of a year elapse between each communication
and I will in time never fear me, I shall improve in procrastination as I get older.
(My hand is trembling like that of an old man so I don't expect you'll be able
to read my writing never mind put the letter by in a drawer and I'll read it
to you next time I see you)—Little Haworth has been all in a bustle about
Church-rates[2] since you were here—we had a most stormy meeting in the
School-room—Papa took the chair and Mr Collins[3] and Mr Weightman acted
as his supporters one on each side—There was violent opposition—which set
Mr Collins' Irish blood in a ferment and if Papa had not kept him quiet partly by
persuasion, and partly by compulsion he would have given the Dissenters their

kail through the reek.[4] (a Scotch proverb which I'll explain another time)—He and Mr Weightman both bottled up their wrath for that time but it was only to explode with redoubled force at a future period—We had two sermons on Dissent and its consequences preached last Sunday one in the afternoon by Mr Weightman and one in the evening by Mr Collins—all the Dissenters were invited to come and hear and they actually shut up their chapels and came in a body; of course the church was crowded. Miss Celia Amelia[5] delivered a noble, eloquent high-Church, Apostolical succession[6] discourse—in which he banged the Dissenters most fearlessly and unflinchingly—I thought they had got enough for one while, but it was nothing to the dose that was thrust down their throats in the evening—a keener, cleverer, bolder and more heart-stirring harangue I never heard than that which Mr Collins delivered from Haworth Pulpit last Sunday Evening—he did not rant—he did not cant he did not whine, he did not snivel: he just got up and spoke with the boldness of a man who is impressed with the truth of what he is saying who has no fear of his enemies and no dread of consequences—his Sermon lasted an hour yet I was sorry when it was done   I do not say that I agree either with him or Mr Weightman in all or half their opinions—I consider them bigoted, intolerant and wholly unjustifiable on the grounds of common sense—my conscience will not let me be either a Puseyite[7] or a Hookist[8] nay if I were [a] Dissenter I would have taken the first opportunity of kicking or horse-whipping both the Gentlemen for their stern bitter attack on my religion and its teachers—but in spite of all this I admired the noble integrity which could dictate so fearless an opposition against so strong an antagonist. I have been painting a portrait of Agnes Walton[9] for our friend Miss Celia Amelia—you would laugh to see how his eyes sparkle with delight when he looks at it like a pretty child pleased with a new play-thing. Good bye to you let me have no more of your humbug about *Cupid* &c. you know as well as I do it is all groundless trash

C Brontë

Mr Weightman has given another [lecture][10] at the Keighley Mechanic's Institute,[11] and Papa has also given a lecture—both are spoken of very highly in the Newspaper[12] and it is mentioned as a matter of wonder that such displays of intellect should emanate from the Village of Haworth "situated amongst the bogs and Mountains and until very lately supposed to be in a state of Semi-barbarism." Such are the words of the newspaper.

MS HM 24422.

1. Helen of Troy, wife of Menelaus—a play on the name Ellen.
2. Rates levied for the maintenance of the church fabric. Nonconformists, who received no benefit, had in many places resisted recent increased levies. Mr Brontë had suggested that both churchmen and dissenters should give voluntary sums, and any shortfall should be made up by a church collection.

3. Revd John Collins, MA, b. 1801, curate to Revd Theodore Dury of Keighley. By 12 Nov. 1840 Collins had shown himself to be vicious and dissolute, and his wife had asked Mr Brontë what she could do. Because of Collins's 'drunken, extravagant, profligate habits', they owed debts they could never pay, and were faced by ruin. 'He treated her and her child savagely . . . Papa advised her to leave him for ever, and go home, if she had a home to go to. She said this was what she had long resolved to do; and she would leave him directly,' as soon as Mr Busfeild, Dury's successor at Keighley, had dismissed him (CB to Ellen Nussey, 12 Nov. 1840).

4. He would let the Dissenters 'have it', in an abusive tirade. 'Kail' is 'cabbage' and 'reek' 'thick smoke' in Scottish dialect.

5. Mr Weightman.

6. The doctrine that the power of Christian ministry can derive only from ordination by a bishop whose own ordination derives from a continuous succession of bishops going back ultimately to the early church.

7. A follower of Edward Bouverie Pusey (1800–82), a leader of the Oxford Movement, and one of the authors of *Tracts for the Times* (1833 onwards) aimed at the purification of the Anglican church from rationalist and latitudinarian tendencies.

8. A follower of Walter Farquhar Hook (1798–1875), vicar of Leeds 1837–59, dean of Chichester 1859–75. In 1838 he had preached at the Chapel Royal a sermon, 'Hear the Church', affirming the apostolical succession of English bishops.

9. Born at Crackenthorpe, a few miles from Mr Weightman's birthplace, Appleby in Westmoreland.

10. CB wrote 'letter'.

11. Founded 1825. Mr Brontë joined it in the year ending 8 Apr. 1833.

12. Not traced.

12. *To Ellen Nussey, [?29 September 1840]*

[Haworth]

"The wind bloweth where it listeth. Thou hearest the sound thereof, but canst not tell whence it cometh, nor whither it goeth."[1] That, I believe, is Scripture, though in what chapter or book, or whether it be correctly quoted, I can't justly say. However, it behoves me to write a letter to a young woman of the name of E N with whom I was once acquainted, "in life's morning march, when my spirit was young."[2] This young woman asked me to write to her some time since, though having nothing to say—I e'en put it off, day by day, till at last, fearing that she will "curse me by her gods,"[3] I feel constrained to sit down and tack a few lines together, which she may call a letter or not as she pleases. Now if the young woman expects sense in this production, she will find herself miserably disappointed. I shall dress her a dish of salmagundi,[4]—I shall cook a hash—compound a stew—toss up an omelette soufflée à la Française, and send it to her with my respects. The wind, which is very high up in our hills of Judea,[5] though, I suppose, down in the Philistine flats of Batley parish it is nothing to speak of, has produced the same effects on the contents of my knowledge-box that a quaigh of usquebaugh[6] does upon those of most other bipeds. I see everything *couleur de rose*, and am strongly inclined to dance a jig, if I knew how. I think I must partake of the nature of a pig or an ass—both which animals are strongly affected by a high wind. From what quarter the wind blows I cannot tell, for I never could in my life; but I should very much like to know how the great brewing-tub of Bridlington Bay works,[7] and what sort of yeasty froth rises just now on the waves.

A woman of the name of Mrs Brooke,[8] it seems, wants a teacher. I wish she would have me; and I have written to another woman denominated Peg Wooler, to tell her so. Verily, it is a delightful thing to live here at home, at full liberty to do just what one pleases. But I recollect some fable or other about grasshoppers and ants by a scrubby old knave, yclept Æsop; the grasshoppers sung all the summer and starved all the winter.

A distant relation of mine, one Patrick Boanerges,[9] has set off to seek his fortune, in the wild, wandering, adventurous, romantic, knight-errant-like capacity of clerk on the Leeds and Manchester Railroad. Leeds and Manchester, where are they? Cities in the wilderness—like Tadmor, alias Palmyra—are they not? I know Mrs. Ellen is burning with eagerness to hear something about W[illiam] W[eightman], whom she adores in her heart, and whose image she cannot efface from her memory. I think I'll plague her by not telling her a word. To speak heaven's truth, I have precious little to say, inasmuch as I seldom see him, except on a Sunday, when he looks as handsome, cheery and good tempered as usual. I have indeed had the advantage of one long conversation since his return from Westmoreland, when he poured out his whole warm fickle soul in fondness and admiration of Agnes W. Whether he is in love with her or not I can't say; I can only observe that it sounds very like it. He sent us a prodigious quantity of game while he was away. A brace of wild ducks, a brace of black grouse, a brace of partridges, ditto of snipes, ditto of curlews, and a large salmon. There is one little trait respecting him which lately came to my knowledge, which gives a glimpse of the better side of his character. Last Saturday night he had been sitting an hour in the parlour with Papa; and as he went away, I heard Papa say to him—"what is the matter with you? You seem in very low spirits to-night." "Oh, I don't know. I've been to see a poor young girl, who, I'm afraid, is dying." "Indeed, what is her name?" "Susan Bland,[10] the daughter of John Bland, the superintendent." Now Susan Bland is my oldest and best scholar in the Sunday-school; and when I heard that, I thought I would go as soon as I could to see her. I did go, on Monday afternoon, and found her very ill and weak, and seemingly far on her way to that bourne whence no traveller returns.[11] After sitting with her some time, I happened to ask her mother if she thought a little port wine would do her good. She replied that the doctor had recommended it, and that when Mr. Weightman was last there, he had sent them a bottle of wine and a jar of preserves. She added, that he was always good-natured to poor folks, and seemed to have a deal of feeling and kind-heartedness about him. This proves that he is not all selfishness and vanity. No doubt, there are defects in his character, but there are also good qualities. God bless him! I wonder who, with his advantages, would be without his faults. I know many of his faulty actions, many of his weak points; yet, where I am, he shall always find rather a defender than an accuser. To be sure, my opinion will go but a very little way to decide his character; what of that? People should do right as far as their ability extends. You are not to suppose from all this, that Mr. W and I are on very amiable terms; we are not at all. We are distant, cold and reserved. We seldom speak; and when we do, it is only to exchange the most trivial and commonplace remarks. If you were to ask Mr. W's opinion of my character just now, he would say that at first he thought me a cheerful chatty kind of body, but that on farther acquaintance he found me of a capricious changeful temper never to be reckoned on. He does not know that I have regulated my manner by his, that I was cheerful and chatty so long as he was respectful, and that when he grew almost contemptuously familiar I found it necessary to adopt a degree of reserve which was not natural, and therefore was very painful to me. I find this reserve very convenient, and consequently I intend to keep it up.

MS untraced. Text: *Nussey*, supplemented by C. K. Shorter, *The Brontës' Life and Letters* (1908), letter 76.

1. Cf. John 3: 8.
2. See Thomas Campbell, 'The Soldier's Dream', stanza 4: 'I flew to the pleasant fields traversed so oft | In life's morning march, when my bosom was young.'
3. Cf. 1 Samuel 17: 43.
4. A dish of chopped meat, anchovies, eggs, and onions; a miscellany.
5. Hilly Haworth is as unlike low-lying Birstall and Batley as the hills of Judaea are unlike the Philistine plain of Shephela.
6. A wooden drinking-cup of whisky (Scottish dialect).
7. Ferments.
8. Possibly Mrs Thomas Brooke of Northgate House near Huddersfield.
9. The bombastic Branwell Brontë is compared to James and John, named by Christ 'Boan-erges'—'sons of thunder'—in Mark 3: 17.
10. Possibly the daughter of 'John Bland, Warp Dresser', 83, Main Street, Haworth.
11. *Hamlet* iii. i. 79–80.

13. *To Ellen Nussey, [20 November 1840]*

[Haworth]

My dearest Nell

That last letter of thine treated of matters so high and important I cannot delay answering it for a day—Now Nell I am about to write thee a discourse and a piece of advice which thou must take as if it came from thy Grandmother—but in the first place—before I begin with thee, I have a word to whisper in the ear of Mr Vincent[1] and I wish it could reach him.

In the name of St Chrysostom, St Simeon and St Jude,[2] why does not that amiable young gentleman come forward like a man and say all that he has to say to yourself personally—instead of trifling with kinsmen and kinswomen?—Mr Vincent I say—walk or ride over to Brookroyd some fine morning—where you will find Miss Ellen sitting in the drawing room making a little white frock for the Jew's basket[3]—and say "Miss Ellen I want to speak to you." Miss Ellen will of course civilly answer "I'm at your service Mr Vincent" and then when the room is cleared of all but <u>yourself</u> and <u>herself</u> just take a chair near her, insist upon her laying down that silly Jew-basket work, and listening to <u>you</u>. Then begin in a clear distinct, deferential, but determined voice—"Miss Ellen I have a question to put to you, a very important question—will you take me as your husband, for better for worse—? I am not a rich man, but I have sufficient to support us—I am not a great man but I love you honestly and truly—Miss Ellen if you knew the world better, you would see that this is an offer not to be despised—a kind attatched heart, and a moderate competency"—do this Mr Vincent and you may succeed—go on writing sentimental and love-sick letters to Henry[4] and I would not give sixpence for your suit.

So much for Mr Vincent—now Nell your turn comes to swallow the black bolus[5]—called a friend's advice—Here I am under difficulties because I don't know Mr V—if I did—I would give you my opinion roundly in two words. Is the man a fool? is he a knave a humbug, a hypocrite a ninny a noodle? If he is any or all of these things of course there is no sense in trifling with him—cut him short at once—blast his hopes with lightning rapidity and keenness.

Is he something better than this? has he at least common sense—a good disposition a manageable temper? then Nell consider the matter. You feel a disgust towards him <u>now</u>—an utter repugnance—very likely—but be so good as to remember you don't know him—you have only had three or four days' acquaintance with him—longer and closer intimacy might reconcile you to a wonderful extent—and now I'll tell you a word of truth: at which you may be offended or not as you like—From what I know of your character—and I think I know it pretty well—I should say you will never <u>love before marriage</u>—After that ceremony is over, and after you have had some months to settle down, and to get accustomed to the creature you have taken for your worse half—you will probably make a most affectionate and happy wife—even if the individual should not prove <u>all</u> you could wish—you will be indulgent towards his little follies and foibles—and will not feel much annoyance at them. This will especially be the case if he should have sense sufficient to allow you to guide him in important matters.

Such being the case Nell—I hope you will not have the romantic folly to wait for the awakening of what the French call "<u>Une grande passion</u>"—My good girl "une grande passion" is "<u>une grande folie</u>". I have told you so before—and I tell it you again. Mediocrity in all things is wisdom—mediocrity in the sensations is superlative wisdom. When you are as old as I am Nell—(I am sixty at least being your Grandmother) you will find that the majority of those worldly precepts—whose seeming coldness—shocks and repels us in youth—are founded in wisdom. Did you not once say to me in all childlike simplicity "I thought Charlotte—no young ladies should fall in love, till the offer was actually made". I forget what answer I made at the time—but I now reply after due consideration—"Right as a glove"—the maxim is just—and I hope you will always attend to it—I will even extend and confirm it—no young lady should fall in love till the offer has been made, accepted—the marriage ceremony performed and the first half year of wedded life has passed away—a woman may then begin to love, but with great precaution—very coolly—very moderately—very rationally—If she ever loves so much that a harsh word or a cold look from her husband cuts her to the heart—she is a fool—if she ever loves so much that her husband's will is her law—and that she has got into a habit of watching his looks in order that she may anticipate his wishes she will soon be a neglected fool.—Did I not once tell you of an instance of a Relative of mine[6] who cared for a young lady[7] till he began to suspect that she cared more for him and then instantly conceived a sort of contempt for her—? You know to what I allude—never as you value your ears mention the circumstance—but I have two studies—<u>you</u> are my study for the success the credit, and the respectability of a quiet, tranquil character. Mary is my study—for the contempt, the remorse—the misconstruction which follow the developement[8] of feelings in themselves noble, warm—generous—devoted and profound—but which being too freely revealed—too frankly bestowed—are not estimated at their real value. God bless her—I never hope to see in this world a character more truly noble—she would <u>die</u> willingly for one she loved—her intellect and her attainments are of the very highest standard—yet during her last visit here—she so conducted herself on one or two occasions that Mr Weightman thought her mad—do not for a moment suspect that she acted in a manner really wrong—her conduct was merely wrought to a pitch of great intensity and irregularity seldom equalled—but it produced a most unfortunate impression. I did not value her the less for it, because I understood it,[9] yet I doubt whether Mary will ever marry.

I think I may as well conclude the letter for after all I can give you no advice worth receiving—all I have to say may be comprised in a very brief sentence. On one hand don't accept if you are <u>certain</u> you cannot <u>tolerate</u> the man—on the other hand don't refuse because you cannot <u>adore</u> him. As to little Walter Mitchell[10]—I think he will not die for love of anybody—you might safely coquette with him a trifle if you were so disposed—without fear of having a broken heart on your Conscience—I am not quite in earnest in this recommendation—nor am I in some other parts of this letter but[11] . . .

The enclosed note is for Mercy in reply to a few lines from her—I have just received a note from Henry—his account makes the matter rather more uncertain than Anne's—he talks of a Father being in the case, and of the possibility of his raising objections to your own want of fortune. I am sure Ellen you will have prudence enough to communicate this business to as few as possible in its present stage. Impress upon Mercy's mind the necessity of her being equally discreet. When you have once decided whether to refuse or accept—it will not so much signify.[12] His reverence Henry expresses himself very strongly on the subject of young ladies saying "No" when they mean "Yes"—He assures me he means nothing personal. I hope not. Assuredly I quite agree with him, in his disapprobation of such a senseless course—It is folly indeed for the tongue to stammer a negative—when the heart is proclaiming an affirmative. Or rather it is an act of heroic self-denial of which I for one confess myself wholly incapable—I would not tell such a lie to gain a thousand pounds—Write to me again soon and let me know how all goes on—What made you say I admired Hippocrates?[13] It is a confounded "fib"—I tried to find something admirable in him and failed.

MS HM 24426.

1. Revd Osman Parke Vincent (?1813–85). He moved from one parish to another, mainly in the south of England, before becoming rector of St Mildred's, Bread Street, London, in 1872.
2. St John Chrysostom, the golden-mouthed (c.345–407), St Simeon (see Luke 2: 25–32), and the first-century apostle Judas (not Iscariot), patron saint of desperate causes.
3. See Letter 10.
4. Ellen's brother, Revd Henry Nussey (1812–60). See Letter 2 n. 17.
5. A large, round, soft, bitter pill.
6. Charlotte's brother Branwell.
7. Mary Taylor.
8. Disclosure.
9. The words from 'yet during her last visit' to 'I understood it' are heavily deleted in dark ink, presumably by Ellen Nussey, and the reading given is conjectural.
10. Walter Mitchell, eldest son of the surgeon Thomas Mitchell of Birstall, had qualified as an apothecary on 20 Sept. 1838.
11. Words from 'nor am I' to 'but' deleted, and followed by three illegible deleted words.
12. The passage from 'I am not quite' to 'so much signify' is heavily deleted in dark ink, presumably by Ellen Nussey.
13. Perhaps Walter Mitchell; an allusion to the Greek physician Hippocrates, b. 460 BC. Ellen never married.

14. *To Hartley Coleridge,*[1] *10 December 1840*

[Haworth]

Sir

I was almost as much pleased to get your letter as if it had been one from Professor Wilson[2] containing a passport of admission to Blackwood—You do not certainly flatter me very much nor suggest very brilliant hopes to my imagination—but on the whole I can perceive that you write like an honest man and a gentleman—and I am very much obliged to you both for the candour and civility of your reply. It seems then Messrs Percy and West[3] are not gentlemen likely to make an impression upon the heart of any Editor in Christendom? well I commit them to oblivion with several tears and much affliction but I hope I can get over it.

Your calculation that the affair might have extended to three Vols is very moderate—I felt myself actuated by the pith and perseverance of a Richardson[4] and could have held the distaff and spun day and night till I had lengthened the thread to thrice that extent—but you, like a most pitiless Atropos,[5] have cut it short in its very commencement—I do not think you would have hesitated to do the same to the immortal Sir Charles Grandison if Samuel Richardson Esqr. had sent you the first letters of Miss Harriet Byron[6]—and Miss Lucy Selby for inspection—very good letters they are Sir, Miss Harriet sings her own praises as sweetly as a dying swan—and her friends all join in the chorus, like a Company of wild asses of the desert. It is very edifying and profitable to create a world out of one's own brain and people it with inhabitants who are like so many Melchisedecs[7]—"Without father, without mother, without descent, having neither beginning of days, nor end of life". By conversing daily with such beings and accustoming your eyes to their glaring attire and fantastic features—you acquire a tone of mind admirably calculated to enable you to cut a respectable figure in practical life—If you have ever been accustomed to such society Sir you will be aware how distinctly and vividly their forms and features fix themselves on the retina of that "inward eye" which is said to be "the bliss of solitude".[8] Some of them are so ugly—you can liken them to nothing but the grotesque things carved by a besotted pagan for his temple—and some of them so preternaturally beautiful that their aspect startles you as much as Pygmalion's Statue[9] must have startled him—when life began to animate its chiselled features and kindle up its blind, marble eyes.

I am sorry Sir I did not exist forty or fifty years ago when the Lady's magazine[10] was flourishing like a green bay tree—in that case I make no doubt my aspirations after literary fame would have met with due encouragement—Messrs Percy and West should have stepped forward like heroes upon a stage worthy of their pretensions and I would have contested the palm with the Authors of Derwent Priory[11]—of the Abbey[12] and of Ethelinda.[13]—You see Sir I have read the Lady's Magazine and know something of its contents—though I am not quite certain of the correctness of the titles I have quoted for it is long, very long since I perused the antiquated print in which those tales were given forth—I read them before I knew how to criticize or object—they were old books belonging to my mother or my Aunt; they had crossed the Sea, had suffered ship-wreck and were discoloured with brine[14]—I read them as a treat on holiday afternoons or by stealth when I should have been minding my lessons—I shall never see anything which will interest me so much again—One black day my father burnt them because they contained foolish love-stories. With all my heart I wish I had been born in time to contribute to the Lady's magazine.

The idea of applying to a regular Novel-publisher—and seeing all my characters at length in three Vols, is very tempting—but I think on the whole I had better lock up this precious manuscript—wait till I get sense to produce something which shall at least <u>aim</u> at an object of some kind and meantime bind myself apprentice to a chemist and druggist if I am a young gentleman or to a Milliner and Dressmaker if I am a young lady.

You say a few words about my politics intimating that you suppose me to be a high Tory belonging to that party which claims for its head his Serene highness the Prince of the Powers of the Air. I would have proved that to perfection if I had gone on with the tale—I would have made old Thornton[15] a just representative of all the senseless, frigid prejudices of conservatism—I think I would have introduced a Puseyite too and polished-off the High Church with the best of Warren's jet blacking.[16]

I am pleased that you cannot quite decide whether I belong to the soft or the hard sex—and though at first I had no intention of being enigmatical on the subject—yet as I accidentally omitted to give the clue at first, I will venture purposely to withhold it now—as to my handwriting, or the ladylike tricks you mention in my style and imagery—you must not draw any conclusion from those—Several young gentlemen curl their hair and wear corsets—Richardson and Rousseau—often write exactly like old women—and Bulwer and Cooper and Dickens and Warren[17] like boarding-school misses. Seriously Sir, I am very much obliged to you for your kind and candid letter—and on the whole I wonder you took the trouble to read and notice the demi-semi novelette of an anonymous scribe who had not even the manners to tell you whether he was a man or woman or whether his common-place "C T"[18] meant Charles Tims or Charlotte Tomkins.

You ask how I came to hear of you—or of your place of residence[19] or to think of applying to you for advice—These things are all a mystery Sir—It is very pleasant to have something in one's power—and to be able to give a Lord Burleigh shake of the head[20] and to look wise and important even in a letter.

I did not suspect you were your Father

MS Texas.

1. Hartley Coleridge (1796–1849), poet and miscellaneous writer; eldest son of the poet Samuel Taylor Coleridge. In their boyhood Hartley and his brother Derwent had written stories about an imaginary world, 'Ejuxria', as the young Brontës had written about Angria and Gondal. Promising as a youth, he was dismissed from his fellowship at Oriel College Oxford for intemperance. The Brontës admired his contributions to *Blackwood's Edinburgh Magazine* and Charlotte had sent him one of her stories, dealing with the rivalry between two brothers, and attempting a realism absent from the exotic tales of her Angrian heroes and villains. See Christine Alexander, *The Early Writings of Charlotte Brontë* (Oxford: Blackwell, 1983), 204–9.
2. John Wilson (1785–1854), the 'Christopher North' of the 'Noctes Ambrosianae' in *Blackwood's Edinburgh Magazine*, 1822–35; Professor of Moral Philosophy at Edinburgh University since 1820.
3. Arthur Ripley West and Alexander Percy, later renamed Ashworth, characters in CB's juvenilia.

4. All the novels of Samuel Richardson (1689–1761) are long, and the 7-volume epistolary novel *Sir Charles Grandison* (1753–4) has also an immense cast of characters.

5. The eldest of the three Fates, who severs the thread of life spun by Lachesis and drawn from the distaff by Clotho.

6. Harriet Byron is beloved by and eventually married to Sir Charles Grandison; Lucy Selby is her cousin and principal correspondent.

7. Melchisedec was the priest-king to whom Abraham gave tribute. See Genesis 14: 18 and Hebrews 7: 3.

8. From Wordsworth's poem, 'I wandered lonely as a cloud', lines 21 and 22.

9. Pygmalion fell in love with the beautiful statue he had carved. At his request Aphrodite turned it into a living woman, whom he married.

10. *The Lady's Magazine: or Entertaining Companion for the Fair Sex* (1770–1848).

11. *Derwent Priory: A Novel. In a Series of Letters* [By A. Kendall.] *Lady's Magazine* 1796–7; rpt. in 2 vols. 1798.

12. Possibly *Grasville Abbey, A Romance*, by G[eorge] M[oore]; *Lady's Magazine* 1793–7, rpt. in 3 vols. 1801.

13. Probably *Ethelinde, or the Recluse of the Lake* (1789), by Charlotte Smith (1749–1806), excerpted in a number of miscellanies..

14. Before her marriage Maria Branwell had sent for her books from Penzance, but the box containing them had been dashed to pieces by the sea when the vessel containing it was wrecked, and all but a few items were lost.

15. A dialect-speaking character in the juvenilia; a private joke, since Thornton was based on the radical Joshua Taylor of Gomersal.

16. Shoe blacking made by the firm of Robert Warren, 30, Strand, London.

17. Edward George Earle Lytton Bulwer, later Bulwer-Lytton (1803–73), James Fenimore Cooper (1789–1851), Charles Dickens (1812–70), and Samuel Warren (1807–77).

18. Either 'Captain Tree' or 'Charles Townshend', pseudonyms used by Charlotte Brontë in her juvenilia.

19. CB addressed her letter to 'Hartley Coleridge Esqr. | Knabbe | Rydal | nr Ambleside | Westmoreland'. Branwell Brontë, who is said to have met Coleridge in Bradford, had visited him at 'Knabbe' (Nab Cottage) on 1 May 1840.

20. In Sheridan's *The Critic* (1779), Lord Burleigh sits without speaking, '*shakes his head, and exit*'; Puff expounds his meaning at length. (III. i.)

15. *To Ellen Nussey, 3 March 1841*

[Upperwood House,
Rawdon]

My dear Ellen

I have not written to you for a long time. [CB is afraid Ellen will be angry with her but she has been very busy.] I told you some time since that I meant to get a situation and when I said so my resolution was quite fixed—I felt that however often I was disappointed I had no intention of relinquishing my efforts—After being severely baffled two or three times—after a world of trouble in the way of correspondence and interviews—I have at length succeeded and am fairly established in my new place—It is in the family of Mr. White, of Upperwood House, Rawdon.[1] . . .

The House is not very large but exceedingly comfortable and well regulated—the grounds are fine and extensive—In taking this place I have made a large sacrifice in the way of salary, in the hope of securing comfort—by which word I do not mean to express good eating & drinking or warm fire or a soft bed—but the society of cheerful faces & minds and hearts not dug out of a lead mine or cut from a marble quarry. My salary is not really more than £16. per annum, though it is nominally £20 but the expense of washing will be deducted therefrom. My pupils are two in number, a girl of eight and a boy of six.[2] As to my employers, you will not expect me to say much respecting their characters when I tell you that I only arrived here yesterday—I have not the faculty of telling an individual's disposition at first sight—before I can venture to pronounce on a character I must see it first under various lights and from various points of view—All I can say therefore is both Mr and Mrs White seem to me <u>now</u> good sort of people. I have as yet had no cause to complain of want of considerateness or civility. My pupils <u>are</u> wild and unbroken but <u>apparently</u> well-disposed. I wish I may be able to say as much next time I write to you—My earnest wish and endeavour will be to please them—if I can but feel that I am giving satisfaction & if at the same time I can keep my health I shall I hope be moderately happy—but no one but myself can tell how hard a Governesse's work is to me—for no one but myself is aware how utterly averse my whole mind and nature are from the employment—Do not think that I fail to blame myself for this or that I leave any means unemployed to conquer this feeling. Some of my greatest difficulties lie in things that would appear to you comparatively trivial. I find it so hard to repel the rude familiarity of the children—I find it so difficult to ask either servants or mistress for anything I want, however much I want it. It is less pain to me to endure the greatest inconvenience than to go into the kitchen to request its removal. I am a fool—Heaven knows I cannot help it.

Now Ellen can you tell me whether it is considered improper for Governesses to ask their friends to come and see them—I do not mean of course to stay—but just for a call of an hour or two—If it is not absolute treason I do fervently request that you will contrive in some way or other to let me have a sight of your face—yet I feel at the same time, that I am making a very foolish and almost impracticable demand yet Rawdon is only four miles from Bradford . . . How is Mr Vincent?[3]

I dare say you have received a Valentine this year from our bonny-faced friend the Curate of Haworth.[4] I got a precious specimen a few days before I left home—but I knew better how to treat it than I did those we received a year ago—I am up to the dodges and artifices of his Lordship's character, he knows I know him—and you cannot conceive how quiet & respectful he has long been—Mind I am not writing against him—I never <u>will</u> do that—I like him very much—I honour and admire his generous, open disposition & sweet temper—but for all the tricks, wiles and insincerities of love the gentleman has not his match for 20 miles round—He would fain persuade every woman under

30 whom he sees that he is desperately in love with her—I have a great deal more to say but I have not a moment's time to write it in—My dear Ellen, <u>do</u> write to me soon don't forget—good-bye.

C Brontë

MS untraced. An incomplete text based on Ellen Nussey's version as printed by Horsfall Turner, with additions from printed versions by C. K. Shorter and Wise and Symington, and quotations and facsimiles in sale catalogues.

1. John White (?1790–1860), a Bradford merchant; the house was near Apperley Lane, about five miles from Bradford.
2. Sarah Louisa White (b. 1832) who was to marry Samuel Walter Atkinson of Huddersfield, and Jasper Leavens White (?1834–?65).
3. See Letter 13 n. 1.
4. William Weightman.

16. *To Ellen Nussey, 19 July 1841*

[Haworth]

My dear Ellen

We waited long—and anxiously for you on the Thursday that you promised to come—I quite wearied my eyes with watching from the window—eye-glass in hand and sometimes spectacles on nose—However you are not to blame—I believe you have done right in going to Earnley and as to the disappointment we endured why all must suffer disappointment at some period or other of their lives—but a hundred things I had to say to you will now be forgotten and never said—there is a project hatching in this house—which both Emily and I anxiously wished to discuss with you—The project is yet in its infancy—hardly peeping from its shell—and whether it will ever come out—a fine, full-fledged chicken—or will turn addle and die before it cheeps, is one of those considerations that are but dimly revealed by the oracles of futurity. Now dear Nell don't be nonplussed by all this metaphorical mystery—I talk of a plain and every day occurrence—though in Delphic[1] style—I wrap up the information in figures of speech concerning eggs, chickens, etcetera etceterorum.

To come to the point—Papa and Aunt talk by fits & starts of our—id est—Emily Anne & myself commencing a School[2]—! I have often you know said how much I wished such a thing—but I never could conceive where the capital was to come from for making such a speculation—I was well aware indeed, that Aunt <u>had</u> money—but I always considered that she was the last person who would offer a loan for the purpose in question—A loan however she <u>has</u> offered or rather intimates that she perhaps <u>will</u> offer in case pupils can be secured,—an eligible situation obtained &c. &c.

This sounds very fair—but still there are matters to be considered which throw something of a damp upon the Scheme—I do not expect that Aunt will risk more than 150£ on such a venture—& would it be possible to establish a respectable (not by any means a <u>shewy</u>) school—and to commence housekeeping with a capital of <u>only</u> that amount? Propound the question to your sister Anne—if you think <u>she</u> can answer it—if not, don't say a word on the subject—As to getting into debt that is a thing we could none of us reconcile our minds to for a moment—We do not care how modest—how humble our commencement be so it be made on sure grounds & have a safe foundation—

In thinking of all possible and impossible places where we could establish a School—I have thought of Burlington[3]—or rather of the neighbourhood of Burlington—do you remember whether there was any other school there besides that of Miss Jackson? This is of course a perfectly crude, random idea—There are a hundred reasons why it should be an impracticable one—We have no connexions—no acquaintance there—it is far from home &c. Still I fancy the ground in the East-Riding is less fully occupied than in the West—Much inquiry & consideration will be necessary of course before any plan is decided on—and I fear much time will elapse before any plan is executed. Can events be so turned as that you shall be included as an associate in our projects?[4] This is a question I have not at present the means to answer—

I must not conclude this note without even mentioning the name of our revered friend William Weightman—He is quite as bonny—pleasant—light-hearted—good-tempered—generous, careless, crafty, fickle & unclerical as ever—he keeps up his correspondence with Agnes Walton—During the last Spring he went to Appleby & stayed upwards of a month—in the interim he wrote to Papa several times & from his letters—which I have seen—he appears to have a fixed design of obtaining Miss Walton's hand & if she can be won by a handsome face—by a cheerful & frank disposition & highly cultivated talents—if she can be satisfied with these things & will not exact further the pride of a sensitive mind & the delicacy of a feeling one—in this case he will doubtless prove successful—

Write to me as soon as you can and address to Rawden—I shall not leave my present situation—till my future prospects assume a more fixed & definite aspect—Good bye dear Ellen

C B

MS BPM Gr. E4.

1. Oracular; from the oracle of Apollo at Delphi.
2. This idea was not finally dropped until 1845, when the sisters had failed to secure a single pupil for their projected school.
3. Bridlington, on the east coast of Yorks. See Letter 8 n. 2 . A Miss Clarissa Jacks had an Academy at Prospect Place, Bridlington Quay.
4. A conjectural reading for a heavily deleted passage.

17. *To Ellen Nussey, 7 August 1841*

Upperwood-House

My dear Ellen

This is Saturday evening—I have put the children to-bed and now I am going to sit down and answer your letter. I am again by myself—Housekeeper and Governess—for Mr & Mrs White are staying with a Mrs Duncome[1] of Brook-Hall near Tadcaster—to speak truth though I am solitary while they are away—it is still by far the happiest part of my time—the children are now under at least <u>decent</u> control—the servants are very observant and attentive to me and the absence of the Master & Mistress relieves me from the heavy duty of endeavouring to seem always easy, cheerful & conversible with those whose ideas and feelings are nearly as incomprehensible to <u>me</u>, as probably mine (if I shewed them unreservedly) would be to <u>them</u>.

Martha Taylor it appears is in the way of enjoying great advantages[2]—so is Mary—for you will be surprised to hear that she is returning immediately to the Continent with her brother John[3]—not however to <u>stay</u> there but to take a month's tour and recreation—I am glad it has been so arranged—it seemed hard that Martha should be preferred so far before her elder Sister—I had a long letter from Mary and a packet—containing a present of a very handsome black silk scarf & a pair of beautiful kid gloves bought at Brussels—of course I was in one sense pleased with the gift—pleased that they should think of me—so far off—amidst the excitements of one of the most splendid capitals of Europe—and yet it felt irksome to accept it—I should think Mary & Martha have not more than sufficient pocket-money to supply themselves—I wish they had testified their regard by a less expensive token.

Mary's letter spoke of some of the pictures & cathedrals she had seen—pictures the most exquisite—& cathedrals the most venerable—I hardly know what swelled to my throat as I read her letter—such a vehement impatience of restraint & steady work—such a strong wish for wings—wings such as wealth can furnish—such an urgent thirst to see—to know—to learn—something internal seemed to expand boldly for a minute—I was tantalized with the consciousness of faculties unexercised—then all collapsed and I despaired.

My dear Nell—I would hardly make that confession to any one but yourself—and to you rather in a letter than "viva voce"—these rebellious & absurd emotions were only momentary—I quelled them in five minutes—I hope they will not revive—for they were acutely painful—No further steps have been taken about the project[4] I mentioned to you—nor probably will be for the present—But Emily & Anne & I keep it in view—it is our polar-star & we look to it under all circumstances of despondency—I begin to suspect I am writing in a strain which will make you think I am unhappy—this is far from being the case—on the contrary I know my place is a favourable one for a

Governess—what dismays & haunts me sometimes is a conviction that I have
no natural knack for my vocation—if teaching only—were requisite it would be
smooth & easy—but it is the living in other people's houses—the estrangement
from one's real character—the adoption of a cold frigid—apathetic exterior that
is painful.

   On the whole I am glad you went with Henry to Sussex—our disappointment
was bitter enough—but that is gone by now—and it is as well you have got
a change—You will not mention our School-scheme to any one at present—a
project not actually commenced is always uncertain—Write to me often my
dear Nell—you *know* your letters are valued—Give my regards to your brother
& Sister and believe me

>   Your loving child (as you choose to call me so)
>   C B

I am well in health—. I have one aching feeling at my heart (I must allude to it
though I had resolved not to)—it is about Anne—she has so much to endure—far
far more than I have—when my thoughts turn to her—they always see her as
a patient, persecuted stranger[5]—amongst people more grossly insolent, proud
& tyrannical than your imagination unassisted can readily depict—I know what
concealed susceptibility is in her nature—when her feelings are wounded I wish
I could be with her to administer a little balm—She is more lonely—less gifted
with the power of making friends even than I am—drop the subject.

MS HM 24428.

1. Possibly related to the Duncombes of Copgrove, Boroughbridge, Yorks.
2. Mary Taylor had taken her younger sister to Mme Goussaert's expensive 'Château de Koekelberg' finishing school in Brussels.
3. John Taylor (1813–1901) who travelled to the Continent on business for the family firm.
4. The plan to set up a school, mentioned in Letter 16 of 19 July.
5. Anne was a governess in the family of Revd Edmund Robinson at Thorp Green Hall near York from May 1840 to June 1845, her pupils being Lydia Mary, Elizabeth Lydia ('Bessy'), and Mary; she may also have taught Latin to Mr Robinson's son Edmund. In Anne's novel, *Agnes Grey*, the heroine's experiences at Horton Lodge are partly based on Anne's at Thorp Green.

18. *To Elizabeth Branwell,*[1] *29 September 1841*

>   Upperwood House, Rawdon.

Dear Aunt,
   I have heard nothing of Miss Wooler yet since I wrote to her intimating that
I would accept her offer.[2] I cannot conjecture the reason of this long silence,
unless some unforeseen impediment has occurred in concluding the bargain.
Meantime, a plan has been suggested and approved by Mr. and Mrs. White,
and others, which I wish now to impart to you. My friends recommend me, if
I desire to secure permanent success, to delay commencing the school for six

months longer, and by all means to contrive, by hook or by crook, to spend the intervening time in some school on the continent. They say schools in England are so numerous, competition so great, that without some such step towards attaining superiority we shall probably have a very hard struggle, and may fail in the end. They say, moreover, that the loan of £100, which you have been so kind as to offer us, will, perhaps, not be all required now, as Miss Wooler will lend us the furniture; and that, if the speculation is intended to be a good and successful one, half the sum, at least, ought to be laid out in the manner I have mentioned, thereby insuring a more speedy repayment both of interest and principal.

I would not go to France or to Paris. I would go to Brussels, in Belgium. The cost of the journey there, at the dearest rate of travelling, would be £5; living is there little more than half as dear as it is in England, and the facilities for education are equal or superior to any other place in Europe. In half a year, I could acquire a thorough familiarity with French. I could improve greatly in Italian, and even get a dash of German, i.e., providing my health continued as good as it is now. Martha Taylor is now staying in Brussels, at a first-rate establishment there. I should not think of going to the Château de Kockleberg, where she is resident, as the terms are much too high; but if I wrote to her, she, with the assistance of Mrs. Jenkins, the wife of the British Consul,[3] would be able to secure me a cheap and decent residence and respectable protection. I should have the opportunity of seeing her frequently, she would make me acquainted with the city; and, with the assistance of her cousins,[4] I should probably in time be introduced to connections far more improving, polished, and cultivated, than any I have yet known.

These are advantages which would turn to vast account, when we actually commenced a school—and, if Emily could share them with me, only for a single half-year, we could take a footing in the world afterwards which we can never do now. I say Emily instead of Anne; for Anne might take her turn at some future period, if our school answered. I feel certain, while I am writing, that you will see the propriety of what I say; you always like to use your money to the best advantage; you are not fond of making shabby purchases; when you do confer a favour, it is often done in style; and depend upon it £50, or £100, thus laid out, would be well employed. Of course, I know no other friend in the world to whom I could apply on this subject except yourself. I feel an absolute conviction that, if this advantage were allowed us, it would be the making of us for life. Papa will perhaps think it a wild and ambitious scheme; but who ever rose in the world without ambition? When he left Ireland to go to Cambridge University, he was as ambitious as I am now. I want us _all_ to go on. I know we have talents, and I want them to be turned to account. I look to you, aunt, to help us. I think you will not refuse. I know, if you consent, it shall not be my fault if you ever repent your kindness. With love to all, and the hope that you are all well,—Believe me, dear aunt, your affectionate niece,

C. Brontë.

MS untraced. Text *CBCircle* 96–7 n. 1.

1. See Biographical Notes, p. xxxiii, and Letter 16 for the possibility that Miss Branwell would offer a loan to enable her nieces to set up a school.
2. Margaret Wooler had invited CB to take over Heald's House school, Dewsbury Moor, which Margaret's sister Eliza had relinquished.
3. Revd Evan Jenkins (?1797–1856) was not a consul. He had been the British Chaplain in Brussels since 1826. His brother, Revd David Jenkins of Pudsey near Leeds, was well known to Mr Brontë.
4. The sons and daughters of Abraham Dixon (1779–1850), a commission agent and inventor living in Brussels, and his wife Laetitia, née Taylor (1780–1842).

19. *To Ellen Nussey, [May 1842]*

[Brussels]

Dear Ellen

It is the fashion now a days for persons to send sheets of blank paper instead of letters to their friends in foreign parts—[1]

I was twenty-six years old a week or two since—and at that ripe time of life I am a schoolgirl—a complete school-girl and on the whole very happy in that capacity. It felt very strange at first to submit to authority instead of exercising it—to obey orders instead of giving them—but I like that state of things—I returned to it with the same avidity that a cow that has long been kept on dry hay returns to fresh grass—don't laugh at my simile—it is natural to me to submit and very unnatural to command.

This is a large school in which there are about 40 externes or day-pupils and 12 pensionnaires or boarders—Madame Heger the head is a lady of precisely the same cast of mind degree of cultivation & quality of character as Miss Catherine Wooler[2]—I think the severe points are a little softened because she has not been disappointed & consequently soured—in a word—she is a married instead of a maiden lady—there are 3 teachers in the school Mademoiselle Blanche—mademoiselle Sophie & Mademoiselle Marie[3]—The two first have no particular character—one is an old maid & the other will be one—Mademoiselle Marie is talented & original—but of repulsive & arbitrary manners which have made the whole school except myself and Emily her bitter enemies—no less than seven masters attend to teach the different branches of education—French—drawing—music, singing, writing, arithmetic, and German.

All in the house are Catholics except ourselves one other girl[4] and the gouvernante[5] of Madam's children—an Englishwoman in rank something between a lady's maid and a nursery governess   the difference in Country & religion makes a broad line of demarcation between us & all the rest   we are completely isolated in the midst of numbers—yet I think I am never unhappy—my present life is so delightful so congenial to my own nature compared to that of a Governess—my time constantly occupied passes too rapidly—hitherto both Emily and I have had good health & therefore we have been able to work well. There is one individual of whom I have not yet spoken Monsieur Heger[6] the husband of Madame—he is professor of Rhetoric a man of power as to mind but very choleric and irritable in temperament—a little, black, ugly being with a face that varies in expression, sometimes he borrows the lineaments of an insane Tom-cat—sometimes those of a delirious Hyena—occasionally—but very seldom he discards these perilous attractions and assumes an air not above a hundred degrees removed from what you would call mild & gentleman-like he is very angry with me just at present because I have written a translation which he chose to stigmatize as peu correct[7]—not because it was particularly so in reality but because he happened to be in a bad humour when he read it—he did not tell me so—but wrote the accusation in the margin of my book and asked in brief stern phrase how it happened that my compositions were always better than my translations—adding that the thing seemed to him inexplicable   the fact is some weeks ago in a high-flown humour he forbade me to use either dictionary or grammar—in translating the most difficult English compositions into French this makes the task rather arduous—& compels me every now and then to introduce an English word which nearly plucks the eyes out of his head when he sees it.

Emily and he don't draw well together at all—when he is very ferocious with me I cry—& that sets all things straight.

Emily works like a horse and she has had great difficulties to contend with—far greater than I have had   indeed those who come to a French school for instruction ought previously to have acquired a considerable knowledge of the French language—otherwise they will lose a great deal of time for the course of instruction is adapted to natives & not to foreigners and in these large establishments they will not change their ordinary course for one or two strangers—the few private lessons that monsieur Heger has vouchsafed to give us are I suppose to be considered a great favour & I can perceive they have already excited much spite & jealousy in the school—

You will abuse this letter for being short I daresay, and there are a hundred things which I wish to tell you but I have not time. Do write to me and cherish Christian charity in your heart! Brussels is a beautiful city—the Belgians hate the English—their external morality is more rigid than ours—to lace the stays without any handkerchief on the neck[8] is considered a disgusting piece of

indelicacy—Remember me to Mercy & your Mother, and believe me, my dear
Ellen—Yours, sundered by the sea,

C Brontë

MS Law-Dixon. Text based on a transcript by M. G. Christian, with some readings from Wise &
Symington, letter 131.

1. There had been some coolness between EN and CB since EN's failure to visit Haworth in January,
   before Emily and Charlotte set off for Mme Zoë Heger's school in Brussels. See Biographical
   Notes, p. xxxviii. Their original plan to go to a Brussels school had been changed, on Mrs Evan
   Jenkins's advice, to one in Lille; but she had subsequently recommended Mme Heger's school.
2. Katherine Harriet Wooler (1796–1884), Margaret Wooler's sister and partner at Roe Head school,
   where she taught French and other subjects. She was said to be intelligent, narrow-minded, and
   a severe disciplinarian.
3. Mlle Sophie was well-disposed towards CB; the other two may be portrayed in *Villette* as the
   corrupt Zélie St Pierre and an avaricious teacher 'not yet twenty-five'.
4. Maria Miller, later Mrs W. P. Robertson; said to be fashionable, dashing, and worldly, and
   allegedly the prototype of Ginevra Fanshawe in *Villette*.
5. Martha Trotman.
6. See Biographical Notes p. xxxviii. CB was to become deeply attached to M. Heger, and she used
   many of his traits in creating the talented, vehement, and temperamental M. Paul Emanuel in
   Villette.
7. Not very correct.
8. A ladylike term for the upper part of the bosom.

20. *To Ellen Nussey, [?July 1842]*

[Brussels]

Dear Ellen

I began seriously to think you had no particular intention of writing to me
again—however let us have no reproaches, thank you for your letter.

I consider it doubtful whether I shall come home in September or
not—Madame Heger has made a proposal for both me and Emily to stay
another half year—offering to dismiss her English master and take me as English
teacher—also to employ Emily some part of each day in teaching music to
a certain number of the pupils—for these services we are to be allowed to
continue our studies in French and German—and to have board &c without
paying for it—no salaries however are offered—the proposal is kind and in
a great selfish city like Brussels and a great selfish school containing nearly
ninety pupils (boarders & day-pupils included) implies a degree of interest which
demands gratitude in return—I am inclined to accept it—what think you?

Your letter set my teeth on edge—I can but half divine the significance of a
great part of it but what I guess makes me wish to know all   you must speedily
write again and explain yourself—

I don't deny that I sometimes wish to be in England or that I have brief
attacks of home-sickness—but on the whole I have borne a very valiant heart

so far—and I have been happy in Brussels because I have always been fully occupied with the employments that I like—Emily is making rapid progress in French, German, Music and Drawing—Monsieur & Madame Heger begin to recognise the valuable points of her character under her singularities.

If the national character of the Belgians is to be measured by the character of most of the girls in this school, it is a character singularly cold, selfish, animal and inferior—they are besides very mutinous and difficult for the teachers to manage—and their principles are rotten to the core—we avoid them—which is not difficult to do—as we have the brand of Protestantism and Anglicism[1] upon us

People talk of the danger which protestants expose themselves to in going to reside in Catholic countries—and thereby running the chance of changing to their faith—my advice to all protestants who are tempted to do anything so besotted as turn Catholic—is to walk over the sea on to the continent—to attend mass sedulously for a time—to note well the mum[m]eries thereof—also the idiotic, mercenary, aspect of all the priests—& then if they are still disposed to consider Papistry in any other light than a most feeble childish piece of humbug let them turn papists at once that's all—I consider Methodism, Quakerism & the extremes of high & low Churchism foolish but Roman Catholicism beats them all.

At the same time allow me to tell you that there are some Catholics—who are as good as any christians can be to whom the bible is a sealed book,[2] and much better than scores of Protestants <Don't be alarmed because I say my prayers before> [3]

Give my love to your Mother & Mercy—believe me present occasionally in spirit when absent in flesh

C B

MS HM 24431.

1. Presumably 'Englishness'.
2. In *Villette* ch. 42 M. Paul Emanuel, who is based on M. Heger, is singled out for similar praise.
3. 'Don't . . . before' deleted in MS.

21. *To Ellen Nussey, 10 November [1842]*

Haworth

My dear Ellen

I was not yet returned to England when your letter arrived—We received the first news of Aunt's illness—Wednesday Novbr 2nd—we decided to come home directly—next morning a second letter informed us of her death.[1] We sailed from Antwerp on Sunday—we travelled day & night and got home on

Tuesday morning—of course the funeral and all was over. We shall see her no more—Papa is pretty well—we found Anne at home—she is pretty well also—You say you have had no letter from me for a long time—I wrote to you three weeks ago—When you answer this note I will write to you again more in detail—Martha Taylor's illness was unknown to me till the day before she died[2]—I hastened to Kokleberg the next morning—unconscious that she was in great danger—and was told that it was finished, she had died in the night—Mary was taken away to Bruxelles[3]—I have seen Mary frequently since—she is in no way crushed by the event—but while Martha was ill she was to her, more than a Mother—more than a Sister—watching—nursing—cherishing her—so tenderly, so unweariedly—she appears calm and serious now—no bursts of violent emotion—no exaggeration of distress—I have seen Martha's grave—the place where her ashes lie in a foreign country. Aunt—Martha Taylor—Mr Weightman[4] are now all gone—how dreary & void everything seems—Mr Weightman's illness was exactly what Martha's was—he was ill the same length of time & died in the same manner—Aunts disease was internal obstruction. She also was ill a fortnight.

Good bye my dear Ellen.

MS Widener, Harvard, HEW 1.5.4.

1. After acute suffering, Elizabeth Branwell had died of 'internal obstruction' on 29 Oct. She was buried at Haworth on 3 Nov.
2. Martha Taylor had died of what was probably cholera at the Koekelberg school on 12 Oct., and was buried in the Protestant cemetery beyond the 'porte de Louvain'.
3. i.e. back from the outskirts into the city, to the house where Mary's cousins the Dixons were living in the rue de la Régence.
4. The curate William Weightman had died of cholera, probably caught from a parishioner he had visited. He died after a fortnight's suffering on 6 Sept. at the age of 28, and was buried in Haworth on 10 Sept.

22. To Ellen Nussey, 6 March [1843]

Bruxelles

Dear Nell

Whether you received my last billet or not I do not know, but as an opportunity offers of dispatching to you another I will avail myself of it—I am settled by this time of course—I am not too much overloaded with occupation and besides teaching English I have time to improve myself in German—I ought to consider myself well off and to be thankful for my good fortune—I hope I am thankful—and if I could always keep up my spirits—and never feel lonely or long for companionship or friendship or whatever they call it, I should do very well—As I told you before Monsieur and Mde Heger are the only two persons in the house for whom I really experience regard and esteem and of

course I cannot always be with them nor even often—They told me when I first
returned that I was to consider their sitting-room my sitting-room also and to go
there whenever I was not engaged in the school-room—this however I cannot
do—in the day-time it is a public-room—where music-masters and mistresses
are constantly passing in and out and in the evening I will not and ought not to
intrude on Mr & Mde Heger & their children[1]—thus I am a good deal by myself
out of school-hours—but that does not signify—

I now regularly give English lessons to Mr Heger & his brother-in-law Mr
Chappelle[2] (Mr H's first wife was the sister of Mr C's present wife)   they get
on with wonderful rapidity—especially the first—he already begins to speak
English very decently—if you could see and hear the efforts I make to teach
them to pronounce like Englishmen and their unavailing attempts to imitate,
you would laugh to all eternity.

The Carnival[3] is just over and we have entered upon the gloom and abstinence
of Lent—the first day of Lent we had coffee without milk for breakfast—vinegar
& vegetables with a very little salt-fish for dinner and bread for supper—The
carnival was nothing but masking and mum[m]ery—Mr Heger took me and
one of the pupils into the town to see the masks—it was animating to see the
immense crowds & the general gaiety—but the masks were nothing—

I have been several times to the Dixons   they are very kind to me—this letter
will probably go by Mr Tom[4]—Miss Dixon is certainly an elegant & accomplished
person—my opinion of her is unchanged—for good & otherwise—When she
leaves Bruxelles I shall have no where to go to—I shall be sorry to lose her
society

I hear that Mary Walker is going to be married[5] and that Mr Joe Taylor has
been & is very poorly—what is the matter with him?

I have had two letters from Mary[6]—she does not tell me she has been ill &
she does not complain—but her letters are not the letters of a person in the
enjoyment of great happiness—She has nobody to be so good to her as Mr
Heger is to me—to lend her books to converse with her sometimes &c.

Remember me to Mercy & your Mother, tell me if any chances & changes
have happened—remember me also to Mrs George Allbutt[7] when you see her—

You do no[t] merit that I should prolong this letter—Good-bye to you dear
Nell when I say so—it seems to me that you will hardly hear me—all the waves
of the Channel, heaving & roaring between must deaden the sound—

Go-o-d—b-y-e

C B[8]

MS BPM B.S. 50.4.

1. Marie Pauline (1837–86), Louise Florence (1839–1933, portrayed as 'Fifine' in Villette), Claire
   Zoë Marie (1840–1930), and Prospère Édouard Augustin (1842–67). There would be two more
   children: Julie Marie Victorine (1843–1928) and Paul François Xavier (1846–1925).

2. Pianist and Professor at the Conservatoire Royal in Brussels; M. Heger's first wife was Marie-Joséphine Noyer (d. 1833).
3. The eight days of festival preceding the 'farewell to flesh' on Ash Wednesday (1 Mar. 1843).
4. Thomas Dixon (1821–65), son of Abraham Dixon and brother of Mary (1809–97), for whom see the Biographical Notes, p. xxxvii. He was to be an engineer.
5. A daughter of the late Joshua Walker of Oakwell House; she was to marry Revd Richard Greaves Micklethwait on 17 Jan. 1844.
6. Mary Taylor.
7. Anna Maria, née Brooke (b. 1818), a former Roe Head school pupil, who had married Dr George Allbutt of Batley on 6 Aug. 1842.
8. The last half-page of the letter contains a sketch by Charlotte of herself, diminutive and plain, waving 'Good bye' across the sea to an attractively dressed Ellen Nussey, now 'Mrs O P Vincent', accompanied by a top-hatted bespectacled gentleman, 'The Chosen'. See Letter 13 n. 1, and illustration no. 6. Ellen never married.

23. To Branwell Brontë, 1 May 1843

Brussels

Dear B

I hear you have written a letter to me; this letter however as usual I have never received which I am exceedingly sorry for, as I have wished very much to hear from you—are you sure that you put the right address and that you paid the English postage 1 s/6d—without that, letters are never forwarded. I heard from papa a day or two since—all appears to be going on reasonably well at home—I grieve only that Emily[1] is so solitary but however you & Anne will soon be returning for the holidays which will cheer the house for a time[2]—Are you in better health and spirits and does Anne continue to be pretty well—? I understand papa has been to see you[3]—did he seem cheerful and well? Mind when you write to me you answer these questions as I wish to know—Also give me a detailed account as to how you get on with your pupil and the rest of the family. I have received a general assurance that you do well and are in good odour—but I want to know particulars—

As for me I am very well and wag on[4] as usual, I perceive however that I grow exceedingly misanthropic and sour—you will say this is no news, and that you never knew me possessed of the contrary qualities, philanthropy & sugariness—daß ist wahr (which being translated means that is true) but the fact is the people here are no go whatsoever—amongst 120 persons, which compose the daily population of this house I can discern only 1 or 2 who deserve anything like regard—This is not owing to foolish fastidiousness on my part—but to the absence of decent qualities on theirs—they have not intellect or politeness or good-nature or good-feeling—they are nothing—I don't hate them—hatred would be too warm a feeling—They have no sensations themselves and they excite none—but one wearies from day to day of caring nothing, fearing nothing, liking nothing hating nothing—being nothing, doing nothing—yes, I teach &

sometimes get red-in-the-face with impatience at their stupidity—but don't think I ever scold or fly into a passion—if I spoke warmly, as warmly as I sometimes used to do at Roe-Head they would think me mad—nobody ever gets into a passion here—such a thing is not known—the phlegm that thickens their blood is too gluey to boil—they are very false in their relations with each other—but they rarely quarrel & friendship is a folly they are unacquainted with—The black Swan Mr Heger is the sole veritable exception to this rule (for Madame, always cool & always reasoning is not quite an exception) but I rarely speak to Mr now for not being a pupil I have little or nothing to do with him—from time to time he shews his kind-heartedness by loading me with books[5] –so that I am still indebted to him for all the pleasure or amusement I have—

Except for the total want of companionship I have nothing to complain—of— I have not too much to do—sufficient liberty—& I am rarely interfered with—I lead an easiful, stagnant, silent life—for which when I think of Mrs Sedgwick[6] I ought to be very thankful.

Be sure you write to me soon—& beg of Anne to inclose a small billet in the same letter—it will be a real charity to do me this kindness—tell me every thing you can think of.

It is a curious metaphysical fact that always in the evening when I am in the great Dormitory alone—having no other company than a number of beds with white curtains I always recur as fanatically as ever to the old ideas the old faces & the old scenes in the world below.[7]

Give my love to Anne
And believe me
Yourn[8]

Dear Anne

Write to me
Your affectionate Schwester[9]
CB

Mr Heger has just been in & given me a little German Testament as a present[10] —I was surprised for since a good many days he has hardly spoken to me—

MS BL Ashley 161.

1. 'Emily' deleted and 'papa' written above it in dark ink, not by CB.
2. In January 1843 Branwell had become a tutor to Edmund (1831–69), the son of Anne Brontë's employer, Revd Edmund Robinson of Thorp Green.
3. Mr Brontë attended the York assizes on 11 and 20 Mar. 1843 as a witness at the trial of men accused of forging a deed, and may have taken the opportunity to visit Thorp Green. See the article by Sarah Fermi and Dorinda Kinghorn in BST 21. 1 and 2, 15–24.
4. Jog along.
5. The gifts would include the works of Bernardin de St Pierre, given to CB on 15 Aug. 1843, and Les Fleurs de la poésie française depuis le commencement du XVIe siècle, given on 1 Jan. 1844, the morning when she left Brussels.

6. Thus, for Mrs J. B. Sidgwick of Stonegappe, near Skipton. See Letter 7.
7. The fantasy world of Angria, shared with Branwell for many years. See Letter 14 nn. 1 and 2.
8. Yours (northern dialect).
9. Sister (German).
10. *Das neue Testament* (London, printed for the British and Foreign Bible Society, 1835), inscribed by CB 'Herr Heger hat mir dieses Buch gegeben | Brußel | Mai 1843 | CB'. (M. Heger gave me this book; Brussels, May 1843). Now in BPM.

24. *To Emily Jane Brontë, 2 September 1843*

Bruxelles

Dear E. J.,

Another opportunity of writing to you coming to pass, I shall improve it by scribbling a few lines. More than half the holidays are now past, and rather better than I expected. The weather has been exceedingly fine during the last fortnight, and yet not so Asiatically hot as it was last year at this time. Consequently I have tramped about a great deal and tried to get a clearer acquaintance with the streets of Bruxelles. This week, as no teacher is here except Mdlle. Blanche,[1] who is returned from Paris, I am always alone except at meal-times, for Mdlle. Blanche's character is so false and so contemptible I can't force myself to associate with her. She perceives my utter dislike and never now speaks to me—a great relief.

However, I should inevitably fall into the gulf of low spirits if I stayed always by myself here without a human being to speak to, so I go out and traverse the Boulevards and streets of Bruxelles sometimes for hours together. Yesterday I went on a pilgrimage to the cemetery,[2] and far beyond it on to a hill where there was nothing but fields as far as the horizon. When I came back it was evening; but I had such a repugnance to return to the house, which contained nothing that I cared for, I still kept threading the streets in the neighbourhood of the Rue d'Isabelle and avoiding it. I found myself opposite to Ste. Gudule,[3] and the bell, whose voice you know, began to toll for evening salut. I went in, quite alone (which procedure you will say is not much like me), wandered about the aisles where a few old women were saying their prayers, till vespers begun. I stayed till they were over. Still I could not leave the church or force myself to go home—to school I mean. An odd whim came into my head. In a solitary part of the Cathedral six or seven people still remained kneeling by the confessionals. In two confessionals I saw a priest. I felt as if I did not care what I did, provided it was not absolutely wrong, and that it served to vary my life and yield a moment's interest. I took a fancy to change myself into a Catholic and go and make a real confession to see what it was like.[4] Knowing me as you do, you will think this odd, but when people are by themselves they have singular fancies. A penitent was occupied in confessing. They do not go into the sort of pew or cloister which the priest occupies, but kneel down on the steps and confess through a grating. Both the confessor and the penitent whisper very low, you can hardly hear their voices. After I had watched two or three penitents go and return I approached at last and knelt down in a niche which was just vacated. I had to kneel there ten minutes waiting, for on the other side was another penitent invisible to me. At last that went away[5] and a little wooden door inside the grating opened, and I saw the priest leaning his ear towards me. I was obliged to begin, and yet I did not know a word of the formula with which they always commence their confessions. It was a funny position. I felt precisely as I did when alone on the Thames at midnight.[6] I commenced with saying I was a foreigner and had been brought up a Protestant. The priest asked if I was a Protestant then. I somehow could not tell a lie and said 'yes.' He replied that in that case I could not 'jouir du bonheur de la confesse';[7] but I was determined to confess, and at last he said he would allow me because it might be the first step towards returning to the true church. I actually did confess—a real confession. When I had done he told me his address, and said that every morning I was to go to the rue du Parc—to his house—and he would reason with me and try to convince me of the error and enormity of being a Protestant!!! I promised faithfully to go. Of course, however, the adventure stops there, and I hope I shall never see the priest again. I think you had better not tell papa of this. He will not understand that it was only a freak, and will perhaps think I am going to turn Catholic. Trusting that you and papa are well, and also Tabby and the Holyes,[8] and hoping you will write to me immediately,—I am, yours,

C. B.

MS untraced. Text *CBCircle* 117–18.

1. See Letter 19 n. 3. The Hegers and the school pupils were presumably away on holiday.
2. The Protestant cemetery where Martha Taylor had been buried in Oct. 1842.
3. The Collegiate church of Saint-Michel and Sainte-Gudule, founded 1226.
4. CB uses this event in chapter 15 of *Villette*, where Lucy Snowe's 'pressure of affliction' is said to be neither a sin nor a crime.
5. The text, based on C. K. Shorter, *Charlotte Brontë and her Circle* (1896), 117–18, may be corrupt. No manuscript has been traced.
6. i.e. when CB returned alone to Brussels, having travelled from Haworth to London by train, then by cab to London Bridge wharf, where she went on board the *Earl of Liverpool* in the middle of the night.
7. I could not enjoy the privilege of confession.
8. Interpreted by C. K. Shorter as Charlotte's 'irreverent appellation for the curates', Revd James William Smith and Revd Joseph Brett Grant. Wise & Symington print 'Hoyles', with a footnote, 'A family with whom Rev. W. Weightman, curate of Haworth, is understood to have lived until his death on 6 Sept., 1842.' But the 1841 Census for Haworth shows that Mr Weightman was then lodging with the widowed Mrs Grace Ogden at Cook Gate, Haworth. In the absence of a manuscript, the reading must remain uncertain.

25. To Ellen Nussey, 13 October [1843]

Brussels

Dear Ellen

I was glad to receive your last letter but when I read it—its contents gave me some pain—it was melancholy indeed that so soon after the death of a sister[1] you should be called away from a distant county by the news of the severe illness of a brother[2]—and that after your return home your sister Anne should fall ill too—A note I received yesterday from Mary Dixon[3] informs me that Anne is now better but that George is scarcely expected to recover—is this true—? I hope not—for his sake and for yours—His loss would indeed be a blow to his mother and sisters—a blow which I hope providence will long avert—do not my dear Ellen fail to write to me soon—to inform me how affairs get on at Brookroyd—I cannot fail to be anxious on the subject—your family being amongst the number of the oldest & kindest friends I have. I trust the season of your afflictions will soon pass—it has been a long one—

Mary Taylor is getting on well[4]—as she deserves to [do]—I often hear from her—her letters and yours are one of my few pleasures—she urges me very much to leave Brussels and go to her—but at present however tempted to take such a step I should not feel justified in doing so—To leave a certainty for a complete uncertainty would be to the last degree imprudent.

Notwithstanding Brussels is indeed desolate to me now—since Mary Dixon left I have had no friend—I had indeed some very kind acquaintances in the family of Dr Wheelwright[5]—but they too are gone now—they left in latter part of August—and I am completely alone—I cannot count the Belgians as anything—Madame Heger is a politic—plausible and interested person—I no longer trust her—It is a curious position to be so utterly solitary in the midst of numbers—sometimes this solitude oppresses me to an excess—one day lately I felt as if I could bear it no longer—and I went to Mde Heger and gave her notice—If it had depended on her I should certainly have soon been at liberty but Monsieur Heger—having heard of what was in agitation—sent for me the day after—and pronounced with vehemence his decision that I should not leave—I could not at that time have persevered in my intention without exciting him to passion—so I promised to stay a while longer—how long that while will be I do not know—I should not like to return to England [to] do nothing—I am too old for that now—but if I could hear of a favourable occasion for commencing a school—I think I should embrace it.

I have much to say Ellen—many little odd things queer and puzzling enough—which I do not like to trust to a letter, but which one day perhaps or rather one evening—if ever we should find ourselves again by the fireside at Haworth or at Brookroyd with our feet on the fender—curling our hair—I may communicate to you—

We have as yet no fires here and I suffer much from cold otherwise I am well in health—. Mr George Dixon[6] will take this letter to England—he is a pretty-looking & pretty behaved young man—apparently constructed without a back-bone—by which I don't allude to his corporeal spine—which is all right enough—but to his character.

Farewell dear Ellen—I hope by the time you receive this Mr George[7] will be quickly gathering strength   he has been severely tried—I hope also your Sister Anne will be quite well—give my love to your Mother & Sisters and my good wishes to Mr George—anything you like to yourself dear Nell—

C B—

MS HM 24433.

1. The invalid Sarah Walker Nussey (1809–43) had died of a painful infection in the small intestine on 16 June.
2. George Nussey (1814–85), whose recurrent bouts of mental illness were becoming more frequent.
3. See Letter 22 and Biographical Notes, p. xxxvii.
4. Mary Taylor was in Germany, teaching English to German students, and paying for tuition in music and German. She received music lessons from Friedrich Halle, father of Sir Charles Hallé.
5. Dr Thomas Wheelwright (1786–1861), a London physician who had brought his family to Brussels for their education. His daughters were Laetitia Elizabeth (1828–1911), Emily (1829–88), Frances (1831–1913), Sarah Ann (1834–1900), and Julia (b. 1835) who contracted typhus or typhoid fever at the pensionnat Heger and died on 17 Nov. 1842.
6. George Dixon (1820–98), working for the Birmingham firm of Rabone, makers and exporters of precision tools, later to become an educational reformer and MP for Birmingham.
7. Ellen Nussey's brother.

26. To Ellen Nussey, 23 January 1844

[Haworth]

My dear Ellen

It was a great disappointment to me to hear that you were in the south of England[1]—I had counted upon seeing you soon as one of the great pleasures of my return home now I fear our meeting will be postponed for an indefinite time. Every one asks me what I am going to do now that I am returned home and every one seems to expect that I should immediately commence a school—In truth Ellen it is what I should wish to do—I desire it of all things—I have sufficient money for the undertaking—and I hope now sufficient qualifications to give me a fair chance of success—yet I cannot yet permit myself to enter upon life—to touch the object which seems now within my reach and which I have been so long striving to attain—you will ask me why—It is on Papa's account—he is now as you know getting old—and it grieves me to tell you that he is losing his sight—I have felt for some months that I ought not to be away from him—and I feel now that it would be too selfish to leave him (at least so long as Branwell and Anne are absent)[2] in order to pursue selfish interests of my own—with the help of God—I will try to deny myself in this matter and to wait.

I suffered much before I left Brussels—I think however long I live I shall not forget what the parting with Monsr Heger cost me—It grieved me so much to grieve him who has been so true and kind and disinterested a friend—at parting he gave me a sort of diploma[3] certifying my abilities as a teacher—sealed with the seal of the Athénée Royal of which he is professor. He wanted me to take one of his little girls with me—this however I refused to do as I knew it would not have been agreeable to Madame—I was surprised also at the degree of regret expressed by my Belgian pupils when they knew I was going to leave   I did not think it had been in their phlegmatic natures—

When do you think I shall see you Ellen—I have of course much to tell you—and I daresay you have much also to tell me   things which we should neither of us wish to commit to paper   I am much disquieted at not having heard from Mary Taylor for a long time—Joe[4] called at the Rue d'Isabelle with a letter from you—but I was already gone—he brought the letter back with him to England.

I do not know whether you feel as I do Ellen—but there are times now when it appears to me as if all my ideas and feelings except a few friendships and affections are changed from what they used to be—something in me which used to be enthusiasm is tamed down and broken—I have fewer illusions—what I wish for now is active exertion—a stake in life—Haworth seems such a lonely, quiet spot, buried away from the world—I no longer regard myself as young, indeed I shall soon be 28—and it seems as if I ought to be working and braving the rough realities of the world as other people do—It is however my duty to restrain this feeling at present and I will endeavour to do so   Write to me soon my dear Ellen

and believe me as far as it regards yourself
your unchanged friend
C Bronte

Jany 23d—44
Remember me with kindness to your brother Henry—Anne and Branwell have just left us to return to York—they are both wonderously valued in their situation

MS Law-Dixon.

1. EN was with her brother Henry at Earnley, Sussex. In Apr. 1844 he was appointed curate to Revd John le Cornu (?1760–1844) at Hathersage in Derbyshire.
2. Employed as tutor and governess in the Robinson family at Thorp Green, near York.
3. The diploma, dated 29 Dec. 1843, certified CB's competence to teach French.
4. Mary's brother Joseph.

27. To Victoire Dubois,[1] 18 May 1844

[Haworth]

My dear little Victoire

You ask me how I do—and I answer I am much better I thank you—You tell me to return to Belgium—that is not possible—I cannot return to you—but I can think of you all and love you.

I cannot tell you my dear Victoire how much pleasure the packet of letters I received from the pupils of the first Class, gave me—I knew I loved my pupils—but I did not know that they had for me the affection those letters express—I only fear now that they will exaggerate my good qualities and think me better than I really am.

It grieves me to hear that you are not quite satisfied with your present mistress—do not give way to this feeling—Be obedient, docile and studious and then I think she cannot fail to be kind to you—

I had intended to have written a long letter to you but I have not time so to do—I am afraid of missing the occasion to send these letters—[2]

If ever I return to Brussels, which is not likely, I shall certainly come to see you and Clémence—remember me kindly to her—I hope her health is better than it was—Write to me again my dear little Victoire the first opportunity and believe me

Your affectionate and sincere friend
C Brontë

MS BPM B.S. 51.

1. A former pupil of CB at Mme Heger's pensionnat in Brussels.
2. CB would entrust a packet of letters to Mary Taylor, who planned to return to Germany, presumably via Brussels, on 22 May.

28. To Constantin Heger, 24 July [1844][1]

[Haworth]

Monsieur

Je sais bien que ce n'est pas à mon tour de vous écrire, mais puisque Mde Wheelwright va à Bruxelles et veut bien se charger d'une lettre—il me semble que je ne dois pas négliger une occasion si favorable pour vous écrire.

Je suis très contente que l'année scolaire soit presque finie et que l'époque des vacances approche—j'en suis contente pour vous Monsieur—car, on m'a dit que vous travaillez trop et que votre santé en est un peu altérée—C'est pourquoi je ne me permets pas de proférer une seule plainte au sujet de votre long silence—j'aimerais mieux rester six mois sans recevoir de vos nouvelles que d'ajouter un atome au poids, déjà trop lourd, qui vous accable—Je me rappelle bien que c'est maintenant l'époque des compositions, que ce sera bientôt celle des examens et puis, des prix—et pendant tout ce temps, vous êtes condamné à respirer l'atmostphère desséchante des classes—à vous user—à expliquer, à interroger à parler toute la journée et puis le soir vous avez toutes ces malheureuses compositions à lire, à corriger, presqu'à refaire—Ah Monsieur! je vous ai écrit une fois une lettre peu raisonnable, parceque le chagrin me serrait le cœur, mais je ne le ferai plus—je tacherai de ne plus être égoïste et tout en regardant vos² lettres comme un des plus grands bonheurs que je connaisse j'attendrai patiemment pour en recevoir jusqu'à ce qu'il vous plaira et vous conviendra de m'en envoyer. En même temps je puis bien vous écrire de temps en temps une petite lettre—vous m'y avez autorisée—

Je crains beaucoup d'oublier le français, car je suis bien persuadée que je vous reverrai un jour—je ne sais pas comment ni quand—mais cela doit être puisque je le désire tant, et alors je ne voudrais pas rester muette devant vous—ce serait trop triste de vous voir et de ne pas pouvoir vous parler; pour éviter ce malheur—j'apprends, tous les jours, une demie page de français par cœur dans un livre de style familier: et j'ai un plaisir à apprendre cette leçon—monsieur—quand je prononce les mots français il me semble que je cause avec vous.

On vient de m'offrir une place comme première maîtresse dans un grand pensionnat à Manchester, avec un traitement de 100£ i.e. 2500 frs par an—je ne puis pas l'accepter—car en l'acceptant je dois quitter mon père et cela ne se peut pas—J'ai cependant mon projet—(lorsqu'on vit dans la retraite le cerveau travaille toujours—on désire s'occuper—on veut se lancer dans une carrière active) Notre Presbytère est une maison assez grande—avec quelques changements—il y aura de la place pour cinq ou six pensionnaires—si je pouvais trouver ce nombre d'enfants de bonne famille je me dévouerais à leur éducation—Emilie n'aime pas beaucoup l'instruction mais elle s'occuperait toujours du ménage et, quoiqu'un peu recluse, elle a trop bon cœur pour ne pas faire son possible pour le bien-être des enfants—elle est aussi très généreuse et pour l'ordre, l'économie, l'exactitude—le travail assidu—toutes choses très essentielles dans un pensionnat—je m'en charge volontiers.

Voilà mon projet Monsieur, que j'ai déjà expliqué à mon père et qu'il trouve bon—Il ne reste donc que de trouver des élèves—chose assez difficile—car nous demeurons loin des villes et on ne se soucie guère de franchir les montagnes qui nous servent de barrière—mais la tâche qui est sans difficulté est presque sans mérite—il y a un grand intérêt à vaincre les obstacles—je ne dis pas que je réussirai mais je tâcherai de réussir—le seul effort me fera du bien—il n'y a rien que je crains comme la paresse—le désœuvrement—l'inertie—la lethargie des facultés—quand le corps est paresseux, l'esprit souffre cruellement. Je ne connaîtrais pas cette lethargie si je pouvais écrire—autrefois je passais des journées, des semaines, des mois entiers à écrire et pas tout à fait sans fruit puisque

Southey, et Coleridge—deux de nos meilleurs auteurs, à qui j'ai envoyé certains manuscrits en ont bien voulu temoigner leur approbation—mais à present j'ai la vue trop faible pour écrire—si j'écrivais beaucoup je deviendrais aveugle. Cette faiblesse de vue est pour moi une terrible privation—sans cela savez-vous ce que je ferais Monsieur?—j'écrirais un livre et je le dédierais à mon maître de litérature—au seul maître que j'ai jamais eu—à vous Monsieur. Je vous ai souvent dit en français combien je vous respecte—combien je suis redevable à votre bonté, à vos conseils, Je voudrais le dire une fois en Anglais—Cela ne se peut pas—il ne faut pas y penser—la carrière des lettres m'est fermée—celle de l'instruction seule m'est ouverte—elle n'offre pas les mêmes attraits—c'est égal, j'y entrerai et si je n'y vais pas loin, ce ne sera pas manque de diligence. Vous aussi Monsieur—vous avez voulu être avocat—le sort ou la Providence vous a fait professeur—vous êtes heureux malgré cela.

Veuillez presenter à Madame l'assurance de mon estime—je crains que Maria—Louise—Claire ne m'aient déjà oubliée—Prospère et Victorine ne m'ont jamais bien connue—moi je me souviens bien de tous les cinq—surtout de Louise—elle avait tant de caractère—tant de naïveté—tant de vérité dans sa petite figure—

> Adieu Monsieur—
> votre élève reconnaissante
> C Brontë

July 24th.

Je ne vous ai pas prié de m'écrire bientôt, parceque je crains de vous importuner—mais vous êtes trop bon pour oublier que je le désire tout le même—oui—je le désire beaucoup—c'est assez—après tout—faites comme vous voudrez monsieur—si, enfin je recevais une lettre et si je croyais que vous l'aviez écrite par pitié—cela me ferait beaucoup de mal—

Il parait que Mde Wheelwright va à Paris avant d'aller à Bruxelles—mais elle mettra ma lettre à la poste à Boulogne—encore une fois adieu Monsieur—cela fait mal de dire adieu même dans une lettre—Oh c'est certain que je vous reverrai un jour—il le faut bien—puisque aussitôt que j'aurai gagné assez d'argent pour aller à Bruxelles j'y irai—et je vous reverrai si ce n'est que pour un instant.

Translation

Monsieur,

I am well aware that it is not my turn to write to you, but since Mrs Wheelwright[3] is going to Brussels and is willing to take charge of a letter—it seems to me that I should not neglect such a favourable opportunity for writing to you.

I am very pleased that the school year is almost over and that the holiday period is approaching—I am pleased about it on your account, Monsieur—for I have been told that you are working too hard and that as a result your health has deteriorated a little—That is why I refrain from uttering a single complaint about your long silence—I would rather remain six months without hearing from you than add an atom to the burden—already too heavy—which overwhelms you—I well remember that it is now the time for compositions, that it will soon be the time for examinations and after that for prizes—and for the whole period you are condemned to breathe in the deadening aridity of the classes—to wear yourself out—in explaining, questioning, speaking all day long, and then in the evenings you have all those dreary compositions to read, correct, almost re-write—Ah Monsieur! I once wrote you a letter which was hardly rational, because sadness was wringing my heart, but I shall do so no more[4]—I will try to stop being egotistical and though I look on your letters as one of the greatest joys I know, I shall wait patiently to receive them until it pleases and suits you to send them. But all the same I can still write you a little letter from time to time—you have given me permission to do so. I am very much afraid of forgetting French, for I am quite convinced that I shall see you again one day—I don't know how or when—but it must happen since I so long for it, and then I would not like to stay silent in your presence—it would be too sad to see you and not be able to speak to you; to prevent this misfortune—every single day, I learn by heart half a page of French from a book in a colloquial style: and I take pleasure in learning this lesson, Monsieur—when I pronounce the French words I seem to be chatting with you.

I have just been offered a position as principal teacher in a large boarding school in Manchester, with a salary of £100, i.e. 2,500 francs a year—I cannot accept it—because acceptance would mean having to leave my father and that cannot be—Nevertheless I have made a plan: (when one lives in seclusion one's brain is always active—one longs to be busy—one longs to launch out into an active career). Our Parsonage is a fairly large house—with some alterations—there will be room for five or six boarders—if I could find that number of children from respectable families—I would devote myself to their education—Emily is not very fond of teaching but she would nevertheless take care of the housekeeping, and though she is rather withdrawn she has too kind a heart not to do her utmost for the well-being of the children—she is also a very generous soul; and as for order, economy, strict organisation—hard work—all very essential matters in a boarding-school—I willingly make myself responsible for them.

There is my plan, Monsieur, which I have already explained to my father and which he considers a good one.—So all that remains is to find the pupils—a rather difficult matter—for we live a long way from towns and people hardly wish to take the trouble of crossing the mountains which form a barrier round us—but the task which lacks difficulty almost lacks merit—it is very rewarding to surmount obstacles—I do not say that I shall succeed but I shall try to succeed—the effort alone will do me good—I fear nothing so much as idleness—lack of employment—inertia—lethargy of the faculties—when the body is idle, the spirit suffers cruelly. I would not experience this lethargy if I could write—once upon a time I used to spend whole days, weeks, complete months in writing and not quite in vain since Southey and Coleridge—two of our best authors, to whom I sent some manuscripts were pleased to express their approval of them[5]—but at present my sight is too weak for writing—if I wrote a lot I would become blind. This weakness of sight is a terrible privation for me—without it, do you know what I would do, Monsieur?—I would write a book and I would dedicate it to my literature master—to the only master that I have ever had—to you Monsieur. I have often told you in French how much I respect you—how much I am indebted to your kindness, to your advice, I would like to tell you for once in English—That cannot be—it must not be thought of—a literary career is closed to me—only that of teaching is open to me—it does not offer the same attractions—never mind, I shall enter upon it and if I do not go far in it, it will not be for want of diligence. You too, Monsieur—you wanted to be a barrister—fate or Providence has made you a teacher—you are happy in spite of that.

Please assure Madame of my esteem—I am afraid that Maria, Louise and Claire will have already forgotten me—Prospère and Victorine have never known me well—I myself clearly remember all five—especially Louise—she had so much character—so much naïveté—so much *truthfulness* in her little face[6]—

Goodbye Monsieur— | Your grateful pupil,
C. Brontë

July 24th.

I have not asked you to write to me soon because I don't want to seem importunate—but you are too good to forget that I wish it all the same—yes—I wish for it very much—that is enough—after all, do as you please, Monsieur—if in fact I received a letter and thought that you had written *out of pity* for me—that would hurt me very much.

It seems that Mrs Wheelwright is going to Paris before going to Brussels—but she will put my letter in the post at Boulogne—once more goodbye, Monsieur—it hurts to say goodbye even in a letter—Oh it is certain that I shall see you again one day—it really has to be—for as soon as I have earned enough money to go to Brussels I shall go—and I shall see you again if it is only for a moment.

Original MS in French BL Add. 38732 A.

1. An English translation follows. M. Heger had torn up and thrown away the letter, but Mme Heger found it and stuck the pieces together with thin paper strips.
2. CB wrote 'vous'.

3. Elizabeth, wife of Dr Thomas Wheelwright.
4. CB failed to keep her promise. See especially her letters of 8 Jan. and 18 Nov. 1845.
5. Robert Southey had acknowledged that CB had the 'faculty of Verse', but Hartley Coleridge seems to have been less than enthusiastic about her work. See pp. a and 25.
6. Louise Heger was to become a 'remarkable woman—an artist and musician', according to those who knew her. She and her brother Paul presented CB's letters to their father to the British Museum in 1913 because they believed that the truth should always be brought to light. See *BST* II. 59. 259.

29. To Ellen Nussey, [?10 August 1844]

[Haworth]

I did not "swear at the postman" when I saw another epistle from you Nell—and I hope you will not "swear" at me when I tell you that I cannot think of leaving home at present even to have the pleasure of joining you your Mother and Sisters at Harrogate,[1] but I am obliged to you for thinking of me—thank you Nell.

I have seriously entered into the enterprise of keeping a school—or rather taking a limited number of pupils at home that is I have begun to seek in good earnest for pupils—I wrote to Mrs White, not asking her for her daughter[2]—I cannot do that—but informing her of my intentions I received an answer from Mr White expressive of, I believe, sincere regret that I had not informed them a month sooner in which case, he said, they would gladly have sent me their own daughter and also Colonel Stott's[3]—but that now both were promised to Miss Cockhills'[4]—

I was partly disappointed by this answer—and partly gratified—indeed I derived quite an impulse of encouragement from the warm assurance that if I had but applied a little sooner they would certainly have sent me Sarah Louisa I own I had misgivings that nobody would be willing to send a child for education to Haworth—these misgivings are partly done away with—

I have written also to Mrs Busfield[5] of Keighley and enclosed the diploma which Mr Heger gave me before I left Brussels—I have not yet received her answer but I wait for it with some anxiety—I do not expect that she will send me any of her children but if she would, I daresay she could recommend me other pupils—unfortunately she knows us only very slightly

As soon as I can get an assurance of only <u>one</u> pupil—I will have cards of terms printed—and will commence the repairs necessary in the house—I wish all that to be done before winter—

I think of fixing the board and English education at 25£ per annum[6]   do you know what Miss Cockhill's terms are? If not I wish you could get to know and inform me.

I have nothing new to tell you about the Revd Mr Lothario-Lovelace Smith[7]—I think I like him a little bit less every day—I am glad now he did not ask you to marry him—you are far too good for him—Mr Weightman was worth 200 Mr Smiths—tied in a bunch

Good-bye to you, remember me to "Mrs Nussey & family."

I fear by what you say Flossy Junr[8] behaves discreditably & gets his Mistress into scrapes—

C Brontë

MS HM 24434.

1. The natural springs at Harrogate in Yorks. had made the town a popular health resort.
2. Sarah Louisa, daughter of CB's employer at Upperwood House, 1841. See Letter 15.
3. Colonel George Stott, later Stott-Stanhope, of Eccleshill Hall, about two miles from Upperwood House.
4. The school at Oakwell Hall, near Birstall, kept by Hannah, Sarah, and Elizabeth Cockill, distant relatives of Ellen Nussey.
5. Probably Sarah Busfeild, wife of Revd William Busfeild, rector of Keighley from July 1840.
6. A 'card of terms' had been printed by about 22 Aug. 1844, fixing the cost of board and basic education at 'The Misses Bronte's Establishment for the Board and Education of a Limited Number of Young Ladies' at £35 per annum, with French, German, Latin, Music, and Drawing as extras, each at one guinea a quarter. But no pupils were to be found, then or later.
7. Revd James William Smith, Mr Brontë's curate Mar. 1843–Oct. 1844; subsequently a minister in Eastwood parish, Keighley. He was probably the model for Peter Malone in *Shirley*. On 26 Feb. 1848 CB told EN that Smith had absconded from his ministry, having misappropriated a charitable donation and left unpaid debts.
8. EN's dog, the offspring of Anne Brontë's spaniel, Flossy, was to damage a 'book-muslin dress' and 'lace bertha' (a deep collar) in Nov. 1844.

30. *To Constantin Heger, 24 October 1844*[1]

[Haworth]

Monsieur

Je suis toute joyeuse ce matin—ce qui ne m'arrive pas souvent depuis deux ans—c'est parceque un Monsieur de mes connaissances va passer par Bruxelles et qu'il a offert de se charger d'une lettre pour vous—laquelle lettre il vous remettra luimême, ou bien, sa sœur de sorte que je serai certaine que vous l'avez reçue.

Ce n'est pas une longue lettre que je vais écrire—d'abord je n'ai pas le temps—il faut que cela parte tout de suite et ensuite je crains de vous ennuyer. Je voudrais seulement vous demander, si vous avez reçu de mes nouvelles au commencement du mois de Mai et puis au mois d'Août? Voilà six mois que j'attends une lettre de Monsieur—six mois d'attente c'est bien long, cela! Pourtant je ne me plains pas et je serai richement recompensée pour un peu de chagrin—si vous voulez maintenant écrire une lettre et la donner à ce monsieur—ou à sa sœur qui me la remettrait sans faute.

Quelque courte que soit la lettre j'en serai satisfaite—n'oubliez pas seulement de me dire comment vous vous portez Monsieur et comment Madame et les enfants se portent et les maîtresses et les élèves.

Mon père et ma sœur vous presentent leurs respects—l'infirmité de mon père augmente peu à peu—cependant il n'est pas encore tout à fait aveugle—mes sœurs se portent bien mais mon pauvre frère est toujours malade.

Adieu Monsieur, je compte bientôt avoir de vos nouvelles—cette idée me sourit car le souvenir de vos bontés ne s'effacera jamais de ma memoire et tant que ce souvenir durera <?l'affection> le respect qu'il m'a inspiré durera aussi

Votre élève très dévouée
C Brontë

Je viens de faire relier tous les livres que vous m'avez donnés quand j'étais encore à Bruxelles   j'ai un plaisir à les considérer—cela fait tout une petite bibliothèque—Il y a d'abord les ouvrages complets de Bernardin St Pierre—Les Pensées de Pascal—un livre de poësie, deux livres allemands—et (ce qui vaut tout le reste) deux discours de Monsieur le Professeur Heger—prononcés à la Distribution des Prix de l'Athénée royal—
Octbe. 24th 1844

Translation

Monsieur,

I am full of joy this morning—something which has rarely happened to me these last two years—it is because a gentleman of my acquaintance[2] will be passing through Brussels and has offered to take charge of a letter to you—which either he or else his sister will deliver to you, so that I shall be certain you have received it.

I am not going to write a long letter—first of all I haven't the time—it has to go immediately—and then I am afraid of boring you. I would just like to ask you whether you heard from me at the beginning of May and then in the month of August? For all those six months I have been expecting a letter from you, Monsieur—six months of waiting—That is a very long time indeed! Nevertheless I am not complaining and I shall be richly recompensed for a little sadness—if you are now willing to write a letter and give it to this gentleman—or to his sister—who would deliver it to me without fail.

However short the letter may be I shall be satisfied with it—only do not forget to tell me how you are, Monsieur, and how Madame and the children are and the teachers and pupils.

My father and sister[3] send you their regards—my father's affliction is gradually increasing—however he is still not completely blind[4]—my sisters are keeping well but my poor brother is always ill.[5]

Goodbye Monsieur, I am counting on soon having news of you—this thought delights me for the remembrance of your kindness will never fade from my memory and so long as this remembrance endures, the respect it has inspired in me will endure also.

Your very devoted pupil,
C. Brontë

I have just had bound all the books that you gave me when I was still in Brussels. I take pleasure in looking at them—they make quite a little library—First there are the complete works of Bernardin de St. Pierre[6]—the Pensées of Pascal[7]—a book of verse,[8] two German books—and (something worth all the rest) two speeches, by Professor Heger—given at the Prize Distribution of the Athénée Royal.[9]

Oct 24 1844.

Original MS in French, BL Add. 38732 B.

1. An English translation follows. The letter had been torn up by M. Heger, then rescued and pieced together by Mme Heger.
2. Joe Taylor or his sister Mary would deliver the letter.
3. Emily, who remained at Haworth; Anne would be at Thorp Green.
4. Cataracts were developing on both eyes.
5. Branwell's sisters sometimes used this term as a euphemism for 'the worse for drink'. At this period he was still at Thorp Green, where, as Anne later recorded, he 'had much tribulation and ill health'.
6. M. Heger had given CB the works of Jacques-Henri Bernardin de Saint-Pierre (1737–1814) on 15 August 1843. They included *Paul et Virginie* (1787), a tale of parted lovers. Its title is used for the ship in which M. Paul Emanuel leaves 'Labassecour' (Belgium) for Guadaloupe in the West Indies.
7. *Les Pensées* (first published 1670) by Blaise Pascal (1623–62).
8. *Les Fleurs de la poésie française depuis le commencement du XVIe siècle* (Tours, 1841), given to CB 1 Jan. 1844, on the morning she left Brussels.
9. M. Heger gave the prize-giving addresses at the Athénée in 1834 and 1843.

31. *To Constantin Heger, 8 January 1845*[1]

Haworth—Bradford—Yorkshire

M. Taylor est revenue, je lui ai demandé s'il n'avait pas une lettre pour moi—"Non, rien." "Patience"—dis-je—"Sa sœur viendra bientôt"—Mademoiselle Taylor est revenue "Je n'ai rien pour vous de la part de Monsieur Heger" dit-elle "ni lettre ni message."

Ayant bien compris ces mots—je me suis dit, ce que je dirais à un autre en pareille circonstance "Il faut vous résigner et, surtout, ne pas vous affliger d'un malheur que vous n'avez pas merité" Je me suis efforcée à ne pas pleurer à ne pas me plaindre—

Mais quand on ne se plaint pas et qu'on veut se dominer en tyran—les facultés se révoltent—et on paie le calme extérieur par une lutte intérieure presque insupportable

Jour et nuit je ne trouve ni repos ni paix—si je dors je fais des rêves tourmentants où je vous vois toujours sévère, toujours sombre et irrité contre moi—

Pardonnez-moi donc Monsieur si je prends la partie de vous écrire encore—Comment puis-je supporter la vie si je ne fais pas un effort pour en alléger les souffrances?

Je sais que vous serez impatienté quand vous lirez cette lettre—Vous direz encore que je suis exaltée—que j'ai des pensées noires &c. Soit Monsieur—je ne cherche pas à me justifier, je me soumets à toutes sortes de réproches—tout ce que je sais—c'est que je ne puis pas—que je ne veux pas me résigner à perdre entièrement l'amitié de mon maître—j'aime mieux subir les plus grandes douleurs physiques que d'avoir toujours le cœur, lacéré par des regrets cuisants. Si mon maître me retire entièrement son amitié je serai tout à fait sans espoir—s'il m'en donne un peu—très peu—je serai contente—heureuse, j'aurais un motif pour vivre—pour travailler.

Monsieur, les pauvres n'ont pas besoin de grand'chose pour vivre—ils ne demandent que les miettes de pain qui tombent de la table des riches—mais si on leur refuse ces miettes de pain—ils meurent de faim—Moi non plus je n'ai pas besoin de beaucoup d'affection de la part de ceux que j'aime   je ne saurais que faire d'une amitié entière et complète—je n'y suis pas habituée—mais vous me témoigniez, autrefois, un peu d'intérêt quand j'étais votre élève à Bruxelles—et je tiens à conserver ce peu d'intérêt—j'y tiens comme je tiendrais à la vie.

Vous me direz peutêtre—Je ne vous porte plus le moindre intérêt Mademoiselle Charlotte—vous n'êtes plus de Ma Maison—je vous ai oubliée"

Eh bien Monsieur   dites-moi cela franchement—ce sera pour moi un choc—n'importe ce sera toujours moins hideux que l'incertitude.

Je ne veux pas relire cet[t]e lettre—je l'envoie comme je l'ai écrite—Pourtant j'ai comme la conscience obscure qu'il y a des personnes froides et sensées qui diraient en la lisant—"elle déraisonne"—Pour toute vengeance—je souhaite à ces personnes—un seul jour des tourments [que] j'ai subis depuis huit mois—on verrait alors s'elles [ne] déraison[n]eraient pas de même

On souffre en silence tant qu'on a la force et qua[nd] cette force manque on parle sans trop mesurer ses paroles. <Je n'ai pas besoin de souhaiter à Monsieur le bonheur et la prosperité—il jouit de . . . ?autour>

Je souhaite à Monsieur le bonheur et la prospérité

CB

Translation

Mr Taylor returned, I asked him if he had a letter for me—"No, nothing."
"Patience"—I say—"His sister will be coming soon"—Miss Taylor returned[2]
"I have nothing for you from M. Heger" she says "neither letter nor message."

When I had taken in the full meaning of these words—I said to myself, what
I would say to someone else in such a case "You will have to resign yourself to
the fact, and above all, not distress yourself about a misfortune that you have
not deserved." I did my utmost not to cry not to complain—

But when one does not complain, and when one wants to master oneself with
a tyrant's grip—one's faculties rise in revolt—and one pays for outward calm
by an almost unbearable inner struggle

Day and night I find neither rest nor peace—if I sleep I have tormenting
dreams in which I see you always severe, always saturnine and angry with me—

Forgive me then Monsieur if I take the step of writing to you again—How
can I bear my life unless I make an effort to alleviate its sufferings?

I know that you will lose patience with me when you read this letter—You will
say that I am over-excited—that I have black thoughts etc. So be it Monsieur—I
do not seek to justify myself, I submit to all kinds of reproaches—all I know—is
that I cannot—that I will not resign myself to the total loss of my master's
friendship—I would rather undergo the greatest bodily pains than have my heart
constantly lacerated by searing regrets. If my master withdraws his friendship
from me entirely, I shall be absolutely without hope—if he gives me a little
friendship—a very little—I shall be content—happy, I would have a motive for
living—for working.

Monsieur, the poor do not need a great deal to live on—they ask only the
crumbs of bread which fall from the rich men's table[3]—but if they are refused
these crumbs—they die of hunger—No more do I need a great deal of affection
from those I love—I would not know what to do with a whole and complete
friendship—I am not accustomed to it—but you showed a <u>little</u> interest in me in
days gone by when I was your pupil in Brussels—and I cling to the preservation
of this <u>little</u> interest—I cling to it as I would cling on to life.

Perhaps you will say to me—"I no longer take the slightest interest in you
Miss Charlotte—you no longer belong to my household—I have forgotten
you."

Well Monsieur tell me so candidly—it will be a shock to me—that doesn't
matter—it will still be less horrible than uncertainty.

I don't want to re-read this letter—I am sending it as I have written
it—Nevertheless I am as it were dimly aware that there are some cold and
rational people who would say on reading it—"she is raving"—My sole revenge
is to wish these people—a single day of the torments that I have suffered for
eight months—then we should see whether they wouldn't be raving too

1 (*above*). Haworth
Parsonage: ambrotype
photograph taken before
1861.

2 (*left*). Watercolour portrait
of Anne Brontë by Charlotte
Brontë, 17 June 1834. Brontë
Parsonage Museum, C21.

3 (*left*). Self portrait in pencil by Branwell Brontë, *c*.1840. Brontë Parsonage Museum, Bonnell 18 verso.

4 (*below*). Pencil engraving of the 'Gun group' by Branwell Brontë, showing Anne, Charlotte, Branwell, and Emily Brontë.

5. Photograph of the Revd Patrick Brontë in old age. Brontë Parsonage Museum.

6. The last page of Charlotte Brontë's letter to Ellen Nussey of 6 March 1843, including a sketch of herself waving goodbye to Ellen across the sea from Belgium. Brontë Parsonage Museum, MS B.S. 50.4.

One suffers in silence so long as one has the strength and when that strength fails one speaks without measuring one's words too much.

I wish Monsieur happiness and prosperity[4]

C B

Original MS in French, BL 38732 D.

1. An English translation follows. The letter had been torn to pieces by M. Heger, but it was retrieved by Mme Heger, who stitched the fragments together with thread.
2. CB had hoped that her letter to M. Heger of 24 Oct. 1844, taken to him by Joe Taylor, would elicit a reply, to be delivered to her by Joe or Mary Taylor. Mary had decided to give up her teaching post in Germany, and, after returning to Yorkshire, to emigrate to New Zealand.
3. Cf. Luke 16: 20–1.
4. This sentence is preceded by two heavily deleted lines of writing which may read in part, 'Je n'ai pas besoin de souhaiter à Monsieur du bonheur et de la prospérité—il joue . . .'. (I do not need to wish Monsieur happiness and prosperity—he enjoys . . . ').

32. *To Ellen Nussey, 24 March [1845]*

[Haworth]

Dear Ellen

I repeat to you what you say sometimes to me "Take care of yourself". You are not strong enough, not of sufficiently robust fibre to travel 70 miles in an open gig in very cold weather—[1] Don't do it again.

You have done quite right to leave George[2] for a time—your absence cannot harm him—and a total estrangement from the persons and things that were about him in his illness—will in all probability do him good—Do not dear Ellen be disheartened because George's improvement in health is slow—When one thinks of the nature of his illness—of the extreme delicacy of the organ affected (the brain) it is obvious that that organ after the irritation of fever & inflammation could not all at once regain its healthy state—it must have time—but with <u>time</u> I do believe a complete cure will yet be effected—I should not hope it, if George were a man of irregular habits—but as it is—I think there is the best ground for confident hope.

Have you heard any particulars of Mary Taylor's departure—what day she sailed[3]—what passengers were in the ship—in what sort of spirits and health she set off—&c.—glean what intelligence you can and transmit it to me. Yesterday I was much surprised to see a newspaper directed in Mary Taylor's hand—its date was of the 9th March—the Post-Mark I could not make out—it was a Weekly Despatch.[4]

I can hardly tell you how time gets on here at Haworth—There is no event whatever to mark its progress—one day resembles another—and all have heavy lifeless physiognomies—Sunday—baking day & Saturday are the only ones that bear the slightest distinctive mark—meantime life wears away—I shall soon be

30—and I have done nothing yet—Sometimes I get melancholy—at the prospect before and behind me—yet it is wrong and foolish to repine—undoubtedly my Duty directs me to stay at home for the present—There was a time when Haworth was a very pleasant place to me, it is not so now—I feel as if we were all buried here—I long to travel—to work to live a life of action—Excuse me dear Ellen for troubling you with my fruitless wishes—I will put by the rest and not bother you with them.

You <u>must</u> write to me—if you knew how welcome your letters are—you would write very often. Your letters and the French Newspapers[5]—are the only messengers that come to me from the outer world—beyond our Moors; and very welcome messengers they are.

Talking of the French Newspapers—it is a pity I never had any intimation that I was expected to send them to you—otherwise I should not have failed to do so—as it was I concluded of course that they would go to you from Hunsworth—now however you will in all probability receive them first—be sure & send them regularly—

What did Mr & Mrs Hudson[6] say about your looks when they saw you—? Did they not think it marvellous that after a lapse of near 7 years you should be looking nearly as young as ever?

Don't forget to tell me how George is when you write—Give my love to your Mother and sister—is Mrs Sykes[7] with you yet—Do you know anything about Miss Wooler? Write very soon—Good bye dear Ellen.

C Bronte

When you see Joe Taylor ask him for Ellen Taylor's[8] address at Bradford.

March 24th—[45].

I shall be sorry when you are gone to Hathersage[9]—you will be so far off again—how long will they want you to stay? I should say Henry would do wisely to make sure of Miss Prescott immediately—6 months is a long time to wait—adverse things might happen in the mean while.

MS Law-Dixon.

1. Ellen had returned to Birstall from Bridlington on the East Yorks. coast.
2. Ellen's brother.
3. Mary Taylor had sailed on the barque *Louisa Campbell* from Gravesend on 12 Mar., calling at Plymouth on 17 Mar. The ship arrived in Wellington, New Zealand on 24 July.
4. A radical Sunday paper founded 1801, sympathetic to Chartism and republicanism. Reports in the *Dispatch* for 9 Mar. on a shipwreck at Dover and the 'appalling shipwreck' of an East Indiaman and two transport ships in the Far East would add to Charlotte's anxiety about Mary's voyage.
5. Unidentified papers sent to CB from Hunsworth by Mary Taylor's brothers Joseph and John.
6. John Hudson, a gentleman farmer, and his wife Sophia, hosts of CB and EN at Easton, near Bridlington, in Sept. 1839.

7. Not identified.
8. Ellen Taylor (1826–51), orphan daughter of William Taylor (1777–1837) and Margaret, née Moss-
   man (1793–1834). Ellen joined her cousin Mary Taylor in Wellington in Aug. 1849, helping her to
   plan and stock a shop there, but she died of TB on 27 Dec. 1851.
9. Ellen was to help her brother Henry, who planned to improve his vicarage at Hathersage,
   Derbyshire, before his marriage to Emily Prescott (1811/12–1907) of Everton, Lancs. They
   married on 22 May 1845.

33. To Ellen Nussey, [?18 June 1845]

[Haworth]

Dear Nell

You thought I refused you coldly did you?[1] It was a queer sort of coldness
when I would have given my ears to be able to say yes, and felt obliged to say no.

Matters are now however a little changed, Branwell and Anne are both come
home, and Anne I am rejoiced to say has decided not to return to Mr Robinson's—_her_ presence at home certainly makes me feel more at liberty—Then
dear Ellen if all be well I will come and see you at Hathersage—tell me only
when I must come—mention the week and the day—have the kindness also to
answer the following queries if you can—

How far is it from Leeds to Sheffield?[2]

What time in the morning does the Sheffield train start from Leeds?

Can you give me a notion of the cost?—

I think with you that I had better go direct from Haworth and not spend a day
at Brookroyd—

Of course when I come you will let me enjoy your own company in peace
and not drag me out a visiting.[3]

I have no desire at all to see your medical clerical curate[4]—I think he must
be like all the other curates I have seen—and they seem to me a self-seeking,
vain, empty race. At this blessed moment we have no less than three of them in
Haworth-Parish—and God knows there is not one to mend another.[5]

The other day they all three—accompanied by Mr Smith[6] (of whom by the
bye I have grievous things to tell you) dropped or rather rushed in unexpectedly
to tea   It was Monday and I was hot & tired—still if they had behaved quietly
and decently—I would have served them out their tea in peace—but they
began glorifying themselves and abusing Dissenters in such a manner—that
my temper lost its balance and I pronounced a few sentences sharply & rapidly
which struck them all dumb. Papa was greatly horrified also—I don't regret it.

Give my respects (as Joe Taylor says) to Miss Gorham[7]—By the bye I reserve
the greatest part of my opinion of Master Joe's epistle till we meet

I can only say that it is highly characteristic

C Brontë

Write soon   Come to Sheffield to meet me if you can.

MS HM 24440.

1. On 13 June CB had refused Ellen's invitation to stay with her in Hathersage because she was reluctant to leave Mr Brontë, whose rapidly diminishing sight made him depressed and anxious.
2. The railway route via Rotherham would be about forty-two miles.
3. Charlotte's visiting was to include the battlemented North Lees Hall, near Hathersage, where the widowed Mary Eyre lived, and the famous caverns at Castleton.
4. Revd James Yates Rooker, curate of Bamford, near Hathersage.
5. Joseph Brett Grant (?1820–79), curate of Haworth's neighbouring village, Oxenhope, and the model for Mr Donne in Shirley; Revd James Chesterton Bradley (1818–1913), perpetual curate of Oakworth, about two miles from Haworth, and the model for Mr Sweeting; and Revd Arthur Bell Nicholls (1819–1906), Mr Brontë's new curate and CB's future husband. On 26 May Charlotte had described him as 'a respectable young man, [who] reads well, and I hope will give satisfaction' (CBL i. 393). He appears as 'Mr. Macarthey' in Shirley.
6. See Letter 29 n. 7.
7. Ellen's friend Mary Gorham (1826–1917) of Cakeham, Sussex, near Henry Nussey's former curacy at Earnley; she was staying, or about to stay with Ellen in Hathersage. Mary married Revd Thomas Swinton Hewitt on 29 June 1852.

34. To Ellen Nussey, 31 July [1845]

[Haworth]

Dear Ellen

I was glad to get your little packet—it was quite a treasure of interest to me—I think the intelligence about George is cheering—I have read the lines to Miss Ringrose—they are expressive of the affectionate feelings of his nature and are poetical in so much as they are true—faults in expression, rhythm, metre were of course to be expected.[1]

I cannot understand how your brother John should withhold assistance in the matter of ?Joseph[2]—I think he is deeply to blame—he ought from the first to have relieved your Mother entirely from the care of keeping him. It is true he has many calls upon him but this call is certainly one of the most sacred he can have—It is hard—it is wrong to leave such a burthen on his aged Mother's shoulders.

All you say about Mr Rooker amused me much—still I cannot put out of my mind one fear—viz. that you should think too much about him—faulty as he is and as you know him to be—he has still certain qualities which might create an interest in your mind before you were aware—he has the art of impressing ladies by something apparently involuntary in his look & manner—exciting in them the notion that he cares for them while his words and actions are all careless, inattentive and quite uncompromising for himself. It is only men who have seen much of life and of the world and are become in a measure indifferent to female attractions that possess this art—so be on your guard—these are not pleasant or flattering words—but they are the words of one who has known you long enough to be indifferent about being temporarily disagreeable provided she can be permanently useful—

I got home very well[3]—There was a gentleman in the rail-road carriage whom I recognized by his features immediately as a foreigner and a Frenchman—so sure was I of it that I ventured to say to him in French "Monsieur est français n'est-ce pas?" He gave a start of surprise and answered immediately in his own tongue. He appeared still more astonished & even puzzled when after a few minutes further conversation—I enquired if he had not passed the greater part of his life in Germany—He said the surmise was correct—I had guessed it from his speaking French with the German accent.

It was ten o'clock at night when I got home—I found Branwell ill[4]—he is so very often owing to his own fault—I was not therefore shocked at first—but when Anne informed me of the immediate cause of his present illness I was greatly shocked, he had last Thursday[5] received a note from Mr Robinson sternly dismissing him intimating that he had discovered his proceedings which he characterised as bad beyond expression and charging him on pain of exposure to break off instantly and for ever all communication with every member of his family—[6] We have had sad work with Branwell since—he thought of nothing but stunning,[7] or drowning his distress of mind—no one in the house could have rest—and at last we have been obliged to send him from home for a week with some one to look after him—he has written to me this morning and expresses some sense of contrition for his frantic folly—he promises amendment on his return—but so long as he remains at home I scarce dare hope for peace in the house—We must all I fear prepare for a season of distress and disquietude—When I left you I was strongly impressed with the feeling that I was going back to sorrow. I cannot now ask Miss Wooler nor any one else.

Give my love to Miss Rooker—ask her if she will forgive me for disfiguring her album[8]—Write to me again as soon as you can after the Bride & Bridegroom are come home

Good-bye dear Nell
C Brontë

I would not send the lines to Miss Ringrose—they are too defective and unfinished as poetry to be seen.

MS BPM Gr. E 7.

1. George Nussey was engaged to Ellen's friend Amelia Ringrose, b. 1818, daughter of the Hull shipowner and merchant Christopher Leake Ringrose. George's continuing mental illness was to prevent their marriage.
2. Ellen's eldest brother John (1794–1862) of 4 Cleveland Row, London, was a general practitioner and apothecary to George IV and his successors. He might have been expected to help Mrs Nussey with the care of his brother Joseph (1797–1846), who was probably a dissolute alcoholic.
3. CB had returned to Haworth after her visit to Hathersage.

4. CB's euphemism for Branwell's drinking and its consequences.
5. 17 July, not 24 July. In a letter of Oct. 1845 to his friend F. H. Grundy, Branwell wrote of 'Eleven continued nights of sleepless horrors' between his receipt of Mr Robinson's letter and his journey to Liverpool in the care of the sexton John Brown.
6. Branwell alleged that Mr Robinson had discovered an 'attachment' between Branwell and his wife, and had threatened to shoot him if he returned. Branwell convinced his family and many of his friends that Mrs Robinson had been strongly attracted to him. When Mrs Gaskell alleged in the first two editions of her *Life* of CB that Branwell had been 'seduced' she was compelled by a threat of legal action to retract every statement which imputed to an unnamed, but clearly identifiable lady, 'any breach of her conjugal, of her maternal, or of her social duties'. Speculation about this 'seduction' and other possible reasons for Branwell's dismissal—drunken excess, forgery, homosexual advances to his pupil, the young Edmund Robinson (1831–69)—is not supported by firm evidence.
7. Mrs Gaskell alleged that Branwell took opium habitually for the last three years of his life.
8. Ellen told Mary Gorham that CB had written 'a piece of German from memory' in Miss Rooker's autograph album, and a piece of French (lines from C. H. Millevoye's 'La chute des feuilles') in Ellen's.

35. To Ellen Nussey, [4 November 1845]

[Haworth]

Dear Ellen

You do not reproach me in your last but I fear you must have thought me unkind in being so long without answering you—The fact is I had hoped to be able to ask you to come to Haworth—Branwell seemed to have a prospect of getting employment,[1] and I waited to know the result of his efforts in order to say, "dear Ellen come and see us—but the place (a Secretaryship to a Railroad Committee) is given to another person—Branwell still remains at home and while he is here—you shall not come—I am more confirmed in that resolution the more I know of him—I wish I could say one word to you in his favour—but I cannot—therefore I will hold my tongue.

Poor Miss Ringrose's letters interest me much—they are quiet and unpretending but seem affectionate and sincere—Will she and George ever be married? Such an event seems to human eyes very unlikely now—yet that is no proof that it will not one day take place—Oh I wish brighter days would come for all your family—and they may do so, sooner than we can calculate.

We are all obliged to you dear Ellen for your kind suggestion about Leeds but I think our school-schemes are for the present at rest.

Emily and Anne wish me to tell you that they think it very unlikely[2] for little Flossy to be expected to rear so numerous a family—they think you are quite right in protesting against all the pups being preserved—for if kept they will pull their poor little mother to pieces—The French Newspaper I send you to day is the first we have had for an age—two have missed—Be sure I shall always be punctual in dispatching them to you so that when there is a long gap—you will know to what quarter to ascribe the delay. I believe Joe Taylor is at present at

Ilkley[3] or has been there lately—I saw his name in the newspaper in the list of visitors "at this fashionable watering-place".

Do not think about my coming to Brookroyd for the present Ellen—[4] Give my sincere love to your Mother Anne & Mercy and believe me—

Yours faithfully

C B

MS Berg.

1. In October Branwell had applied for the secretaryship of the proposed Manchester, Hebden Bridge, and Keighley, and Leeds and Carlisle Junction Railway Company, but the line was never built.
2. Yorkshire dialect meaning 'unfitting, undesirable'. CB had not realized that the little spaniel was a bitch when she wrote of Ellen as 'his Mistress' in Letter 29.
3. A small spa town on the river Wharfe, sixteen miles from Leeds, with 'hydropathic establishments' which made it a popular resort for invalids.
4. CB does not tell Ellen what was preoccupying her: she had accidentally found some of Emily's poems in manuscript, and Anne had produced hers. The sisters agreed, once Emily's reluctance was overcome, to arrange a selection of their poems, and if possible get them printed.

36. To Constantin Heger, 18 November [1845][1]

Haworth
Bradford Yorkshire

Monsieur

Les six mois de silence sont écoulés; nous sommes aujourd'hui au 18 Nov[embr]e, ma dernière lettre etait datée (je crois) le 18 Mai, je puis donc vous écrire encore, sans manquer à ma promesse.

L'été et l'automne m'ont paru bien longs; à vrai dire il m'a fallu des efforts pénibles pour supporter jusqu'à present la privation que je me suis imposée: vous ne pouvez pas concevoir cela, vous, Monsieur, mais imaginez vous, pour un instant, qu'un de vos enfants est séparé de vous de 160 lieues de distance et que vous devez rester six mois sans lui écrire, sans recevoir de ses nouvelles, sans en entendre parler, sans savoir comment il se porte, alors vous comprendrez facilement tout ce qu'il y a de dure dans une pareille obligation. Je vous dirai franchement, qu'en attendant, j'ai tâché de vous oublier, car le souvenir d'une personne que l'on croit ne devoir plus revoir et que, pourtant, on estime beaucoup, harasse trop l'esprit et quand on a subi cette espèce d'inquiétude pendant un ou deux ans, on est prêt à tout faire pour retrouver le repos. J'ai tout fait, j'ai cherché les occupations, je me suis interdit absolument le plaisir de parler de vous—même à Emilie mais je n'ai pu vaincre ni mes regrets ni mon impatience—c'est humiliant cela—de ne pas savoir maîtriser ses propres pensées, être esclave à un regret, un souvenir, esclave à une idée dominante et fixe qui tyrannise son esprit. Que ne puis-je avoir pour vous juste autant d'amitié que vous avez pour moi—ni plus ni moins? je serais alors si tranquille, si libre—je pourrais garder le silence pendant dix ans sans effort.

Mon père se porte bien mais sa vue est presqu'éteinte, il ne sait plus ni lire ni écrire; c'est, pourtant, l'avis des medecins d'attendre encore quelques mois avant de tenter une opération—l'hiver ne sera pour lui qu'une longue nuit—il se plaint rarement, j'admire sa patience—Si la Providence me destine la même calamité—puisse-t-elle au moins m'accorder autant de patience pour la supporter! Il me semble, monsieur, que ce qu'il y a de plus amère dans les grands malheurs physiques c'est d'être forcé à faire partager nos souffrances à tous ceux qui nous entourent; on peut cacher les maladies de l'âme mais celles qui attaquent le corps et détruisent les facultés, ne se cachent pas. Mon père me permet maintenant de lui lire et d'écrire pour lui, il me témoigne aussi plus de confiance qu'il ne m'en a jamais témoignée, ce qui est une grande consolation.

Monsieur, j'ai une grâce à vous demander: quand vous répondrez à cette lettre, parlez-moi un peu de vous-même—pas de moi car, je sais, que si vous me parlez de moi ce sera pour me gronder et, cette fois, je voudrais voir votre aspect bienveillant; parlez-moi donc de vos enfants; jamais vous n'aviez le front sévère quand Louise et Claire et Prosper, étaient près de vous. Dîtes-moi aussi quelquechose du Pensionnat, des élèves, des Maîtresses—Mesdemoiselles Blanche, Sophie et Justine restent-elles toujours à Bruxelles? Dîtes-moi où vous avez voyagé pendant les vacances—n'avez-vous pas été sur les bords du Rhin? N'avez-vous pas visité Cologne ou Coblentz? Dîtes-moi enfin ce que vous voulez mon maître mais dîtes-moi quelquechose. Écrire à une ci-devant sous-maîtresse (non—je ne veux pas me souvenir de mon emploi de sous-maîtresse je le renie) mais enfin, écrire à une ancienne élève ne peut être une occupation fort intéressante pour vous—je le sais—mais pour moi c'est la vie. Votre dernière lettre m'a servi de soutien—de nourriture pendant six mois—à present il m'en faut une autre et vous me le donnerez—pas parceque vous avez pour moi de l'amitié—vous ne pouvez en avoir beaucoup—mais parcequ[e] vous avez l'âme compatissante et que vous ne condamneriez personne à de longues souffrances pour vous épargner quelques moments d'ennui. Me défendre à vous écrire, refuser de me répondre ce sera m'arracher la seule joie que j'ai au monde, me priver de mon dernier privilège—privilège auquel je ne consentirai jamais à renoncer volontairement. Croyez-moi mon maître, en m'écrivant vous faites un bon œuvre—tant que je vous crois assez content de moi, tant que j'ai l'espoir de recevoir de vos nouvelles je puis être tranquille et pas trop triste mais quand un silence morne et prolongé semble m'avertir de l'éloignement de mon maître à mon égard—quand de jour en jour j'attends une lettre et que de jour en jour le désappointement vient me rejeter dans un douloureux accablement et que cette douce joie de voir votre écriture, de lire vos conseils me fuit comme une vaine vision, alors, j'ai la fièvre—je perds l'appétit et le sommeil—je dépéris

Puis-je vous écrire encore au mois de Mai prochain? J'aurais voulu attendre toute une année—mais c'est impossible—c'est trop long.

C Brontë

[The remainder of the letter is in English. See the last two paragraphs after the translation below.]

Monsieur,

The six months of silence have elapsed; to-day is the 18th November, my last letter was dated (I believe) the 18th May;[2] therefore I can write to you again without breaking my promise.

The summer and autumn have seemed very long to me; to tell the truth I have had to make painful efforts to endure until now the privation I imposed on myself: you, Monsieur—you cannot conceive what that means—but imagine for a moment that one of your children is separated from you by a distance of 160 leagues, and that you have to let six months go by without writing to him, without receiving news of him, without hearing him spoken of, without knowing how he is, then you will easily understand what hardship there is in such an obligation. I will tell you candidly that during this time of waiting I have tried to forget you, for the memory of a person one believes one is never to see again,[3] and whom one nevertheless greatly respects, torments the mind exceedingly and when one has suffered this kind of anxiety for one or two years, one is ready to do anything to regain peace of mind. I have done everything, I have sought occupations,[4] I have absolutely forbidden myself the pleasure of speaking about you—even to Emily, but I have not been able to overcome either my regrets or my impatience—and that is truly humiliating—not to know how to get the mastery over one's own thoughts, to be the slave of a regret, a memory, the slave of a dominant and fixed idea which has become a tyrant over one's mind. Why cannot I have for you exactly as much friendship as you have for me—neither more nor less? Then I would be so tranquil, so free—I could keep silence for ten years without effort.

My father is well but his sight has almost gone, he can no longer read or write; nevertheless the doctors' advice is to wait a few months longer before attempting an operation[5]—for him the winter will be nothing but a long night—he rarely complains, I admire his patience—If Providence ordains that the same calamity should be my own fate—may He at least grant me as much patience to endure it! It seems to me, Monsieur, that what is most bitterly painful in great bodily afflictions is that we are compelled to make all those who surround us sharers in our sufferings; we can hide the troubles of the soul, but those which attack the body and destroy its faculties cannot be hidden. My father now lets me read to him and write for him, he also shows more confidence in me than he has ever done before, and that is a great consolation.

Monsieur, I have a favour to ask you: when you reply to this letter, talk to me a little about yourself—not about me, for I know that if you talk to me about myself it will be to scold me, and this time I would like to see your kindly aspect; talk to me then about your children; your forehead never had a severe look when Louise and Claire and Prospère[6] were near you. Tell me also something about the School, the pupils, the teachers—are Mesdemoiselles Blanche, Sophie and Justine[7] still in Brussels? Tell me where you travelled during the holidays—haven't you been through the Rhineland? Haven't you visited Cologne or Coblenz? In a word, tell me what you will, my master, but tell me something. Writing to a former assistant teacher (no,—I don't want to remember my position as an assistant teacher, I disown it) well then, writing to an old pupil cannot be a very interesting occupation for you—I know that—but for me it is life itself. Your last letter has sustained me—has nourished me for six months—now I need another and you will give it me—not because you have any friendship for me—you cannot have much—but because you have a compassionate soul and because you would not condemn anyone to undergo long suffering in order to spare yourself a few moments of tedium. To forbid me to write to you, to refuse to reply to me—that will be to tear from me the only joy I have on earth—to deprive me of my last remaining privilege—a privilege which I will never consent to renounce voluntarily. Believe me, my master, in writing to me you do a good deed[8]—so long as I think you are fairly pleased with me, so long as I still have the hope of hearing from you, I can be tranquil and not too sad, but when a dreary and prolonged silence seems to warn me that my master is becoming estranged from me—when day after day I await a letter and day after day disappointment flings me down again into overwhelming misery, when the sweet delight of seeing your writing and reading your counsel flees from me like an empty vision—then I am in a fever—I lose my appetite and my sleep—I pine away.

May I write to you again next May? I would have liked to wait a full year—but it is impossible—it is too long—

C. Brontë

I must say one word to you in English—I wish I could write to you more cheerful letters, for when I read this over, I find it to be somewhat gloomy—but forgive me my dear master—do not be irritated at my sadness—according to the words of the Bible: "Out of the fullness of the heart, the mouth speaketh["][9] and truly I find it difficult to be cheerful so long as I think I shall never see you more. You will perceive by the defects in this letter that I am forgetting the French language—yet I read all the French books I can get, and learn daily a portion by heart—but I have never heard French spoken but once since I left Brussels[10]—and then it sounded like music in my ears—every word was most precious to me because it reminded me of you—I love French for your sake with all my heart and soul.

Farewell my dear Master—may God protect you with special care and crown you with peculiar blessings

C B.

Original MS in French, with English postscript, BL Add. 38732C.

1. An English translation follows. This letter has remained intact.
2. This letter does not survive.
3. The French original, 'une personne que l'on croit ne devoir plus revoir' may imply obligation as well as futurity. Contrast p. 49, 'je vous reverrai'.
4. One occupation was the transformation of memories of Heger and Brussels into *The Professor* and poems on the theme of master and pupil.
5. Mr Brontë was operated on for cataract on 25 Aug. 1846.
6. See Letter 22 n. 1.
7. See Letter 19 n. 3. Mlle Justine has not been identified.
8. M. Heger's rejection of Charlotte's pleas is implied in her poem, written in Dec. 1847, 'He saw my heart's woe discovered my soul's anguish . . . But once a year he heard a whisper low and dreary . . . He was mute as is the grave.' See Victor A. Neufeldt, *The Poems of Charlotte Brontë* (1985), 340.
9. Cf. Matthew 12: 34 and Luke 6: 45.
10. See Letter 34.

37. *To Messrs Aylott and Jones,*[1] *28 January 1846*

[Haworth]

Gentlemen

May I request to be informed whether you would undertake the publication of a Collection of short poems in 1 vol. oct[avo]?[2]—

If you object to publishing the work at your own risk—would you undertake it on the Author's account?—

I am Gentlemen
Your obdt. hmble. Servt.
C Brontë

Address

Revd P Brontë

Haworth Bradford—Yorkshire

MS BPM Bon. 169.

1. Aylott & Jones of Paternoster Row, London, a small firm of booksellers and publishers, had a preference for publishing theological works, but they agreed to publish the poems offered to them by 'C Brontë', and in Jan. 1850 they were to publish the first number of *The Germ: Thoughts towards Nature in Poetry, Literature and Art* for D. G. Rossetti and his Pre-Raphaelite colleagues.

2. In her 'Biographical Notice of Ellis and Acton Bell', prefixed to her edition of *Wuthering Heights* and *Agnes Grey* in 1850, CB recalled her discovery of some of Emily's poems, her conviction that they were 'not common effusions' but vigorous and genuine, and Anne's offer of her own poems. 'It took hours to reconcile [Emily] to the discovery I had made, and days to persuade her that such poems merited publication.'

38.　*To Margaret Wooler,*[1] *30 January 1846*

[Haworth]

My dear Miss Wooler

I have not yet paid my usual visit to Brookroyd—it is indeed more than a year since I was there, but I frequently hear from Ellen and she did not fail to tell me that you were gone into Worcestershire,[2] she was unable however to give me your exact address—had I known it I should have written to you long since.

I thought you would wonder how we were getting on when you heard of the Railway Panic[3] and you may be sure that I am very glad to be able to answer your kind enquiries by an assurance that our small capital is as yet undiminished. The York and N. Midland is, as you say, a very good line—yet I confess to you I should wish, for my own part, to be wise in time—I cannot think that even the very best lines will continue for many years at their present premiums and I have been most anxious for us to sell our shares ere it be too late—and to secure the proceeds in some safer if, for the present, less profitable—, investment. I cannot however persuade my Sisters to regard the affair precisely from my point of view and I feel as if I would rather run the risk of loss than hurt Emily's feelings by acting in direct opposition to her opinion—she managed in a most handsome and able manner for me when I was at Brussels and prevented by distance from looking after my own interests—therefore I will let her manage still and take the consequences. Disinterested and energetic she certainly is and if she be not quite so tractable or open to conviction as I could wish I must remember perfection is not the lot of humanity and as long as we can regard those we love and to whom we are closely allied, with profound and never-shaken esteem, it is a small thing that they should vex us occasionally by, what appear to us, unreasonable and headstrong notions. You my dear Miss Wooler know full as well as I do the value of sisters' affection to each other; there is nothing like it in this world, I believe, when they are nearly equal in age and similar in education, tastes and sentiments.

You ask about Branwell; he never thinks of seeking employment and I begin to fear that he has rendered himself incapable of filling any respectable station in life, besides, if money were at his disposal he would use it only to his own injury—the faculty of self-government is, I fear almost destroyed in him　You ask me if I do not think that men are strange beings—I do indeed, I have often thought so—and I think too that the mode of bringing them up is strange, they are not half sufficiently guarded from temptation—Girls are protected as if they were something very frail and silly indeed while boys are turned loose on the world as if they—of all beings in existence, were the wisest and the least liable to be led astray.

I am glad you like Bromsgrove, though I daresay there are few places you would <u>not</u> like with Mrs Moore for a companion. I always feel a peculiar satisfaction when I hear of your enjoying yourself because it proves to me that there is really such a thing as retributive justice even in this world—You worked hard, you denied yourself all pleasure, almost all relaxation in your youth and the prime of your life—now you are free—and that while you have still, I hope, many years of vigour and health in which you can enjoy freedom—Besides I have another and very egotistical motive for being pleased—it seems that even "a lone woman" can be happy, as well as cherished wives and proud mothers—I am glad of that—I speculate much on the existence of unmarried and never-to-be married women nowadays and I have already got to the point of considering that there is no more respectable character on this earth than an unmarried woman who makes her own way through life quietly perseveringly—without support of husband or brother and who having attained the age of 45 or upwards—retains in her possession a well-regulated mind—a disposition to enjoy simple pleasures—fortitude to support inevitable pains, sympathy with the sufferings of others & willingness to relieve want as far as her means extend—

I once had the pleasure of seeing Mrs Moore at Rouse-Mill[4]—will you offer her my respectful remembrances—I wish to send this letter off by to-day's post I must therefore conclude in haste—Believe me My dear Miss Wooler

Yours most affectionately

C Brontë

Write to me again when you have time—

MS Fitzwilliam.

1. CB's former teacher at Roe Head school. See Biographical Notes p. xlvi.
2. Miss Wooler was staying with a relative, Mrs Moore, in Bromsgrove, Worcs.
3. The Brontë sisters had previously sought Miss Wooler's advice on their investments. In late 1845 there had been a rapid increase in the flotation of fraudulent railway schemes, with lists of fictitious subscribers. Many deluded shareholders had been impoverished or left destitute. The York and North Midland line, a sound venture opened in 1839, was now linked with the North Midlands line, making possible rail travel from York to London.
4. The Wooler family home and corn mill in Batley.

39. *To Messrs Aylott and Jones, 6 February 1846*

[Haworth]

Gentlemen

I send you the M.S. as you desired.

You will perceive that the Poems are the work of three persons—relatives—
their separate pieces are distinguished by their respective signatures—[1]

I am Gentlemen

Yrs. truly

C Brontë

Feby. 6th./ 46

I am obliged to send it in two parcels on account of the weight—

MS BPM Bon. 171.

1. The volume was to be entitled *Poems by Currer, Ellis and Acton Bell*. It contained twenty-one poems by Emily, twenty-one by Anne (signed 'Ellis' and 'Acton' respectively) and nineteen by Charlotte (signed 'Currer'). Most are arranged so that a poem by Currer is followed by one each by Ellis and Acton. It was published, bound in green cloth, on or about 22 May, at 4 shillings. Only two copies were sold, but it was well reviewed in *The Critic* and *The Athenaeum* for 4 July, and in the *Dublin University Magazine*, vol. 28, for Oct. 1846.

40. *To Messrs Aylott and Jones, 6 April 1846*

[Haworth]

Gentlemen

C. E & A Bell are now preparing for the Press a work of fiction—consisting of
three distinct and unconnected tales[1] which may be published either together as
a work of 3 vols. of the ordinary novel-size, or separately as single vols—as shall
be deemed most advisable.

It is not their intention to publish these tales on their own account.

They direct me to ask you whether you would be disposed to undertake the
work—after having of course by due inspection of the M.S. ascertained that its
contents are such as to warrant an expectation of success.

An early answer will oblige as in case of your negativing the proposal—inquiry
must be made of other Publishers—

I am Gentlemen

Yrs truly

C Brontë

MS BPM Bon. 179.

1. Emily Brontë's *Wuthering Heights* and Anne's *Agnes Grey* would be published together as 3 vols. by Thomas Cautley Newby in Dec. 1847, *Agnes Grey* being vol. iii. The third 'tale' was CB's *The Professor*, posthumously published in June 1857 by Smith, Elder & Co.

41. *To Messrs Aylott and Jones, 11 April 1846*

[Haworth]

Gentlemen

I beg to thank you in the name of C. E. & A Bell for your obliging offer of advice; I will avail myself of it to request information on two or three points.

It is evident that unknown authors have great difficulties to contend with before they can succeed in bringing their works before the public; can you give me any hint as to the way in which these difficulties are best met. For instance, in the present case, where a work of fiction is in question, in what form would a publisher be most likely to accept the M.S.—? whether offered as a work of 3 vols or as tales which might be published in numbers or as contributions to a periodical?[1]

<Is it usual to ?intr> What publishers would be most likely to receive favourably a proposal of this nature?

Would it suffice to <u>write</u> to a publisher on the subject or would it be necessary to have recourse to a personal interview?

Your opinion and advice on these three points or on any other which your experience may suggest as important—would be esteemed by us a favour

I am Gentlemen

Yrs truly

C Brontë

MS BPM Bon. 180.

1. Circulating libraries benefited from discounts on large numbers of 3-volume novels, normally priced at 31s. 6d., the market being dominated by the publishers Henry Colburn and Richard Bentley. Serial publication in cheap monthly or weekly parts had been given new prominence by Dickens's *Pickwick Papers* (1836–7). Dickens's *Oliver Twist* appeared in instalments in *Bentley's Miscellany* (1837–9), and Thackeray had published instalments of his early fiction in e.g. *Punch* and *Fraser's Magazine*.

42. *To Ellen Nussey, 17 June 1846*

[Haworth]

Dear Ellen

I was glad to perceive by the tone of your last letter that you are beginning to be a little more settled and comfortable. I should think Dr Belcombe[1] is quite right in opposing George's removal home—if he has such an impression of suffering connected with all recollections of Brookroyd—depend upon it, it would be misery to him to return there—and I fear misery to you to have him amongst you; you would all be too often, painfully and forcibly reminded of the difference between what he <u>is</u> and what he <u>was</u>; and if there is a chance of his final recovery (which I would still hope) that chance is far more likely to become certainty if he remains in the hands of those who understand his complaint and can watch its symptoms.

We—I am sorry to say—have been somewhat more harrassed than usual lately—The death of Mr Robinson—which took place about three weeks or a month ago[2]—served Branwell for a pretext to throw all about him into hubbub and confusion with his emotions—&c. &c. Shortly after came news from all hands that Mr Robinson had altered his will before he died and effectually prevented all chance of a marriage between his widow and Branwell by stipulating that she should not have a shilling if she ever ventured to reopen any communication with him—Of course he then became intolerable—to papa he allows rest neither day nor night—and he is continually screwing money out of him sometimes threatening that he will kill himself if it is withheld from him—He says Mrs R—is now insane—that her mind is a complete wreck—owing to remorse for her conduct towards Mr R—(whose end it appears was hastened by distress of mind)—and grief for having lost him.[3]

I do not know how much to believe of what he says but I fear she is very ill—Branwell declares now that he neither can nor will do anything for himself—good situations have been offered more than once—for which by a fortnight's work he might have qualified himself—but he will do nothing—except drink, and make us all wretched—

Do not say a word about this to any one dear Ellen—I know no one but yourself to whom I would communicate it—

I had a note from Ellen Taylor[4] a week ago—in which she remarks that letters were received from New Zealand a month since or more and that all was well—but that they were on business and not sent anywhere[5]—Mary's name was not mentioned—but I suppose she was included in the expression that all was well—I thought it singular that J Taylor had never intimated to any of Mary's friends that tidings of her had been heard—He was not aware I am sure of Ellen Taylor's writing to me—so don't mention this circumstance either—there may be reasons for the reserve with which we are unacquainted—at any rate do not speak of it unless you should hear others speak of it—

I should like to hear from you again soon
Believe me yrs
C B____

June 17th.—46
I am greatly obliged to your sister Anne—for so kindly making me an exception to her rule of exclusion[6]—and I hope one day to see Brookroyd again—though I think it will not be just yet—these are not times of amusement. Love to all—

MS BPM Gr. E ii.

1. Henry S. Belcombe (1790–1856), senior physician to the York County Hospital, the York Retreat, and to the private asylum, Clifton Green House, York. George Nussey was cared for at the Clifton Asylum from 1845 to 1853, when he was moved to Lime Tree House Asylum, York.

2. Branwell's former employer had died on 26 May at the age of 46, having suffered from 'Dyspepsia many years Phthisis 3 months'. He had altered his will on 2 Jan. 1846 to prevent his eldest daughter Lydia Mary, who had eloped with an actor, Henry Roxby, from benefiting from his own marriage settlement. There was no clause under which his widow would forfeit her inheritance on remarriage: he left his possessions to her, his son Edmund, and his daughters Elizabeth and Mary. Neither was there any stipulation about communication with Branwell.

3. The Robinson papers in the BPM show that Mrs Robinson, while mourning the death of her 'Angel Edmund', was coping fairly efficiently with business matters. She married a wealthy relative, Sir Edward Dolman Scott of Great Barr, on 8 Nov. 1848, soon after his first wife's death in Aug. 1848.

4. Ellen (1826–51), the orphaned daughter of Mary Taylor's uncle William Taylor (1777–1837), was staying with her cousins Joe and John Taylor at Hunsworth.

5. i.e. these letters from Mary, written from New Zealand, would not be circulated amongst her friends, since they concerned her brothers John, Joe, and Waring, who all helped her financially.

6. Ellen Nussey's dissolute brother Joseph (b. 1797) had died on 29 May 1846. The family would be exhausted and in mourning after a long period of nursing.

43. *To Henry Colburn,*[1] *4 July 1846*

[Haworth]

Sir

I request permission to send for your inspection the M.S of a work of fiction in 3 vols. It consists of three tales,[2] each occupying a volume and capable of being published together or separately, as thought most advisable. The authors of these tales have already appeared before the public.

Should you consent to examine the work, would you, in your reply, state at what period after transmission of the M.S. to you, the authors may expect to receive your decision upon its merits—

I am Sir
Yours respectfully
C Bell

Address Mr Currer Bell
  Parsonage,
    Haworth
     Bradford
      Yorkshire.
July 4th—46
Henry Colburn Esqr.

MS Parrish Collection, Princeton.

1. Henry Colburn (d. 1855), publisher of fiction, and proprietor of various journals. He did not publish the 'Bells' ' novels, and may not have agreed to see them, since his note on the verso of this letter reads in part '[t]he Authors, & what they have written & state that this information is necessary before I can decide on allowing the M.S—to be sent to me Also to request them to state the nature of the stories | HC.'

2. See Letter 40 n. 1. In her 'Biographical Notice' CB recalled that 'These MSS. were perseveringly obtruded upon various publishers for the space of a year and a half; usually, their fate was an ignominious and abrupt dismissal.'

44. *To Ellen Nussey, 10 July 1846*

[Haworth]

Dear Ellen

I see you are in a dilemma and one of a peculiar and difficult nature—Two paths lie before you—you conscientiously wish to choose the right one—even though it be the most steep, strait and rugged—but you do not know which is the right one—you cannot decide whether Duty and Religion command you to go out into the cold and friendless world and there to earn your bread by Governess drudgery—or whether they enjoin your continued stay with your aged Mother—neglecting for the present every prospect of independency for yourself and putting up with daily inconvenience—sometimes even with privations.

Dear Ellen I can well imagine that it is next to impossible for you to decide for yourself in this matter—so I will decide it for you—at least I will tell you what is my earnest conviction on the subject—I will shew you candidly how the question strikes me.

The right path is that which necessitates the greatest sacrifice of self-interest—which implies the greatest good to others—and this path steadily followed will lead I believe in time to prosperity and to happiness though it may seem at the outset to tend quite in a contrary direction—

Your Mother is both old and infirm; old and infirm people have few sources of happiness—fewer almost than the comparatively young and healthy can conceive—to deprive them of one of these is cruel—If your Mother is more composed when you are with her—Stay with her—If she would be unhappy in case you left her—stay with her—It will not apparently, as far [as] shortsighted humanity can see—be for your advantage to remain at Brookroyd—nor will you be praised and admired for remaining at home to comfort your Mother—Yet probably your own Conscience will approve you and if it does—stay with her.

I recommend you to do—what I am trying to do myself—

Who gravely asked you "whether Miss Brontë was not going to be married to her papa's Curate"?

I scarcely need say that never was rumour more unfounded—it puzzles me to think how it could possibly have originated—A cold, far-away sort of civility are the only terms on which I have ever been with Mr Nicholls[1]—I could by no means think of mentioning such a rumour to him even as a joke—it would make me the laughing-stock of himself and his fellow-curates for half a year to come—They regard me as an old maid, and I regard them, one and all, as highly uninteresting, narrow and unattractive specimens of the "coarser sex".

The coldness and neglect of your brothers for their struggling, suffering Mother and Sisters irritates me more than I can or at least ought to express—I had fully calculated on Joshua inviting you at least to pay him a lengthened visit.[2]

Write to me again soon whether you have anything particular to say or not—Give my sincere love to your Mother and Sisters

C Brontë

The enigmas are very smart and well-worded—[3]

MS BPM Gr. E 10.

1. The Revd Arthur Bell Nicholls (1819–1906), Mr Brontë's curate since May 1845. CB's early coolness had changed into a genuine affection by the time she married him on 29 June 1854, though she still had reservations about his Puseyism and his not being intellectual. See the Biographical Note, pp. xl–xli.
2. Conjectural reading of a passage heavily deleted by EN. The Revd Joshua Nussey (1798–1871), vicar of Oundle since 1845, had at least visited his mother and sisters after the death of his brother Joseph, and had urged Henry Nussey to do likewise; but Henry and his wife had begged to be excused 'on a/c of the expense to both yrselves & us.'
3. Polite riddles or enigmas could be found in contemporary ladies' magazines and 'pocket companions'.

45. To Ellen Nussey, [9 August 1846]

[Haworth]

Dear Nell

Anne and I both thank you for your kind invitation—and our thanks are not mere words of course[1]—they are very sincere both as addressed to yourself and your Mother and Sisters—but we cannot accept it and I think even you will consider our motives for declining valid this time.

In a fortnight I hope to go with papa to Manchester to have his eyes couched[2]—Emily and I made a pilgrimage there a week ago to search out an operator and we found one in the person of a Mr Wilson[3]—He could not tell from description whether the eyes were ready for an operation—Papa must therefore necessarily take a journey to Manchester to consult him—if he judges the cataract ripe—we shall remain—if on the contrary he thinks it not yet sufficiently hardened we shall have to return—and papa must remain in darkness a while longer.

Poor Bessie Hirst![4] I was thinking about her only a day or two before I got your letter. Do you know whether she suffered much pain or whether her death was easy?

I am sorry to hear so indifferent an account of Mrs Henry[5]—I certainly never did expect she would make an <u>agreeable</u> addition to your family after reading Mrs Prescott's letter to you respecting her—yet though not <u>agreeable</u> she may still be well-principled and well intentioned—let us hope she is so—for in that case she will never go far wrong—There is a defect in your reasoning about the feelings a wife ought to experience in paying money for her husband. Who holds the purse will wish to be Master, Ellen; depend on it whether Man or woman—Who provides the cash will now and then value himself (or herself) upon it—and even in the case of ordinary Minds, reproach the less wealthy partner—besides no husband ought to be an object of charity to his wife—as no wife to her husband   Sisterly affection makes you partial and misleads your usually correct judgment—No dear Nell—it is doubtless pleasant to marry <u>well</u> as they say—but with all pleasures are mixed bitters—I do not wish for you a very rich husband—I should not like you to be regarded by any man even as <u>"a sweet object of charity"</u>

Give my sincere love to all
Yours
C Brontë

MS HM 24445.

1. Customary or ordinary words—i.e. a mere empty formula.
2. To have the opaque crystalline lens depressed in order to restore vision.
3. The oculist William James Wilson, MRCS (d. 1855), honorary surgeon at Manchester Royal Infirmary 1826–55, with a private practice at 72 Mosley Street.
4. Elizabeth, daughter of William Hirst of Marsh House, Gomersal, died of TB on 2 Aug. 1846.
5. Henry Nussey's wife, née Emily Prescott.

46. To Ellen Nussey, 26 August [1846]

[Manchester][1]

Dear Ellen

The operation is over—it took place yesterday—Mr Wilson performed it, two other surgeons assisted—Mr Wilson says he considers it quite successful but papa cannot yet see anything—The affair lasted precisely a quarter of an hour—it was not the simple operation of couching Mr Carr[2] described but the more complicated one of extracting the cataract—Mr Wilson entirely disapproves of couching.[3]

Papa displayed extraordinary patience and firmness—the surgeons seemed surprised. I was in the room all the time, as it was his wish that I should be there—of course I neither spoke nor moved till the thing was done—and then I felt that the less I said either to papa or the surgeons, the better—papa is now confined to his bed in a dark room and is not to be stirred for four days—he is to speak and to be spoken to as little as possible—

I am greatly obliged to you for your letter and your kind advice which gave me extreme satisfaction because I found I had arranged most things in accordance with it—and as your theory coincides with my practice I feel assured the latter is right[4]—I hope Mr Wilson will soon allow me to dispense with the nurse—She is well enough no doubt but somewhat too obsequious &c. and not I should think to be much trusted—yet I am obliged to trust her in some things—

Your friend Charlotte has had a letter from Mary Taylor[5]—and she was only waiting to hear from one Ellen Nussey that she had received a similar document in order to communicate the fact—if the said Ellen had not got one too—Charlotte would have said nothing about it for fear of inflicting a touch of pain—I have not my letter here or I should send it to you   it was written on the voyage—she refers me to "the long one" for later news—I have not yet seen it.

Greatly was I amused by your accounts of Joe Taylor's flirtations—and yet something saddened also—I think Nature intended him for something better than to fritter away his time in making a set of poor, unoccupied spinsters unhappy—The girls unfortunately are forced to care for him and such as him because while their minds are mostly unemployed, their sensations are all unworn and consequently fresh and keen—and he on the contrary has had his fill of pleasure and can with impunity make a mere pastime of other people's torments. This is an unfair state of things, the match is not equal   I only wish I had the power to infuse into the souls of the persecuted a little of the quiet strength of pride—of the supporting consciousness of superiority (for they are superior to him because purer) of the fortifying resolve of firmness to bear the present and wait the end. Could all the virgin population of Birstal and Gomersal receive and retain these sentiments—Joe Taylor would eventually have to vail his crest before them.[6]

Perhaps luckily their feelings are not so acute as one would think and the gentleman's shafts consequently don't wound so deeply as he might desire—I hope it is so.

Give my best love to your Mother and Sisters.

Write soon

C Brontë

MS HM 24447.

1. CB and her father were in lodgings at 83 Mount Pleasant, Boundary Street, Oxford Road, Manchester.
2. William Carr (1784–1861), surgeon, of Little Gomersal.
3. In her *Life* of CB, Mrs Gaskell wrote: 'Charlotte told me that her tale [*The Professor*] came back upon her hands, curtly rejected by some publisher, on the very day when her father was to

submit to his operation. But she had the heart of Robert Bruce within her . . . Not only did "The Professor" return again to try his chance among the London publishers, but she began, in this time of care and depressing inquietude,—in those grey, weary, uniform streets . . . there and then, did the brave genius begin "Jane Eyre" ' (ch. 15).

4. In a letter written on 21 Aug. CB had told Ellen that she was 'somewhat puzzled in managing about provisions—we board ourselves.'

5. After a $4\frac{1}{2}$-month voyage from 12 Mar. to 24 July 1845, Mary had joined her brother Waring in his house and shop in Herbert Street, Wellington, New Zealand.

6. Cf. Shakespeare, *I Henry VI*, V. iii. 24–6.

47. To Ellen Nussey, 14 October 1846

[Haworth]

Dear Ellen

I read your letter with attention—not on my own account—for any project which infers the necessity of my leaving home is impracticable to me—but on yours.

If your brother Richard[1] has really interest to get you—I will not say several—but two or three pupils—he would be performing a really kind and brotherly act to secure you that number—Be assured Ellen that you could instruct them without mine or any other assistance—if they were not more advanced than it is at all usual for children to be, at the ages of 10–11–12—[2] There would not be work for two teachers—and what is more to the purpose—there would assuredly not be profit for two—after deducting an equitable sum for your Mother—At the present rate of competition it would be vain to expect a great number of pupils at first—nor would a great number be necessary if there were only yourself to be maintained out of your earnings—£20 clear gain—would be a very comfortable thing in that case, but if at the end of the year—you had to halve it with another, it would be a very different affair—A Master or two might be necessary to help you with the accomplishments—but the expense of paying them would be nothing to the subtraction of an equal share for a regular co-adjutor.

Take courage—try the matter by yourself—Your Sisters can keep the house—you can devote yourself to the schoolroom.

I talk in this wise way, and yet to say the truth—had I no will or interest to consult but my own—were I an isolated being without ties or duties connected with others I should probably with pleasure and promptitude have cast in my lot with yours—and struggled to double the £20 which I should scruple to share—But if I could leave home Ellen—I should not be at Haworth now—I know life is passing away and I am doing nothing—earning nothing—a very bitter knowledge it is at moments—but I see no way out of the mist—More than one very favourable opportunity has now offered which I have been obliged to put aside—probably when I am free to leave home I shall neither be able to find place nor employment—perhaps too I shall be quite past the prime of life—my faculties will be rusted—and my few acquirements in a great measure forgotten—These ideas sting me keenly sometimes—but whenever I consult my Conscience it affirms that I am doing right in staying at home—and bitter are its upbraidings when I yield to an eager desire for release—I returned to Brussels after Aunt's death against my conscience—prompted by what then seemed an irresistible impulse[3]—I was punished for my selfish folly by a total withdrawal for more than two year[s] of happiness and peace of mind—I could hardly expect success if I were to err again in the same way—

I should like to hear from you again soon—Bring Richard to the point and make him give you a <u>clear</u> not a <u>vague</u> account of what pupils he really could procure you—people often think they can do great things in that way till they have tried—but getting pupils is unlike getting any other sort of goods.

C Brontë

MS HM 24449.

1. Richard Nussey (1803–72), a woollen manufacturer and merchant, who carried on the Nussey family business. He married Elizabeth Charnock of Leeds in 1846, and after her father John Charnock's death in 1847, Richard inherited his two mills in Meadows Lane, Leeds.
2. EN's school project did not materialize.
3. CB had wished to improve her knowledge of French, and therefore her qualifications for teaching; her longing to see and be taught by M. Heger could not be openly admitted. In a note probably written in the 1890s, Ellen chose to explain CB's 'sad suffering' by alleging that Mr Brontë 'in conjunction with Mr. S[mith] . . . had fallen into habits of intemperance'. 'Mr Smith' was the curate J. W. Smith, said to be the original of 'Peter Augustus Malone' in *Shirley*. It is true that Mr Brontë had to deny rumours that he was drinking too much, in a letter to a Mr Greenwood of 4 Oct. 1843, where he attributes the slanders to his use of an eye-lotion.

48. *To Ellen Nussey, 19 January 1847*

[Haworth]

Dear Ellen

I thank you again for your last letter which I found as full or fuller of interest than either of the preceding ones—it is just written as I wish you to write to me—not a detail too much—a correspondence of that sort is the next best thing to actual conversation—though it must be allowed that between the two there is a wide gulph still—

I imagine your face—voice—presence very plainly when I read your letters—still—imagination is not reality and when I return them to their envelope and put them by in my desk—I feel the difference sensibly enough—

My curiosity is a little piqued about that Countess you mention[1]—what is her name? you have not yet given it—I cannot decide from what you say whether she is really clever or only eccentric—the two sometimes go together but are often seen apart—I generally feel inclined to fight very shy of eccentricity and have no small horror of being thought eccentric myself—by which observation I don't mean to insinuate that I class myself under the head clever—God knows a more consummate ass in sundry important points has seldom browzed the green herb of his bounties than I[2]—Oh Lord Nell—I'm in danger sometimes of falling into self-weariness—

I used to say and to think in former times that you would certainly be married—I am not so sanguine on that point now—It will never suit you to accept a husband you cannot love or at least respect—and it appears there are many chances against your meeting with such a one under favourable circumstances—besides from all I can hear and see Money seems to be regarded as almost the Alpha and Omega of requisites in a wife—Well Nell if you are destined to be an old maid I don't think you will be a repining one—I think you will find resources in your own mind and disposition which will help you to get on—

As to society I don't understand much about it—but from the few glimpses I have had of its machinery it seems to me to be a very strange, complicated affair indeed—wherein Nature is turned upside down—Your well-bred people appear to me figuratively speaking to walk on their heads—to see everything the wrong way up—a lie is with them truth—truth a lie—eternal and tedious botheration is their notion of happiness—sensible pursuits their ennui—

—But this may be only the view ignorance takes of what it cannot understand—I refrain from judging them therefore—but if I was called upon to swop (you know the word I suppose?) to swop tastes and ideas and feelings with **Mrs Joshua Nussey**[3] for instance—I should prefer walking into a good Yorkshire kitchen fire—and concluding the bargain at once by an act of voluntary combustion—Is she a frog or a fish—? She is certainly a specimen of some kind of cold-blooded animal—**To live with a decent girl like you day after day and never to thaw is intolerable**—All here is as usual—

Write again soon
Yours faithfully
C Brontë

MS BPM B.S. 57.5.

1. Not identified.
2. Cf. Job 6: 5 and Genesis 1: 30.
3. Mrs Anne Elizabeth Nussey, née Alexander (1788–1875) sister of Henry Alexander, a director of the East India Company. For Ellen's brother Joshua see Letter 44 n. 2. Ellen was staying at his vicarage in Oundle, Northants.

49. *To Ellen Nussey, 1 March 1847*

Haworth

Dear Ellen

Even at the risk of appearing very exacting I can't help saying that I should like a letter as long as your last every time you write—Short notes give one the feeling of a very small piece of a very good thing to eat—they set the appetite on edge and don't satisfy it—a letter leaves you more contented—and yet, after all, I am very glad to get notes so don't think, when you are pinched for time and materials that it is useless to write a few lines—be assured a few lines are very acceptable as far as they go—and though I like long letters I would by no means have you to make a task of writing to me.

Dear Nell—as you wish to avoid making me uneasy—say nothing more about my going to Brookroyd at present—Let your visit to Sussex[1] be got over—let the summer arrive—and then we shall see how matters stand by that time. To confess the truth I really should like you to come to Haworth before I again go to Brookroyd—and it is natural and right that I should have this wish—to keep friendship in proper order the balance of good offices must be preserved—otherwise a disquieting and anxious feeling creeps in and destroys mutual comfort—In summer—and in fine weather your visit here might be much better managed than in winter—we could go out more be more independent of the house and of one room—Branwell has been conducting himself very badly lately—I expect from the extravagance of his behaviour and from mysterious hints he drops—(for he never will speak out plainly) that we shall be hearing news of fresh debts contracted by him soon—[2]

The Misses Robinson[3]—who had entirely ceased their correspondence with Anne for half a year after their father's death have lately recommenced it—for a fortnight they sent her a letter almost every day—crammed with warm protestation of endless esteem and gratitude—they speak with great affection too of their Mother—and never make any allusion intimating acquaintance with her errors—It is to be hoped they are and always will remain in ignorance on that point—especially since—I think—she has bitterly repented them. We take special care that Branwell does not know of their writing to Anne.

Have you yet found any document which will give you a claim to a larger proportion of the sum you expect from the Railway people?[4] What a grievous pity it seems that you could not get the whole—It could never have come in better—

Poor George's condition from what you say seems stationary—if he does not improve much neither does he retrograde—perhaps he may when it is least expected—take a sudden turn for the better—the brain may resume its proper healthy action and all may yet be well—[5]

Give my love to your Mother and Sisters—Write again soon

I am yours faithfully
C Brontë

My health is better—I lay the blame of its feebleness on the cold weather more than on an uneasy mind. For after all I have many things to be thankful for.

MS Law-Dixon.

1. No visit to Ellen's friend Mary Gorham at Cakeham is recorded in 1847.
2. In Dec. 1846 a Sheriff's Officer had 'invited' Branwell 'to pay his debts or to take a trip to York', i.e. to be imprisoned for debt. 'Of course his debts had to be paid,' CB told Ellen—presumably by Mr Brontë. In c.Jan. 1847 Branwell had written to his friend Joseph Bentley Leyland, 'I wish Mr Thos Nicholson of the "Old Cock" [Halifax] would send me my bill of what I owe to him, and, the moment that I receive my outlaid cash, or any sum which may fall into my hands through the hands of one whom I may never see again, I shall settle it' (Wise & Symington Letter 278). Dr John Crosby, doctor to the Robinsons of Thorp Green, and a member of the society of Oddfellows' 'Loyal Providence Lodge' at Great Ouseburn, has been suggested as a possible source of financial help to Branwell, but proof is lacking.
3. The Robinsons' two younger daughters, Elizabeth Lydia and Mary.
4. Some property owned by the Nusseys abutted on or formed part of land needed for new railroads.
5. The conjectural reading of this heavily deleted paragraph is that of Dr Mildred Christian, who saw the original MS. For George Nussey's mental illness see Letters 25, 34, 42, and notes.

50. *To Thomas de Quincey,*[1] *16 June 1847*

[Haworth]

Sir

My Relatives, Ellis and Acton Bell and myself, heedless of the repeated warnings of various respectable publishers, have committed the rash act of printing a volume of poems.

The consequences predicted have, of course, overtaken us; our book is found to be a drug; no man needs it or heeds it; in the space of a year our publisher has disposed but of two copies, and by what painful efforts he succeeded in getting rid of those two, himself only knows.

Before transferring the edition to the trunk-makers,[2] we have decided on distributing as presents a few copies of what we cannot sell—we beg to offer you one in acknowledgment of the pleasure and profit we have often and long derived from your works—

I am Sir
Yours very respectfully
Currer Bell.

MS Berg.

1. De Quincey (1785–1859) was one of several authors, including Hartley Coleridge, Ebenezer Elliott, John Gibson Lockhart, Alfred Tennyson, Wordsworth, and possibly Dickens, to whom CB and her sisters sent copies of their poems. Their letters to the first four of these closely resemble that to De Quincey; those to Wordsworth and Dickens have not been traced.
2. For use as a lining in leather travelling trunks.

51. To Messrs Smith, Elder & Co.,[1] 15 July 1847

Gentlemen

I beg to submit to your consideration the accompanying Manuscript[2]—I should be glad to learn whether it be such as you approve and would undertake to publish—at as early a period as possible—

[Signature cut out]

Address—Mr Currer Bell
Under cover to Miss Brontë
  Haworth
    Bradford
      Yorkshire

MS BPM SG 1.

1. A London firm founded as a bookseller's and stationer's in 1816 by George Smith (1789–1846) and Alexander Elder (1790–1876). They became publishers in 1819, and moved to 65 Cornhill in 1824. Under the energetic leadership of the younger George Smith (1824–1901) from 1844 onwards, the firm's publishing had rapidly expanded, and was to diversify also into banking and the export of books and other commodities to the Far East. See the Biographical Notes for the younger George Smith and his reader William Smith Williams, pp. xliii and xlv.
2. The MS of *The Professor*, already refused by six other publishers.

52. To Messrs Smith, Elder & Co., 7 August 1847

[Haworth]

Gentlemen

I have received your communication of the 5th. inst. for which I thank you.[1]

Your objection to the want of varied interest in the tale is, I am aware, not without grounds—yet it appears to me that it might be published without serious risk if its appearance were speedily followed up by another work from the same pen of a more striking and exciting character. The first work might serve as an introduction and accustom the public to the author's name, the success of the second might thereby be rendered more probable.

I have a second narrative[2] in 3 vols. now in progress and nearly completed, to which I have endeavoured to impart a more vivid interest than belongs to the Professor; in about a month I hope to finish it—so that if a publisher were found for "the Professor", the second narrative might follow as soon as was deemed advisable—and thus the interest of the public (if any interest were roused) might not be suffered to cool.

Will you be kind enough to favour me with your judgment on this plan—

I am Gentlemen
Yours very respectfully
C Bell—

MS BPM SG 3.

1. W. S. Williams had advised George Smith that *The Professor* had 'great literary power', but he doubted whether it would succeed as a publication. CB was cheered by Mr Williams's courteous discussion of her novel's 'merits and demerits' and his suggestion that a 3-volume work 'would meet with careful attention'.
2. *Jane Eyre.*

53. *To Messrs Smith, Elder & Co., 12 September 1847*

[Brookroyd, Birstall][1]

Gentlemen

I have received your letter and thank you for the judicious remarks and sound advice it contains. I am not however in a position to follow the advice; my engagements will not permit me to revise 'Jane Eyre' a third time, and perhaps there is little to regret in the circumstance; you probably know from personal experience that an author never writes well till he has got into the full spirit of his work, and were I to retrench, to alter and to add now when I am uninterested and cold, I know I should only further injure what may be already defective. Perhaps too the first part of 'Jane Eyre' may suit the public taste better than you anticipate—for it is true and Truth has a severe charm of its own.[2] Had I told all the truth, I might indeed have made it far more exquisitely painful—but I deemed it advisable to soften and retrench many particulars lest the narrative should rather displease than attract.

I adopt your suggestion respecting the title; it would be much better to add the words "an autobiography."

In accepting your terms, I trust much to your equity and sense of justice.[3] You stipulate for the refusal of my two next works at the price of one hundred pounds each. One hundred pounds is a small sum for a year's intellectual labour, nor would circumstances justify me in devoting my time and attention to literary pursuits with so narrow a prospect of advantage did I not feel convinced that in case the ultimate result of my efforts should prove more successful than you now anticipate, you would make some proportionate addition to the remuneration you at present offer. On this ground of confidence in your generosity and honour, I accept your conditions.

I shall be glad to know when the work will appear. I shall be happy also to receive any advice you can give me as to choice of subject or style of treatment in my next effort—and if you can point out any works peculiarly remarkable for the qualities in which I am deficient, I would study them carefully and endeavour to remedy my errors.

Allow me in conclusion to express my sense of the punctuality, straight-forwardness and intelligence which have hitherto marked your dealings with me.

And believe me Gentlemen

Yours respectfully

C Bell.

Since you have no use for 'the Professor', I shall be obliged if you will return the MS.S.[4] Address as usual to Miss Brontë &c.

MS BPM SG 3/1B.

1. On 24 Aug. CB had sent the manuscript of *Jane Eyre* to Smith, Elder & Co. by rail, asking the firm to enclose letters to 'Mr. Currer Bell' in an envelope addressed to 'Miss Brontë'. From 9 to 23 Sept. she stayed with the Nusseys at Brookroyd., and by 18 Sept. she had received the first proofs of *Jane Eyre*, forwarded to her from Haworth. She corrected them at Brookroyd without revealing the nature of her work to Ellen.
2. Lowood school in *JE* is based upon CB's memories of her experiences as a child of 8 at the Clergy Daughters' School at Cowan Bridge, Lancs., founded by the Revd William Carus Wilson and others. Her elder sisters Maria and Elizabeth had died as a result of illnesses which began or grew worse at Cowan Bridge.
3. Smith, Elder paid CB £100 for the copyright of *JE*, later adding sums to make a total of £500.
4. CB made three attempts to revise *The Professor*. See Letter 59 n. 1.

54. *To Messrs Smith, Elder & Co., 24 September 1847*

Haworth[1]

Gentlemen

I have to thank you for punctuating the sheets before sending them to me as I found the task very puzzling—and besides I consider your mode of punctuation a great deal more correct and rational than my own.

I am glad you think pretty well of the first part of "Jane Eyre" and I trust, both for your sakes and my own the public may think pretty well of it too.

Henceforth I hope I shall be able to return the sheets promptly and regularly.

I am Gentlemen

Yours respectfully

C Bell

MS BPM SG 4.

1. CB was writing on the day after her return from her visit to Birstall. She had returned some of the proof-sheets of *Jane Eyre* from Birstall on 18 Sept., noting that the errors were 'not numerous', and adding that she perfectly understood that she was not to publish "The Professor" or any other work till after the appearance of the two books of which Smith, Elder were to have the refusal.

55. *To Messrs Smith, Elder & Co., 19 October 1847*

[Haworth]

Gentlemen

The six copies of "Jane Eyre" reached me this morning.[1] You have given the work every advantage which good paper, clear type and a seemly outside can supply—if it fails—the fault will lie with the author—you are exempt.

I now await the judgment of the press and the public

I am Gentlemen
Yrs. respectfully
C Bell.

MS Parrish Collection, Princeton.

1. CB was writing on the day of publication. The novel was published as '*Jane Eyre. An Autobiography*. Edited by Currer Bell. 3 vols. post 8vo' at £1. 11s. 6d.

56. *To W. S. Williams, 28 October 1847*

[Haworth]

Dear Sir

Your last letter was very pleasant to me to read, and is very cheering to reflect on. I feel honoured in being approved by Mr. Thackeray because I approve Mr. Thackeray.[1] This may sound presumptuous perhaps, but I mean that I have long recognized in his writings genuine talent such as I admired, such as I wondered at and delighted in. No author seems to distinguish so exquisitely as he does dross from ore, the real from the counterfeit. I believed too he had deep and true feelings under his seeming sternness—now I am sure he has. One good word from such a man is worth pages of praise from ordinary judges.

You are right in having faith in the reality of Helen Burns's character: she was real enough: I have exaggerated nothing there: I abstained from recording much that I remember respecting her, lest the narrative should sound incredible. Knowing this, I could not but smile at the quiet, self-complacent dogmatism with which one of the journals lays it down that "such creations as Helen Burns are very beautiful but very untrue".[2]

The plot of "Jane Eyre" may be a hackneyed one; Mr. Thackeray remarks that it is familiar to him; but having read comparatively few novels, I never chanced to meet with it, and I thought it original—. The critic of the Athenæum's work, I had not had the good fortune to hear of.[3]

The Weekly Chronicle seems inclined to identify me with Mrs. Marsh.[4] I never had the pleasure of perusing a line of Mrs. Marsh's in my life—but I wish very much to read her works and shall profit by the first opportunity of doing so. I hope I shall not find I have been an unconscious imitator.

I would still endeavour to keep my expectations low respecting the ultimate success of "Jane Eyre"; but my desire that it should succeed augments—for you have taken much trouble about the work, and it would grieve me seriously if your active efforts should be baffled and your sanguine hopes disappointed: excuse me if I again remark that I fear they are rather <u>too</u> sanguine; it would be better to moderate them. What will the critics of the Monthly Reviews and Magazines be likely to see in "Jane Eyre" (if indeed they deign to read it) which will win from them even a stinted modicum of approbation? It has no learning, no research, it discusses no subject of public interest. A mere domestic novel will I fear seem trivial to men of large views and solid attainments.

Still—efforts so energetic and indefatigable as yours ought to realize a result in some degree favourable, and I trust they will.

I remain, dear Sir
Yours respectfully
C Bell.

Octbr. 28th./47

I have just recd. "the Tablet" and the "Morning Advertiser"[5]—neither paper seems inimical to the book—but I see it produces a very different effect—on different natures. I was amused at the analysis in the Tablet—it is oddly expressed in some parts—I think the critic did not always seize my meaning—he speaks for instance of "Jane's inconceivable alarm at Mr. Rochester's repelling manner—I do not remember that

MS Pierpont Morgan, MA 2696.

1. Thackeray wrote to W. S. Williams on 23 Oct. that he had 'lost (or won if you like) a whole day in reading' *Jane Eyre*. 'It is a fine book though . . . The plot of the story is one with wh. I am familiar. . . . It is a woman's writing, but whose?' Thackeray had been deeply distressed when his wife Isabella became insane in 1840. In 1847 she was being cared for in a private home, as she was to be for the rest of her life.
2. CB quotes the *Atlas* newspaper for 23 Oct. 1847; but the reviewer had also praised *JE* as 'one of the most powerful domestic romances which have been published for many years'. Charlotte later told Mrs Gaskell that her eldest sister Maria, who patiently suffered cruel treatment at Cowan Bridge, was the original of Helen Burns.
3. Henry Fothergill Chorley, reviewing *JE* in the *Athenaeum* for 23 Oct. 1847, compared it with his own novel, *Sketches of a Seaport Town* (1834).

4. The reviewer in the *Weekly Chronicle* for 23 Oct. thought the author's 'simple, penetrating style' and 'love of nature' were characteristic of Anne Marsh (1791–1874), author of the recent best-seller, *Emilia Wyndham* (1845).

5. The Roman Catholic *Tablet* found *JE* challenging and unconventional, but a 'healthful exercise' which deserved to succeed. Jane's original 'inconceivable alarm' at Rochester's repelling manner is followed by 'various phases of amusement at enduring and defying his haughty abruptness.' It would be 'marvellous' if Rochester were 'a portrait from a man's hands, notwithstanding the masculine firmness of the touch and the breadth of the handling'. (23 Oct. 1847.) *The Morning Advertiser* for 26 Oct. found *JE* deeply interesting, exciting, fresh, and original, though occasionally melodramatic, odd, or eccentric.

57. *To G. H. Lewes,*[1] *6 November 1847*

[Haworth]

Dear Sir

Your letter reached me yesterday; I beg to assure you that I appreciate fully the intention with which it was written, and I thank you sincerely for both its cheering commendation and valuable advice.

You warn me to beware of Melodrame[2] and you exhort me to adhere to the real. When I first began to write, so impressed was I with the truth of the principles you advocate that I determined to take Nature and Truth as my sole guides and to follow in their very footprints; I restrained imagination, eschewed romance, repressed excitement:[3] over-bright colouring too I avoided, and sought to produce something which should be soft, grave and true.

My work (a tale in 1 vol.) being completed, I offered it to a publisher. He said it was original, faithful to Nature, but he did not feel warranted in accepting it, such a work would not sell. I tried six publishers in succession; they all told me it was deficient in "startling incident" and "thrilling excitement", that it would never suit the circulating libraries, and as it was on those libraries the success of works of fiction mainly depended they could not undertake to publish what would be overlooked there—"Jane Eyre" was rather objected to at first [on] the same grounds—but finally found acceptance.

I mention this to you, not with a view of pleading exemption from censure, but in order to direct your attention to the root of certain literary evils—if in your forthcoming article in "Frazer" you would bestow a few words of enlightenment on the public who support the circulating libraries, you might, with your powers, do some good.

You advise me too, not to stray far from the ground of experience as I become weak when I enter the region of fiction; and you say "real experience is perennially interesting and to all men..."

I feel that this also is true, but, dear Sir, is not the real experience of each individual very limited? and if a writer dwells upon that solely or principally is he not in danger of repeating himself, and also of becoming an egotist?

Then too, Imagination is a strong, restless faculty which claims to be heard and exercised, are we to be quite deaf to her cry and insensate to her struggles? When she shews us bright pictures are we never to look at them and try to reproduce them?—And when she is eloquent and speaks rapidly and urgently in our ear are we not to write to her dictation?

I shall anxiously search the next number of "Frazer" for your opinions on these points.

Believe me, dear Sir,
Yours gratefully
C Bell

MS BL Add. 39763.

1. George Henry Lewes (1817–78), journalist, novelist, dramatist, and writer on philosophy and physiology. At this period he was happily married to Agnes, née Jervis, whose later infidelity led to Lewes's partnership with 'George Eliot' from 1854.
2. Thus in MS. Lewes was to make the same criticism in *Fraser's Magazine* for Dec. 1847: JE's 'deep, significant reality' brings into stronger relief its defects of 'melodrama and improbability, which smack of the circulating library'. In fact Lewes's own novels, *Ranthorpe* (1847) and *Rose, Blanche, and Violet* (1848) are often marred by melodramatic scenes and absurdly inflated style.
3. CB's early writings are full of these qualities; but in 1839 she wrote her 'Farewell to Angria', and longed to 'turn to a cooler region'. *The Professor* was written as a 'study of real life'.

58. *To W. S. Williams, 10 November 1847*

[Haworth]

Dear Sir,

I have received the "Britannia" and the "Sun," but not the "Spectator," which I rather regret, as censure, though not pleasant, is often wholesome.[1]

Thank you for your information regarding Mr Lewes. I am glad to hear that he is a clever and sincere man; such being the case, I can await his critical sentence with fortitude: even if it goes against me, I shall not murmur; ability and honesty have a right to condemn where they think condemnation is deserved. From what you say, however, I trust rather to obtain at least a modified approval.

Your account of the various surmises respecting the identity of the brothers Bell, amused me much:[2] were the enigma solved, it would probably be found not worth the trouble of solution; but I will let it alone; it suits ourselves to remain quiet and certainly injures no one else.

The Reviewer, who noticed the little book of poems, in the "Dublin Magazine,"[3] conjectured that the soi-disant three personages were in reality but one, who, endowed with an unduly prominent organ of self-esteem, and consequently impressed with a somewhat weighty notion of his own merits, thought them too vast to be concentrated in a single individual, and accordingly divided himself into three, out of consideration, I suppose, for the nerves of the much-to-be-astounded public! This was an ingenious thought in the reviewer; very original and striking, but not accurate. We are three.

A prose work by Ellis and Acton will soon appear:[4] it should have been out, indeed, long since; for the first proof-sheets were already in the press at the commencement of last August, before Currer Bell had placed the M.S. of "Jane Eyre" in your hands. Mr. N<ewby>,[5] however, does not do business like Messrs. Smith and Elder; a different spirit seems to preside at 72. Mortimer Street to that which guides the helm at 65, Cornhill. Mr. N<ewby> shuffles, gives his word and breaks it; Messrs. Smith and Elder's performance is always better than their promise. My relatives have suffered from exhausting delay and procrastination, while I have to acknowledge the benefits of a management, at once business-like and gentlemanlike, energetic and considerate.

I should like to know if Mr. N<ewby> often acts as he has done to my relatives, or whether this is an exceptional instance of his method.[6] Do you know, and can you tell me anything about him? You must excuse me for going to the point at once, when I want to learn anything; if my questions are importunate,[7] you are, of course, at liberty to decline answering them.—I am yours respectfully,

C. Bell.

MS untraced. Text: *CBL* i. 561–2.

1. The Tory *Britannia* for 6 Nov. criticized the novel's alleged lack of construction, Jane's 'purposeless' adventures, and some 'revolting' passages, but praised the deep thought and high feeling which foretold a promising literary career. On the same day the *Sun*, a daily newspaper, praised *JE*'s originality, vigorous expression of feeling, and delineation of character. Despite some unnatural incidents, the novel was entertaining and ennobling. In contrast the radical *Spectator* condemned its artifice, contrived dialogue, and improbability, Rochester's hardness, peculiarity, and impropriety, and in general the low tone of behaviour. The reviewer nevertheless conceded 'considerable skill in the plan, and great power' (6. Nov. 1847).
2. J. G. Lockhart reported two surmises to Miss Rigby (later Lady Eastlake) on 13 Nov. 1848: 'The common rumour is that they are brothers of the weaving order in some Lancashire town. At first it was generally said Currer was a lady, and Mayfair circumstantialised by making her the *chère amie* of Mr. Thackeray' (Charles Eastlake Smith (ed.), *Journals and Correspondence of Lady Eastlake* (1895), i. 222). The Mayfair rumour probably circulated after the publication of the second edition of *JE*, with its dedication to Thackeray, in January 1848.
3. The *Dublin University Magazine* 28 (1846), 385–7.
4. *Wuthering Heights* and *Agnes Grey* were published together in Dec. 1847, *Agnes Grey* forming the third of the three volumes.
5. Thomas Cautley Newby (?1798–1882) began publishing in the late 1820s, and retired in 1874. CB's indignation on her sisters' behalf was caused by his tardy publication, delayed until *JE* proved to be a best-seller, and by his hard bargaining. In 1848 his advertisements implied that 'Acton Bell's' second novel was the work of the successful Currer Bell.
6. In his *Autobiography* Anthony Trollope recalled that Newby had paid him nothing for his first novel, *The Macdermots of Ballycloran* (1847), but he admitted that Newby 'probably did not sell fifty copies of the work'.
7. Other versions of this letter read 'impertinent', which may well be correct.

59. *To W. S. Williams, 14 December 1847*

[Haworth]

Dear Sir

I have just received your kind and welcome letter of the 11th. I shall proceed at once to discuss the principal subject of it.

Of course a second work has occupied my thoughts much. I think it would be premature in me to undertake a serial now; I am not yet qualified for the task: I have neither gained a sufficiently firm footing with the public, nor do I possess sufficient confidence in myself, nor can I boast those unflagging animal spirits, that even command of the faculty of composition, which, as you say and I am persuaded, most justly, is an indispensable requisite to success in serial literature. I decidedly feel that ere I change my ground, I had better make another venture in the 3 vol. novel form.

Respecting the plan of such a work, I have pondered it, but as yet with very unsatisfactory results. Three commencements have I essayed, but all three displease me. A few days since I looked over "the Professor." I found the beginning very feeble, the whole narrative deficient in incident and in general attractiveness; yet the middle and latter portion of the work, all that relates to Brussels, the Belgian school &c. is as good as I can write; it contains more pith, more substance, more reality, in my judgment, than much of "Jane Eyre". It gives, I think, a new view of a grade, an occupation, and a class of characters—all very common-place, very insignificant in themselves, but not more so than the materials composing that portion of "Jane Eyre" which seems to please most generally—.

My wish is to recast "the Professor", add as well as I can, what is deficient, retrench some parts, develop others—and make of it a 3-vol. work; no easy task, I know, yet I trust not an impracticable one.[1]

I have not forgotten that "the Professor" was set aside in my agreement with Messrs. Smith & Elder—therefore before I take any step to execute the plan I have sketched, I should wish to have your judgment on its wisdom. You read or looked over the M.S.—what impression have you now respecting its worth? And what confidence have you that I can make it better than it is?

Feeling certain that from business reasons as well as from natural integrity you will be quite candid with me, I esteem it a privilege to be able thus to consult you.

Believe me, dear Sir,
Yours respectfully
C. Bell—

"Wuthering Heights" is, I suppose, at length published—at least Mr. Newby has sent the authors their six copies—I wonder how it will be received. I should say it merits the epithets of "vigorous" and "original" much more decidedly than "Jane Eyre" did. "Agnes Grey" should please such critics as Mr. Lewes—for it is "true" and "unexaggerated" enough.

The books are not well got up—they abound in errors of the press.[2] On a former occasion I expressed myself with perhaps too little reserve regarding Mr. Newby—yet I cannot but feel, and feel painfully that Ellis and Acton have not had the justice at his hands that I have had at those of Messrs. Smith & Elder.

MS Taylor Collection, Princeton.

1. A single-page draft of a preface, written before *Shirley* was begun, explains that the narrator has cut out the first seven chapters of *The Professor* (BPM MS Bonnell 109; Clarendon edition of *The Professor*, Appendix III). A longer draft of 18 leaves (Princeton University Library, Clarendon *Shirley*, Appendix D) renames the Crimsworth brothers John Henry and William Moore, and begins to develop the character of John Henry's wife Julia. Fragmentary paragraphs and calculations of the extra material needed to expand *The Professor* also survive (Pierpont Morgan Library, Clarendon *Professor* App. II).
2. Newby both printed and published the three carelessly produced volumes.

60. *To W. S. Williams, 21 December 1847*

[Haworth]

Dear Sir

I am, for my own part, dissatisfied with the preface I sent—I fear it savours of flippancy. If you see no objection, I should prefer substituting the enclosed.[1] It is rather more lengthy, but it expresses something I have long wished to express.

Mr. Smith is kind indeed to think of sending me "the Jar of honey";[2] when I receive the book I will write to him.

I cannot thank you sufficiently for your letters, and I can give you but a faint idea of the pleasure they afford me; they seem to introduce such light and life to the torpid retirement where we lie like dormice. But—understand this distinctly; you must never write to me except when you have both leisure and inclination. I know your time is too fully occupied and too valuable to be often at the service of any one individual.

You are not far wrong in your judgment respecting "Wuthering Heights" & "Agnes Grey". Ellis has a strong, original mind, full of strange though sombre power: when he writes poetry that power speaks in language at once condensed, elaborated and refined—but in prose it breaks forth in scenes which shock more than they attract—Ellis will improve, however, because he knows his defects. "Agnes Grey" is the mirror of the mind of the writer. The orthography & punctuation of the books are mortifying to a degree—almost all the errors that were corrected in the proof-sheets appear intact in what should have been the fair copies. If Mr. Newby always does business in this way, few authors would like to have him for their publisher a second time.

Believe me, dear Sir,

Yours respectfully

C Bell.

MS Pforzheimer.

1. The final version of CB's preface to the second edition of *Jane Eyre*, which would be published on 22 Jan. 1848, includes a solemn tribute to Thackeray as 'the first social regenerator of the day', and ends with CB's dedication of the edition to him.
2. Leigh Hunt's *A Jar of Honey from Mount Hybla*, an illustrated Christmas gift-book of pastoral poetry and legends, issued by Smith, Elder by 15 Dec.

61. *To ?W. S. Williams, 31 December 1847*

[Haworth]

Dear Sir

I think, for the reasons you mention, it is better to substitute <u>Author</u> for <u>Editor</u>.[1] I should not be ashamed to be considered the author of "Wuthering Heights" and "Agnes Grey", but, possessing no real claim to that honour, I would rather not have it attributed to me, thereby depriving the true authors of their just meed.

You do very rightly and very kindly to tell me the objections made against "Jane Eyre"; they are more essential than the praises. I feel a sort of heart-ache when I hear the book called "godless" and "pernicious" by good and earnest-minded men—but I know that heart-ache will be salutary—at least I trust so.[2]

What is meant by the charges of "<u>trickery</u>" and "<u>artifice</u>" I have yet to comprehend.[3] It was no art in me to write a tale—it was no trick in Messrs. Smith & Elder to publish it. Where do the trickery and artifice lie?

I have received the Scotsman, and was greatly amused to see Jane Eyre likened to Rebecca Sharp[4]—the resemblance would hardly have occurred to me.

I wish to send this note by to-day's post and must therefore conclude in haste

I am, dear Sir

Yours respectfully | C Bell

MS Parrish Collection, Princeton.

1. i.e. of *Jane Eyre*. The title-page of the 2nd edition begins 'JANE EYRE: | **An Autobiography** | BY CURRER BELL.'
2. In *The Mirror of Literature, Amusement and Instruction* for Dec. 1847 George Searle Phillips ('January Searle') alleged that in *Jane Eyre* 'Religion is stabbed in the dark—our social distinctions attempted to be levelled, and all absurdly moral notions done away with.'
3. In *The Spectator* for 6 Nov. 1847 JE is said to have 'too much artifice'; its author 'resorts to trick' and 'everything is *made* to change just in the nick of time' (p. 1074).

4. The *Scotsman* found *JE* striking, powerful, and original; Jane was 'mentally' 'a sort of Becky
   Sharpe . . . in her self-possession and dexterous management' (22 Dec. 1847, p. [3]). In the Nov.
   1847 number of Thackeray's serialized *Vanity Fair*, Becky Sharp, as Mrs Rawdon Crawley, had
   been received by the Pitt Crawleys and had decided she 'could be a good woman' if she had 'five
   thousand a year'.

62. *To W. S. Williams, 4 January 1848*

[Haworth]

Dear Sir,

Your letter made me ashamed of myself that I should ever have uttered
a murmur, or expressed by any sign that I was sensible of pain from the
unfavourable opinions of some misjudging but well-meaning people. But indeed,
let me assure you, I am not ungrateful for the kindness which has been given me
in such abundant measure; I can discriminate the proportions in which blame
and praise have been awarded to my efforts; I see well that I have had less of the
former and more of the latter than I merit; I am not therefore crushed, though I
may be momentarily saddened by the frown, even of the good.

It would take a great deal to crush me, because I know, in the first place, that
my own intentions were correct; that I feel in my heart a deep reverence for
Religion, that impiety is very abhorrent to me; and in the second, I place firm
reliance on the judgment of some who have encouraged me. You and Mr. Lewes
are quite as good authorities in my estimation as Mr. Dilke[1] or the editor of the
Spectator,[2] and I would not under any circumstances, or for any opprobrium
regard with shame what my friends had approved: none but a coward would let
the detraction of an enemy outweigh the encouragement of a friend. You must
not therefore fulfil your threat of being less communicative in future; you must
kindly tell me all.

Miss Kavanagh's[3] view of the Maniac coincides with Leigh Hunt's. I agree
with them that the character is shocking, but I know that it is but too natural.
There is a phase of insanity which may be called moral madness, in which all
that is good or even human seems to disappear from the mind and a fiend-nature
replaces it. The sole aim and desire of the being thus possessed is to exasperate,
to molest, to destroy, and preternatural ingenuity and energy are often exercised
to that dreadful end. The aspect in such cases, assimilates with the disposition;
all seems demonized. It is true that profound pity ought to be the only sentiment
elicited by the view of such degradation, and equally true is it that I have not
sufficiently dwelt on that feeling; I have erred in making <u>horror</u> too predominant.
Mrs. Rochester indeed lived a sinful life before she was insane, but sin is itself a
species of insanity: the truly good behold and compassionate it as such.

"Jane Eyre" has got down into Yorkshire; a copy has even penetrated into this
neighbourhood: I saw an elderly clergyman[4] reading it the other day, and had the

satisfaction of hearing him exclaim "Why—they have got _____ School, and Mr _____ here, I declare! and Miss _____ (naming the originals of Lowood, Mr Brocklehurst, and Miss Temple). He had known them all: I wondered whether he would recognize the portraits, and was gratified to find that he did and that moreover he pronounced them faithful and just—he said too that Mr__ (Brocklehurst) "deserved the chastisement he had got."

He did not recognize "Currer Bell"—What author would be without the advantage of being able to walk invisible? One is thereby enabled to keep such a quiet mind. I make this small observation in confidence.

What makes you say that the notice in the "Westminster Review" is not by Mr. Lewes? It expresses precisely his opinions, and he said he would perhaps insert a few lines in that periodical.[5]

I have sometimes thought that I ought to have written to Mr. Lewes to thank him for his review in "Frazer";[6] and indeed I did write a note, but then it occurred to me that he did not require the author's thanks, and I feared it would be superfluous to send it, therefore I refrained; however though I have not expressed gratitude I have felt it.

I wish you too, many, many happy new years, and prosperity and success to you and yours—

Believe me &c
Currer Bell

I have recd. The Courier[7] and the Oxford Chronicle.[8]

MS HM 26008.

1. The antiquary and critic Charles Wentworth Dilke (1789–1864), editor (1830–46) of the *Athenaeum*, to which he continued to contribute. Perhaps CB thought he had reviewed *JE* in the *Athenaeum* for 23. Oct. 1847; but the reviewer was H. F. Chorley.
2. Robert Stephen Rintoul (1787–1858).
3. Julia Kavanagh (1824–77), novelist and biographer. She was befriended by W. S. Williams, whose description of her character and needy circumstances led CB to ask for a copy of the 2nd edn. of *JE* to be sent to her.
4. Possibly Mr Brontë's friend Revd Thomas Crowther, who had sent his daughters to Cowan Bridge school ('Lowood') in the 1830s. The 'originals' of Mr Brocklehurst and Miss Temple were the Revd William Carus Wilson (1791–1859) and Ann Evans, later Mrs James Connor (?1794–1857). See Brett Harrison, 'The real "Miss Temple"', *Brontë Society Transactions* 16. 85. 361–4.
5. Lewes had praised the originality and lifelike characters of *JE* as 'the best novel of the season'; it was 'certainly from the pen of a lady, and a clever one too' (*Westminster Review*, 48 (1848), 581–4).
6. In *Fraser's Magazine* for Dec. 1847, Lewes had found much to praise, especially *JE*'s reality. Nevertheless, he detected some of the 'phantasmagoria' popular with circulating library readers: 'St. John Rivers, the missionary, has a touch of the circulating library, but not enough to spoil the truth of the delineation.' See Letter 57 n. 2.
7. The *Courier* reviewer considered that *JE* marked the dawn of 'a new era of novel writing': 'we are no longer to groan beneath ill-written chronicles of fashionable life, nor dreadfully conceived details of melo-dramatic hue. ...We are strongly inclined to suspect that it is written by a woman, from the fact that the female characters are more truly and pleasingly sketched than the male' (1 Jan. 1848, pp. 9–10).

8. The *Oxford Chronicle* reviewer considered *JE* superior to most contemporary fiction because it presented 'character as it is to be met with in common life, and much that is calculated to interest and to improve the taste of the young' (1 Jan. 1848, p. [4]).

63. To G. H. Lewes, 12 January 1848

[Haworth]

Dear Sir

Mr. Williams did well on the whole to tell you I regretted not having sent the note of thanks I wrote, as I am thus afforded the opportunity of repairing that omission.

I thank you then sincerely for your generous review, and it is with a sense of double content I express my gratitude, because I am now sure the tribute is not superfluous or obtrusive. You were not severe on "Jane Eyre" you were very lenient: I am glad you told me my faults plainly in private, for in your public notice you touch on them so lightly, I should perhaps have passed them over thus indicated, with too little reflection.

I mean to observe your warning about being careful how I undertake new works:[1] my stock of materials is not abundant but very slender, and besides neither my experience, my acquirements, nor my powers are sufficiently varied to justify my ever becoming a frequent writer.

I tell you this because your article in "Frazer" left on me an uneasy impression that you were disposed to think better of the author of "Jane Eyre" than that individual deserved, and I would rather you had a correct than a flattering opinion of me, even though I should never see you.

If I ever <u>do</u> write another book, I think I will have nothing of what you call "melodrame"; I <u>think</u> so, but I am not sure. I <u>think</u> too I will endeavour to follow the counsel which shines out of Miss Austen's "mild eyes"; "to finish more, and be more subdued"; but neither am I sure of that.[2] When authors write best, or at least, when they write most fluently, an influence seems to waken in them which becomes their master, which will have its own way, putting out of view all behests but its own, dictating certain words, and insisting on their being used, whether vehement or measured in their nature; new moulding characters, giving unthought-of turns to incidents, rejecting carefully elaborated old ideas, and suddenly creating and adopting new ones. Is it not so? And should we try to counteract this influence? Can we indeed counteract it?

I am glad that another work of yours will soon appear;[3] most curious shall I be to see whether you will write up to your own principles, and work out your own theories. You did not do it altogether in "Ranthorpe", at least not in the latter part;[4] but the first portion was, I think, nearly without fault; then it had a pith, truth, significance in it which gave the book sterling value: but to write so one must have seen and known a great deal, and I have seen and known very little.

Why do you like Miss Austen so very much? I am puzzled on that point.

What induced you to say that you would rather have written "Pride & Prejudice" or "Tom Jones" than any of the Waverly Novels?[5]

I had not seen "Pride & Prejudice" till I read that sentence of yours, and then I got the book and studied it. And what did I find? An accurate daguerreotyped portrait of a common-place face; a carefully-fenced, highly cultivated garden with neat borders and delicate flowers—but no glance of a bright vivid physiognomy—no open country—no fresh air—no blue hill—no bonny beck.[6] I should hardly like to live with her ladies and gentlemen in their elegant but confined houses. These observations will probably irritate you, but I shall run the risk.

Now I can understand admiration of George Sand—for though I never saw any of her works which I admired throughout (even "Consuelo"[7] which is the best, or the best I have read, appears to me[8] to couple strange extravagance with wondrous excellence) yet she has a grasp of mind which if I cannot fully comprehend, I can very deeply respect; she is sagacious and profound; Miss Austen is only shrewd and observant. Am I wrong—or were you hasty in what you said?

If you have time, I should be glad to hear you further on this subject—if not—or if you think the questions frivolous do not trouble yourself to reply.

I am yours respectfully
C. Bell.

MS BL Add. 39763.

1. If the author had led a 'quiet, secluded life', new works should be 'planned and executed with excessive circumspection; for, unless a novel be built out of real experience, it can have no real success' (*Fraser's Magazine*, 36. 691).
2. 'What we most heartily enjoy and applaud, is truth in the delineation of life and character . . . Fielding and Miss Austen are the greatest novelists in our language' (*Fraser's Magazine*, 36. 687).
3. Lewes's second novel, *Rose, Blanche and Violet* (3 vols., Apr. 1848) has a complicated and incredible plot, and a melodramatic villainess—an adulterous stepmother with 'tiger eyes'.
4. Published anonymously in 1 vol., April 1847. The early chapters are based in part on Lewes's own experiences in the company of medical students, playwrights, and journalists; the later chapters are contrived and theatrical.
5. Thus in MS, for Sir Walter Scott's novels, of which the first was *Waverley* (1814), all well known and admired by CB. She disliked the novels of Henry Fielding, whose *Tom Jones* was published in 1749, and regarded him as cynical and immoral.
6. A northern word for a stream.
7. 1842–3. Sand's portrayal of the talented, conventual-looking pupil of a temperamental master may be echoed in Frances Henri, CB's heroine in *The Professor*.
8. CB wrote 'appears to me to me'.

64. *To G. H. Lewes, 18 January 1848*

[Haworth]

Dear Sir

I must write to you one more note, though I had not intended to trouble you again so soon. I have to agree with you, and to differ from you.

You correct my crude remarks on the subject of the "influence" well: I accept your definition of what the effects of that influence should be; I recognize the wisdom of your rules for its regulation.

About "Ranthorpe" I am right. By the last part of that work I understand only from page 271 to the end;[1] the first portion, in which I include the episode of the Hawbuckes, is the best. You yourself admit it. You say "the great merit of the book lies in its views of literature and literary life, and in the reflections." So I think, and it is in the first part these views are disclosed, and these reflections made. I like them. The views are just, the reflections profound; both are instructive.

What a strange sentence comes next in your letter! You say I must familiarize my mind with the fact that "Miss Austen is not a poetess, has no 'sentiment' (you scornfully enclose the word in inverted commas) no eloquence, none of the ravishing enthusiasm of poetry"—and then you add, I <u>must</u> "learn to acknowledge her as one of the greatest artists, of the greatest painters of human character, and one of the writers with the nicest sense of means to an end that ever lived."

The last point only will I ever acknowledge. Can there be a great Artist without poetry? What I call—what I will bend to as a great Artist, there cannot be destitute of the divine gift. But by <u>poetry</u> I am sure you understand something different to what I do—as you do by "sentiment". It is <u>poetry</u>, as I comprehend the word which elevates that masculine George Sand, and makes out of something coarse, something godlike. It is "sentiment", in my sense of the term, sentiment jealously hidden, but genuine, which extracts the venom from that formidable Thackeray, and converts what might be only corrosive poison into purifying elixir. If Thackeray did not cherish in his large heart deep feeling for his kind, he would delight to exterminate; as it is, I believe he wishes only to reform.

Miss Austen, being as you say without "sentiment", without <u>poetry</u>, may be—<u>is</u> sensible, real (more <u>real</u> than <u>true</u>) but she cannot be great.

I submit to your anger which I have now excited (for have I not questioned the perfection of your darling?) the storm may pass over me. Nevertheless I will, when I can (I do not know when that will be as I have no access to a circulating library) diligently peruse all Miss Austen's works, as you recommend.

I have something else to say. You mention the authoress of "Azeth the Egyptian":[2] you say you think I should sympathize "with her daring imagination and pictorial fancy." Permit me to undeceive you: with infinitely more relish can I sympathize with Miss Austen's clear common sense and subtle shrewdness. If you find no inspiration in Miss Austen's page, neither do you find there windy wordiness: to use your words once again, she exquisitely adapts her means to her end: both are very subdued, a little contracted, but never absurd. I have not read "Azeth", but I did read or begin to read a tale in the "New Monthly" from the same pen,[3] and harsh as the opinion may sound to you, I must candidly avow that I thought it both turgid and feeble: it reminded me of some of the most inflated and emptiest parts of Bulwer's novels:[4] I found in it neither strength, sense, nor originality.

You must forgive me for not always being able to think as you do, and still believe me

Yours gratefully
C Bell.

MS BL Add. 39763.

1. See Letter 57 n. 2. *Ranthorpe* includes an improbable scene in which the hero pursues a murderer, but is himself suspected of the murder. CB apparently approves of the sentimentality and high-flown renunciations of the Hawbucke episodes.
2. T. C. Newby had published *Azeth, the Egyptian, a Novel* by Eliza Lynn, later Linton (1822–98) in Dec. 1846. H. F. Chorley had noted its 'over-wrought, tedious,—florid' descriptions in an otherwise favourable review in the *Athenaeum*, 23. Jan. 1847.
3. *The Priest of Isis*, in *The New Monthly Magazine*, vols. 80 and 81, June–Sept. 1847, a historical novel ornamented with much overblown rhetoric.
4. The novelist and dramatist Edward George Earle Lytton Bulwer, later Bulwer-Lytton (1803–73). In her letter to Hartley Coleridge of 10 Dec. 1840 CB had mockingly declared that 'Bulwer and Cooper and Dickens and Warren' often wrote 'like boarding-school misses'.

65. *To W. S. Williams, 28 January 1848*

[Haworth]

Dear Sir

I need not tell you that when I saw Mr. Thackeray's letter enclosed under your cover, the sight made me very happy. It was some time before I dared open it, lest my pleasure in receiving it should be mixed with pain on learning its contents—lest—in short—the dedication should have been in some way unacceptable to him.[1]

And, to tell you the truth, I fear this must have been the case: he does not say so; his letter is most friendly in its noble simplicity—; but he apprises me at the commencement of a circumstance which both surprised and dismayed me.

I suppose it is no indiscretion to tell you this circumstance, for you doubtless know it already. It appears that his private position is in some point similar to that I have ascribed to Mr. Rochester; that thence arose a report that "Jane Eyre" had been written by a Governess in his family; and that the Dedication coming now has confirmed everybody in the surmise.

Well may it be said that Fact is often stranger than Fiction! The coincidence struck me as equally unfortunate and extraordinary. Of course I knew nothing whatever of Mr. Thackeray's domestic concerns: he existed for me only as an author: of all regarding his personality, station, connections, private history—I was, (and am still in a great measure) totally in the dark: but I am very, very sorry that my inadvertent blunder should have made his name and affairs a subject for common gossip.

The very fact of his not complaining at all—and addressing me with such kindness notwithstanding the pain and annoyance I must have caused him—increases my chagrin. I could not half express my regret to him in my answer, for I was restrained by the consciousness that that regret was just worth nothing at all—quite valueless for healing the mischief I had done.

Can you tell me anything more on this subject? Or can you guess in what degree the unlucky coincidence would affect him—whether it would pain him much and deeply? for he says so little himself on the topic, I am at a loss to divine the exact truth—but I fear—

Do not think, my dear Sir, from my silence respecting the advice you have at different times given me for my future literary guidance, that I am heedless of or indifferent to your kindness. I keep your letters, and not unfrequently refer to them. Circumstances may render it impracticable for me to act up to the letter of what you counsel, but I think I comprehend the spirit of your precepts—and trust I shall be able to profit thereby.[2] Details—Situations which I do not understand, and cannot personally inspect, I would not for the world meddle with, lest I should make even a more ridiculous mess of the matter than Mrs. Trollope did in her "Factory Boy"—besides—not one feeling, on any subject—public or private, will I ever affect that I do not really experience—yet though I must limit my sympathies—though my observation cannot penetrate where the very deepest political and social truths are to be learnt—though many doors of knowledge which are open for you, are for ever shut for me—though I must guess, and calculate, and grope my way in the dark and come to uncertain conclusions unaided and alone—where such writers as Dickens and Thackeray having access to the shrine and image of Truth, have only to go into the temple, lift the veil a moment and come out and say what they have seen—yet with every disadvantage, I mean still, in my own contracted way to do my best. Imperfect my best will be, and poor—and compared with the works of the true Masters—of that greatest modern Master, Thackeray, in especial (for it is him I at heart reverence with all my strength) it will be trifling—but I trust not affected or counterfeit.

> Believe me, my dear Sir,
> Yours with regard & respect
> Currer Bell.

MS Berg.

1. For the dedication, see Letter 60 n. 1, and for the insanity of Thackeray's wife, see Letter 56 n. 1.

2. Possibly Mr Williams had suggested that CB should write a novel comparable to Disraeli's *Coningsby* (1844) or *Sybil* (1845), designed to arouse public concern for the 'Condition of England'. Frances Trollope (1780–1863), the mother of Anthony Trollope, had written *The Life and Adventures of Michael Armstrong, the Factory Boy* (1839–40), 'to draw the attention of her countrymen to the fearful evils of the Factory System'. The work was spoilt by her exaggeration, inadequate knowledge, and unrealistic character-drawing.

66. *To W. S. Williams, 11 March 1848*

[Haworth]

Dear Sir

I have just received the copy of the 2nd. edition, and will look over it, and send the corrections as soon as possible: I will also, since you think it advisable, avail myself of the opportunity of a 3rd. edition to correct the mistake respecting the authorship of "Wuthering Heights" & "Agnes Grey."[1]

As to your second suggestion, it is, one can see at a glance, a very judicious and happy one; but I cannot adopt it, because I have not the skill you attribute to me. It is not enough to have the artist's eye; one must also have the artist's hand to turn the first gift to practical account. I have, in my day, wasted a certain quantity of Bristol board and drawing-paper, crayons and cakes of colour, but when I examine the contents of my portfolio now, it seems as if during the years it has been lying closed, some fairy had changed what I once thought sterling coin into dry leaves, and I feel much inclined to consign the whole collection of drawings to the fire; I see they have no value.[2] If then "Jane Eyre" is ever to be illustrated, it must be by some other hand than that of its author. But I hope no one will be at the trouble to make portraits of my characters: Bulwer- and Byron-heroes and heroines are very well—they are all of them handsome—; but my personages are mostly unattractive in look and therefore ill-adapted to figure in ideal portraits—At the best, I have always thought such representations futile.

You will not easily find a second Thackeray. How he can render with a few black lines and dots, shades of expression so fine, so real; traits of character so minute, so subtle, so difficult to seize and fix—I cannot tell; I can only wonder and admire.[3] Thackeray may not be a painter, but he is a wizard of a draughtsman; touched with his pencil, paper lives. And then his drawing is so refreshing; after the wooden limbs, one is accustomed to see pourtrayed by common-place illustrators, his shapes of bone and muscle, clothed with flesh, correct in proportion and anatomy, are a real relief—All is true in Thackeray: if Truth were again a Goddess, Thackeray should be her high-priest.

I read my preface over with some pain: I did not like it: I wrote it when I was a little enthusiastic, like you about the French Revolution;[4] I wish I had written it in a cool moment—I should have said the same things, but in a different manner. One may be as enthusiastic as one likes about an author who has been dead a century or two; but I see it is a fault to bore the public with enthusiasm about a living author. I promise myself to take better care in future. Still I will think as I please.

Are the London republicans—and you amongst the number—cooled down yet. I suppose not—because your French brethren are acting very nobly: the abolition of slavery, and of the punishment of death for political offences are two glorious deeds; but how will they get over the question of the organization of labour?[5] Such theories will be the sand-bank on which their vessel will run aground if they don't mind. Lamartine, there is no doubt, would make an excellent legislator for a nation of Lamartines—but where is that nation? I hope these observation[s] are sceptical and cool enough.

> Believe me, my dear Sir,
> Yours sincerely
> C Bell.

MS Eng 871, Houghton Library, Harvard University.

1. In her note to the 3rd edition of *Jane Eyre*, dated '*April 13th*, *1848*', but actually written on or by 13 Mar., CB explains that her 'claim to the title of novelist rests on this one work alone'.
2. Many of CB's drawings and paintings, made between 1828 and 1845, had been copies of engravings in Thomas Bewick's *A History of British Birds*, or in annuals such as *Friendship's Offering* and the *Forget Me Not*. She had, however, made some sensitive portraits of her sister Anne. See Christine Alexander and Jane Sellars, *The Art of the Brontës*, Cambridge University Press, 1995.
3. Thackeray illustrated many of his books, including *Vanity Fair*.
4. The Revolution which had begun with violent popular demonstrations in Paris against Louis Philippe (1773–1850; King of the French 1830–48) and his government after he had banned a patriotic banquet on 22 Feb. 1848. CB's preface to the second edition of *JE* might well cause offence by her superlative praise of Thackeray as a critic of society, and by her fiercely expressed defiance of critics who had attacked her supposed attitude to religion.
5. In *L'Organisation du travail* (1839) Louis Blanc had opposed capitalism and advocated workshops financed by the state but controlled by the workers. Alphonse de Lamartine (1790–1869), acting head of the French provisional government, had averted the threat of a mob rising on 25 Feb. 1848 by proclaiming the right of all citizens to employment, at whatever cost, under the inspection of the state or of associations organized by it. As CB foresaw, Lamartine's idealism was distrusted, and he failed to win general support.

67. *To Ellen Nussey, 3 May 1848*

[Haworth]

Dear Ellen,

All I can say to you about a certain matter is this: the report—if report there be—and if the lady,[1] who seems to have been rather mystified, had not dreamt what she fancied had been told to her—must have had its origin in some absurd misunderstanding. I have given no one a right either to affirm, or hint, in the most distant manner, that I am "publishing"[2]—(humbug!) Whoever has said it—if any one has, which I doubt—is no friend of mine. Though twenty books were ascribed to me, I should own none. I scout the idea utterly. Whoever, after I have distinctly rejected the charge, urges it upon me, will do an unkind and an ill-bred thing. The most profound obscurity is infinitely preferable to vulgar notoriety; and that notoriety I neither seek nor will have. If then any Birstalian or Gomersalian should presume to bore you on the subject,—to ask you what "novel" Miss Brontë has been "publishing,"—you can just say, with the distinct firmness of which you are perfect mistress, when you choose, that you are authorized by Miss Brontë to say, that she repels and disowns every accusation of the kind. You may add, if you please, that if any one has her confidence, you believe you have, and she has made no drivelling confessions to you on the subject. I am not absolutely at a loss to conjecture from what source this rumour has come; and I fear it has far from a friendly origin. I am not certain, however, and I should be very glad if I could gain certainty. Should you hear anything more, let me know it. I was astonished to hear of Miss Dixon[3] being likely to go to the West Indies; probably this too is only rumour. Your offer of "Simeon's Life"[4] is a very kind one, and I thank you for it. I dare say Papa would like to see the work very much, as he knew Mr. Simeon. Laugh or scold A[nn][5] out of the publishing notion; and believe me through all chances and changes, whether calumniated or let alone.

Yours faithfully,

C. Brontë.

MS untraced. Text based on Ellen Nussey's version in surviving copies of the Horsfall Turner printing.

1. Not identified.
2. In her *Life* of CB, Mrs Gaskell alleged that Charlotte had 'pledged her word to her sisters' that the secret of their authorship should not be revealed through her (ch. 16).
3. Mary Dixon, cousin of Mary Taylor. See Biographical Notes, p. xxxvii. Mary Dixon's brothers Joshua and Tom lived and worked in America for a time, and she had other relatives abroad, but it is unlikely that she joined them.
4. *Memoirs of the Life of the Rev'd Charles Simeon* (1847), ed. Revd William Carus. Mr Brontë had heard Simeon preach at Holy Trinity church, Cambridge, and was in sympathy with the Church of England evangelical movement in which he was a prominent leader.
5. Ellen's sister Ann Nussey.

68. *To W. S. Williams, 12 May 1848*

[Haworth]

My dear Sir

I take a large sheet of paper because I foresee that I am about to write another long letter, and for the same reason as before, viz—that yours interested me.

I have received the M[orning] Chron[icle][1] and was both surprised and pleased to see the passage you speak of, in one of its leading articles: an allusion of that sort seems to say more than a regular notice. I <u>do</u> trust I may have the power so to write in future as not to disappoint those who have been kind enough to think and speak well of "Jane Eyre"; at any rate I will take pains; but still whenever I hear my one book praised, the pleasure I feel is chastened by a mixture of doubt and fear; and, in truth, I hardly wish it to be otherwise: it is much too early for me to feel safe, or to take as my due the commendation bestowed.

Some remarks in your last letter on teaching commanded my attention. I suppose you never were engaged in tuition yourself, but if you had been, you could not have more exactly hit on the great qualification—I had almost said—the <u>one</u> great qualification necessary to the task: the faculty, not merely of acquiring but of <u>imparting</u> knowledge; the power of influencing young minds; that natural fondness for—that innate sympathy with children, which, you say, Mrs Williams[2] is so happy as to possess. He or She who possesses this faculty, this sympathy—though perhaps not otherwise highly accomplished—need never fear failure in the career of instruction. Children will be docile with them, will improve under them; parents will consequently repose in them confidence; their task will be comparatively light, their path comparatively smooth. If the faculty be absent, the life of a teacher will be a struggle from beginning to end. No matter how amiable the disposition, how strong the sense of duty, how active the desire to please; no matter how brilliant and varied the accomplishments, if the governess has not the power to win her young charge, the secret to instil gently and surely her own knowledge into the growing mind entrusted to her, she will have a wearing, wasting existence of it. To <u>educate</u> a child as, I daresay Mrs. Williams has educated her children, probably with as much pleasure to herself as profit to them, will indeed be impossible to the teacher who lacks this qualification; but, I conceive, should circumstances—as in the case of your daughters—compel a young girl notwithstanding to adopt a governesse's profession, she may contrive to <u>instruct</u> and even to instruct well. That is—though she cannot form the child's mind, mould its character, influence its disposition and guide its conduct as she would wish, she may give lessons—even good, clear, clever lessons in the various branches of knowledge; she may earn and doubly earn her scanty salary; as a daily governess, or a school-teacher she may succeed, but as a resident governess she will never—(except under peculiar and exceptional circumstances) be happy. Her deficiency will harass her not so much in school-time as in play-hours; the moments that would be rest and recreation to the governess who understood and could adapt herself to children, will be almost torture to her who has not that power; many a time, when her charge turns unruly on her hands, when the responsibility which she would wish to discharge faithfully and perfectly, becomes unmanageable to her, she will wish herself a housemaid or kitchen-girl, rather than a baited, trampled, desolate, distracted governess.

The Governesse's Institution[3] may be an excellent thing in some points of view—but it is both absurd and cruel to attempt to raise still higher the standard of acquirements. Already Governesses are not half nor a quarter paid for what they teach—nor in most instances is half or a quarter of their attainments required by their pupils. The young Teacher's chief anxiety, when she sets out in life, always is, to know a great deal; her chief fear that she should not know enough; brief experience will, in most instances, shew her that this anxiety has been misdirected. She will rarely be found too ignorant for her pupils; the demand on her knowledge will not often be larger than she can answer; but on her patience—on her self-control the requirement will be enormous; on her animal spirits (and woe be to her if these fail!) the pressure will be immense.

I have seen an ignorant nursery-maid who could scarcely read or write—by dint of an excellent, serviceable sanguine-phlegmatic temperament which made her at once cheerful and unmoveable; of a robust constitution and steady, unimpressionable nerves which kept her firm under shocks, and unharassed under annoyances—manage with comparative ease a large family of spoilt children, while their Governess lived amongst them a life of inexpressible misery; tyrannized over, finding her efforts to please and teach utterly vain, chagrined, distressed, worried—so badgered so trodden-on, that she ceased almost at last to know herself, and wondered in what despicable, trembling frame her oppressed mind was prisoned—and could not realize the idea of evermore being treated with respect and regarded with affection—till she finally resigned her situation and went away quite broken in spirit and reduced to the verge of decline in health.

Those who would urge on Governesses more acquirements do not know the origin of their chief sufferings. It is more physical and mental strength, denser moral impassibility that they require, rather than additional skill in arts or sciences. As to the forcing system, whether applied to Teachers or Taught—I hold it to be a cruel system.

It is true the world demands a brilliant list of accomplishments; for £20. per ann. it expects in one woman the attainments of several professors—but the demand is insensate—and I think should rather be resisted than complied with. If I might plead with you in behalf of your daughters—I should say—Do not let them waste their young lives in trying to attain manifold accomplishments. Let them try rather to possess thoroughly, fully one or two talents, then let them endeavour to lay in a stock of health, strength, cheerfulness; let them labour to attain self-control, endurance, fortitude, firmness; if possible, let them learn from their mother something of the precious art she possesses—these things, together with sound principles, will be their best supports—their best aids through a governesse's life.

As for that one who—you say has a nervous horror of exhibition[4]—I need not beg you to be gentle with her—I am sure you will not be harsh—but she must be firm with herself, or she will repent it in after-life—She should begin by degrees to endeavour to overcome her diffidence. Were she destined to enjoy an independent, easy existence she might respect her natural disposition to seek retirement and even cherish it as a shade-loving virtue—but since that is not her lot; since she is fated to make her way in the crowd—and to depend on herself, she should say—I will try and learn the art of self-possession—not that I may display my accomplishments—but that I may have the satisfaction of feeling that I am my own mistress—and can move and speak, undaunted by the fear of man. While however—I pen this piece of advice—I confess that it is much easier to give than to follow. What the sensations of the nervous are under the gaze of publicity none but the nervous know—and how powerless Reason and Resolution are to control them would sound incredible except to the actual sufferers.

The rumours you mention respecting the authorship of "Jane Eyre" amused me inexpressibly. The gossips are, on this subject, just where I should wish them to be; i.e. as far from the truth as possible—and as they have not a grain of fact to found their fictions upon—they fabricate pure inventions.[5] Judge Erle[6] must—I think have made up his Story—expressly for a hoax—the other <u>fib</u> is amazing—so circumstantial! Called on the author forsooth! Where did he live I wonder? In what purlieu of Cockayne?[7] Here I must stop—lest if I run on further I should fill another sheet—

Believe me yours sincerely Currer Bell

P.S. I must, after all, add a morsel of paper—for I find—on glancing over yours—that I have forgotten to answer a question you ask respecting my next work—I have not therein so far treated of governesses, as I do not wish it to resemble its predecessor. I often wish to say something about the "condition of women" question—but it is one respecting which so much "cant" has been talked, that one feels a sort of repugnance to approach it. It is true enough that the present market for female labour is quite overstocked—but where or how could another be opened? Many say that the professions now filled only by men should be open to women also—but are not their present occupants and candidates more than numerous enough to answer every demand? Is there any room for female lawyers, female doctors, female engravers, for more female artists, more authoresses? One can see where the evil lies—but who can point out the remedy? When a woman has a little family to rear and educate and a houshold to conduct, her hands are full, her vocation is evident—when her destiny isolates her—I suppose she must do what she can—live as she can—complain as little—bear as much—work as well as possible. This is not high theory—but I believe it is sound practice—good to put into execution while philosophers and legislators ponder over the better ordering of the Social System. At the same time, I conceive that when Patience has done its utmost and

Industry its best, whether in the case of Women or Operatives, and when both are baffled and Pain and Want triumphant—the Sufferer is free—is entitled—at last to send up to Heaven any piercing cry for relief—if by that cry he can hope to obtain succour.

MS BPM Gr. F 3.

1. On 9 May the *Chronicle* printed an article on the Governesses' Benevolent Institution, expressing compassion for the plight of governesses, and observing that the influential writing of Martineau, Edgeworth, Jane Austen, and especially the 'powerful authoress of "Jane Eyre" ' might do good. The writer had no doubt that *JE* was 'from a woman's pen'.
2. Née Margaret Eliza Hills (1805–87), married to Mr Williams on 14 Jan. 1826. They had eight children.
3. The Governesses' Benevolent Institution, supported by subscribers, was formed in June 1841 to alleviate the hardships of governesses. By May 1847 it could provide annuities, a savings bank, and a home for governesses during the intervals between their engagements. In addition, the 'Queen's College for Female Education, and for granting Certificates of Qualification to Governesses' had opened in Harley Street, London, on 1 May 1848.
4. At this date Mr Williams was especially concerned about his 18-year-old daughter Fanny Emily, who may be referred to here.
5. See Letter 58 n. 2.
6. Sir William Erle (1793–1880), justice of the Court of Queen's Bench from Oct. 1846. I have not traced his 'Story', or 'the other fib'.
7. Here, 'an imaginary country, the abode of luxury and idleness'.

69. *To W. S. Williams, 8 July 1848*

Chapter Coffee-House[1]
[London]

My dear Sir

Your invitation is too welcome not to be at once accepted. I should much like to see Mrs. Williams[2] and her children, and very much like to have a quiet chat with yourself. Would it suit you if we came to-morrow, after dinner—say about 7 o'clock and spent Sunday Evening with you?

We shall be truly glad to see you whenever it is convenient to you to call.

I am, my dear Sir
Yours faithfully
C Brontë

MS BPM Gr. F 4.

1. On 7 July Charlotte had received an abrupt letter from George Smith. He had been negotiating with Harper's, the American firm which had published *Jane Eyre* in Jan. 1848, to sell them advance copies of 'Currer's' next work. Smith had now heard that a new novel by 'Currer Bell' had been promised to a different American publisher. T. C. Newby, the English publisher of *Agnes Grey* and *Wuthering Heights*, had assured the rival American firm that to the best of his knowledge, 'Currer Bell' had written all three published novels in addition to a new work, *The Tenant of Wildfell Hall*. Since 'Currer' had promised her next novel to Smith, Elder, George Smith was alarmed and angry. Charlotte and Anne immediately decided to go to London to prove

their separate identities to Smith, and confront Newby with his lie. They had hurried through a thunderstorm to Keighley station and travelled by rail to Leeds, from where they 'whirled up' by the night-train to London. Arriving early in the morning, they took a room at the old-fashioned 'Chapter Coffee-House' near Paternoster Row, where Charlotte and Emily had stayed with their father in 1842 on their way to Brussels. They found their way to 65 Cornhill, where they greeted George Smith by giving him his own letter addressed to 'Currer Bell'. Astonished recognition was followed by a meeting with W. S. Williams, and eager invitations to meet Thackeray and G. H. Lewes. They refused, insisting that they should remain incognito, but agreed to meet Smith's mother and two sisters, Eliza and Sarah, and to accompany them to a performance of *The Barber of Seville* at Covent Garden, where they ruefully admired the ladies' fashionable clothes in contrast to their own simple country dresses. See Charlotte's lively account in her letter to Mary Taylor of 4 Sept. 1848 in *CBL* ii. 111–15.

2. For Mrs Williams, see Letter 68. There were eight children, Margaret Ellen, the eldest, Fanny Emily, William Francis ('Frank'), Mary Louisa, Robert Henry, Richard Smith, Thornton Arthur, and Ann Catherine, the youngest, who would later become a famous soprano singer.

70. *To W. S. Williams, 13 July 1848*

[Haworth]

My dear Sir

We reached home safely yesterday, and in a day or two I doubt not we shall get the better of the fatigues of our journey.

It was a somewhat hasty step to hurry up to Town as we did, but I do not regret having taken it. In the first place, mystery is irksome, and I was glad to shake it off with you and Mr. Smith, and to shew myself to you for what I am, neither more nor less, thus removing any false expectations that may have arisen under the idea that "Currer Bell" had a just claim to the masculine cognomen, he, perhaps, somewhat presumptuously, adopted—that he was, in short, of the "nobler sex."

I was glad also to see you and Mr. Smith, and am very happy now to have such pleasant recollections of you both, and of your respective families.[1] My satisfaction would have been complete could I have seen Mrs. Williams—the appearance of your children tallied on the whole accurately with the description you had given of them. Fanny was the one I saw least distinctly—I tried to get a clear view of her countenance, but her position in the room did not favour my efforts.

I have just read your article in the "John Bull";[2] it very clearly and fully explains the cause of the difference obvious between ancient and modern paintings. I wish you had been with us when we went over the Exhibition and the National Gallery[3]—a little explanation from a judge of Art would doubtless have enabled us to understand better what we saw; perhaps, one day, we may have this pleasure.

Accept my own thanks and my sister's for your kind attention to us while in Town, and believe me

Yours sincerely

Charlotte Brontë

I trust Mrs. Williams is quite recovered from her indisposition

MS Pierpont Morgan, MA 2696.

1. George Smith was then living with his mother, his sisters Eliza, Sarah, and Isabella, and his brother Alexander, at 4, Westbourne Place, Bayswater—at that date a new, quiet suburb. The Williams family lived at 3 Campden Hill Terrace, Kensington.
2. In *John Bull* for 1 and 3 July 1848 Mr Williams contrasted the 'want of atmosphere' in modern paintings with the 'luminous brilliancy' of the works of old masters.
3. At this period the Royal Academy shared the premises of the National Gallery in Trafalgar Square, opened in 1838.

71. *To Ellen Nussey, 28 July 1848*

[Haworth]

Dear Ellen

There were passages in your last letter which touched me, but I shall not dwell on them.

I am writing now, simply because I want to hear from you again—not because I have anything of the slightest interest to say. I observe in your letters you have not said much about Mary Gorham.[1] I hope you find reason to like her as well as ever; and indeed I cannot doubt that this is the case, as from your account of her I should conjecture that she is not of those characters that deteriorate with time and experience, or even that change, except for the better. Perhaps the presence of the two other young ladies[2] would, at first, keep you a little apart from her—but since you wrote last you will have been with her more alone, and can tell me more about her.

I should suppose the brothers,[3] from what you say, are of the better end of mankind; Mrs Gorham I always stand a little in awe of; I fancy her somewhat cold and severe, even suspicious. I think I confuse her character with that of our old friend Mrs. Taylor;[4] doubtless I do her great injustice. As to Mr. Gorham, he seems a noentity[5] to me; I daresay you may have described him to me at some time, but if so I have forgotten the very outlines of the portrait; you must sketch it again.

Anne continues to hear constantly—almost daily from her old pupils, the Robinsons—They are both now engaged to different gentlemen—and if they do not change their minds—which they have already done two or three times—will probably be married in a few months.[6] Not one spark of love does either of them profess for her future husband—One of them openly declares that interest alone guides her—and the other, poor thing! is acting according to her mother's wish, and is utterly indifferent herself to the man chosen for her. The lightest-headed of the two sisters takes a pleasure in the spectacle of her fine wedding-dresses and costly bridal presents—the more thoughtful can derive no gratification from these things and is much depressed at the contemplation of her future lot—Anne does her best to cheer and counsel her—and she seems to cling to her quiet, former governess as her only true friend. Of Mrs. R—I have not patience to speak—a worse mother a worse woman, I may say, I believe hardly exists—the more I hear of her the more deeply she revolts me—but I do not like to talk about her in a letter.[7]

Branwell is the same in conduct as ever—his constitution seems much shattered—Papa—and sometimes all of us have sad nights with him—he sleeps most of the day, and consequently will lie awake at night—But has not every house its trial? Write to me very soon, dear Nell—and believe me

Yours sincerely

C Brontë

MS BPM Gr. E 14.

1. Ellen was visiting her friend Mary Gorham (1826–1917), the daughter of a farmer who lived at Cakeham, near Chichester in Sussex.
2. Probably the Miss Fileys who left Cakeham on 15 July, according to a memorandum in EN's diary for 1849.
3. Revd John Gorham, MA Cantab. (1823–66), and James Gorham. The 'better end' is a dialect term for 'better kind or class'.
4. Mary Taylor's mother, Mrs Joshua Taylor (?1781–1856), model for the formidable and unpleasant Mrs Yorke in *Shirley*.
5. Thus in MS, for 'nonentity'.
6. Bessy Robinson (Elizabeth Lydia) was threatened in Dec. 1848 with a breach of promise case by her fiancé, Mr Milner. The matter had to be settled at law, Bessy's mother, Lydia Robinson, having to pay £85. 19s. 5d. and a separate sum of £6. 5s. 4d. Bessy was to marry William Jessop, a Derbyshire ironmaster, on 27 Nov. 1851. Bessy's sister Mary married the manufacturer Henry Clapham of Keighley on 19 Oct. 1848, and after his death in 1855, married the Revd George Hume Innes Pocock, vicar of Pentrich, Derbyshire.
7. CB may have believed that Mrs Robinson had seduced and then betrayed Branwell Brontë.

72. *To W. S. Williams, 31 July 1848*

[Haworth]

My dear Sir

I have lately been reading "Modern Painters",[1] and I have derived from the work much genuine pleasure and, I hope, some edification; at any rate it made me feel how ignorant I had previously been on the subject which it treats. Hitherto I have only had instinct to guide me in judging of art; I feel now as if I had been walking blindfold—this book seems to give me eyes—I <u>do</u> wish I had pictures within reach by which to test the new sense. Who can read these glowing descriptions of Turner's works without longing to see them? However eloquent and convincing the language in which another's opinion is placed before you, you still wish to judge for yourself. I like this author's style much; there is both energy and beauty in it: I like himself too, because he is such a hearty admirer. He does not give Turner half-measure of praise or veneration; he eulogizes, he reverences him (or rather his genius) with his whole soul. One can sympathize with that sort of devout, serious admiration (for he is no rhapsodist) one can respect it; and yet possibly many people would laugh at it. I am truly obliged to Mr. Smith for giving me this book, not having often met with one that has pleased me more.

You will have seen some of the notices of "Wildfell Hall".[2] I wish my Sister felt the unfavourable ones less keenly. She does not say much, for she is of a remarkably taciturn, still, thoughtful nature, reserved even with her nearest of kin, but I cannot avoid seeing that her spirits are depressed sometimes. The fact is neither she nor any of us expected that view to be taken of the book which has been taken by some critics: that it had faults of execution, faults of art was obvious; but faults of intention or feeling could be suspected by none who knew the writer. For my own part I consider the subject unfortunately chosen—it was one the author was not qualified to handle at once vigourously and truthfully—the simple and natural—quiet description and simple pathos are, I think, Acton Bell's forte. I liked "Agnes Grey" better than the present work.[3]

Permit me to caution you not to speak of my sisters when you write to me—I mean do not use the word in the plural. "Ellis Bell" will not endure to be alluded to under any other appellation than the "nom de plume". I committed a grand error in betraying <her> his identity to you and Mr. Smith—it was inadvertent—the words "we are three sisters" escaped me before I was aware—I regretted the avowal the moment I had made it; I regret it bitterly now, for I find it is against every feeling and intention of "Ellis Bell."

I was greatly amused to see in the "Examiner" of this week one of Newby's little cobwebs neatly swept away by some dexterous brush.[4] If Newby is not too old to profit by experience, such an exposure ought to teach him that "Honesty is indeed the best policy."

Your letter has just been brought to me—I must not pause to thank you—I should say too much. Our life is, and always has been, one of few pleasures, as you seem in part to guess; and for that reason we feel what passages of enjoyment come in our way, very keenly; and I think if you knew how pleased I am to get a long letter from you, you would laugh at me.

In return, however, I smile at you for the earnestness with which you urge on us the propriety of seeing something of London Society. There would be an advantage in it—a great advantage; yet it is one that no power on earth could induce "Ellis Bell" for instance to avail himself of—and even for "Acton" and "Currer", the experiment of an introduction to society would be more formidable than you, probably, can well imagine. An existence of absolute seclusion and unvarying monotony, such as we have long—I may say indeed—ever been habituated to tends I fear to unfit the mind for lively and exciting scenes—to destroy the capacity for social enjoyment.

The only glimpses of society I have ever had, were obtained in my vocation of governess—and some of the most miserable moments I can recall, were passed in drawing-rooms full of strange faces. At such times, my animal spirits would ebb gradually till they sank quite away—and when I could endure the sense of exhaustion and solitude no longer, I used to steal off, too glad to find any corner where I could really be alone.

Still, I know very well, that though that experiment of seeing the world might give acute pain for the time, it would do good afterwards; and as I have never that I remember, gained any important good without incurring proportionate suffering—I mean to try to take your advice some day—in part at least—to put off, if possible that troublesome egotism which is always judging and blaming itself—and to try—country spinster as I am—to get a view of some sphere where civilized humanity is to be contemplated.

I smile at you again for supposing that I could be annoyed by what you say respecting your religious and philosophical views, that I could blame you for not being able when you look amongst sects and creeds, to discover any one which you can exclusively and implicitly adopt as yours. I perceive myself that some light falls on Earth from Heaven—that some rays from the Shrine of Truth pierce the darkness of this Life and World—but they are few, faint and scattered—and who without presumption can assert that he has found the only true path upwards?

Yet Ignorance, Weakness and Indiscretion must have their creeds and forms; they must have their props—they cannot walk alone. Let them hold by what is purest in doctrine and simplest in ritual—something they must have.

I never read Emerson[5]—but the book which has had so healing an effect on your mind must be a good one. Very enviable is the writer whose words have fallen like a gentle rain on a soil that so needed and merited refreshment, whose influence has come like a genial breeze to lift a spirit which circumstances seem so harshly to have trampled. Emerson—if he has cheered you—has not written in vain.

May this feeling of self-reconcilement, of inward peace and strength continue! May you still be lenient with—be just to yourself! I will not praise nor flatter you—I should hate to pay those enervating compliments which tend to check the exertions of a mind that aspires after excellence, but I must permit myself to remark that if you had not something good and superior in you, something better, whether more <u>shewy</u> or not, than is often met with—the assurance of your friendship would not make one so happy as it does—nor would the advantage of your correspondence be felt as such a privilege.

I hope Mrs. Williams' state of health may soon improve and her anxieties lessen—blamable indeed are those who sow division where there ought to be peace—and specially deserving of the ban of society—

I thank both you and your family for keeping our secret—It will indeed be a kindness to us to persevere in doing so—and I own I have a certain confidence in the honourable discretion of a houshold of which you are the head.

Believe me
Yours very sincerely
C Brontë

W. S. Williams Esq—
This letter was partly written before I received yours. CB

MS Taylor Collection, Princeton.

1. Two volumes of *Modern Painters* (1843, 1846) by John Ruskin, published by Smith, Elder, were included in a parcel of books given to Charlotte and Anne to take home with them from London. *Modern Painters* was begun as a vindication of the genius of J. W. M. Turner.
2. Anne Brontë's second novel, *The Tenant of Wildfell Hall*, published on or about 27 June. While there had been unreserved praise by some reviewers, the influential *Spectator* for 8 July found that despite the novel's power, the writer seemed to have a 'morbid love for the coarse, not to say the brutal', and the *Athenaeum* for the same date found the novel 'most interesting' but complained that the Bells had a 'fancy for dwelling upon what is disagreeable'.
3. CB did not include *Tenant* in her edition of her sisters' works in 1850.
4. A correspondent had sent in one of Newby's advertisements from *The Times*, proclaiming his publication of 'Mrs Mackenzie Daniel's New Novel *My Sister Minnie*' and quoting in its praise seven notices, including 'Its merits cannot fail to secure success', allegedly from the *Examiner*, which disclaimed any such notice.
5. Ralph Waldo Emerson (1803–82), a leading exponent of transcendentalism. Mr. Williams had probably read his *Essays* of 1841 and 1844, and might have heard his London lectures at the Scientific and Literary Institution in Portman Square in June 1848.

73. To W. S. Williams, 14 August 1848

[Haworth]

My dear Sir

My Sister Anne thanks you, as well as myself, for your just critique on "Wildfell Hall." It appears to me that your observations exactly hit both the strong and weak points of the book, and the advice which accompanies them, is worthy of, and shall receive our most careful attention.

The first duty of an Author is—I conceive—a faithful allegiance to Truth and Nature; his second, such a conscientious study of Art as shall enable him to interpret eloquently and effectively the oracles delivered by those two great deities. The "Bells" are very sincere in their worship of Truth, and they hope so to apply themselves to the consideration of Art as to attain, one day, the power of speaking the language of conviction in the accents of persuasion; though they rather apprehend that whatever pains they take to modify and soften, an abrupt word or vehement tone will now and then occur to startle ears polite, whenever the subject shall chance to be such as moves their spirits within them.

I have already told you, I believe, that I regard Mr. Thackeray as the first of Modern Masters, and as the legitimate High Priest of Truth; I study him accordingly with reverence: he—I see—keeps the mermaid's tail below water, and only hints at the dead men's bones and noxious slime amidst which it wriggles;[1] but—his hint is more vivid than other men's elaborate explanations, and never is his satire whetted to so keen an edge as when with quiet mocking irony he modestly recommends to the approbation of the Public his own exemplary discretion and forbearance. The world begins to know Thackeray rather better than it did two years—or even a year ago—but as yet it only half knows him. His mind seems to me a fabric as simple and unpretending as it is deep-founded and enduring—there is no meretricious ornament to attract or fix a superficial glance: his great distinction of the Genuine is one that can only be fully appreciated with time. There is something, a sort of "still profound" revealed in the concluding part of "Vanity Fair" which the discernment of one generation will not suffice to fathom—a hundred years hence—if he only lives to do justice to himself—he will be better known than he is now. A hundred years hence, some thoughtful critic—standing and looking down on the deep waters—will see shining through them the pearl without price of a purely original mind—such a mind as the Bulwers[2] &c. his contemporaries—have not: not acquirements gained from study—but the thing that came into the world with him—his inherent genius: the thing that made him—I doubt not different as a child from other children, that caused him, perhaps, peculiar griefs and struggles in life—and that now makes him as a writer, unlike other writers. Excuse me for recurring to this theme—I do not wish to bore you.

You say, Mr Huntingdon[3] reminds you of Mr. Rochester—does he? Yet there is no likeness between the two; the foundation of each character is entirely different. Huntingdon is a specimen of the naturally selfish sensual, superficial man whose one merit of a joyous temperament only avails him while he is young and healthy, whose best days are his earliest, who never profits by experience, who is sure to grow worse, the older he grows. Mr. Rochester has a thoughtful nature and a very feeling heart; he is neither selfish nor self-indulgent; he is ill-educated, mis-guided, errs, when he does err, through rashness and inexperience: he lives for a time as too many other men live—but being radically better than most men he does not like that degraded life, and is never happy in it. He is taught the severe lessons of Experience and has sense to learn wisdom from them—years improve him—the effervescence of youth foamed away, what is really good in him still remains—his nature is like wine of a good vintage, time cannot sour—but only mellows him. Such at least was the character I meant to pourtray.

Heathcliffe,[4] again, of "Wuthering Heights", is quite another creation. He exemplifies the effects which a life of continued injustice and hard usage may produce on a naturally perverse, vindictive and inexorable disposition. Carefully trained and kindly treated, the black gypsey-cub might possibly have been reared into a human being, but tyranny and ignorance made of him a mere demon. The worst of it is, some of his spirit seems breathed through the whole narrative in which he figures: it haunts every moor and glen, and beckons in every fir-tree of the "Heights."

I must not forget to thank you for the "Examiner" and "Atlas" newspapers.[5] Poor Mr. Newby! It is not enough that the "Examiner" nails him by both ears to the pillory, but the "Atlas" brands a token of disgrace on his forehead. His is a deplorable plight, and he makes all matters worse by his foolish little answers to his assailants. It is a pity that he has no kind friend to suggest to him that he had better not bandy words with the "Examiner"—His plea about the "printer" was too ludicrous, and his second note is pitiable. I only regret that the names of "Ellis & Acton Bell" should perforce be mixed up with his proceedings. My sister Anne wishes me to say that should she ever write another work, Mr. Smith will certainly have the first offer of the copyright.

I hope Mrs. Williams health is more satisfactory than when you last wrote—with every good wish to yourself & your family

Believe me, my dear Sir,
Yours sincerely
C Brontë

MS Berg.

1. In the final number of *Vanity Fair*, published in July 1848, Thackeray boasts with 'modest pride' that he has presented the 'syren' Becky with due decorum, never showing 'the monster's hideous tail above water . . . Those who like may peep down . . . and see it writhing and twirling, diabolically hideous and slimy, flapping amongst bones, or curling round corpses' (ch. 64).
2. Bulwer Lytton. See Letter 14 n. 16, and CB's reference to 'the most inflated and emptiest parts of Bulwer's novels' in Letter 64.
3. The dissipated husband of the heroine in *Tenant*.
4. Thus in MS.
5. See the previous letter, n. 4. Newby alleged in the *Examiner* for 5 August that the erroneous reference to a review of Mrs Daniel's novel 'was caused by the printer omitting *Glasgow*, the extract being from the *Glasgow Examiner*'. Newby had also advertised *Tenant* by referring, in the *Morning Herald* for 29 July, to a 'very warm eulogium from "The Examiner"'. The book was not noticed in the *Examiner* till the afternoon of that day.' The reviewer of *Tenant* in the *Atlas* for 12 Aug. 1848 objected to Newby's quotations from alleged reviews of *Agnes Grey* on the fly-leaf of *Tenant*: the words 'this is a colossal performance' were an inaccurate quotation from a review of *Wuthering Heights*.

74. *To W. S. Williams, ?early September 1848*

My dear Sir

We are very much obliged to you for sending the notice from "the Rambler".[1] It is indeed acting the part of a true friend to apprise an author faithfully of what opponents say, and profess to think of his works. Your own comments also demand our best thanks; I have read them with attention and feel their justice.

Defects there are both in "Jane Eyre" and "Wildfell Hall" which it will be the authors' wisdom and duty to endeavour to avoid in future; other points there are to which they deem it incumbent on them firmly to adhere, whether such adherence bring popularity or unpopularity, praise or blame. The standard heros and heroines of novels, are personages in whom I could never, from childhood upwards, take an interest, believe to be natural, or wish to imitate: were I obliged to copy these characters, I would simply—not write at all. Were I obliged to copy any former novelist, even the greatest, even Scott, in anything, I would not write—Unless I have something of my own to say, and a way of my own to say it in, I have no business to publish; unless I can look beyond the greatest Masters, and study Nature herself, I have no right to paint; unless I can have the courage to use the language of Truth in preference to the jargon of Conventionality, I ought to be silent.

I am glad you have seen and approve of the preface to the 2nd. editn. of "Wildfell Hall"; I, too, thought it sensible.[2]

I have not yet thanked you for the letter you wrote on your return from Ramsgate. Your holiday was short, but you seem to have enjoyed it fully. It seems hard that a mind which can so well appreciate the sweet, quiet pleasures of the Country—should be doomed to the drudging life of the city; your lot reminds one but too forcibly of that of the caged bird—but you do well to bear it with fortitude—and to cultivate content even in a position for which you certainly were not naturally intended. Is it not a mark of the truest courage to endure serenely evils we cannot remedy—? And if we are patient and persevering, may not Providence in time work out for us the deliverance we are unable to achieve alone? Judging from the tone of your letters, your mind is more at ease now than it was six months ago—is it too much to hope that your prospects and position will continue to improve—and that your mental peace will thus be permanently confirmed? Much of your domestic happiness must depend on the restoration of your wife's health, and on the prosperity of your promising family—I trust that her complete recovery—and their continued welfare—may combine to cheer and comfort you. Mr. Smith is certainly most happy in his selection of the books he gives me; I read Lamb's letters[3] with a sort of sad pleasure I cannot describe; a more touching history than that of himself and his Sister, was never imagined: we like Human Nature the better for their gentle sakes—Yet Charles Lamb was not perfect—he had his piteous frailty—(I wish it had been absent by the by—without that single fault his character would have been pure as moonlight). Mary Lamb too had her terrible calamity—How different were their lives and Natures to those attributed to the idealized creations of Romance!

The description of London Literary Society in those days is singularly vivid and interesting; does it at all resemble what is to be met with there now?

I am glad the little vol. of the Bells' poems is likely to get into Mr. Smith's hands.[4] I should feel unmixed pleasure in the chance of its being brought under respectable auspices before the public, were Currer Bell's share in its contents absent—but of that portion I am by no means proud—much of it was written in early youth—I feel it now to be crude and rhapsodical. Ellis Bell's is of a different stamp—of its sterling excellence I am deeply convinced, and have been from the first moment the M.S. fell by chance into my hands. The pieces are short, but they are very genuine: they stirred my heart like the sound of a trumpet when I read them alone and in secret. The deep excitement I felt forced from me the confession of the discovery I had made—I was sternly rated at first for having taken an unwarrantable liberty—this I expected—for Ellis Bell is of no flexible or ordinary materials—but by dint of entreaty and reason—I at last wrung out a reluctant consent to have the "rhymes" (as they were contemptuously termed) published—The author never alludes to them—or when she does—it is with scorn—but I know—no woman that ever lived—ever wrote such poetry before—condensed energy, clearness, finish—strange, strong pathos are their characteristics—utterly different from the weak diffusiveness—the laboured yet most feeble wordiness which dilute the writings of even very popular poetesses.[5] This is my deliberate and quite impartial opinion to which I should hold if all the critics in the periodical press held a different one—as I should to the supremacy of Thackeray in fiction—

Believe me
Yours sincerely
C Bell—

MS BL Ashley 164.

1. The reviewer of *Tenant* in this Catholic journal believed that it was written by the same female author as *Jane Eyre*. Both novels were clever, but offensive, sensual, and full of vulgar characters. The heroine of *Tenant* recounts 'disgusting and revolting scenes' detailing with offensive minuteness 'debauchery, blasphemy, and profaneness'. In both novels the heroines' religious sentiments are 'either false and bad, or . . . vague and unmeaning' (*The Rambler*, vol. 3, pt. ix, 65–6).

2. Anne's preface is dated 'July 22nd, 1848'. She responded forcefully to critics who failed to understand her intentions in writing the novel: 'I wished to tell the truth, for truth always conveys its own moral to those who are able to receive it. . . . if I have warned one rash youth from following' in the steps of Huntingdon and his profligate companions 'or prevented one thoughtless girl from falling into the very natural error of my heroine, the book has not been written in vain'.

3. *Final Memorials of Charles Lamb, consisting chiefly of his Letters not before published, with sketches of some of his companions.* By Thomas Noon Talfourd, 2 vols. (Moxon, July 1848). Talfourd writes sympathetically of Lamb's drinking, as a relief from the 'distressful drama' of the family's tragedy. In one of her fits of insanity, Lamb's sister Mary had killed their mother.
4. Aylott and Jones decided to dispose of their unsold stock of the Bells' *Poems* to Smith, Elder and Co., who acquired 961 copies—probably the remainder of a print-run of 1,000 copies—before 7 Nov. 1848.
5. CB disliked the 'wordy, intricate, obscure style' of Elizabeth Barrett Browning. Other popular poetesses were Camilla Toulmin (1812–95), Caroline Norton (1808–77), and Eliza Cook (1818–89).

75. To W. S. Williams, 2 October 1848

[Haworth]

My dear Sir

"We have buried our dead out of our sight."[1] A lull begins to succeed the gloomy tumult of last week. It is not permitted us to grieve for him who is gone as others grieve for those they lose; the removal of our only brother must necessarily be regarded by us rather in the light of a mercy than a chastisement. Branwell was his Father's and his sisters' pride and hope in boyhood, but since Manhood, the case has been otherwise. It has been our lot to see him take a wrong bent; to hope, expect, wait his return to the right path; to know the sickness of hope deferred, the dismay of prayer baffled, to experience despair at last; and now to behold the sudden early obscure close of what might have been a noble career.

I do not weep from a sense of bereavement—there is no prop withdrawn, no consolation torn away, no dear companion lost—but for the wreck of talent, the ruin of promise, the untimely dreary extinction of what might have been a burning and a shining light.[2] My brother was a year my junior; I had aspirations and ambitions for him once—long ago—they have perished mournfully—nothing remains of him but a memory of errors and sufferings—There is such a bitterness of pity for his life and death—such a yearning for the emptiness of his whole existence as I cannot describe—I trust time will allay these feelings.

My poor Father naturally thought more of his only son than of his daughters, and much and long as he had suffered on his account—he cried out for his loss like David for that of Absalom—My Son! My Son! And refused at first to be comforted[3]—and then—when I ought to have been able to collect my strength, and be at hand to support him—I fell ill with an illness whose approaches I had felt for some time previously—and of which the crisis was hastened by the awe and trouble of the death-scene—the first I had ever witnessed.[4] The past has seemed to me a strange week—Thank God—for my Father's sake—I am better now—though still feeble—I wish indeed I had more general physical strength—the want of it is sadly in my way. I cannot do what I would do, for want of sustained animal spirits—and efficient bodily vigour.

My unhappy brother never knew what his sisters had done in literature—he was not aware that they had ever published a line; we could not tell him of our efforts for fear of causing him too deep a pang of remorse for his own time misspent, and talents misapplied—Now he will <u>never</u> know. I cannot dwell longer on the subject at present; it is too painful.

I thank you for your kind sympathy—and pray earnestly that your sons may all do well and that you may be spared the sufferings my Father has gone through.

Yours sincerely

C Brontë

MS Pierpont Morgan, MA 2696.

1. Cf. Genesis 23: 4. Branwell Brontë had died on 24 Sept. The shock of his death had prostrated CB, who had had to ask her sister Anne to inform Mr Williams of the bereavement. The local doctor John Bateman Wheelhouse had been called in on Saturday 23 Sept., when Branwell was unable to rise from his bed, and had told the family that death was imminent. The death certificate stated the cause as 'Chronic bronchitis—Marasmus' (wasting with no apparent disease). CB believed he had died of tuberculosis. His heavy drinking and dependence on opiates were no doubt contributory causes.
2. John 5: 35.
3. Cf. 2 Samuel 18: 33 and Psalm 77: 2.
4. Mrs Brontë died in 1821, and Charlotte's sister Elizabeth in 1825. On both occasions CB was at home, but was probably not present at the point of death. When their sister Maria died at Haworth on 6 May 1825, Charlotte and Emily were still at the Cowan Bridge Clergy Daughters' School.

76. To W. S. Williams, 6 October 1848

[Haworth]

My dear Sir

I thank you for your last truly friendly letter, and for the number of "Blackwood" which accompanied it;[1] both arrived at a time when a relapse of illness had depressed me much, both did me good—especially the letter. I have only one fault to find with your expressions of friendship; they make me ashamed, because they seem to imply that you think better of me than I merit. I believe you are prone to think too highly of your fellow-creatures in general—to see too exclusively the good points of those for whom you have a regard. Disappointment must be the inevitable result of this habit. Believe all Men, and women too, to be dust and ashes—a spark of the divinity now and then kindling in the dull heap—that is all.

When I looked on the noble face and forehead of my dead brother (Nature had favoured him with a fairer outside, as well as a finer constitution than his Sisters) and asked myself what had made him go ever wrong, tend ever downwards, when he had so many gifts to induce to, and aid in an upward course—I seemed to receive an oppressive revelation of the feebleness of humanity; of the inadequacy of even genius to lead to true greatness if unaided by religion and principle. In the value, or even the reality of these two things he would never believe till within a few days of his end, and then all at once he seemed to open his heart to a conviction of their existence and worth. The remembrance of this strange change now comforts my poor Father greatly. I myself, with painful, mournful joy, heard him praying softly in his dying moments, and to the last prayer which my father offered up at his bedside, he added "amen". How unusual that word appeared from his lips—of course you who did not know him, cannot conceive. Akin to this alteration was that in his feelings towards his relatives—all bitterness seemed gone.

When the struggle was over—and a marble calm began to succeed the last dread agony—I felt as I had never felt before that there was peace and forgiveness for him in Heaven. All his errors—to speak plainly—all his vices seemed nothing to me in that moment; every wrong he had done, every pain he had caused, vanished; his sufferings only were remembered; the wrench to the natural affections only was felt. If Man can thus experience total oblivion of his fellow's imperfection—how much more can the Eternal Being who made man, forgive his creature!

Had his sins been scarlet in their dye—I believe now they are white as wool[2]—He is at rest—and that comforts us all—long before he quitted this world—Life had no happiness for him.

"Blackwoods" mention of "Jane Eyre" gratified me much—and will gratify me more, I daresay, when the ferment of other feelings than that of literary ambition, shall have a little subsided in my mind.

The doctor has told me I must not expect too rapid a restoration to health, but to-day, I certainly feel better.

I am thankful to say my Father has hitherto stood the storm well, and so have my <u>dear</u> sisters to whose untiring care and kindness I am chiefly indebted for my present state of convalescence.

Believe me, my dear Sir
Yours faithfully
C Brontë

MS BPM Bon 204.

1. *Blackwood's Edinburgh Magazine*, 64 (Oct. 1848), containing 'a few words about novels' by 'Aquilius', i.e. Revd John Eagles (1783–1855). *JE* is praised as 'very pathetic', 'very singular; and so like truth', uniting 'the strongest passion and the strongest principle'. 'It is not a book for Prudes . . . it is for the enjoyment of a feeling heart and vigorous understanding.'
2. Cf. Isaiah 1: 18.

77. To W. S. Williams, 22 November 1848

My dear Sir

I put your most friendly letter into Emily's hands as soon as I had myself perused it, taking care however not to say a word in favour of homœopathy,[1] that would not have answered; it is best usually to leave her to form her own judgment and especially not to advocate the side you wish her to favour; if you do she is sure to lean in the opposite direction, and ten to one will argue herself into non-compliance. Hitherto she has refused medicine, rejected medical advice—no reasoning, no entreaty has availed to induce her to see a physician; after reading your letter she said "Mr. Williams' intention was kind and good, but he was under a delusion—Homœopathy was only another form of Quackery". Yet she may reconsider this opinion and come to a different conclusion; her second thoughts are often the best.

The North American Review is worth reading—there is no mincing the matter there—what a bad set the Bells must be! What appalling books they write![2] To-day as Emily appeared a little easier, I thought the Review would amuse her so I read it aloud to her and Anne. As I sat between them at our quiet but now somewhat melancholy fireside, I studied the two ferocious authors. Ellis the "man of uncommon talents but dogged, brutal and morose", sat leaning back in his easy chair drawing his impeded breath as he best could, and looking, alas! piteously pale and wasted—it is not his wont to laugh—but he smiled half-amused and half in scorn as he listened. Acton was sewing, no emotion ever stirs him to loquacity, so he only smiled too, dropping at the same time a single word of calm amazement to hear his character so darkly pourtrayed. I wonder what the Reviewer would have thought of his own sagacity, could he have beheld the pair, as I did. Vainly too might he have looked round for the masculine partner in the firm of "Bell & Co."[3] How I laugh in my sleeve when I read the solemn assertions that "Jane Eyre" was written in partnership, and that it "bears the marks of more than one mind, and one sex."

The wise critics would certainly sink a degree in their own estimation if they knew that yours or Mr. Smith's was the first masculine hand that touched the M.S. of "Jane Eyre"—and that till you or he read it, no masculine eye had scanned a line of its contents—no masculine ear heard a phrase from its pages. However the view they take of the matter rather pleases me than otherwise—if they like I am not unwilling they should think a dozen ladies and gentlemen aided at the compilation of the book—Strange patch-work it must seem to them, this chapter being penned by Mr., and that by Miss or Mrs. Bell; that character or scene being delineated by the husband—that other by the wife! The gentleman of course doing the rough work—the lady getting up the finer parts. I admire the idea vastly.

I have read "Madeleine".[4] It is a fine pearl in simple setting. Julia Kavanagh has my esteem—I would rather know her than many far more brilliant personages—somehow my heart leans more to her than to Eliza Lynn for instance.[5] Not that I have read either "Amymone" or "Azeth"—but I have seen extracts from them which I found it literally impossible to digest. They presented to my imagination Lytton Bulwer in petticoats—an overwhelming vision. By the by the American Critic talks admirable sense about Bulwer[6]—Candour obliges me to confess that.

I must abruptly bid you goodbye for the present

Yours sincerely Currer Bell.

MS BL Ashley 2452.

1. A system founded by Christian Friedrich Samuel Hahnemann (1755–1843) by which diseases are treated with very small doses of drugs which would produce in a healthy person symptoms like those of the disease. Emily Brontë had been suffering since October from a persistent cold and cough, pain in the chest, and shortness of breath. Yet, as Charlotte told Mr Williams on 2 Nov., 'she neither seeks nor will accept sympathy . . . you must look on, and not dare to say a word; a painful necessity for those to whom her health and existence are as precious as the life in their veins. When she is ill there seems to be no sunshine in the world for me.'

2. In the *North American Review* for Oct. 1848, Edwin Percy Whipple asserted that *Jane Eyre* fever had rapidly infected New England when it was hinted that 'it was a book which no respectable man should bring into his family circle'. *Wuthering Heights* (announced as by the same author, 'Acton Bell') was eagerly purchased, but created widespread disappointment: in it a 'complete science of human brutality' was developed; and in *Tenant*, the author 'succeeds in making profligacy disgusting', but 'fails in making virtue pleasing. His depravity is total depravity.'

3. *Jane Eyre* 'bears the marks of more than one mind and one sex', showing that Currer Bell 'divides the authorship . . . with a brother and sister'. The novel's prevailing masculine tone . . . the shocking 'profanity, brutality, and slang' of Mr. Rochester, and scenes exhibiting 'mere animal appetite, and . . . courtship after the manner of kangaroos' all hint that the author of *Wuthering Heights* is at work; but some 'niceties of thought and emotion' reveal a woman's hand. The 'whole firm of Bell & Co. seem to have a sense of the depravity of human nature peculiarly their own' (*North American Review*, 47. 355–7).

4. *Madeleine, a Tale of Auvergne*, by Julia Kavanagh (1824–77); published by Bentley in Oct. 1848. Kavanagh claims that her novel is founded on reality, and is intended to display the power of religious faith, and the heroic devotedness of a simple peasant girl.

5. See Letter 64 n. 2. *Amymone; A Romance of the Days of Pericles*. By the author of 'Azeth the Egyptian' was published by Bentley in 1848.

6. Bulwer Lytton's *Harold, the Last of the Saxon Kings* (1848) was one of the 'Novels of the Season' reviewed with those of the Bells. The reviewer declared that Bulwer presented an effete hothouse world in a sombre and unsatisfying tone and with a superficial rhetoric: 'The heart never speaks its own language in Bulwer's writings' (*North American Review*, 47. 366).

78. To Ellen Nussey, 23 November 1848

[Haworth]

Dear Ellen

Whatever my inclination may be to let all correspondence alone for the present—I feel that to you at least I ought to write a line.

I told you Emily was ill in my last letter—she has not rallied yet—she is <u>very</u> ill: I believe if you were to see her your impression would be that there is no hope: a more hollow, wasted pallid aspect I have not beheld. The deep tight cough continues; the breathing after the least exertion is a rapid pant—and these symptoms are accompanied by pain in the chest and side.

Her pulse, the only time she allowed it to be felt, was found to be at 115 per minute. In this state she resolutely refuses to see a doctor; she will give no explanation of her feelings, she will scarcely allow her illness to be alluded to. Our position is, and has been for some weeks, exquisitely painful. God only knows how all this is to terminate. More than once I have been forced boldly to regard the terrible event of her loss as possible and even probable. But Nature shrinks from such thoughts. I think Emily seems the nearest thing to my heart in this world.

Miss Mary Robinson is just married to Mr Henry Clapham, a relation of the Sugdens[1]—a low match for her—she feels it so—she does not, in writing to Anne, even profess to be happy.

Mrs. Robinson is married too—She is now Lady Scott[2]—her daughters say she is in the highest spirits—The new Mrs Clapham is said to be cutting a prodigious dash. She infuriates the Keighley gentry with her pride and assumption of superiority. She & her sister[3] threaten to pay us a visit—they have written to ask if they can bring the carriage up to the house—we have told them "yes," as we think if they bring it once through those breakneck turnings—they will not be in a hurry to try the experiment again—it is our wish and intention to have as little to do with them as possible, and sorry we are that they have brought their grandeur and weakness so near.

Write to me soon, dear Ellen, and believe me

Yours sincerely
C Brontë

MS BPM Gr. E 16.

1. Anne Brontë's former pupil, youngest daughter of Mrs Lydia Robinson, had married Henry Clapham, son of Samuel Blakey Clapham, the owner of a worsted spinning mill in Keighley, on 19 Oct. 1848. The Sugdens were wealthy relatives of the mill-owning Greenwoods of Haworth.
2. Mrs Robinson and her family had finally left Thorp Green in Mar. 1847, and had gone to live with relatives. Mrs Robinson chose to stay at Great Barr Hall, near Birmingham, the home of her cousin Catherine Juliana, wife of the wealthy Sir Edward Dolman Scott (?1797–1851). Catherine, already ill, had died in Aug. 1848. Mrs Robinson and Sir Edward married in Bath on 8 Nov. the same year, and returned to live at Great Barr Hall.
3. Elizabeth Lydia ('Bessy').

79. *To W. S. Williams, 7 December 1848*

[Haworth]

My dear Sir

I duly received Dr. Curie's work on Homœopathy,[1] and ought to apologize for having forgotten to thank you for it. I will return it when I have given it a more attentive perusal than I have yet had leisure to do. My sister has read it, but as yet she remains unshaken in her former opinion: she will not admit there can be efficacy in such a system. Were I in her place it appears to me that I should be glad to give it a trial, confident that it can scarcely do harm and might do good.

I can give no favourable report of Emily's state. My Father is very despondent about her. Anne and I cherish hope as well as we can—but her appearance and her symptoms tend to crush that feeling. Yet I argue that the present emaciation, cough, weakness, shortness of breath are the results of inflammation now, I trust, subsided, and that with time, these ailments will gradually leave her, but my father shakes his head and speaks of others of our family once similarly afflicted,[2] for whom he likewise persisted in hoping against hope, and who are now removed where hope and fear fluctuate no more. There were, however, differences between their case and hers—important differences I think—I <u>must</u> cling to the expectation of her recovery; I <u>cannot</u> renounce it.

Much would I give to have the opinion of a skilful professional man. It is easy, my dear sir, to say there is nothing in medicine and that physicians are useless but we naturally wish to procure aid for those we love when we see them suffer—most painful is it to sit still, look on and do nothing. Would that my sister added to her many great qualities the humble one of tractability! I have again and again incurred her displeasure by urging the necessity of seeking advice, and I fear I must yet incur it again and again. Let me leave the subject—I have no right thus to make you a sharer in our sorrows.

I am indeed surprised that Mr. Newby should say that he is to publish another work by Ellis and Acton Bell.[3] Acton has had quite enough of him. I think I have before intimated that that author never more intends to have Mr. Newby for a publisher. Not only does he seem to forget that engagements made should be fulfilled—but by a system of petty and contemptible manœuvring he throws an air of charlatanry over the works of which he has the management: this does not suit the "Bells"; they have their own rude north-country ideas of what is delicate, honourable and gentlemanlike: Newby's conduct in no sort corresponds with these notions; they have found him—I will not say what they have found him; two words that would exactly suit him are at my pen point, but I shall not take the trouble to employ them.

Ellis Bell is at present in no condition to trouble himself with thoughts either of writing or publishing; should it please Heaven to restore his health and strength he reserves to himself the right of deciding whether or not Mr. Newby has forfeited every claim to his second work.

I have not yet read the 2nd. No. of Pendennis;[4] the first I thought rich in indication of ease, resource, promise—but it is not Thackeray's way to develop his full power all at once: "Vanity Fair" began very quietly—it was quiet all through, but the stream as it rolled gathered a resistless volume and force—such—I doubt not—will be the case with "Pendennis".

You must forget what I said about Eliza Lynn[5]—she may be the best of human beings—and I am but a narrow-minded fool to express prejudice against a person I have never seen.

Believe me, my dear Sir, in haste

Yours sincerely

C Brontë

MS BPM Gr. F 6.

1. Dr Paul Francis Curie (MD Paris 1823), a homoeopathic physician and lecturer, was the author of *Principles of Homœopathy* (1836), *Practice of Homœopathy* (1837), and other works.
2. Maria Brontë (1813–25) and Elizabeth Brontë (1815–25).
3. A letter from Newby, dated 15 Feb. 1848, begins 'Dear Sir' and goes on, 'I am much obliged by your kind note & shall have great pleasure in making arrangements for your next novel.' Since it was found in Emily Brontë's writing desk, along with five reviews of *Wuthering Heights*, it may have been directed to her.
4. Thackeray's *The History of Pendennis* appeared in parts from Nov. 1848 to Dec. 1850, and in 2 vols. in 1850. The quietness of the opening was deliberate.
5. See Letter 64 nn. 2 and 3. W. S. Williams may have known her personally.

80. *To Ellen Nussey, 23 December 1848*

[Haworth]

Dear Ellen

Emily suffers no more either from pain or weakness now. She never will suffer more in this world—she is gone after a hard, short conflict. She died on Tuesday, the very day I wrote to you. I thought it very possible then she might be with us still for weeks and a few hours afterwards she was in Eternity—Yes—there is no Emily in Time or on Earth now—yesterday, we put her poor, wasted mortal frame quietly under the Church pavement. We are very calm at present, why should we be otherwise?—the anguish of seeing her suffer is over—the spectacle of the pains of Death is gone by—the funeral day is past—we feel she is at peace—no need now to tremble for the hard frost and keen wind—Emily does not feel them. She has died in a time of promise—we saw her torn from life in its prime—but it is God's will—and the place where she is gone is better than that she has left.

God has sustained me in a way I marvel at through such agony as I had not conceived. I now look at Anne and wish she were well and strong—but she is neither, nor is papa—Could you now come to us for a few days? I would not ask you to stay long. Write and tell me if you could come next week and what day and by what train—I would try to send a gig for you to Keighley—You will I trust find us tranquil

C Brontë

Try to come—I never so much needed the consolation of a friend's presence. Pleasure, of course, there would be none for you in the visit, except what your kind heart would teach you to find in doing good to others.[1]

MS Berg.

1. Ellen stayed at the parsonage from 28 Dec. 1848 until 9 Jan. 1849. In early January the Leeds doctor Thomas Pridgin Teale (1800–67) was called in to give his opinion on Anne's condition. He examined her, using a stethoscope, and diagnosed an advanced stage of pulmonary tuberculosis.

81. *To W. S. Williams, 25 December 1848*

[Haworth]

My dear Sir

I will write to you more at length when my heart can find a little rest—now I can only thank you very briefly for your letter which seemed to me eloquent in its sincerity.[1]

Emily is nowhere here now—her wasted mortal remains are taken out of the house; we have laid her cherished head under the church-aisle beside my mother's my two sisters', dead long ago, and my poor, hapless brother's.[2] But a small remnant of the race is left—so my poor father thinks.

Well—the loss is ours—not hers, and some sad comfort I take, as I hear the wind blow and feel the cutting keenness of the frost, in knowing that the elements bring her no more suffering—their severity cannot reach her grave—her fever is quieted, her restlessness soothed, her deep, hollow cough is hushed for ever; we do not hear it in the night nor listen for it in the morning: we have not the conflict of the strangely strong spirit and the fragile frame before us—relentless conflict—once seen, never to be forgotten. A dreary calm reigns round us, in the midst of which we seek resignation.

My father and my Sister Anne are far from well—as to me, God has hitherto most graciously sustained me—so far I have felt adequate to bear my own burden and even to offer a little help to others—I am not ill—I can get through daily duties—and do something towards keeping hope and energy alive in our mourning houshold. My Father says to me almost hourly "Charlotte, you must bear up—I shall sink if you fail me." these words—you can conceive are a stimulus to nature. The sight too of my Sister Anne's very still but deep sorrow wakens in me such fear for her that I dare not falter. Somebody <u>must</u> cheer the rest.

So I will not now ask why Emily was torn from us in the fullness of our attachment, rooted up in the prime of her own days in the promise of her powers—why her existence now lies like a field of green corn trodden down—like a tree in full bearing—struck at the root;[3] I will only say, sweet is rest after labour and calm after tempest[4] and repeat again and again that Emily knows that now.

Yours sincerely
C Brontë

MS BL Ashley 2452.

1. Mr Williams had written to CB on 21 Dec. after hearing the 'mournful intelligence' of Emily Brontë's death on 19 Dec. 'in the arms of those who loved her'. With deep and delicately expressed sympathy, he wished that the family's sorrow might be 'relieved by the blessed rays of consolation'. See his letter in *CBL* ii. 155–7.
2. Mrs Maria Brontë, née Branwell (1783–1821), had died after months of agonizing pain from what was probably uterine cancer on 15 Sept. 1821. CB's elder sisters Maria (?1813–6 May 1825) and Elizabeth (1815–15 June 1825) both died of pulmonary tuberculosis. Her brother Branwell (1817–48) died of 'chronic bronchitis and marasmus' (wasting of the flesh) on 24 Sept. 1848, his illness no doubt exacerbated by drink and opium. See Letters 75 and 76.
3. Cf. Joel 1: 10 and 12: 'The field is wasted, the land mourneth; for the corn is wasted ... The vine is dried up ... and the apple tree, even all the trees of the field, are withered: because joy is withered away from the sons of men.'
4. Cf. Psalm 107: 29–30: 'He maketh the storm a calm, so that the waves thereof are still. | Then are they glad because they be quiet; so he bringeth them unto their desired haven.'

82. *To W. S. Williams, ?13 January 1849*

[Haworth]

(a) My dear Sir

In sitting down to write to you I feel as if I were doing a wrong and a selfish thing; I believe I ought to discontinue my correspondence with you till times change and the tide of calamity which of late days has set so strongly in against us, takes a turn. But the fact is, sometimes I feel it absolutely necessary to unburden my mind. To papa I must only speak cheeringly, to Anne only encouragingly, to you I may give some hint of the dreary truth.

Anne and I sit alone and in seclusion as you fancy us, but we do not study; Anne cannot study now, she can scarcely read; she occupies Emily's chair—she does not get well. A week ago we sent for a Medical Man[1] of skill and experience from Leeds to see her; he examined her with the Stethoscope; his report I forbear to dwell on for the present; even skilful physicians have often been mistaken in their conjectures.

My first impulse was to hasten her away to a warmer climate, but this was forbidden—she must not travel—she is not to stir from the house this winter—the temperature of her room is to be kept constantly equal.

Had leave been given to try change of air and scene, I should hardly have known how to act—I could not possibly leave papa—and when I mentioned his accompanying us the bare thought distressed him too much to be dwelt upon. Papa is now upwards of seventy years of age; his habits for nearly thirty years have been those of absolute retirement—any change in them is most repugnant to him and probably could not at this time especially—when the hand of God is so heavy upon his old age, be ventured upon without danger.

When we lost Emily I thought we had drained the very dregs of our cup of trial, but now when I hear Anne cough as Emily coughed, I tremble lest there should be exquisite bitterness yet to taste. However I must not look forwards, nor must I look backwards. Too often I feel like one crossing an abyss on a narrow plank—a glance round might quite unnerve.

So circumstanced, my dear Sir, what claim have I on your friendship—what right to the comfort of your letters? My literary character is effaced for the time—and it is by that only you know me—care of Papa and Anne is necessarily my chief present object in life to the exclusion of all that could give me interest with my Publishers or their connexions—Should Anne get better, I think I could rally and become Currer Bell once more—but if otherwise—I look no farther—sufficient for the day is the evil thereof.[2]

Anne is very patient in her illness—as patient as Emily was unflinching. I recall one sister and look at the other with a sort of reverence as well as affection—under the test of suffering neither have faltered.

All the days of this winter have gone by darkly and heavily like a funeral train; since September sickness has not quitted the house—it is strange—it did not use to be so—but I suspect now all this has been coming on for years: (b) unused any of us to the possession of robust health, we have not noticed the gradual approaches of decay; we did not know its symptoms; the little cough, the small appetite, the tendency to take cold at every variation of atmosphere have been regarded as things of course[3]—I see them in another light now.

If you answer this write to me as you would to a person in an average state of tranquillity and happiness—I want to keep myself as firm and calm as I can; while papa and Anne want me I hope, I pray never to fail them; were I to see you I should endeavour to converse on ordinary topics and I should wish to write on the same, besides it will be less harassing to yourself to address me as usual.

May God long preserve to you the domestic treasures you value and when bereavement at last comes may He give you strength to bear it.—

Yours sincerely,
C. Brontë

MSS (a) BPM Bon 205. (b) untraced. Text: *CBL* ii. 168.

1. Thomas Pridgin Teale.
2. Cf. Matthew 6: 34.
3. Customary things.

83. *To George Smith, 22 January 1849*

[Haworth]

My dear Sir

I think it is to yourself I should address what I have to say respecting a suggestion conveyed through Mr. Williams on the subject of your friend, Dr. Forbes.[1]

The proposal was one which I felt it advisable to mention to my Father, and it is his reply which I would now beg to convey to you.

I am enjoined, in the first place, to express my Father's sense of the friendly and generous feeling which prompted the suggestion, and in the second place to assure you that did he think any really useful end could be answered by a visit from Dr. Forbes he would—notwithstanding his habitual reluctance to place himself under obligations—unhesitatingly accept an offer so delicately made. He is however convinced that whatever aid human skill and the resources of science can yield my Sister is already furnished her in the person of her present medical attendant, in whom my father has reason to repose perfect confidence, and he conceives that to bring down a Physician from London would be to impose trouble in quarters where we have no claim, without securing any adequate result.

Still—having reported my Father's reply—I would beg to add a request of my own, compliance with which would—it appears to me—secure us many of the advantages of your proposal without subjecting yourself or Dr. Forbes to its inconveniences. I would state Mr. Teale's opinion of my Sister's case, the course of treatment he has recommended to be adopted—and should be most happy to obtain, through you, Dr. Forbes' opinion on the regimen prescribed.

Mr. Teale said it was a case of tubercular consumption with congestion of the lungs—yet he intimated that the malady had not yet reached so advanced a stage as to cut off all hope; he held out a prospect that a truce and even an arrest of disease might yet be procured; till such truce or arrest could be brought about, he forbade the excitement of travelling, enjoined strict care and prescribed the use of cod-liver oil and carbonate of iron. It would be a satisfaction to know whether Dr. Forbes approves these remedies—or whether there are others he would recommend in preference.[2]

To be indebted to you for information on these points would be felt as no burden either by my sister or myself; your kindness is of an order which will not admit of entire rejection from any motives—where there cannot be full acceptance there must at least be considerate compromise.

Believe me, My dear Sir

Yours sincerely

C Brontë

MS BPM SG 20.

1. Dr. John Forbes (1787–1861), knighted 1853; a distinguished specialist in tuberculosis, physician to the hospital for Consumption and Diseases of the Chest. He was to become the Queen's physician.
2. On 1 Feb. CB wrote to Mr Williams: 'Whether my hopes are quite fallacious or not I do not know, but sometimes I fancy that the remedies prescribed by Mr. Teale and approved—as I was glad to learn—by Dr. Forbes are working a good result.'

84. *To W. S. Williams, ?10 February 1849*

[Haworth]

My dear Sir

My sister still continues better; she has less languor and weakness, her spirits are improved; this change gives cause, I think, both for gratitude and hope.

I am glad that you and Mr. Smith like the commencement of my present work—I wish it were <u>more than a commencement</u>, for how it will be re-united after the long break, or how it can gather force of flow when the current has been checked—or rather drawn off so long—I know not.[1]

I sincerely thank you both for the candid expression of your objections—what you say with reference to the first chapter shall be duly weighed—At present I feel reluctant to withdraw it—because as I formerly said of the Lowood-part of "Jane Eyre"—it <u>is</u> <u>true</u>—The curates and their ongoings are merely photographed from the life[2]—I should like you to explain to me more fully the ground of your objections—is it because you think this chapter will render the work liable to severe handling by the press? Is it because knowing as you now do the identity of "Currer Bell"—this scene strikes you as unfeminine—? Is it because it is intrinsically defective and inferior—? I am afraid the two first reasons would not weigh with me—the last would.

Anne and I thought it very kind in you to preserve all the notices of the Poems so carefully for us—some of them, as you said, were well worth reading—we were glad to find that our old friend "the Critic" has again a kind word for us[3]—I was struck with one curious fact—viz. that four of the notices are fac-similes of each other—how does this happen—? I suppose they copy.

Your generous indignation against the "Quarterly" touched me[4]—but do not trouble yourself to be angry on Currer Bell's account—except where the May-Fair gossip and Mr. Thackeray's name were brought in—he was never stung at all—but he certainly thought that passage and one or two others quite unwarrantable—However slander without a germ of truth is seldom injurious—it resembles a rootless plant and must soon wither away.[5]

The critic would certainly be a little ashamed of herself if she knew what foolish blunders she had committed—if she were aware how completely Mr. Thackeray & Currer Bell are strangers to each other—that "Jane Eyre" was written before the author had seen one line of "Vanity Fair", and that if C Bell had known that there existed in Mr. Thackeray's private circumstances the shadow of a reason for fancying personal allusion—so far from dedicating the book to that gentleman—he would have regarded such a step as ill-judged, insolent and indefensible, and would have shunned it accordingly.

Believe me my dear Sir
Yours sincerely | C Brontë

MS Eng 871, Houghton Library, Harvard University.

1. *Shirley* had been 'laid aside' after Branwell Brontë's death on 24 Sept. 1848.
2. David Sweeting was based on Revd James Chesterton Bradley (?1818–1913), curate at Keighley and Oakworth, Peter Augustus Malone on Revd James William Smith (b. ?1815), curate at Haworth and then at Eastwood, Keighley, Mr Donne on Revd Joseph Brett Grant (?1820–79), curate at Haworth and then vicar of Oxenhope, and Mr Macarthey on Revd. A. B. Nicholls (1819–1906).
3. CB refers to reviews of the Bells' *Poems*, reissued by Smith, Elder in 1848. The *Critic* for 15 Dec. 1848 found in Currer Bell's poems 'the same originality, truth and power so conspicuous in "Jane Eyre"'. Ellis Bell was less objective and more 'metaphysical' than his brothers, but all showed wide sympathy, expansive humanity, a poet's eye to nature, and a Christian's views of the comparative claims of the seen and the unseen.
4. The *Quarterly Review* for Dec. 1848 published a long review of *Vanity Fair*, *Jane Eyre*, and the *Governesses' Benevolent Institution report for 1847* by Elizabeth Rigby (1809–93), later Lady Eastlake. Admitting that *JE* was in some respects masterly, she criticized the unattractive hero and heroine and their improbable actions. The novel was merely another *Pamela*, coarse in language and lax in tone, combining genuine power with 'horrid taste', rudeness, and vulgarity. The book was 'throughout the personification of an unregenerate and undisciplined spirit', 'pre-eminently an anti-Christian composition', a 'murmuring against God's appointment . . . the tone of the mind and thought which has overthrown authority and violated every code human and divine abroad, and fostered Chartism and rebellion at home, is the same which has also written Jane Eyre'.
5. Miss Rigby had written, 'Jane Eyre is sentimentally assumed to have proceeded from the pen of Mr. Thackeray's governess.' The insanity of Thackeray's wife was known to many in 'Mayfair' society. The plot of *Jane Eyre*, and CB's dedication of the second edition to him, had led to persistent rumours that it was written by a former governess in his household who had become his mistress.

85. *To Margaret Wooler, 24 March 1849*

Haworth

My dear Miss Wooler

I have delayed answering your letter in the faint hope that I might be able to reply favourably to your enquiries after my Sister's health.[1] This, however, it is not permitted me to do. Her decline is gradual and fluctuating, but its nature is not doubtful. The symptoms of cough, pain in the side and chest, wasting of flesh, strength and appetite—after the sad experience we have had—cannot be regarded by us as equivocal. In Spirit she is resigned: at heart she is—I believe—a true Christian: She looks beyond this life—and regards her Home and Rest as elsewhere than on Earth. May God support her and all of us through the trial of lingering sickness—and aid her in the last hour when the struggle which separates soul from body must be gone through!

We saw Emily torn from the midst of us when our hearts clung to her with intense attachment and when—loving each other as we did—well—it seemed as if—might we but have been spared to each other—we could have found complete happiness in our mutual society and affection—She was scarcely buried when Anne's health failed—and we were warned that Consumption had found another victim in her, and that it would be vain to reckon on her life. These things would be too much if Reason, unsupported by Religion—were condemned to bear them alone.

I have cause to be most thankful for the strength which has hitherto been vouchsafed both to my Father and myself. God, I think, is specially merciful to Old Age—and for my own part—trials which in perspective would have seemed to me quite intolerable—when they actually came—I endured without prostration. Yet I must confess that in the time which has elapsed since Emily's death there have been moments of solitary—deep—inert affliction far harder to bear—than those which immediately followed our loss—The crisis of bereavement has an acute pang which goads to exertion—the desolate after feeling sometimes paralyzes.

I have learnt that we are not to find solace in our own strength; we must seek it in God's omnipotence. Fortitude is good—but fortitude itself must be shaken under us to teach us how weak we are.

With best regards to yourself and all dear to you—and sincere thanks for the interest you so kindly continue to take in me and my Sister,

Believe me my dear Miss Wooler
Yours faithfully
C Brontë

MS Fitzwilliam.

1. Miss Wooler would know Anne well, for she had been a pupil in her school from mid-Oct. 1835 to the end of 1837, and possibly longer.

86. To Ellen Nussey, c. 12 and 14 May 1849

[Haworth]

(a) Dear Ellen

I returned Mary Taylor's letter to Hunsworth as soon as I had read it   Thank God she was safe up to that time but I do not think the earthquake was then over—I shall long to hear tidings of her again.[1]

Anne was worse during the warm weather we had about a week ago—she grew weaker and both the pain in her side and her cough were worse—strange to say since it is colder, she has appeared rather to revive than sink. I still hope that if she gets over May she may last a long time.

We have engaged lodgings at Scarbro—We stipulated for a good sized sitting-room and an airy double-bedded lodging room—with a sea-view—and—if not deceived—have obtained these desiderata at No 2 Cliff—Anne says it is one of the best situations in the place—[2] It would not have done to have taken lodgings either in the town or on the bleak, steep coast where Miss Wooler's house is situated—If Anne is to get any good she must have every advantage. Miss Outhwaite left her in her will a small legacy of £200 and she cannot employ her money better than in obtaining what may prolong existence if it does not restore health[3]—We hope to leave home on the 23rd. and I think it will be advisable to rest at York and stay all night there—I hope this arrangement will suit you as it will give you more time to see George.[4]

We reckon on your society—dear Ellen—as a real privilege and pleasure. We shall take little luggage and shall have to buy bonnets and dresses and several other things either at York or Scarbro' which place do you think would be best? Oh—if it would please God to strengthen and revive Anne how happy we might be together! His will—however—must be done—and if she is not to recover—it remains to pray for strength and patience

CB

(b) I wish it seemed less like a dreary mockery in us to talk of buying bonnets &c. Anne was very ill yesterday. She had difficulty of breathing all day, even when sitting perfectly still. Today she seems better again. I long for the moment to come when the experiment of the sea-air will be tried. Will it do her good? I cannot tell. I can only wish.

MSS (a) Widener, Harvard HEW 1.5.4; (b) untraced. Text: *CBL* ii. 209.

1. Mary Taylor's letter from New Zealand to her brothers at Hunsworth must have described the earthquake which shook Wellington on and after 16 Oct. 1848, devastating buildings all round the homes of Mary and her relations. By 20 Oct. the Te Aro end of the town was a wreck; but Waring Taylor's house in Herbert Street, where Mary lived, survived with only the loss of its chimneys.
2. By 12 Apr. Anne's physician, Dr Teale, had agreed that she could go, as she wished, to Scarborough on the Yorkshire coast. She had stayed there several times with the Robinsons when she was a governess, and knew that the lodgings in the 'Cliff' had a magnificent view over the south bay. Miss Wooler's house was in the north bay.
3. Anne's godmother, Frances Outhwaite, had died on 14 Feb. 1849.
4. The journey was postponed to 24 May, since Anne was too ill to travel on the 23rd. Ellen's brother George was being cared for in the Clifton House asylum in York.

87. *To W. S. Williams, 30 May 1849*

[Scarborough]

My dear Sir

My poor Sister is taken quietly home at last. She died on Monday[1]—With almost her last breath she said she was happy—and thanked God that Death was come, and come so gently. I did not think it would be so soon. You will not expect me to add more at present.

> Yours faithfully
> C Brontë

MS Berg.

1. 28 May.

88. *To W. S. Williams, 4 June 1849*

2. Cliff. Scarbro'

My dear Sir

I hardly know what I said when I wrote last—I was then feverish and exhausted—I am now better—and—I believe—quite calm.

You have been informed of my dear Sister Anne's death—let me now add that she died without severe struggle—resigned—trusting in God—thankful for release from a suffering life—deeply assured that a better existence lay before her—she believed—she hoped, and declared her belief and hope with her last breath.—Her quiet—Christian death did not rend my heart as Emily's stern, simple, undemonstrative end did—I let Anne go to God and felt He had a right to her.

I could hardly let Emily go—I wanted to hold her back then—and I want her back hourly now—Anne, from her childhood seemed preparing for an early death—Emily's spirit seemed strong enough to bear her to fulness of years—They are both gone—and so is poor Branwell—and Papa has now me only—the weakest—puniest—least promising of his six children—Consumption has taken the whole five.

For the present Anne's ashes rest apart from the others—I have buried her here at Scarbro' to save papa the anguish of the return and a third funeral.[1]

I am ordered to remain at the sea-side a while—I cannot rest here but neither can I go home—Possibly I may not write again soon—attribute my silence neither to illness nor negligence. No letters will find me at Scarbro' after the 7th. I do not know what my next address will be—I shall wander a week or two on the east coast and only stop at quiet lonely places[2]—No one need be anxious about me as far as I know—Friends and acquaintance seem to think this the worst time of suffering—they are sorely mistaken—Anne reposes now—what have the long desolate hours of her patient pain and fast decay been?

Why life is so blank, brief and bitter I do not know—Why younger and far better than I are snatched from it with projects unfulfilled I cannot comprehend—but I believe God is wise—perfect—merciful.

I have heard from Papa—he and the servants knew when they parted from Anne they would see her no more—all try to be resigned—I knew it likewise and I wanted her to die where she would be happiest—She loved Scarboro'—a peaceful sun gilded her evening.

Yours sincerely
C Brontë

MS BL Ashley 2452.

1. On 30 May, the day of the funeral, Ellen Nussey registered Anne's death, giving her age as 28 instead of 29 years, and the cause of death as 'Consumption 6 months'. The funeral took place at Christ Church, Vernon Road, Scarborough, because the parish church, St Mary's, was being rebuilt; but Anne was buried in St Mary's churchyard, high up on the cliff near the castle. Miss Wooler was the only mourner apart from Charlotte and Ellen.
2. CB and Ellen travelled to the small fishing town of Filey, about seven miles south of Scarborough, on 7 June, staying at Cliff House in North Street (now Belle Vue Street), which then had an uninterrupted view of the sea.

89. *To W. S. Williams, 13 June 1849*

Filey.

My dear Sir

When I wrote to you last I thought it probable I might not address you again soon—but this evening I will write because I feel in the mood to do so without, I trust, paining you.

You have been kind enough to take a certain interest in my afflictions, and I feel it a sort of duty to tell you how I am enabled to sustain them. The burden is lightened far beyond what I could expect by more circumstances than one. Papa is resigned and his health is not shaken. An immediate change of scene has done me good—All I meet are kind—my friend Ellen is affectionately so. You—on whom I have no claim—write to me in the strain best tending to consolation.

Then—my Sister died happily; nothing dark, except the inevitable shadow of Death overclouded her hour of dissolution—the doctor—a stranger—who was called in—wondered at her fixed tranquillity of spirit and settled longing to be gone. He said in all his experience he had seen no such death-bed, and that it gave evidence of no common mind—Yet to speak the truth—it but half consoles to remember this calm—there is piercing pain in it. Anne had had enough of life such as it was—in her twenty-eighth year she laid it down as a burden.[1] I hardly know whether it is sadder to think of that than of Emily turning her dying eyes reluctantly from the pleasant sun. Had I never believed in a future life before, my Sisters' fate would assure me of it.

There must be Heaven or we must despair—for life seems bitter, brief—blank. To me—these two have left in their memories a noble legacy. Were I quite solitary in the world—bereft even of Papa—there is something in the past I can love intensely and honour deeply—and it is something which cannot change—which cannot decay—which immortality guarantees from corruption.

They have died comparatively young—but their short lives were spotless—their brief career was honourable—their untimely death befel amidst all associations that can hallow, and not one that can desecrate.

A year ago—had a prophet warned me how I should stand in June 1849—how stripped and bereaved—had he foretold the autumn, the winter, the spring of sickness and suffering to be gone through—I should have thought—this can never be endured. It is over. Branwell—Emily—Anne are gone like dreams—gone as Maria and Elizabeth went twenty years ago. One by one I have watched them fall asleep on my arm—and closed their glazed eyes—I have seen them buried one by one—and—thus far—God has upheld me. From my heart I thank Him.

I thank too the friends whose sympathy has given me inexpressible comfort and strength—You, amongst the number.

Filey, where, we have been for the last week—is a small place with a wild rocky coast—its sea is very blue—its cliffs are very white—its sands very solitary—it suits Ellen and myself better than Scarbro' which is too gay. I would stay here another week—but Ellen says I must go to-morrow to Bridlington[2]—and after I have been a week there, I intend to return home to Papa. May I retain strength and cheerfulness enough to be a comfort to him and to bear up against the weight of the solitary life to come—it will be solitary—I cannot help dreading the first experience of it—the first aspect of the empty rooms which once were tenanted by those dearest to my heart—and where the shadow of their last days must now—I think—linger for ever. Ellen lives much too far off to see me often—her home is twenty miles distant from mine; but I trust in the power which has helped me hitherto.

I hope that your little invalid daughter[3] is now quite well, and that her parents are relieved from anxiety on her account.

Should you write to me again soon—and I shall be glad to hear from you—address—Miss Brontë

J. Hudson's Esqr.
Easton
Bridlington
CB—

1. Anne was born on 17 Jan. 1820, and was therefore 29.
2. On the coast some twelve miles south-east of Filey. CB and Ellen had stayed in the town for a week in 1839, after spending four weeks at the home of John and Sophia Hudson in the hamlet of Easton, about one mile inland. See Letter 9.
3. Probably Mr Williams's youngest daughter, Anna, born 6 Aug. 1845.

90. *To Ellen Nussey, 23 June 1849*

[Haworth]

Dear Ellen

I intended to have written a line to you to-day if I had not received yours.

We did indeed part suddenly[1]—it made my heart ache that we were severed without the time to exchange a word—and yet perhaps it was better.

I got home a little before eight o'clock. All was clean and bright waiting for me—Papa and the servants were well—and all received me with an affection which should have consoled. The dogs seemed in strange ecstasy.[2] I am certain they regarded me as the harbinger of others—the dumb creatures thought that as I was returned—those who had been so long absent were not far behind.

I left Papa soon and went into the dining room—I shut the door—I tried to be glad that I was come home—I have always been glad before—except once—even then I was cheered.[3] But this time joy was not to be the sensation. I felt that the house was all silent—the rooms were all empty—I remembered where the three were laid—in what narrow dark dwellings—never were they to reappear on earth. So the sense of desolation and bitterness took possession of me—the agony that was to be undergone—and was not to be avoided came on—I underwent it & passed a dreary evening and night and a mournful morrow—to-day I am better.

I do not know how life will pass—but I certainly do feel confidence in Him who has upheld me hitherto. Solitude may be cheered and made endurable beyond what I can believe. The great trial is when evening closes and night approaches—At that hour we used to assemble in the dining-room—we used to talk—Now I sit by myself—necessarily I am silent.—I cannot help thinking of their last days—remembering their sufferings and what they said and did and how they looked in mortal affliction—perhaps all this will become less poignant in time. Let me thank you once more, dear Ellen, for your kindness to me which I do not mean to forget—How did they think you looking at home?—Papa thought me a little stronger—he said my eyes were not so sunken. I am glad to hear a good account of your Mother and a tolerable one of Mercy—I hope she will soon recover her health—Give my love to her and to all—Write again very soon and tell me how poor Miss Heald[4] goes on—

Yours sincerely
C Brontë

Satdy

MS Law-Dixon.

1. CB and EN had probably used the Bridlington branch of the York and North Midland railway. The sudden parting may have been caused by Charlotte's need to catch a Keighley train from Leeds.
2. Keeper, Emily's fierce, faithful bulldog who had followed her coffin to the grave, and Flossy, Anne's affectionate spaniel.
3. CB had the comfort of her sisters' company on her return from Brussels in Nov. 1842 after the deaths of Elizabeth Branwell and William Weightman, in Jan. 1844 after the parting from M. Heger, and after leaving Hathersage in July 1845 to face the shock of Branwell's dismissal.
4. Harriet Heald (?1802–54), sister of the vicar of Birstall, Revd William Margetson Heald (1803–75). She had been seriously ill in Oct. 1848, and again in the spring of 1849.

91. *To W. S. Williams, 16 August 1849*

[Haworth]

My dear Sir

Since I last wrote to you—I have been getting on with my book as well as I can, and I think I may now venture to say that in a few weeks I hope to have the pleasure of placing the M.S. in Mr. Smith's hands: I shall be glad when it is fairly deposited in those hands.[1]

The North British Review duly reached me. I read attentively all it says about E. Wyndham, J. Eyre, and F. Hervey.[2] Much of the article is clever—and yet there are remarks which—for me—rob it of importance.

To value praise or stand in awe of blame we must respect the source whence the praise and blame proceed—and I do not respect an inconsistent critic. He says "if 'Jane Eyre' be the production of a woman—she must be a woman unsexed."

In that case the book is an unredeemed error and should be unreservedly condemned. "Jane Eyre" is a woman's autobiography—by a woman it is professedly written—if it is written as no woman would write—condemn it—with spirit and decision—say it is bad—but do not first eulogize and then detract.

I am reminded of the "Economist".[3] The literary critic of that paper praised the book if written by a man—and pronounced it "odious" if the work of a woman.

To such critics I would say—"to you I am neither Man nor Woman—I come before you as an Author only—it is the sole standard by which you have a right to judge me—the sole ground on which I accept your judgment."

There is a weak comment, having no pretence either to justice or discrimination—on the works of Ellis and Acton Bell[4]—The critic did not know that
those writers had passed from Time and from Life. I have read no review since
either of my sisters died which I could have wished <u>them</u> to read—none even
which did not render the thought of their departure more tolerable to me. To
hear myself praised beyond them was cruel—to hear qualities ascribed to them
so strangely the reverse of their real characteristics was scarce supportable—It is
sad even now—but they are so remote from Earth—so safe from its turmoils—I
can bear it better. But on one point do I now feel vulnerable—I should grieve to
see my father's peace of mind perturbed on my account: for which reason I keep
my author's existence as much as possible out of his way—I have always given
him a carefully diluted and modified account of the success of "Jane Eyre"—just
what would please without startling him. The book is not mentioned between
us once a month—The "Quarterly" I kept to myself—it would have worried
papa. To that same "Quarterly" I must speak in the introduction to my present
work—just one little word—you once, I remember, said that review was written
by a lady—Miss Rigby—are you sure of this?[5]

Give no hint of my intention of discoursing a little with the "Quarterly". It
would look too important to speak of it beforehand. All plans are best conceived
and executed without noise.

Believe me—
Yours sincerely
CB—

MS BPM Gr. F8.

1. CB had finished writing *Shirley* before 8 Sept., when Smith, Elder's managing clerk, James Taylor,
   collected the MS from Haworth.
2. The Scottish advocate James Lorimer (1818–90) reviewed the three novels in the *North British
   Review* for Aug. 1849. He praised *Fanny Hervey; or The Mother's Choice* (1849) by Mrs Stirling,
   gave moderate praise to Anne Marsh's *Emilia Wyndham* (1848), considering that she wrote 'as
   an English gentlewoman should write', and admitted that, unlike Marsh, Currer Bell was never
   tedious. He praised and found fault with *JE* by turns, finding in it elements of the revolting and
   improbable, but acquitting the author of the *Quarterly*'s charge of vulgarity.
3. The *Economist* for 27 Nov. 1847 praised *JE* enthusiastically. Though the reviewer found some
   coarseness, and some too-obvious art in construction, he wrote nothing resembling CB's
   statement here.
4. Lorimer found the faults of *JE* 'magnified a thousand-fold' in *WH* and *Tenant*, despite the vivid
   realism of their sketches of nature 'in her rougher moods'. He did not finish reading *WH*, repelled
   by 'a perfect pandemonium of low and brutal creatures' and disgusting language. *Tenant* had
   a better beginning and 'poetical justice' at the end, but it brought the reader into 'the closest
   possible proximity with naked vice', with coarseness never really found in gentlefolk, and a style
   marked by vulgar slang and provincialisms.
5. CB's 'A Word to the Quarterly', dated 29 Aug. 1849, was rejected by her publishers, and was
   not printed until 1975, when it appeared in *Brontë Society Transactions*, 16. 85. 329–32; reprinted
   in *CBL* ii. 242–5. It is an ill-conceived, clumsily satirical response to Elizabeth Rigby's review
   of *JE* in the *Quarterly Review* for Dec. 1848, written as from the 'old bachelor', Currer Bell.
   The postscript accuses Rigby of being 'callous, harsh and unsympathizing' towards governesses,

whereas she had written that no other class 'more deserves and demands earnest and judicious befriending'. But Rigby had no wish to prevent the isolation of the governess by removing the distance between her and her superiors—her employers. CB expressed her indignation in *Shirley* by putting Miss Rigby's harshest words into the mouths of 'Mrs and Miss Hardman'.

92. *To W. S. Williams, 24 August 1849*

[Haworth]

My dear Sir

I think the best title for the book would be "Shirley" without any explanation or addition—the simpler and briefer, the better.

If Mr. Taylor[1] calls here on his return to Town, he might take charge of the M.S.; I would rather entrust it to him than send it by the ordinary conveyance. Did I see Mr. Taylor when I was in London? I cannot remember him.

I would with pleasure offer him the homely hospitalities of the Parsonage for a few days, if I could at the same time offer him the company of a brother or if my Father were young enough and strong enough to walk with him on the moors and shew him the neighbourhood, or if the peculiar retirement of papa's habits were not such as to render it irksome to him to give much of his society to a stranger even in the house: without being in the least misanthropical or sour-natured—papa habitually prefers solitude to society, and Custom is a tyrant whose fetters it would now be impossible for him to break. Were it not for difficulties of this sort, I believe I should ere this have asked you to come down to Yorkshire. Papa—I know, would receive any friend of Mr. Smith's with perfect kindness and good-will, but I likewise know that, unless greatly put out of his way—he could not give a guest much of his company, and that, consequently, his entertainment would be but dull.

You will see the force of these considerations, and understand why I only ask Mr. Taylor to come for a day instead of requesting the pleasure of his company for a longer period; you will believe me also, and so will he, when I say I shall be most happy to see him.

He will find Haworth a strange uncivilized little place such as—I daresay—he never saw before. It is twenty miles distant from Leeds; he will have to come by rail to Keighley (there are trains every two hours I believe) he must remember that at a station called Shipley the carriages are changed—otherwise they will take him on to Skipton or Colne, or I know not where; when he reaches Keighley, he will yet have four miles to travel—a conveyance may be hired at the Devonshire Arms;[2] there is no coach or other regular communication.

I should like to hear from him before he comes and to know on what day to expect him that I may have the M.S. ready—if it is not quite finished, I might send the concluding chapter or two by post.

I advise you to send this letter to Mr. Taylor—it will save you the trouble of much explanation—and will serve to apprise him of what lies before him; he can then weigh well with himself whether it would suit him to take so much trouble for so slight an end.

>   Believe me, my dear Sir
>   Yours sincerely
>   C Brontë

MS BPM Bon 211.

1. James Taylor. CB had asked for his opinion on the first volume of *Shirley* in a letter to Mr Williams of 4 Feb. 1849: 'Your mention of Mr. Taylor suggests to me that possibly you and Mr. Smith might wish him to share the little secret of the M.S. . . . admit him to the confidence by all means . . . I shall be glad of another censor.'
2. In Church Street, Keighley.

93. To ?W. S. Williams[1], 21 September 1849

[Haworth]

My dear sir

I am obliged to you for preserving my secret, being at least as anxious as ever (more anxious, I cannot well be) to keep quiet. You asked me in one of your letters lately whether I thought I should escape identification in Yorkshire. I am so little known, that I think I shall.[2] Besides the book is far less founded on the Real—than perhaps appears. It would be difficult to explain to you how little actual experience I have had of life, how few persons I have known and how very few have known me.

As an instance how the characters have been managed—take that of Mr. Helstone. If this character had an original, it was in the person of a clergyman who died some years since at the advanced age of eighty. I never saw him except once—at the consecration of a Church—when I was a child of ten years old. I was then struck with his appearance and stern, martial air. At a subsequent period I heard him talked about in the neighbourhood where he had resided—some mentioned him with enthusiasm—others with detestation—I listened to varied anecdotes, balanced evidence against evidence and drew an inference.

The original of Mr. Hall[3] I have seen—he knows me slightly, but he would as soon think I had closely observed him or taken him for a character—he would as soon, indeed, suspect me of writing a book—a novel—as he would his dog—Prince. Margaret Hall called "Jane Eyre" a "wicked book", on the authority of the "Quarterly"—an expression which—coming from her—I will here confess—struck somewhat deep—It opened my eyes to the harm the Quarterly had done—Margaret would not have called it "wicked" if she had not been told so.

No matter—whether known or unknown—misjudged or the contrary—I am resolved not to write otherwise. I shall bend as my powers tend. The two human beings who understood me and whom I understood are gone: I have some that love me yet and whom I love without expecting or having a right to expect that they shall perfectly understand me: I am satisfied; but I must have my own way in the matter of writing. The loss of what we possess nearest and dearest to us in this world, produces an effect upon the character: we search out what we have yet left that can support, and when found, we cling to it with a hold of new-strung tenacity.

The faculty of imagination lifted me when I was sinking three months ago, its active exercise has kept my head above water since—its results cheer me now—for I feel they have enabled me to give pleasure to others—I am thankful to God who gave me the faculty—and it is for me a part of my religion to defend this gift and to profit by its possession.

Yours sincerely

CB.

MS BPM Gr. F9.

1. Almost certainly to Williams. CB's letters to George Smith at this period deal with finance.
2. Once *Shirley* was published, on 26 Oct., the secret of 'Currer Bell's' identity was soon out. Local people, places, and dialect were recognized at an early date by a Haworth man, probably John Driver, son of the Haworth grocer, who lived in Liverpool and revealed his suspicions to a Liverpool paper. In the Birstall and Cleckheaton area, the Taylors of Gomersal were identified as the Yorkes; and Revd Hammond Roberson (1757–1841), who had sided with the mill-owners when Rawfolds Mill near Cleckheaton was attacked by Luddites on 11 Apr. 1812, as Matthewson Helstone.
3. Revd William Margetson Heald (1803–75), vicar of Birstall 1836–75. His sister was Harriet Heald (?1802–54). In fact, once rumours of the character's identity had circulated, Mr Heald wryly acknowledged that the portrayal of 'Mr Hall' as 'black, bilious & of dismal aspect' and occasionally using dialect, seemed to 'sit very well' on him. (Letter from Heald to Ellen Nussey, 8 Jan. 1850.)

94. To Ellen Nussey, ?24 September 1849

[Haworth]

(a) Dear Ellen

You have to fight your way through labour and difficulty at home[1]—it appears—but I am truly glad now you did not come to Haworth—as matters have turned out you would have found only discomfort and gloom—both Tabby and Martha[2] are ill in bed. Martha's illness has been most serious—she was seized with internal inflamation[3] ten days ago; Tabby's lame leg has broken out—she cannot stand or walk—I have one of Martha's Sisters to help me—and her mother comes up sometimes. There was one day last week when I fairly broke down for ten minutes—sat & cried like a fool—Martha's illness was at its height—a cry from Tabby had called me into the kitchen and I had found her laid on the floor—her head under the kitchen-grate—she had fallen from her chair in attempting to rise—Papa had just been declaring that Martha was in iminent[4] danger—I was myself depressed with head-ache & sickness—that day—I hardly knew what to do or where to turn—

Thank God—Martha is now convalescent—Tabby—I trust will be better soon—Papa is pretty—well—I have the satisfaction of knowing that my Publishers are delighted with what I sent them—this supports me (b)—but Life is a battle May we all be enabled to fight it well.

Yours faithfully
CB.

MSS (a) Widener, Harvard (b) Bodleian Autog. b.9.no.264.

1. Living arrangements at Brookroyd were being changed to accommodate Ellen's sister Ann and her husband, Robert Clapham (?1788–1855), the land-agent for the manor of Batley, after their marriage on 26 Sept. 1849.
2. The parsonage servants Tabitha Aykroyd and Martha Brown, the daughter of the sexton John Brown and his wife Mary.
3. Thus in MS.
4. Thus in MS.

95. To W. S. Williams, 1 November 1849

[Haworth]
My dear Sir

I reached home yesterday, and found your letter and one from Mr. Lewes[1] and one from the Peace Congress Committee[2] awaiting my arrival. The last document it is now too late to answer—for it was an invitation to Currer Bell to appear on the platform at their meeting at Exeter Hall last Tuesday! A wonderful figure Mr. Currer Bell would have cut under such circumstances. Should the "Peace Congress" chance to read "Shirley" they will wash their hands of its author.

I am glad to hear that Mr. Thackeray is better[3]—but I did not know he had been seriously ill; I thought it was only a literary indisposition. You must tell me what he thinks of "Shirley" if he gives you any opinion on the subject.

I am also glad to hear that Mr. Smith is pleased with the commercial prospects of the work. I try not to be anxious about its literary fate—and if I cannot be quite stoical I think I am still tolerably resigned.

Mr. Lewes does not like the opening chapter—wherein he resembles you.

I have permitted myself the treat of spending the last week with my friend Ellen; her residence is in a far more populous and stirring neighbourhood than this—whenever I go there I am unavoidably forced into society—clerical society chiefly.

During my late visit I have too often had reason—sometimes in a pleasant—sometimes in a painful form to fear that I no longer walk invisible—"Jane

Eyre" it appears has been read all over the district—a fact of which I never dreamt—a circumstance of which the possibility never occurred to me—I met sometimes with new deference, with augmented kindness—old schoolfellows and old teachers too, greeted me with generous warmth—and again—ecclesiastical brows lowered thunder on me. When I confronted one or two large-made priests[4] I longed for the battle to come on—I wish they would speak out plainly. You must not understand that my schoolfellows and teachers were of the Clergy Daughters School[5]—in fact I was never there but for one little year as a very little girl—I am certain I have long been forgotten—though for myself I remember all and everything clearly: early impressions are ineffaceable.

I have just received the "Daily News".[6] Let me speak the truth—when I read it my heart sickened over it. It is not a good review—it is unutterably false. If "Shirley" strikes all readers as it has struck that one—but—I shall not say what follows.

On the whole I am glad a decidedly bad notice has come first—a notice whose inexpressible ignorance first stuns and then stirs me. Are there no such men as the Helstones and Yorkes?[7]

Yes there are.

Is the first chapter disgusting or vulgar?

It is not: it is real.

As for the praise of such a critic—I find it silly and nauseous—and I scorn it.

Were my Sisters now alive they and I would laugh over this notice—but they sleep—they will wake no more for me—and I am a fool to be so moved by what is not worth a sigh—

Believe me

Yours sincerely

CB—

You must excuse me if I seem hasty—I fear I really am not so firm as I used to be—nor so patient: whenever any shock comes, I feel that almost all supports have been withdrawn.

MS Pierpont Morgan, MA 2696.

1. George Henry Lewes. See Letter 57 n. 1.
2. A movement advocating the principles of perpetual peace, supported by the American pacifist Elihu Burritt, and the Society of Friends, had led to a second Peace Congress in Paris in Aug. 1849. The London meeting on 30 Oct. 1849 to which CB had been invited was chaired by William Ewart, MP (1798–1869). Exeter Hall in the Strand (opened 1831 and now demolished) was used for religious, charitable, and musical events.
3. Thackeray had been ill with a badly sprained ankle and what may have been cholera from 17 Sept.
4. Not identified. The reference might be to CB's godfather, Revd Thomas Atkinson, vicar of Hartshead, or Revd Thomas Allbutt, vicar of Dewsbury.

5. The school at Cowan Bridge, depicted as Lowood in *Jane Eyre*. CB refers here to the schoolfellows and teachers encountered at Margaret Wooler's schools at Roe Head, Mirfield, and Dewsbury Moor, 1831–June 1832, 1835–8.
6. 'The three curates and their junketting [are] . . . quite as vulgar, as unnecessary, and as disgusting' as the commencement of *Jane Eyre*. 'If you do not mind these monstrosities at the entrance, you will be both welcomed and repaid by the graceful and the beautiful. . . . The merit of the work lies in the variety, beauty, and truth of its female characters. Not one of its men are genuine. There are no such men.' (Unsigned review, *Daily News*, 31 Oct. 1849.)
7. See Letter 93 n. 2 and Biographical Notes, p. xliv.

96. *To Ellen Nussey, 16 November 1849*

[Haworth]

Dear Ellen

Amelia's letter gave me a full and true account of your visit to Hunsworth[1]—it was really very interesting and very well-written—all the little details so nicely put in—making such a graphic whole. I can gather from it that she <u>was</u> an object of special attention. Joe Taylor has written to me to ask "an opinion of Miss Ringrose"—perhaps you had better not tell her this—it might embarrass her painfully when he sees her again—and he is certain to call. I gave him a faithful opinion—I said she was what I called truly amiable, actively useful—genuinely good-natured—sufficiently sensible—neither unobservant nor without discrimination but <u>Not</u> highly intellectual, brilliant or profound. I did not of course say whether I thought she would suit him or not—I did not treat the subject as if I suspected he had any thoughts of her—I simply answered his question without the slightest comment.

You are not to suppose any of the characters in Shirley intended as literal portraits—it would not suit the rules of Art—nor my own feelings to write in that style—we only suffer Reality to <u>suggest</u>—never to <u>dictate</u>—the heroines are abstractions and the heros also—qualities I have seen, loved and admired are here and there put in as decorative gems to be preserved in that setting. Since you say you could recognize the originals of all except the heroines—pray whom did you suppose the two Moores to represent?[2]

I send you a couple of reviews—the one in the "Examiner" is written by Albany Fonblanque[3]—who is called the most brilliant political writer of the day—a man whose dictum is much thought of in London. The one in the "Standard of Freedom" is written by William Howitt a quaker![4] You must take care of the papers—bring them with [you] in your box when you come to Haworth. I have some thoughts of getting my London trip over <u>before</u> you come—as then I shall have something to tell you.[5]

[Goodbye for the present
Yours faithfully CB][6]

Amelia gives only a poor account of you—take care of yourself. I have the
dressmaker with me just now—I don't know how I shall like her—her manners
&c. are not to my taste—whether she is a "good hand" I don't yet know. I
should be pretty well if it were not for headaches and indigestion—my chest has
been better lately.

MS Widener, Harvard.

1. Ellen's friend Amelia Ringrose (1818–?1861 or later), daughter of the ship-owner Christopher
   Leake Ringrose of Tranby Lodge, near Hull, had formerly been engaged to Ellen's brother
   George. The engagement had been broken off when George's mental illness proved intractable.
   She was to marry Joseph Taylor of Hunsworth on 2 Oct. 1850.
2. Louis and Robert Moore derive in part from pairs of brothers, one usually quiet and intellectual,
   the other more active and worldly, in Charlotte and Branwell Brontë's early writings: William
   and Edward Percy, William and Edward Ashworth, William and Edward Crimsworth in *The
   Professor*, and William and John Henry Moore in the fragment, 'John Henry'.
3. The radical journalist Albany Fonblanque (1793–1872) found in *Shirley* a 'peculiar power'. Despite
   its lack of humour and some repulsive qualities, it had freshness, lively interest, irresistible 'grasp
   of reality', and a 'power of exciting, elevating, pleasing and instructing, which belongs only to
   genius of the most unquestionable kind'. Internal evidence proved that the author was a woman
   (*Examiner*, 3 Nov. 49, 692–4.)
4. William Howitt (1792–1879), author of many 'improving' works for the working-class, compared
   Shirley with Mrs Gaskell's *Mary Barton* in its vigour, comprehension of character, independence
   of feeling, and fine impartiality about the questions at issue. The characters displayed 'the hand
   of real genius, and the deep and searching glance of woman's intuition' (*Standard of Freedom*, 10
   Nov. 49, 11).
5. EN stayed at Haworth from c.27 Dec. 1849–17 Jan. 1850. CB stayed in London 29 Nov.–14 Dec.
   1849, arriving home 15 Dec. after a night spent in Derby.
6. Original valediction and signature removed; replaced by text supplied by Ellen Nussey.

97. *To Elizabeth Gaskell, 17 November 1849*

[Haworth]

Currer Bell <u>must</u> answer Mrs. Gaskell's letter[1]—whether forbidden to do so or
not—and She must acknowledge its kind, generous sympathy with all her heart.

Yet Mrs. Gaskell must not pity Currer Bell too much: there are thousands
who suffer more than she: dark days she has known; the worst, perhaps, were
days of bereavement, but though CB. is the survivor of most that were dear to
her, she has one near relative still left, and therefore cannot be said to be quite
alone.

Currer Bell will avow to Mrs. Gaskell that her chief reason for maintaining an
incognito is the fear that if she relinquished it, strength and courage would leave
her, and she should ever after shrink from writing the plain truth.

MS BPM B.S. 71.7(a).

1. Writing to W. S. Williams on ?17 Nov., CB referred to a letter he had forwarded from Mrs
   Gaskell, whose *Mary Barton* she had read by 1 Feb. 1849: 'She said I was not to answer it—but
   I cannot help doing so. Her note brought the tears to my eyes: she is a good—she is a great

woman—proud am I that I can touch a chord of sympathy in souls so noble.' After receiving
the present letter, Mrs Gaskell wrote, allegedly to Catherine Winkworth, 'Currer Bell (aha! what
will you give me for a secret?) She's a she—that I will tell you—who has sent me 'Shirley''
(Elizabeth Haldane, *Mrs Gaskell and her Friends* (1930), 119–20).

98. *To Ellen Nussey, ?5 December 1849*

4 Westbourne Place
Bishop's Road
Paddington
London

Dear Ellen

I have just remembered that as you do not know my address you cannot write
to me till you get it—it is as above.

I came to this big Babylon last Thursday, and have been, in what seems to
me a sort of whirl ever since, for changes, scenes and stimulus which would
be a trifle to others, are much to me. I found when I mentioned to Mr. Smith
my plan of going to Dr. Wheelwright's,[1] it would not do at all—he would have
been seriously hurt: he made his Mother write to me, and thus I was persuaded
to make my principal stay at his house. So far I have found no reason to regret
this decision. Mrs. Smith received me at first like one who has had the strictest
orders to be scrupulously attentive—I had fire in my bedroom evening and
morning—two wax candles—&c. &c. and Mrs. S. & her daughters[2] seemed to
look on me with a mixture of respect and alarm—but all this is changed—that
is to say the attention and politeness continue as great as ever—but the alarm
and enstrangement[3] are quite gone—she treats me as if she liked me and I
begin to like her much—kindness is a potent heart-winner. I had not judged too
favourably of her son on a first impression—he pleases me much: I like him better
even as a son and brother than as a man of business. Mr. Williams too is really
most gentlemanly and well-informed—his weak points he certainly has—but
these are not seen in society. Mr. Taylor—the little man—has again shewn his
parts. Of him I have not yet come to a clear decision: abilities he has—for he
rules the Firm (which Dr. Wheelwright told me the other day is considerably
the largest publishing concern in London)[4]—he keeps 40 young men under
strict control by his iron will—his young Superior likes him which—to speak
truth—is more than I do at present—in fact—I suspect he is of the Helstone[5]
order of men—rigid, despotic and self-willed—He tries to be very kind and
even to express sympathy sometimes—and he does not manage it—he has a
determined, dreadful nose in the middle of his face which when poked into
my countenance cuts into my soul like iron[6]—Still he is horribly intelligent,
quick, searching, sagacious—and with a memory of relentless tenacity: to turn

to Williams after him or to Smith himself is to turn from granite to easy down or warm fur.

I have seen Thackeray.[7]

No more at present from yours &c.

C Brontë

How is Amelia getting on? What more of J[oe] Taylor—give my love to her. Write!

MS Pierpont Morgan, MA 2696.

1. 29, Lower Phillimore Place, Kensington, the home of Dr Thomas Wheelwright and his family, whom CB had met in Brussels.
2. Mrs Elizabeth Smith, née Murray, and her daughters Eliza, Sarah, and Isabella.
3. Thus in MS.
4. After the firm had surmounted a financial crisis in 1848–9, Smith expanded its Indian agency and established a banking department; profits rose steadily, and the clerks at Cornhill eventually numbered 150.
5. Revd Matthewson Helstone in *Shirley*, a man 'almost without sympathy'.
6. See the photograph of Taylor's gravestone, with its life-size sculpture of his face, reproduced in Charlotte Cory, 'Letter from Bombay', *Times Literary Supplement*, 16 Aug. 2002, p.14.
7. George Smith invited Dr John Forbes and Thackeray to meet CB on Tuesday, 4 Dec. Smith recalled that Thackeray affronted Charlotte by failing to respect her anonymity: he went from Smith's house to the Garrick Club and boasted, 'Boys! I have been dining with "Jane Eyre"'' (Smith, 'Recollections', i. 113).

99. To Revd Patrick Brontë, 5 December 1849

[Westbourne Place, London]

Dear Papa

I must write another line to you to tell you how I am getting on. I have seen a great many things since I left home about which I hope to talk to you at future tea-times at home. I have been to the theatre and seen Macready in Macbeth.[1] I have seen the pictures in the National Gallery.[2] I have seen a beautiful exhibition of Turner's paintings,[3] and yesterday I saw Mr. Thackeray. He dined here with some other gentlemen. He is a very tall man—above six feet high, with a peculiar face—not handsome—very ugly indeed—generally somewhat satirical and stern in expression, but capable also of a kind look. He was not told who I was—he was not introduced to me—but I soon saw him looking at me through his spectacles and when we all rose to go down to dinner—he just stept quietly up and said 'Shake hands' so I shook hands—He spoke very few words to me—but when he went away he shook hands again in a very kind way. It is better—I should think to have him for a friend than an enemy—for he is a most formidable looking personage. I listened to him as he conversed with the other gentlemen—all he says is most simple but often cynical, harsh and contradictory.

I get on quietly—most people know me I think, but they are far too well-bred to shew that they know me—so that there is none of that bustle or that sense of publicity I dislike.

I hope you continue pretty well—be sure to take care of yourself: the weather here is exceedingly changeful and often damp and misty—So that it is necessary to guard against taking cold. I do not mean to stay in London above a week longer—but I shall write again two or three days before I return. You need not give yourself the trouble of answering this letter unless you have something particular to say. Remember me to Tabby and Martha.

I remain, dear papa
Your affectionate daughter
C Brontë

MS Berg.

1. William Charles Macready (1793–1873). On 14 Feb. 1850 CB wrote to Margaret Wooler: 'I twice saw Macready act—once in "Macbeth" and once in "Othello"—I astounded a dinner-party by honestly saying I did not like him. It is the fashion to rave about his splendid acting—anything more false and artificial—. . . I could scarcely have imagined.'
2. Opened to the public in 1838.
3. In her letter to Margaret Wooler of 14 Feb., CB wrote, 'One or two private collections of Turner's best water-colour drawings were indeed a treat.' She might have seen the collection of Benjamin Godfrey Windus (?1790–1867) at Tottenham Green, and that of Elhanan Bicknell (1788–1861) at Herne Hill.

100. *To Ellen Nussey, 9 December 1849*

London

Dear Ellen

I was very glad to get the two notes from Brookroyd, yours and Amelia's. I am only going to pen a very hasty reply now—as there are several people in the room and I cannot write in company—only I fear if I delay you will think me negligent.

You seem to suppose I must be very happy—dear Nell—and I see you have twenty romantic notions in your head about me—. These last you may dismiss at once—

As to being happy—I am under scenes and circumstances of excitement—but I suffer acute pain sometimes—mental pain—I mean. At the moment Mr. Thackeray presented himself—I was thoroughly faint from inanition—having eaten nothing since a very slight breakfast—and it was then seven o'clock in the evening—excitement and exhaustion together made savage work of me that evening—what he thought of me—I cannot tell. This evening I am going to meet Miss Martineau[1]—she has written to me most kindly—She knows me only as Currer Bell—I am going alone—how I shall get on I do not know.

If Mrs. Smith were not kind—I should sometimes be miserable—but she treats me almost affectionately—her attentions never flag.

I have seen many things—I hope some day to tell you what—Yesterday I went over the New Houses of Parliament[2] with Mr. Williams—An attack of rheumatic fever—has kept poor Mr. Taylor out of the way—since I wrote last—I am sorry for <u>his</u> sake.

It grows quite dark—I must stop—I shall not stay in London a day longer than I first intended—on these points I form my resolutions and will not be shaken.

The thundering 'Times' has attacked me savagely.[3]

Yours sincerely

C Brontë

Sunday.

Love to Amelia and thanks—I can hardly tell what to say about her & J[oe] T[aylor]. I do not like to think about it—I shudder sometimes

MS Berg.

1. Harriet Martineau (1802–76). See Biographical Note, p. xl. Martineau was staying at the home of her cousin Richard and his wife Lucy Martineau in London. Mrs Martineau recalled their first sight of CB—'a neat little woman, a <u>very</u> little sprite of a creature nicely dressed; & with nice tidy bright hair . . . she was . . . so innocent and un Londony that we were quite charmed with her' (BST 19. 1 and 2. 46, 47.)

2. The greater part of the old Houses of Parliament had been destroyed by fire on 16. Oct. 1834. The new buildings, still incomplete, were designed by Charles Barry (1795–1860), assisted by A. W. N. Pugin (1812–52), who provided the detail drawings.

3. On 7 Dec. *The Times* published a violent attack on *Shirley*. Despite the author's imaginative power, graphic description, and analytic skill, the novel was disfigured by coarseness, unnatural dialogues and plot, 'manufactured' characters, puerile love-entanglements, and the feeble contrivance of Caroline's illness and magical recovery. As for Mrs Pryor, 'a drearier gentlewoman it has seldom been our lot to meet'. Despite occasional flashes of genius, *Shirley* was 'at once the most high-flown and the stalest of fictions'. CB's hosts had 'mislaid' the *Times* out of consideration for her, but she insisted on seeing it, and was seen with 'tears stealing down the face and dropping on the lap' (Gaskell *Life*, ch. 18).

101. *To Ellen Nussey, 19 December 1849*

Haworth—

Dear Ellen

Here I am at Haworth once more.[1] I feel as if I had come out of an exciting whirl—Not that the hurry or stimulus would have seemed much to one accustomed to society and change—but to me they were very marked. My strength and spirits too often proved quite insufficient for the demand on their exertions—I used to bear up as well and as long as I possibly could—for whenever

I flagged I could see Mr. Smith became disturbed—he always thought something had been said or done to annoy me—which never once happened—for I met with perfect good-breeding even from antagonists—men who had done their best or worst to write me down:[2] I explained to him over and over again that my occasional silence was only failure of the power to talk—never of the will—but still he always seemed to fear there was another cause underneath.

Mrs. Smith is rather a stern woman—but she has sense and discrimination—She watched me very narrowly—when I was surrounded by gentlemen—she never took her eye from me—I liked the surveillance—both when it kept guard over me amongst many or only with her cherished and valued Son—She soon—I am convinced—saw in what light I viewed both her George and all the rest—Thackeray included. Her George is a very fine specimen of a young English Man of business—so I regard him and I am proud to be one of his props. Thackeray is a Titan of Mind—his presence and powers impress me deeply in an intellectual sense—I do not see him or know him as a man. All the others are subordinate to these—I have esteem for some and—I trust—courtesy for all. I do not of course know what they thought of me but I believe most of them expected me to come out in a more marked, eccentric, striking light—I believe they desired more to admire and more to blame. I felt sufficiently at my ease with all except Thackeray—and with him I was painfully stupid.

Now dear Nell—when can you come to Haworth[3]—Settle and let me know as soon as you can. Give my best love to all—I enclose a word for Amelia. Have things come to any crisis in that quarter? I cannot help thinking of the lion mated with the lamb—the leopard with the kid[4]—it does not Content me—the first year or two may be well enough—I do not like to look forward any farther.

[Yours sincerely
C Brontë][5]

MS Berg.

1. CB reached home on 15 Dec.
2. Guests at a dinner party given by the Smiths on 13 Dec. included five critics—those of *The Times*, *Athenaeum*, *Examiner*, *Spectator*, and *Atlas*. Like *The Times*, the *Atlas* saw much to criticize in *Shirley*, despite some merits: it was destitute of invention, minor characters were mostly unreal and repulsive, and the curates, pointlessly introduced, were 'like a bevy of goblins in a pantomime'. For the *Examiner*, see Letter 96 n. 3. H. F. Chorley, writing in the *Athenaeum*, considered that the curates provided some clever comedy, but he criticized the 'languid movement' of the tale, and the use of melodramatic coincidence. The *Spectator* found the novel clear, powerful, and vigorous, but objected to its ill-drawn protagonists, and 'ingrained rudeness'.
3. CB hoped that Ellen would come to Haworth for three weeks, from 27 Dec. Amelia Ringrose left Brookroyd on the day this letter was written.
4. Cf. Isaiah 11: 6.
5. Signature cut off.

102. *To W. S. Williams, 3 January 1850*

[Haworth]

My dear Sir

I have to acknowledge the receipt of the "Morning Chronicle" with a good review—and of the "Church of Engl[an]d Quarterly" and the "Westminster" with bad ones:[1] I have also to thank you for your letter which would have been answered sooner had I been alone, but just now I am enjoying the treat of my friend Ellen's society and she makes me indolent and negligent—I am too busy talking to her all day to do anything else. You allude to the subject of female friendship and express wonder at the infrequency of sincere attachments amongst women—As to married women, I can well understand that they should be absorbed in their husbands and children—but single women often like each other much and derive great solace from their mutual regard—Friendship however is a plant which cannot be forced—true friendship is no gourd springing in a night and withering in a day. When I first saw Ellen I did not care for her—we were schoolfellows—in the course of time we learnt each others faults and good points—we were contrasts—still we suited—affection was first a germ, then a sapling—then a strong tree: now—no new friend, however lofty or profound in intellect,—not even Miss Martineau herself—could be to me what Ellen is, yet she is no more than a conscientious, observant, calm, well-bred Yorkshire girl. She is without romance—if she attempts to read poetry—or poetic prose aloud—I am irritated and deprive her of the book—if she talks of it I stop my ears—but she is good—she is true—she is faithful and I love her.

Since I came home Miss Martineau has written me a long and truly kind letter—she invites me to visit her at Ambleside—I like the idea—whether I can realize it or not—it is pleasant to have in prospect.

You ask me to write to Mrs. Williams; I would rather she wrote to me first, and let her send any kind of letter she likes, without studying mood or manner.

[Yours sincerely,
C. Brontë][2]

MS BPM B.S. 73.

1. The *Chronicle* for 25 Dec. 1849 affirmed that *Shirley* must be by a man, and praised the 'uprightness' of thought, purity of heart and feeling, and successful characterization; it was 'a veritable triumph of psychology'. The *Church of England Quarterly Review* for Jan. 1850 deplored CB's irreverent use of scripture, and the depiction of curates who were useless as moral examples because they were not true to present times. But the female characters were sketched with a delicacy lacking in *JE*, and the novel deserved popularity because it appealed to pure sympathies instead of the baser passions. The *Westminster* considered *Shirley* feeble in comparison with *JE*: in the third volume 'we can lay down the book in the middle of a chapter,—and go to sleep'. Nevertheless its discriminating spirit and desire to heal class antagonism were commendable (*Westminster Review* 52. 418–19).
2. Valediction and signature lacking in MS; text supplied from *CBL* ii. 323.

103. *To Ellen Nussey, ?28 January 1850*

[Haworth]

Dear Ellen

I cannot but be concerned to hear of your Mother's illness; write again soon—if it be but a line, to tell me how she gets on. This shadow will I trust and believe, be but a passing one—but it is a foretaste and warning of what <u>must</u> come one day—Let it prepare your mind, dear Ellen, for that great trial which, if you live, it <u>must</u> in the course of a few years be your lot to undergo. That cutting asunder of the ties of nature is the pain we most dread and which we are most certain to experience.

Perhaps you will have seen J. T[aylor] ere this. I had a brief note from him dated Hull—he had seen Mr. R[ingrose] whom he found "inimical though not avowedly so—desirous to refuse but wanting a pretext". "Such a reception" he says "would—six week[1] ago, have made him give it up". He does not mention whether he saw Amelia. He will go on.

Lewes' letter made me laugh—I cannot respect him for it.[2] J. K. Shuttleworth's letter did not make me laugh—he has written again since.[3]

I have received to-day a note from a Miss Alexander[4] of Lupset Cottage, Wakefield—daughter—she says—of Dr. Alexander—Do you know anything of her—?

[Mary Taylor seems in good health and spirits and in the way of doing well.][5] I shall feel anxious to hear again.

Mr. Nicholls[6] has finished reading "Shirley"—he is delighted with it—John Brown's wife seriously thought he had gone wrong in the head as she heard him giving vent to roars of laughter as he sat alone—clapping his hands and stamping on the floor. He would read all the scenes about the curates aloud to papa—he triumphed in his own character.

What Mr. Grant will say is another question.[7]

[Signature lacking in MS.]

MS Widener, Harvard HEW. 1.5.1.

1. Thus in MS. Joseph Taylor married Amelia Ringrose on 2 Oct. 1850.
2. G. H. Lewes's praise of *JE* had left Charlotte unprepared for his harsh review of *Shirley* in the *Edinburgh Review* for Jan. 1850. He found most of the characters disagreeable; the curates were irrelevant and unamusing, and there was no 'passionate link', no unity. The novel was an inartistic 'portfolio of random sketches'. Most hurtfully, he claimed that the reason so few women attained intellectual eminence was that their grand function and preoccupation must be maternity. CB, who wished to be judged as an author, not a woman, had responded with a brusque personal note to Lewes: 'I can be on my guard against my enemies, but God deliver me from my friends!' In his reply Lewes 'remonstrated' with her, and he later claimed that his review 'was dictated by real admiration and friendship'.
3. Sir James Phillips Kay-Shuttleworth, 1st Baronet (1804–77.) See Biographical Notes, p. xxxix. He had invited CB to visit him and his family at Gawthorpe Hall, Padiham, near Burnley, Lancs., some eighteen miles from Haworth.

4. Harriet Alexander, daughter of Dr Disney Alexander, who had a medical practice in Wakefield.
5. Original text cut off; words supplied by Ellen Nussey.
6. Mr Nicholls lodged at the house of John Brown, the sexton. His portrayal as the 'Irish curate, Mr. Macarthey' in *Shirley* is comparatively benign.
7. Revd Joseph Brett Grant, MA (d. 1879) was the prototype of the quarrelsome, 'densely self-satisfied' Mr Donne in *Shirley*, who turned out 'far better than expected' in the end.

104. *To Ellen Nussey, ?5 February 1850*

[Haworth]

Dear Ellen

I am truly glad to hear of the happy change in your Mother's state—I hope nothing will occur to give it a check—The relief when a hope of recovery succeeds to the dread of danger must be sweet indeed—I remember it was what I intensely longed for—but what it was not seen good I should enjoy.

Thank you for the scrap of information respecting Sir J. K. S[huttleworth].

Mr. Morgan[1] has finished reading "Jane Eyre" and writes not in blame but in the highest strain of eulogy—! He says it thoroughly fascinated and enchained him—&c. &c. &c.

Martha came in yesterday—puffing and blowing and much excited—"I've heard sich news" she began—"What about?" "Please ma'am you've been and written two books—the grandest books that ever was seen—My Father has heard it at Halifax and Mr. George Taylor and Mr. Greenwood and Mr. Merrall at Bradford[2]—and they are going to have a meeting at the Mechanic's Institute and to settle about ordering them."

"Hold your tongue, Martha, and be off." I fell into a cold sweat.

"Jane Eyre" will be read by John Brown by Mrs Taylor and Betty[3]—God help keep & deliver me! Good by'e CB.

MS Berg.

1. Mr Brontë's friend, Revd William Morgan (?1782–1858), incumbent of Christ Church, Bradford. He was probably the model for Dr Boultby in *Shirley*.
2. The church warden George Taylor (1801–65) of the Manor House, Stanbury; one of the many local Greenwoods—probably the church trustee Joseph Greenwood, JP (1786–1856) of Spring Head; and one of the wealthy Merralls of Haworth. The mill-owner Michael Merrall (1811–81) was the treasurer and later the chairman of the Haworth Mechanics' Institute, founded in the late 1840s.
3. Not definitely identified, but 'Betty' was possibly George Taylor's daughter Elizabeth, later the wife of Revd Francis Marriner.

105. *To George Smith, 16 March 1850*

[Haworth]

My dear Sir

I return Mr. Thornton Hunt's[1] note after reading it carefully. I tried very hard to understand all he says about "Art", but, to speak truth, my efforts were crowned with incomplete success. There is a certain jargon in use amongst critics on this point, through which it is physically and morally impossible for me to see daylight—One thing however I see plainly enough, and that is Mr. Currer Bell needs improvement and ought to strive after it—and this (D.V.)[2] he honestly intends to do—taking his time, however—and following as his guides Nature and Truth; if these lead to what the Critics call "Art" it <will all come right in the end> is all very well—but if not that grand desideratum has no chance of being run after or caught.

The puzzle is that while the people in the South object to my delineation of Northern life and manners, the people of Yorkshire and Lancashire approve: they say it is precisely that contrast of rough Nature with highly artificial cultivation which forms one of their main characteristics; Such or something very similar has been the observation made to me lately whilst I have been from home by members of some of the ancient East Lancashire families[3] whose mansions lie on the hilly borderland between the two counties—the question arises whether do the London critics or the old Northern Squires understand the matter best?

Any promise you require respecting the books shall be willingly given, provided only I am allowed the Jesuits' privilege of a mental reservation, giving license to forget such promise whenever oblivion shall appear expedient.[4]

The last two or three numbers of "Pendennis"[5] will not, I daresay, be generally thought sufficiently exciting—but still I like them—Though the story lingers, (for me), the interest does not flag. Here and there we feel the pen has been guided by a tired hand, that the mind of the writer has been somewhat clouded and depressed by his recent illness or by some other cause, but Thackeray still proves himself greater when he is weary than other writers are when they are fresh.—The Public of course will have no compassion for his fatigue and make no allowance for the ebb of inspiration—but some true-hearted readers here and there, while grieving that such a man should be obliged to write when he is not in the mood, will wonder that under such circumstances he should write so well.

The parcel of books will come I doubt not, at such time as it shall suit the good pleasure of the railway officials to send it on—or rather to yield it up to the repeated and humble solicitations of Haworth Carriers—till when I wait in all reasonable patience and resignation—looking with docility to that model of active self-helpfulness Punch kindly offers the "Women of England" in his "Unprotected Female".[6]

Offering you my excessive sympathy in that painful operation of a "Removal" to which you allude[7]—and a much sincerer sympathy to your Mother and Sisters—for you I daresay have not been allowed to suffer much.

I am my dear Sir

Yours sincerely　　C Brontë

MS BPM SG 34.

1. Thornton Leigh Hunt (1810–73), journalist, editor, and art critic, eldest son of Leigh Hunt and friend of G. H. Lewes, whose wife Agnes was pregnant with Thornton's son Edmund, b. 16 Apr. 1850.
2. *Deo volente*: God willing.
3. CB had stayed with the Kay-Shuttleworths at Gawthorpe Hall, near Burnley, from 12 to 15 or 16 March. She might have met one of the Towneleys of Towneley Hall, about four miles from Gawthorpe.
4. George Smith had perhaps exacted a promise that CB would not thank him for the parcel of books which arrived on 18 Mar., since he disliked such expressions of gratitude. The twenty books were probably on loan. They included the first 3 vols. of Cuthbert Southey's life of his father, Robert Southey, the letters of Charles Lamb, Jane Austen's *Sense and Sensibility*, *Emma*, and *Pride and Prejudice*, Lewes's play, *The Noble Heart* (1850), and some works on educational themes: *Thoughts on Self-Culture, addressed to Women*, 2 vols. (1850), by Maria Georgina Grey and A. Emily Shirreff, and Alexander John Scott, *Suggestions on Female Education: Two Introductory lectures on English Literature and Moral Philosophy, delivered in the Ladies' College* [in Bedford Square], Dec. 1849.
5. Numbers 12–14 of Thackeray's novel, published by Bradbury & Evans. His illness from Sept. 1849 had caused three months' hiatus in publication, and a weakening in the technique and effect of the work.
6. Twenty satirical 'Scenes from the life of an unprotected female' in *Punch*, 3 Nov. 1849–20 Apr. 1850. 'Mrs. Martha Struggles' is shown travelling in the wrong direction, repeatedly misdirected, baffled, and discomfited, but surviving to marry the 'inevitable one', Mr Jones.
7. The Smiths moved from 4 Westbourne Place to a larger house at 76 (later renumbered 112, then 103) Gloucester Terrace in Bayswater.

106. *To W. S. Williams, 3 April 1850*

[Haworth]

My dear Sir

I have received the "Dublin Review"[1] and your letter enclosing the Indian Notices.[2] I hope these reviews will do good; they are all favourable and one of them (the Dublin) is very able. I have read no critique so discriminating since that in the "Revue des deux Mondes";[3] it offers a curious contrast to Lewes's in the "Edinburgh"[4] where forced praise, given by jerks and obviously without real and cordial liking, and censure crude, conceited and ignorant were mixed in random lumps forming a very loose and inconsistent whole. Against the teaching of some (even clever) men one instinctively revolts. They may possess attainments, they may boast varied knowledge of life and of the world, but if, of the finer perceptions, of the more delicate phases of feeling they be destitute and incapable—of what avail is the rest? Believe me, my dear Sir, while hints well worth consideration may come from unpretending sources, from minds not highly cultured but naturally fine and delicate, from hearts kindly, feeling and unenvious, learned dictums delivered with pomp and sound may be perfectly empty, stupid and contemptible. No man ever yet—"by aid of Greek climbed Parnassus"[5] or taught others to climb it. It is true of "Art" as of Religion—"Out of the mouths of babes and sucklings (figuratively) God has ordained praise." The wisdom of this world, with reference to it, is often mere foolishness—[6]

I enclose for your perusal a scrap of paper[7]—which came into my hands without the knowledge and, I fear, against the consent of the writer—He is a poor working man of this village—a thoughtful, reading, feeling being—whose mind is too keen for his frame and wears it out—I have not spoken to him above thrice in my life, for he is a dissenter and has rarely come in my way—the document is a sort of record of his feelings after the perusal of "Jane Eyre": it is artless and earnest, genuine and generous—you must return it to me, for I value it more than testimonies from higher sources. He said "Miss Brontë if she knew he had written it would scorn him", but indeed Miss Brontë does not scorn him—she only grieves that a mind of which this is the emanation should be kept crushed by the leaden hand of Poverty, by the trials of uncertain health and the claims of a large family.

As to the "Times,"[8] as you say—the acrimony of its critique has proved, in some measure, its own antidote; to have been more effective—it should have been juster. I think it has had little weight here in the North; it may be that annoying remarks, if made, are not suffered to reach my ear, but certainly, while I have heard little condemnatory of "Shirley"—more than once have I been deeply moved by manifestations of even enthusiastic approbation. I deem it unwise to dwell much on these matters, but for once I must permit myself to remark that the generous pride many of the Yorkshire people have taken in the matter has been such as to awake and claim my gratitude—especially since it has afforded a source of reviving pleasure to my Father in his old age. The very Curates—poor fellows! shew no resentment; each characteristically finds solace for his own wounds in crowing over his brethren. Mr. Donne[9] was—at first, a little disturbed; for a week or two he fidgetted about the neighbourhood in some disquietude—but he is now soothed down, only yesterday I had the pleasure of making him a comfortable cup of tea and seeing him sip it with revived complacency. It is a curious fact that since he read "Shirley" he has come to the house oftener than ever and been remarkably meek and assiduous to please.—Some people's natures are veritable enigmas—I quite expected to have one good scene at the least with him, but as yet nothing of the sort has occurred—and if the other curates do not tease him into irritation, he will remain quiet now.

Are you aware whether there are any grounds for that conjecture in the "Bengal Hurkaru"[10] that the critique in the "Times" was from the pen of Mr. Thackeray? I should much like to know this. If such were the case—(and I feel as if it were by no means impossible) the circumstance would open a most curious and novel glimpse of a very peculiar disposition. Do you think it likely to be true?

The account you give of Mrs. Williams' health is not cheering, but I should think her indisposition is partly owing to the variable weather, at least if you have had the same keen frost and cold east winds in London from which we have lately suffered in Yorkshire. I trust the milder temperature we are now enjoying may quickly confirm her convalescence. With kind regards to Mrs. W—believe me, my dear Sir

Yours sincerely   C Brontë

MS Berg.

1. Henry Bagshawe's review of *JE* and *Shirley* in this Catholic quarterly praised the 'raciness and charm', thought and imagination of these novels. Though not suitable for the very young, they were moral in their natural portrayal of life and their lack of distorted or false principles. The only severe criticism is given to a degree of exaggeration and abruptness, especially in dealing with religion, and to the 'flippant attack' on the Litany of Loretto as jargon (*Dublin Review*, 28. 209–33).
2. Although he had not read *Shirley* by 2 Feb. 1850, the reporter in the *Bengal Hurkaru and the India Gazette* for that date disagreed with the damning review in *The Times* which his paper reprinted. On the strength of passages quoted there and in the more favourable *Examiner* review, he was sure readers would welcome another production from the gifted writer of *JE*. I have not traced other Indian notices published by the date of this letter.
3. In this journal Eugene Forçade, convinced that *Shirley* was by a woman, praised the characters, effective drama, and the 'naturalness, fire, spirit and fantasy of the dialogue', though he considered the multiplicity of scenes led to diffuseness and tedium unrelieved by the passion of *JE*. He did not condemn it for being spiced with revolt against certain social conventions (*Revue des deux mondes*, 15 Nov. 49).
4. See Letter 103 n. 2.
5. Robert Burns. 'First Epistle to John Lapraik', stanza 12: 'A set o' dull, conceited Hashes, | Confuse their brains in *Colledge-classes!* They *gang in* stirks, and *come out* Asses, | Plain truth to speak; | An' syne they think to climb Parnassus | By dint o' Greek!'
6. Cf. Psalm 8: 2 and 1 Corinthians 3: 19.
7. Written by the Haworth stationer, John Greenwood (1807–63), formerly a woolcomber. He had provided the Brontë sisters with large quantities of writing paper.
8. See Letter 100 n. 3.
9. Revd Joseph Brett Grant of Oxenhope.
10. After commenting on the literary sensation produced by Currer Bell's novels, the reviewer in the *Hurkaru* remarked: 'We may be wrong in our conjecture, but we are inclined to believe that [*The Times*'] criticism . . . is from the pen of Mr. Thackeray' (2 Feb. 1850, 135). The conjecture was wrong.

107. *To W. S. Williams, 12 April 1850*

[Haworth]

My dear Sir

I own I was glad to receive your assurance that the Calcutta paper's surmise was unfounded. It is said that when we <u>wish</u> a thing to be true, we are prone to believe it true, but I think, (judging from myself) we adopt with a still prompter credulity the rumour which shocks.

It is very kind in Dr. Forbes to give me his book;[1] I hope Mr. Smith will have the goodness to convey my thanks for the present. You can keep it to send with the next parcel, or perhaps I may be in London myself before May is over; that invitation I mentioned in a previous letter is still urged upon me,[2] and well as I know what penance its acceptance would entail in some points, I also know the advantage it would bring in others. My Conscience tells me it would be the act of a moral poltroon to let the fear of suffering stand in the way of improvement. But suffer—I shall. No matter.

The perusal of Southey's Life[3] has lately afforded me much pleasure; the autobiography with which it commences is deeply interesting and the letters which follow are scarcely less so, disclosing as they do a character most estimable in its integrity and a nature most amiable in its benevolence, as well as a mind admirable in its talent. Some people assert that Genius is inconsistent with domestic happiness, and yet Southey was happy at home and made his home happy; he not only loved his wife and children <u>though</u> he was a poet, but he loved them the better <u>because</u> he was a poet. He seems to have been without taint of worldliness; London, with its pomps and vanities, learned coteries with their dry pedantry rather scared than attracted him; he found his prime glory in his genius, and his chief felicity in home-affections. I like Southey.

I have likewise read one of Miss Austen's works "Emma"[4]—read it with interest and with just the degree of admiration which Miss Austen herself would have thought sensible and suitable—anything like warmth or enthusiasm; anything energetic, poignant, heart-felt, is utterly out of place in commending these works: all such demonstration the authoress would have met with a well-bred sneer, would have calmly scorned as outré and extravagant. She does her business of delineating the surface of the lives of genteel English people curiously well; there is a Chinese fidelity, a miniature delicacy in the painting: she ruffles her reader by nothing vehement, disturbs him by nothing profound: the Passions are perfectly unknown to her; she rejects even a speaking acquaintance with that stormy Sisterhood; even to the Feelings she vouchsafes no more than an occasional graceful but distant recognition; too frequent converse with them would ruffle the smooth elegance of her progress. Her business is not half so much with the human heart as with the human eyes, mouth, hands and feet; what sees keenly, speaks aptly, moves flexibly, it suits her to study, but what throbs fast and full, though hidden, what the blood rushes through, what is the unseen seat of Life and the sentient target of Death—this Miss Austen ignores; she no more, with her mind's eye, beholds the heart of her race than each man, with bodily vision sees the heart in his heaving breast. Jane Austen was a complete and most sensible lady, but a very incomplete, and rather insensible (not senseless) woman; if this is heresy—I cannot help it. If I said it to some people (Lewes for instance) they would directly accuse me of advocating exaggerated heroics, but I am not afraid of your falling into any such vulgar error.

Believe me
Yours sincerely
C Brontë

MS HM 24394.

1. For Dr (later Sir) John Forbes, who had approved of Mr Teale's treatment of Anne Brontë, see Letter 83 n. 1. CB had met him in London. His recent publications included *Illustrations of Modern Mesmerism from Personal Investigation* (1845) and *A Physician's Holiday, or a Month in Switzerland in the Summer of 1848* (1849).
2. The Kay-Shuttleworths of Gawthorpe Hall had invited CB to visit them at their London house in Gloucester Square, very near to the Smiths' new home at 76 (later 112) Gloucester Terrace.
3. The first three volumes of Revd Charles Cuthbert Southey's life of his father, *The Life and Correspondence of the Late Robert Southey* (1849, 1850) had been especially welcome when CB received the box of books from her publishers on 18 Mar. 1850. The remaining 3 volumes would be published in or by Oct. 1850.
4. See Letter 105 n. 4.

108. *To W. S. Williams, 22 May 1850*

[Haworth]

My dear Sir

I had thought to bring the "Leader" and the "Athenæum"[1] myself this time, and not to have to send them by post, but it turns out otherwise; my journey to London is again postponed and this time indefinitely: Sir J. Kay Shuttleworth's state of health is the cause, a cause I fear not likely to be soon removed. Of late he has been much worse; his sufferings have for some days been almost incessant; the root of them, in his physicians' opinion, lies in an overwrought and exhausted brain, every excitement—company and conversation included—is consequently interdicted.

Once more then I settle myself down in the quietude of Haworth Parsonage, with books for my houshold companions, and an occasional letter for a visitor—a mute society but neither quarrelsome, nor vulgarizing nor unimproving.

One of the pleasures I had promised myself consisted in asking you several questions about the "Leader" which is really—in its way—an interesting paper—I wanted, amongst other things, to ask you the real names of some of

7 (*left*). A drawing of Ellen Nussey as a young girl; artist unknown. Brontë Parsonage Museum.

8 (*below*). Photograph of Ellen Nussey in old age. Brontë Parsonage Museum.

9 (*above*). Pencil portrait of the Revd. William Weightman by Charlotte Brontë, February 1840. Brontë Parsonage Museum.

10 (*right*). Portrait of George Smith as a young man. Brontë Parsonage Museum.

11 (*left*). Photograph of William Smith Williams. Brontë Parsonage Museum.

12 (*below*). Charlotte Brontë's first letter to Smith, Elder and Company, 15 July 1847, sending them the manuscript of *The Professor*. MS BPM SG 1.

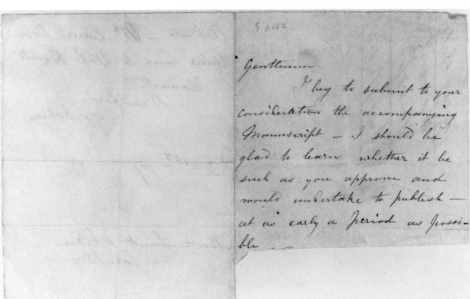

> Gentlemen
> I beg to submit to your consideration the accompanying Manuscript — I should be glad to learn whether it be such as you approve and would undertake to publish — at as early a period as possible —

13 (*right*). Carte-de-visite photograph of Charlotte Brontë, 1854, inscribed on the reverse in ink, 'within a year of CB's death'. Seton-Gordon Collection, Brontë Parsonage Museum, SG 109(a).

14 (*below*). Carte-de-visite photograph of the Revd. A. B. Nicholls, taken at about the time of his marriage to Charlotte Brontë. Brontë Parsonage Museum.

the contributors[2]—and also what Lewes writes besides his "Apprenticeship of Life"—I always think the article headed "Literature" is his. Some of the communications in the "Open Council" department are odd productions—but it seems to me very fair and right to admit them.

Is not the system of this paper altogether a novel one? I do not remember seeing anything precisely like it before.

I have just received yours of this morning; thank you for the enclosed note. The longings for liberty & leisure which May sunshine wakens in you, stir my sympathy—I am afraid Cornhill is little better than a prison for its inmates, on warm Spring or Summer days—It is a pity to think of you all toiling at your desks in such genial weather as this. For my part I am free to walk on the moors—but when I go out there alone—everything reminds me of the times when others were with me and then the moors seem a wilderness, featureless, solitary, saddening—My sister Emily had a particular love for them, and there is not a knoll of heather, not a branch of fern, not a young bilberry leaf not a fluttering lark or linnet but reminds me of her. The distant prospects were Anne's delight, and when I look round, she is in the blue tints, the pale mists, the waves and shadows of the horizon. In the hill-country silence their poetry comes by lines and stanzas into my mind: once I loved it—now I dare not read it—and am driven often to wish I could taste one draught of oblivion and forget much that, while mind remains, I never shall forget. Many people seem to recall their departed relatives with a sort of melancholy complacency—but I think these have not watched them through lingering sickness nor witnessed their last moments—it is these reminiscences that stand by your bedside at night, and rise at your pillow in the morning. At the end of all, however, there exists the great hope—Eternal Life is theirs now.

Believe me yours sincerely

C Brontë

MS Taylor Collection, Princeton.

1. Copies of the *Leader*, the new radical weekly begun by G. H. Lewes and Thornton Hunt on 30 Mar. 1850, had been sent to CB by Smith, Elder since its inception. On 6 Nov. 1849 she had thanked James Taylor for his offer to send her the *Athenaeum*.

2. Lewes wished to open the journal to the free expression of opinion, and the 'Open Council' fulfilled this aim by printing letters to the editor without censorship. Lewes contributed most of the 'Literature' section, using the pseudonym 'Vivian'. The 'Public Affairs' columns were written by Thornton Hunt. See Rosemary Ashton, *G. H. Lewes: A Life* (1991), 97–9, 105–6.

109. *To Revd Patrick Brontë, 4 June 1850*

76 Gloucester Terrace,
Hyde Park Gardens.[1]

Dear Papa,

I was very glad to get your letter this morning, and still more glad to learn that your health continues in some degree to improve. I fear you will feel the present weather somewhat debilitating, at least if it is as warm in Yorkshire as in London. I cannot help grudging these fine days on account of the roofing of the house.[2] It is a great pity the workmen were not prepared to begin a week ago.

Since I wrote I have been to the Opera;[3] to the Exhibition of the Royal Academy, where there were some fine paintings, especially a large one by Landseer of the Duke of Wellington on the field of Waterloo, and a grand, wonderful picture of Martin's from Campbell's poem of the "Last Man," showing the red sun fading out of the sky, and all the soil of the foreground made up of bones and skulls.[4] The secretary of the Zoological Society also sent me an honorary ticket of admission to their gardens, which I wish you could see. There are animals from all parts of the world inclosed in great cages in the open air amongst trees and shrubs—lions, tigers, leopards, elephants, numberless monkies,[5] camels, five or six cameleopards,[6] a young hippopotamus with an Egyptian for its keeper;[7] birds of all kinds—eagles, ostriches, a pair of great condors from the Andes, strange ducks and water-fowl which seem very happy and comfortable, and build their nests amongst the reeds and sedges of the lakes where they are kept. Some of the American birds make inexpressible noises.

There are also all sorts of living snakes and lizards in cages, some great Ceylon toads not much smaller than Flossy,[8] some large foreign rats nearly as large and fierce as little bull-dogs. The most ferocious and deadly-looking things in the place were these rats, a laughing hyena (which every now and then uttered a hideous peal of laughter such as a score of maniacs might produce) and a cobra di capello snake.[9] I think this snake was the worst of all: it had the eyes and face of a fiend, and darted out its barbed tongue sharply and incessantly.

I am glad to hear that Tabby and Martha are pretty well. Remember me to them, and—Believe me, dear papa, your affectionate daughter,

C. Brontë.

I hope you don't care for the notice in Sharpe's Magazine;[10] it does not disturb me in the least. Mr. Smith says it is of no consequence whatever in a literary sense. Sharpe, the proprietor, was an apprentice of Mr. Smith's father.

Text: *CBL* ii. 410–11.

1. George Smith's mother, the widowed Mrs Elizabeth Smith, had invited CB to stay at their home in London. They had moved from 4 Westbourne Place, Bishop's Road, Paddington before 25

May, when Charlotte wrote to Mrs Smith, 'I am sorry you have changed your residence as I shall now again lose my way in going up and down stairs . . .'

2. The stone-flagged roof of Haworth Parsonage was about to be removed and renovated with new supporting timber.

3. CB could have seen Rossini's *Il Barbiere di Siviglia* at Her Majesty's Theatre on Saturday 1 June, but since she had fancied there were things she would like better, when the Smiths took her to that opera on 8 July 1848, they probably took her to Meyerbeer's *Les Huguenots* at Covent Garden. The singers included Giulia Grisi as Valentina and Giovanni Mario as Raoul.

4. Edwin Landseer's 'A dialogue at Waterloo. "But 'twas a famous victory"' depicted Wellington, with his daughter, revisiting the battleground, where a peasant-woman offers to sell him relics: 'Decorations and trappings—nay, the very bones—of some of the dead.' John Martin's sombre picture, now in the Walker Art Gallery, Liverpool, shows creation disarrayed beneath livid clouds, recalling Thomas Campbell's poem, 'The Last Man', where universal death is the result of plague.

5. Thus in source.

6. Giraffes. CB knew that her father would be interested in all she saw at the gardens, for he possessed J. J. Audubon's *Ornithological Biography*, 5 vols. (1831–9), E. T. Bennett's *The Gardens and Menagerie of the Zoological Society Delineated*, i. *Quadrupeds* (1830), and Thomas Bewick's *A History of British Birds*, 2 vols. (1816 edn.).

7. This famous hippopotamus, whose arrival on 25 May had a dramatic effect on the number of visitors to the zoo, was believed to be the first seen in Europe since Roman times.

8. The spaniel that had belonged to Anne Brontë.

9. Properly 'cobra de capello'.

10. *Sharpe's London Journal* for June 1850 found *Shirley* disappointing. Though the novel had some merit, it lacked *JE*'s charm of originality, but retained offensively coarse character portrayal. The heroine—seemingly another self-portrait—was such that 'her sex disowns her—nay, it will even blush for her': unfeminine in thought and expression, she was alien both to good taste and the spirit of romance.

110. *To Ellen Nussey, [12 June 1850]*

[London]

Dear Ellen

Since I wrote to you last,[1] I have not had many moments to myself, except such as it was absolutely necessary to give to rest. On the whole, however, I have thus far got on very well, suffering much less from exhaustion than I did last time—

Of course I cannot in a letter give you a regular chronicle of how my time has been spent—I can only just notify what I deem three of the chief incidents—A sight of the Duke of Wellington at the Chapel Royal[2]—he is a real grand old man—a visit to the House of Commons (which I hope to describe to you some day when I see you) and—last not least—an interview with Mr. Thackeray

He made a morning-call and sat above two hours—Mr. Smith only was in the room the whole time. He described it afterwards as a queer scene, and I suppose it was. The giant sat before me—I was moved to speak to him of some of his short-comings (literary of course) one by one the faults came into my mind and one by one I brought them out and sought some explanation or defence—He did defend himself like a great Turk and heathen—that is to say, the excuses were often worse than the crime itself. The matter ended in decent amity—if all be well I am to dine at his house this evening.[3]

I have seen Lewes too—he is a man with both weaknesses and sins; but unless I err greatly the foundation of his nature is not bad—and were he almost a fiend in character—I could not feel otherwise to him than half sadly half tenderly—a queer word the last—but I use it because the aspect of Lewes's face almost moves me to tears—it is so wonderfully like Emily—her eyes, her features—the very nose, the somewhat prominent mouth, the forehead—even at moments the expression: whatever Lewes does or says I believe I cannot hate him.

Another likeness I have seen too that touched me sorrowfully. Do you remember my speaking of a Miss Kavanagh[4]—a young authoress who supported her mother by her writings? Hearing from Mr. Williams that she had a longing to see me I called on her yesterday—I found a little, almost dwarfish figure to which even *I* had to look down—not deformed—that is—not hunchbacked but long-armed and with a large head and (at first sight) a strange face. She met me half-frankly, half tremblingly; we sat down together and when I had talked with her five minutes that face was no longer strange but mournfully familiar—it was Martha Taylor[5] in every lineament—I shall try to find a moment to see her again. She lives in a poor but clean and neat little lodging—her mother seems a somewhat weak-minded woman who can be no companion to her—her father has quite deserted his wife and child—and this poor little feeble, intelligent, cordial thing wastes her brain to gain a living. She is twenty-five years old.

I have seen considerably more of the Williams' family but would rather communicate my impressions in conversation than by writing—Mr. Williams—his three daughters and his son were here at a ball Mrs. Smith gave last Friday[6]—the ease and grace, the natural gentility of the manners of all five were remarkable—their dress—their appearance were a decoration to the rooms—as Mrs. Smith afterwards remarked—I called at their house yesterday—and I can hardly tell why I came away much pained—others do not see—or at least do not mention—what I seem to see in that family—whether I am partly mistaken I do not know. Mrs. Williams has been here too—her conversation is most fluent and intelligent—her manners perfectly good—of her character—in a moral point of view—I can have now no doubts—and yet I confess there is a something about all excepting the father himself and the eldest daughter—from which I feel inclined to shrink.

I do not intend to stay here at the furthest more than a week longer—but at the end of that time I cannot go home for the house at Haworth is just now unroofed—repairs were become necessary—if I get any cash (of which I see no signs) I should like to go for a week or two to the sea-side—in which case

I wonder whether it would be possible for you to join me—but this point will require deliberation

Meantime with regards to all believe me
Yours faithfully
CB—

Write directly.

MS HM 24471.

1. On 3 June.
2. At St James's Palace. As CB's early writings show, the Duke of Wellington had been her hero since her childhood.
3. The evening party proved to be painfully solemn, since CB was too shy to talk freely. Thackeray's daughter Anne (Lady Ritchie) recalled that 'gloomy and silent evening, when the conversation grew dimmer and more dim', and Thackeray escaped to his club (Anne Ritchie, *Chapters from some Memoirs* (1894), 60–5).
4. Julia Kavanagh, novelist and biographer. See Biographical Notes, p. xxxix, and Letter 62 n. 3.
5. 1819–42. Martha, Mary Taylor's sister, the lively and original 'Miss Boisterous'. She died—possibly of cholera, possibly of a complication of pregnancy—at the Château de Koekelberg, the school just outside Brussels which she and Mary attended.
6. 7 June. Mr Williams probably brought his three older daughters, Margaret Ellen (23), Fanny (21), Louisa (17), and his eldest son, Frank (19).

111. *To Ellen Nussey, 21 June 1850*

76, Gloucester Terrace
Hyde Park Gardens
[London]

Dear Ellen

I am leaving London, if all be well, on Tuesday[1]—and shall be very glad to come to you for a few days, if that arrangement still remains convenient to you—I intend to start at 9 o'clock a.m. by the express train, which arrives in Leeds at 35-minutes past two p.m. I should then be at Batley[2] by about 4 o'clock in the afternoon—would that suit?

My London visit has much surpassed my expectations this time; I have suffered less and enjoyed more than before—rather a trying termination yet remains to me.

Mrs. Smith's youngest son[3] is at school in Scotland, and George—her eldest—is going to fetch him home for the vacation: the other evening he announced his intention of taking one of his sisters with him—and the evening afterwards he further proposed that Miss Brontë should go down to Edinburgh and join them there and see that city and its suburbs—I concluded he was joking—laughed and declined—however it seems he was in earnest; being always accustomed to have his will, he brooks opposition ill. The thing appearing to me perfectly out of the question—I still refused—Mrs. Smith did not at all favour it—you may easily fancy how she helped me to sustain my opposition—but her worthy Son only waxed more determined—his mother is master of the house—but he is master of his mother—this morning she came and entreated me to go—"George wished it so much; he had begged her to use her influence—&c. &c.—"

Now I believe that George and I understand each other very well—and respect each other very sincerely—we both know the wide breach time has made between us—we do not embar[r]ass each other, or very rarely—my six or eight years of seniority, to say nothing of lack of all pretensions to beauty &c. are a perfect safeguard—I should not in the least fear to go with him to China—I like to see him pleased—I greatly <u>dis</u>like to ruffle and disappoint him—so he shall have his mind—and, if all be well—I mean to join him in Edinburgh after I shall have spent a few days with you. With his buoyant animal spirits and youthful vigour he will make severe demands on my muscles and nerves—but I daresay I shall get through somehow—and then perhaps come back to rest a few days longer with you before I go home.

With kind regards to all at Brookroyd—your guests included—

I am—dear Ellen
Yours faithfully
C Brontë

Write by return of post.

MS BPM Gr. E 19.

1. 25 June.
2. The nearest station to Ellen's home in Birstall.
3. Alexander, aged 15 or 16. His eldest sister Eliza would accompany the party.

112. *To W. S. Williams, 20 July 1850*

[Haworth]

My dear Sir

I would not write to you immediately on my arrival at home, because each return to this old house brings with it a phase of feeling which it is better to pass through quietly before beginning to indite letters.

The six weeks of change and enjoyment are past but they are not lost; Memory took a sketch of each as it went by and, especially, a distinct daguerrotype[1] of the two days I spent in Scotland.[2] Those were two very pleasant days. I always liked Scotland as an idea, but now, as a reality, I like it far better; it furnished me with some hours as happy almost as any I ever spent. Do not fear however that

I am going to bore you with description; you will, before now, have received a pithy and pleasant report of all things, to which any addition of mine would be superfluous.

My present endeavours are directed towards recalling my thoughts, cropping their wings drilling them into correct discipline and forcing them to settle to some useful work: they are idle and keep taking the train down to London or making a foray over the Border, especially are they prone to perpetrate that last excursion—and who indeed that has once seen Edinburgh, with its couchant crag-lion,[3] but must see it again in dreams waking or sleeping? My dear Sir, do not think I blaspheme when I tell you that your Great London as compared to Dun-Edin "mine own romantic town"[4] is as prose compared to poetry, or as a great rumbling, rambling, heavy Epic—compared to a lyric brief, bright, clear and vital as a flash of lightning. You have nothing like Scott's Monument,[5] or, if you had that and all the glories of architecture assembled together, you have nothing like Arthur's Seat, and above all you have not the Scotch National Character—and it is that grand character after all which gives the land its true charm, its true greatness.

In dread of becoming enthusiastic I close my letter, prolonging it only to beg that you will give my kind remembrances to Mrs. Williams and your family, and to request that when you write you will tell me how my travelling companions got home and how they now are.

I am yours sincerely
C Brontë

MS BPM Bon 221.

1. Thus, for daguerreotype. Louis Daguerre (1789–1851) had published the details of his photographic invention—the creation of a single copy made by sunlight on an iodized silver plate—in 1839.
2. 3 July until the morning of 6 July.
3. The image recalls Scott's description of 'Arthur's Seat, like a couchant lion of immense size', in *The Heart of Midlothian*, ch. 17.
4. Scott's reference to Edinburgh in *Marmion*, Canto IV, stanza xxx, 617.
5. In East Prince's Street Gardens. Completed in 1844, it has a statue of Scott with his dog Maida, beneath an ornate Gothic canopy.

113. *To Ellen Nussey, 26 August 1850*

Haworth

(a) Dear Ellen

You said I should stay longer than a week in Westmoreland[1]—you ought by this time to know me better—is it my habit to keep dawdling on at a place long after the time I first fixed on departing?

I have got home and I am thankful to say Papa seems—to say the least—no worse than when I left him—yet I wish he were stronger. My visit passed off very well—now that it is over I am glad I went—The scenery is of course grand; could I have wandered about amongst those hills <u>alone</u>—I could have drank[2] in all their beauty—even in a carriage—with company, it was very well.

Sir James was all the while as kind and friendly as he could be—he is in much better health—Lady Shuttleworth never got out—being confined to the house with a cold—but fortunately there was Mrs. Gaskell (the authoress of "Mary Barton") who came to the Briery the day after me—I was truly glad of her companionship[3]—She is a woman of the most genuine talent—of cheerful, pleasing and cordial manners and—I believe—of a kind and good heart. Miss Martineau was from home—she always leaves her house at Ambleside during the Lake Season to avoid the constant influx of visitors to which she would otherwise be subject.[4]

I went out to spend the evening once at Fox-House[5] the residence of Dr. Arnold's widow—there was a considerable party, amongst the rest the son and daughter of the Chevalier Bunsen,[6] the Prussian Ambassador, to whom Lord Brougham lately behaved with such outrageous impertinence in the House of Lords—as you may happen to have seen in the papers.

My previous opinions both of Sir James and Lady Shuttleworth are con- firmed—I honour his intellect—with his heart—I believe I shall never have sympathy—He behaves to me with marked kindness—Mrs. Gaskell said she believed he had for me a sincere and strong friendship—I am grateful for this—yet I scarcely desire a continuation of the interest he professes in me—were he to forget me—I could not feel regret—In observing his behaviour to oth- ers—I find that when once offended his forgiveness is not to be again purchased except perhaps by servile submission. The substratum of his character is hard as flint   To Authors as a class (the imaginative portion of them) he has a natural antipathy.[7] Their virtues give him no pleasure—their faults are wormwood and gall in his soul: he perpetually threatens a visit to Haworth—may this be averted!

Tell me, when you write, how poor Mrs Atkinson[8] is getting on—I have thought of her often—Remember me to your Mother and believe me

Always yours faithfully

C Brontë

I forgot to tell you that about a week before I went to Westmoreland there came an invitation to Harden Grange—Busfield Ferrand's[9] place—which of course I declined. Two or three days after—a large party made (b) their appearance here—consisting of Mrs. Ferrand and sundry other ladies and two gentlemen one tall, stately—black-haired and whiskered who turned out to be Lord John Manners[10]—the other not so distinguished-looking—shy and a little queer—who was Mr. Smythe, the son of lord Strangford.

I found Mrs. Ferrand[11] a true lady in manners and appearance—she is the sister or daughter—I forget which, of Lord Blantyre very gentle and unassuming—not so pretty as Lady Shuttleworth—but I liked her better. Lord John Manners brought in in his hand two brace of grouse for Papa—which was a well-timed present—a day or two before papa had been wishing for some

MS (a) HM 24473 (b) Berg.

1. Sir James Kay-Shuttleworth and his wife had invited CB to visit them at their summer residence, Briery Close, on the hillside above Lake Windermere. She stayed from 19 to ?24 August.
2. Thus in MS.
3. Mrs Gaskell found in CB 'a charming union of simplicity and power'; despite their differing 'about almost everything' they liked each other heartily (ECG to Charlotte Froude, CP letter 78).
4. The writer Harriet Martineau had planned and supervised the building of her own house, The Knoll, on the outskirts of Ambleside, moving into it in 1846. See Biographical Notes, p. xl.
5. Properly Fox How, on the lower slopes of Lough Rigg Fell, built by Thomas Arnold (1795–1842; headmaster of Rugby) as a summer home for the family. His widow, née Mary Penrose (1791–1873) lived there with some of her four daughters.
6. Christian Karl Josias von Bunsen (1791–1860), diplomatist and scholar, Prussian ambassador to London until 1854. The Peeresses' Gallery in the House of Lords was crowded on 17 June, when Lord Stanley was to move a vote of censure on Palmerston's ministry after the 'Don Pacifico' affair. When Bunsen, who was notoriously fat, refused to leave his place in the Gallery and retire to the Ambassadors' quarter, Lord Brougham threatened that he would invoke 'the order of the House', adding, 'It is the more intolerable as he has a place assigned to him in another part, and he is now keeping the room of *two Peeresses.*' The Usher of the Black Rod had to make Bunsen move.
7. Nevertheless Sir James had in his earlier years loved poetry intensely. He had published a masque in 1842, and was to write two novels: *Scarsdale* (1860) and *Ribblesdale* (1874).
8. Probably Mary, née Hirst, wife of Revd Thomas Atkinson of Liversedge; she died on 29 Aug.
9. Thus, for [William] Busfeild Ferrand of Harden Grange, about three miles from Haworth. As MP for Knaresborough (1841–7) he had sponsored the Ten Hours' Factory Act, and had helped to expose the truck system and the harsh administration of the new Poor Law. He was also in sympathy with the Young England movement, led by Disraeli, Lord John Manners, and George Augustus Smythe, who wished to revive a responsible and enlightened feudalism.
10. 1818–1906. He succeeded his brother as Duke of Rutland in 1888. George Augustus Smythe (1818–57) succeeded his father as 7th Viscount Strangford in 1855.
11. The Hon. Fanny Mary Ferrand, daughter of the 11th Lord Blantyre, was W. B. Ferrand's second wife, whom he had married in 1847.

114. *To Revd Charles Cuthbert Southey,*[1] *26 August 1850*

Haworth.

Dear Sir

Your note would have been sooner answered, had not absence from home prevented me from referring to the two letters to which it alludes, and I wished to look at them once more before deciding on their publication.[2]

I have now read them and feel that—truly wise and kind as they are—they ought to be published; I must, however, beg you to suppress my name and likewise to omit the passage which I have marked with a pencil;[3] my own letters to Mr. Southey I do not remember but the passage quoted there seems to me now somewhat silly, and I would rather it were not preserved.

When I wrote to your Father I was very young; I needed the benevolent yet stern advice he gives me, and fortunately I had just sense enough to feel its value and to resolve on its adoption.[4] At this moment I am grateful to his memory for the well-timed check received in my girl-hood at his hand.

May I add that the perusal of his Life and Correspondence arranged by yourself has much deepened the esteem and admiration with which I previously regarded him. You will kindly return the letter enclosed, for it is very precious to me.

I am, my dear Sir

Yours sincerely

C Brontë

MS BPM B.S. 79.5.

1. 1818–?1885, eldest son of the poet Robert Southey; perpetual curate of Setmurthy and curate of Plumbland near Cockermouth 1843–51.
2. CB had received two letters from Robert Southey, written on 12 and 22 Mar. 1837. See Letter 5, her letter to Southey of 16 Mar., and notes. She had already read the first three volumes of Cuthbert Southey's *The Life and Correspondence of the late Robert Southey* (1849, 1850).
3. CB marked for omission two passages including her own 'somewhat silly' words, quoted by Southey in his letter of 12 Mar. from hers of 29 Dec. 1837—a letter for which the original MS has not been located. She had spoken of Southey 'stooping from a throne of light & glory' and of her own ardent desire 'to be for ever known' as a poetess. These phrases were duly omitted in Cuthbert Southey's version of his father's letter in vol. vi of his biography (1850).
4. On the outer wrapper of Robert Southey's letter of 22 Mar. 1837, in which he had emphasized the 'self-government' essential to happiness, and advised CB to 'Take care of over-excitement, & endeavour to keep a quiet mind', CB wrote, 'Southey's Advice | To be kept for ever | Roe Head April 21 | My twenty-first birthday 1837.'

115. *To Elizabeth Gaskell, 27 August 1850*

Haworth.

My dear Mrs. Gaskell

Papa and I have just had tea; he is sitting quietly in his room, and I in mine; "storms of rain" are sweeping over the garden and churchyard; as to the moors—they are hidden in thick fog. Though alone—I am not unhappy; I have a thousand things to be thankful for, and—amongst the rest—that this morning I received a letter from you, and that this evening—I have the privilege of answering it.

I do not know the Life of Sydney Taylor, whenever I have the opportunity I will get it;[1] the little French book[2] you mention shall also take its place on the list of books to be procured as soon as possible. It treats a subject interesting to all women—perhaps, more especially to single women; though indeed—mothers—like you—study it for the sake of their daughters. The "Westminster Review" is not a periodical I see regularly, but some time since I got hold of a number—for last January—I think—in which there was an article entitled "Woman's Mission"[3] (the phrase is hackneyed) containing a great deal that seemed to me just and sensible. Men begin to regard the position of Women in another light than they used to do, and a few Men whose sympathies are fine and whose sense of justice is strong think and speak of it with a candour that commands my admiration. They say—however—and to a certain extent—truly—that the amelioration of our condition depends on ourselves. Certainly there are evils which our own efforts will best reach—but as certainly there are other evils—deep rooted in the foundations of the Social system—which no efforts of ours can touch—of which we cannot complain—of which it is advisable not too often to think.

I have read Tennyson's "In Memoriam"[4]—or rather—part of it; I closed the book when I had got about half-way. It is beautiful; it is mournful; it is monotonous. Many of the feelings expressed, bear, in their utterance, the stamp of Truth, yet if Arthur Hallam had been somewhat nearer Alfred Tennyson—his brother instead of his friend—I should have distrusted this rhymed and measured and printed monument of grief. What change the lapse of years may work—I do not know—but it seems to me that bitter sorrow, while recent, does not flow out in verse.

I promised to send you Wordsworth's "Prelude"[5] and accordingly despatch it by this post; the other little volume[6] shall follow in a day or two.

I shall be glad to hear from you whenever you have time to write to me, but you are never, on any account, to do this except when inclination prompts and leisure permits. I should never thank you for a letter which you had felt it a task to write.

I hope your ancle is better—perhaps Wordsworth will serve to amuse[7] you whilst you nurse it—Amongst your six girls[8] you will doubtless not want ready hand-maidens to attend to your wants and prevent your moving whilst motion is improper.

Good bye, dear Mrs. Gaskell

Believe me
Yours very sincerely
C Brontë

MS Devonshire Collections 2nd series no. 346.1, Chatsworth, by permission of the Duke of Devonshire.

1. *Selections from the Writings of the late J. Sydney Taylor, A.M. Barrister-at-Law: with a brief Sketch of his Life* (1843). Taylor (1795–1841), barrister and journalist, was a fearless liberal who advocated social reform and inveighed against all injustice, including the slave trade.
2. Not identified.

3. An article on [Sarah Lewis], *Woman's Mission* (1849 edn.), in the *Westminster Review* for Jan. 1850, 352–78. The reviewer, like the author, considers that woman's 'genius is <u>influence</u>. Yes; to warm, to cherish into purer life the motive that shall lead to the heroic act.' Women must emerge from 'inactivity of mind', and undertake work 'true to the movement of the soul'.

4. Tennyson's poem in memory of Arthur Henry Hallam (1811–33), published in 1850. Mrs Gaskell had probably praised the poem in her conversations with CB, but she told her friend Charlotte Froude that CB could not bear Tennyson (CP letter 78).

5. After Wordsworth's death on 23 Apr. 1850 his much-revised autobiographical poem, *The Prelude, or Growth of a Poet's Mind* was published, on 20 July.

6. A copy of Smith, Elder's 1848 reissue of *Poems* by Currer, Ellis, and Acton Bell.

7. To while away your time, rather than to divert you.

8. The Gaskells' four daughters, Marianne, Meta, Florence, and Julia, and two guests, Annie and Ellen Green.

116. *To James Taylor, 5 September 1850*

[Haworth]

My dear Sir

The reappearance of the Athenæum is very acceptable[1]—not merely for its own sake—though I esteem the opportunity of its perusal a privilege—but because it comes from Cornhill and, as a weekly token of the remembrance of friends, cheers and gives pleasure. I only fear that its regular transmission may become a task to you—in that case—discontinue it at once.

I did indeed enjoy my trip to Scotland, and yet I saw little of the face of the country—nothing of its grander or finer scenic features—but—Edinburgh, Melrose, Abbotsford[2]—these three in themselves sufficed to stir feelings of such deep interest and admiration that, neither at the time did I regret, nor have I since regretted the want of wider space over which to diffuse the sense of enjoyment. There was room and variety enough to be very happy, and "enough" the proverb says, "is as good as a feast." The Queen was right indeed to climb Arthur's Seat with her husband and children;[3] I shall not soon forget how I felt—when—having reached its summit—we all sat down and looked over the city—towards the Sea and Leith, and the Pentland hills. No doubt you are proud of being a native of Scotland—proud of your Country, her capital, her children and her literature. You cannot be blamed.

The article in the "Palladium"[4] is one of those notices over which an author rejoices with trembling. He rejoices to find his work finely, fully, fervently appreciated—and trembles under the responsibility such appreciation seems to devolve upon him. I am counselled to wait and watch. D. V. I will do so. Yet it is harder work to wait with the hands bound and the observant and reflective faculties, at their silent unseen work, than to labour mechanically.

I need not say how I felt the remarks on "Wuthering Heights"; they woke the saddest yet most grateful feelings; they are true, they are discriminating; they are full of late justice—but it is very late—alas! in one sense—<u>too</u> late. Of this, however, and of the pang of regret for a light prematurely extinguished—it is not wise to speak much. Whoever the author of this article may be—I remain his debtor.

Yet—you see—even here—"Shirley" is disparaged in comparison with "Jane Eyre" and yet I took great pains with "Shirley".[5] I did not hurry; I tried to do my best, and my own impression was that it was not inferior to the former work; indeed I had bestowed on it more time, thought and anxiety—but great part of it was written under the shadow of impending calamity—and the last volume—I cannot deny was composed in the eager, restless endeavour to combat mental sufferings that were scarcely tolerable.

You sent the Tragedy of "Galileo Galilei" by Samuel Brown[6]—in one of the Cornhill parcels—it contained—I remember—passages of very great beauty. Whenever you send any more books (but that must not be till I return what I now have) I should be glad if you would include amongst them the Life of Dr. Arnold[7]—Do you know also the Life of Sydney Taylor? I am not familiar even with the name, but it has been recommended to me as a work meriting perusal. Of course when I name any book—it is always understood that it should be quite convenient to send it.

With thanks for your kind letter

I am, my dear Sir

Yours very sincerely   C Brontë

MS Texas.

1. Taylor had begun to lend copies of the *Athenaeum* to CB in Nov. 1849. Her most recent reference to the loan was on 22 May 1850.
2. For CB's praise of Edinburgh, see Letter 112. On 30 July 1850 she had told Laetitia Wheelwright that the very names of Melrose and Abbotsford possessed 'music and magic'. Abbotsford, about thirty miles from Edinburgh, was built by Sir Walter Scott: a grand house in the Scottish baronial style, in the midst of woodland. About three miles from the house lie the ruins of Melrose Abbey, where the heart of Robert the Bruce was buried at the high altar.
3. The royal family had set out for Edinburgh on 27 Aug., travelling by train, and had stayed at Holyrood Palace. On the morning after their arrival Queen Victoria and her children drove round the park, and climbed Arthur's Seat.
4. An article on 'Currer Bell and *Wuthering Heights*' by the poet Sydney Dobell (1824–74) in the *Palladium* for Sept. 1850 assumed that Currer Bell was a woman who had written *Wuthering Heights* and *Tenant* as well as *JE* and *Shirley*. He considered that *JE* was a 'moral wonder', and though he found some 'disgusting' detail in the portrayal of Heathcliff, he praised *WH* generously, saying that it bore the stamp of genius, and that some pages were 'the masterpiece of a poet'.
5. Dobell attributed the inferiority and evident effort of *Shirley* to overwork, and implied that CB should wait until her brain had 'subsided' from the success of *JE* before writing again.
6. Dr Samuel Brown (1817–56, MD Edinburgh), a scientist who had also been praised for his brilliant literary skills, but had disappointed his friends and the public by his play, *The Tragedy of Galileo Galilei* (1849).
7. Arthur Penrhyn Stanley, *The Life and Correspondence of Thomas Arnold, D.D.*, 2 vols. (1844).

117. *To W. S. Williams, 5 September 1850*

[Haworth]

My dear Sir

I trust your suggestion for Miss Kavanagh's benefit will have all success.¹ It seems to me truly felicitous and excellent and, I doubt not, she will think so too. The last class of female character will be difficult to manage: there will be nice points in it—yet—well-managed—both an attractive and instructive book might result therefrom. One thing may be depended upon in the execution of this plan—Miss Kavanagh will commit no error—either of taste, judgment or principle—and even when she deals with the feelings—I would rather follow the calm course of her quiet pen than the flourishes of a more redundant one, where there is not strength to restrain as well as ardour to impel.

I fear I seemed to you to speak coolly of the beauty of the Lake-scenery. The truth is it was, as scenery, exquisite, far beyond anything I saw in Scotland—but it did not give me half so much pleasure because I saw it under less congenial auspices. Mr. Smith and Sir J. K. Shuttleworth are two different people with whom to travel. I need say nothing of the former; you know him. The latter offers me his friendship and I do my best to be grateful for the gift—but his is a nature with which it is difficult to assimilate and where there is no assimilation—how can there be real regard?—Nine parts out of ten in him are Utilitarian—the tenth is artistic. This tithe of his nature seems to me at war with all the rest—it is just enough to incline him restlessly towards the artist-class—and far too little to make him one of them. The consequent inability to <u>do</u> things which he <u>admires</u>, embitters him I think—it makes him doubt perfections and dwell on faults. Then his notice or presence scarcely tend to set one at ease or make one happy: he is worldly and formal; but I must stop—have I already said too much? I think not—for you will feel it is said in confidence and will not repeat it.

The article in the "Palladium" is indeed such as to atone for a hundred unfavourable or imbecile reviews; I have expressed what I think of it to Mr. Taylor who kindly wrote me a letter on the subject—I thank you also for the newspaper notices and for some you sent me a few weeks ago.

I should much like to carry out your suggestion respecting a reprint of "Wuthering Heights" and "Agnes Grey" in 1 vol. with a prefatory and explanatory notice of the authors—but the question occurs—would Newby claim it?² I could not bear to commit it to any other hands than those of Mr. Smith. "Wildfell Hall" it hardly appears to me desirable to preserve. The choice of subject in that work is a mistake—it was too little consonant with the character—tastes and ideas of the gentle, retiring, inexperienced writer. She wrote it under a strange, conscientious, half-ascetic notion of accomplishing a painful penance and a severe duty. Blameless in deed and almost in thought—there was from her very childhood a tinge of religious melancholy in her mind—this I ever suspected—and I have found, amongst her papers, mournful proofs that such was the case. As to additional compositions, I think there would be none—as I would not offer a line to the publication of which my sisters themselves would have objected. I must conclude or I shall be too late for the post.

Believe me
Yours sincerely
C Brontë

MS Parrish Collection, Princeton.

1. For Julia Kavanagh see Letter 62 n. 3. Perhaps Mr. Williams suggested the idea for her *Women of Christianity Exemplary for Piety and Charity*, published by Smith, Elder in 1852.
2. Newby did not own the copyright of these two novels, published by him on condition that Emily and Anne would share the risk. They had advanced £50, to be repaid when the volumes had sold enough copies to defray expenses; but he had paid them nothing. CB's edition of the novels, with selected poems by Emily and Anne and her 'Biographical Notice' of her sisters, was published on 7 Dec. 1850. Newby eventually sent CB a cheque for £30, acknowledged by her on 18 Mar. 1854, but this was probably part of the proceeds of his sale of the copyright of *Tenant* to the publisher Thomas Hodgson.

118. *To W. S. Williams, 27 September 1850*

[Haworth]

My dear Sir

It is my intention to write a few lines of remark on "W. Heights" which however I proposed to place apart as a brief preface before the tale—I am likewise compelling myself to read it over for the first time of opening the book since my sister's death. Its power fills me with renewed admiration—but yet I am oppressed—the reader is scarcely ever permitted a taste of unalloyed pleasure—every beam of sunshine is poured down through black bars of threatening cloud—every page is surcharged with a sort of moral electricity; and the writer was unconscious of all this—nothing could make her conscious of it. And this makes me reflect—perhaps I too am incapable of perceiving the faults and peculiarities of my own style.

I should wish to revise the proofs, if it be not too great an inconvenience to send them. It seems to me advisable to modify the orthography of the old servant Joseph's speeches[1]—for though—as it stands—it exactly renders the Yorkshire accent to a Yorkshire ear—yet I am sure Southerns must find it unintelligible—and thus one of the most graphic characters in the book is lost on them.

What the probable quantity of new matter will be, I cannot say exactly—but I think it will not exceed thirty or, at the most forty pages—since it is so inconsiderable, would it not be better to place the title thus

Wuthering Heights & Agnes Grey by
E & A Bell
With a Notice of the authors by Currer Bell
and a Selection from their literary Remains?[2]

I only suggest this—if there are reasons rendering the other title prefer-able—adopt it.

I will prepare and send some extracts from reviews.

I grieve to say that I possess no portrait of either of my sisters.[3]

Believe me

Yours sincerely
C. Brontë

MS Eng 871, Houghton Library, Harvard University.

1. CB modified but did not completely remove dialect forms. In ch. 2, for example, the 1st edition reading, ' "T'maisters dahn i' t'fowld. Goa rahnd by th'end ut' laith, if yah went tuh spake tull him" ' becomes in 1850, ' "T'maister's down i' t'fowld. Go round by th'end ot' laith, if ye went to spake to him" ' ('fowld' = fold, 'laith' = barn, 'went' = want).
2. A longer title was decided upon: WUTHERING HEIGHTS | AND AGNES GREY. | BY | ELLIS AND ACTON BELL. | A NEW EDITION REVISED, WITH A BIOGRAPHICAL NOTICE OF THE AUTHORS, | A SELECTION OF THEIR LITERARY REMAINS, | AND A PREFACE, | BY CURRER BELL.
3. CB must have known about Branwell's portraits of his sisters, and her own watercolour portraits of Anne, but it was technically correct to say that she did not 'possess' them, since they were her father's property.

119. *To George Smith, 3 December 1850*

[Haworth]

My dear Sir

Your Will o' the Wisp is a very pleasant and witty sprite,[1] and though not venomous, his pungency may be none the less effective on that account. Indeed I believe a good-natured kind of ridicule is a weapon more appropriate to the present crisis than bitter satire or serious indignation. We are in no danger: Why should we be angry? I only wish the author had rectified some of her rhymes—(such as sedilia and familiar, tiara and bearer) but critics will surely not be severe with the little book.

Mr. M. A. Titmarsh holds out an alluring invitation to the Rhine:[2] I hope thousands will take advantage of the facilities he offers to make the excursion in the "polite society" of the Kickleburys.

As to Mr. Newby—he charms me. First—there is the fascinating coyness with which he shuns your pursuit. For a month, or nearly two months, have you been fondly hoping to win from him an interview,[3] while he has been making himself scarce as violets at Christmas, aristocratically absenting himself from Town, evading your grasp like a Publisher metamorphosed into a Rainbow.

Then, when you come upon him in that fatal way in Regent Street, pin him down and hunt him home with more promptitude than politeness, and with a want of delicate consideration for your victim's fine feelings calculated to awake emotions of regret—that victim is still ready for the emergency. Scorning to stand on the defensive, he at once assumes the offensive. Not only has he realized no profit, he has sustained actual loss! And—to account for this—adds with a sublime boldness of invention—that the author "wished him to spend all possible profits in advertisements"!

Equally well acted too is the artless simplicity of his surprise at the news you communicate; and his pretty little menace of a "chancery injunction" consummates the picture and makes it perfect.

Any statement of accounts he may send, I shall at once transmit to you. In your hands I leave him; deal with him as you list, but I heartily wish you well rid of the business.

On referring to Mr. Newby's letters, I find in one of them, a boast that he is "advertising vigorously". I remember that this flourish caused us to look out carefully for the results of his vast exertions—but though we everywhere encountered "Jane Eyre"—it was as rare a thing to find an advertisement of "Wuthering Heights" as it appears to be to meet with Mr. Newby in Town at an unfashionable season of the year.[4] The fact is he advertised the book very scantily and for a very short time. Of course we never expressed a wish or uttered an injunction on the subject, nor was it likely we should, as it was rather important to us to recover the 50£ we had advanced; more we did not ask.

I would say something about regret for the trouble you have had in your chase of this ethereal and evanescent ornament of "the Trade"[5] but I fear apologies would be even worse than thanks—Both then shall be left out—and you shall only be requested to

Believe me
Yours sincerely
C Brontë

MS BPM SG 42.

1. *A Paper Lantern for Puseyites* by Will o' the Wisp, first published by Smith, Elder in 1843, revised and reissued 1850. The Puseyites were the High Church (Anglo-Catholic) followers of Edward Bouverie Pusey (1800–82). *A Paper Lantern* ridicules their 'Gothic' and Romanizing tendencies in good-humoured doggerel. The 'crisis' had been caused by the Pope's appointment of Nicholas Patrick Stephen Wiseman (1802–65), as Archbishop of Westminster in August, and then his elevation to the Cardinalate on 29 Sept. Wiseman's proclaimed intention to restore England 'to its orbit in the ecclesiastical firmament' caused a hysterical reaction among many English Protestants against 'Papal Aggression'.
2. Smith, Elder published *The Kickleburys on the Rhine* by 'Michael Angelo Titmarsh' (Thackeray) as his Christmas book. Despite a heavy bombardment from *The Times*, it proved successful and immediately went into a second edition.

3. George Smith wished to obtain from Newby on CB's behalf any payments due to her sisters from the publication of their works. Once 'caught', Newby threatened to seek an injunction preventing Smith from publishing Charlotte's edition of their 'Remains' on the ground of infringement of copyright. There is no evidence that Newby had ever acquired copyright in *Wuthering Heights* and *Agnes Grey*.
4. The fashionable London 'season' lasted only from May to July.
5. The publishing and bookselling trade: used in this sense since the late seventeenth century.

120. *To Ellen Nussey, 18 December 1850*

The Knoll. Ambleside

Dear Ellen

I can write to you now for I am away from home[1] and relieved, temporarily at least, by change of air and scene from the heavy burden of depression which I confess has for nearly 3 months been sinking me to the earth. I never shall forget last Autumn. Some days and nights have been cruel—but now—having once told you this—I need say no more on the subject. My loathing of solitude grew extreme; my recollection of my Sisters intolerably poignant; I am better now.

I am at Miss Martineau's for a week—her house is very pleasant both within and without—arranged at all points with admirable neatness and comfort—Her visitors enjoy the most perfect liberty; what she claims for herself she allows them. I rise at my own hour, breakfast alone—(she is up at five, takes a cold bath and a walk by starlight and has finished breakfast and got to her work by 7 o'clock).[2] I pass the morning in the drawing-room—she in her study. At 2 o'clock we meet, work,[3] talk and walk together till 5—her dinner hour—spend the evening together—when she converses fluently, abundantly and with the most complete frankness—I go to my own room soon after ten—she sits up writing letters till twelve. She appears exhaustless in strength and spirits, and indefatigable in the faculty of labour. She is a great and a good woman; of course not without peculiarities but I have seen none as yet that annoy me. She is both hard and warm-hearted, abrupt and affectionate—liberal and despotic. I believe she is not at all conscious of her own absolutism. When I tell her of it, she denys the charge warmly—then I laugh at her.[4] I believe she almost rules Ambleside. Some of the gentry dislike her, but the lower orders have a great regard for her. I will not stay more than a week because about Christmas relations and other guests will come. Sir J & Lady Shuttleworth are coming here to dine on Thursday—I mean to get off going there if I possibly can without giving downright offence. Write to me and say how you are. With kind regards to all I am

Yours faithfully
C Brontë

MS HM 24477.

1. CB stayed with Harriet Martineau at her home, 'The Knoll', from 16 to 23 Dec.
2. When Martineau read quotations from this letter in Mrs Gaskell's *Life* of CB, she was irate about the 'absurd hours' CB had made her keep. At her request, Mrs Gaskell added corrections to the 3rd edn. of the *Life* (Aug. 1857). Martineau insisted that she rose at six, and spoke to CB when the latter came down to breakfast, before beginning work (i.e. her writing) at 8.30 a.m.
3. 'Work' here probably means 'do needlework'.
4. In a letter to the *Daily News* on 24 Aug. 1857, headed 'Mrs Gaskell's Memoirs of Miss Brontë', Martineau asserted that 'scarcely one of Miss Brontë's statements about me is altogether true', but Martineau's memory was fallible; and her deafness may have prevented her from hearing all that Charlotte said at the time.

121. *To George Smith, 7 January 1851*

[Haworth]

My dear Sir

Mr. Thackeray ought to be condemned to build a church and therein to set up two shrines dedicated respectively to St. Bungay and St. Bacon,[1] to which shrines he should moreover be sentenced to make a pilgrimage twice a year with peas in his shoes, and forced in addition to lay on each shrine the offering of a neatly written M.S. being a tale without any allusion to Belgravia in it.

As to you and Mr. Williams—the honours of martyrdom must be awarded you by every well-regulated and feeling mind. Truly you have come out of great tribulation. I would offer you my whole stock of sympathy—were I not restrained by the contrast between the vast demands of the case and the feeble value of the oblation. It is an awful narrative, abounding in thrilling incident; that promise "really to set about writing" a book of which the publication was announced—makes one's hair stand on end. May I ask whether—while the Xmas book, already advertised,[2] was still unwritten—whether—with all this guilt on his head and all this responsibility on his shoulders—Mr. Thackeray managed to retain his usual fine appetite—to make good breakfasts, luncheons and dinners and to enjoy his natural rest—or whether he did not rather send away choice morsels on his plate untouched—and terrify Mrs. Carmichael Smith—Miss Truelove and his daughters[3]—by habitually shrieking out in the dead of the night—under the visitation of a Cornhill nightmare, revealing two wrathful forms at his bedside menacing him with drawn swords and demanding his M.S or his life—?

Allow me to suggest an appropriate revenge. Put out of your head the cherub-vision of the "innocent and happy Publishers" sitting on clouds in Heaven and thence regarding with mild complacency the tortures of perjured authors—descend from this height—turn author yourself and write "The Lion's History of the Man" or "A Revelation of the crimes of popular A-th-rs by a spirited P-b-sh-r". Here is an idea which, properly handled, might "mark an epoch in the history of Modern Literature". I could almost wish you were forced to adopt it and work it out. You little know what you would make of it. You happen not quite to know yourself.

"The King of the Golden River" is a divine fairy tale.[4] Richard Doyle has done it scant justice in his illustrations (which are rather obscurations) but it does not much matter; Mr. Ruskin paints so exquisitely with his pen as to be almost independent of the designer's pencil.

I am glad "the Kickleburys" is likely to be successful: it has that interest and that pith without which Thackeray cannot write—yet I mentally wrung my hands as I laid it down—If Mr. Titmarsh does not mind—erelong there will be a cry of Ichabod![5]

I think you did me a kindness in warding off that copy of "Pendennis"[6] intended to be discharged at my head: the necessary note of acknowledgment would have been written by me under difficulties. To have spoken my mind would have been to displease—and I know, if I had written at all, my mind would have insisted on speaking itself.

"The Stones of Venice"[7] seem nobly laid and chiselled. How grandly the "Quarry" of vast marbles is disclosed! Mr. Ruskin seems to me one of the few genuine writers (as distinguished from bookmakers) of this age. His earnestness even amuses me in certain passages—for I cannot help laughing to think how utilitarians will fume and fret over his deep, serious and (as they will think) fanatical reverence for Art. That pure and severe mind you ascribed to him speaks in every line. He writes like a consecrated Priest of the Abstract and Ideal.

You inquire with a certain tender anxiety about Mr. Newby. I am sorry not to be in a position to soothe your solicitude respecting him. That fabulous "Statement of accounts" has never made its appearance, nor has any wind from any quarter wafted a whisper of explanation. You talk of commencing a correspondence. Let me conjure you, as you value your own peace of mind, not to risk it by hazarding such a step. The sole result will be the wasting of some good stationery—paper, ink and sealing-wax—as well as of some moments of precious time on an object that will not respond to your assiduities. It is Newby's nature to conduct himself in this manner; nothing can change him; and I believe the best thing people who don't approve of his proceedings—can do—is to withdraw in due state and dignity—leaving him to his own little devices, and deeming themselves fortunate in securing their ransom at so cheap a rate as 50£.

I did enjoy my visit to Miss Martineau very much—and I often thought while I was with her what a heathen R. H. Horne was, to compare her "to a sour apple crushed with a hob-nail shoe".[8] She is fallible in some matters of judgment and (as I thought) blunt on some points of feeling—but otherwise a very noble and genial being. I rather tremble at the anticipation of a work she is about to publish conjointly with a Mr. Atkinson[9]—she read me some passages of it which partially mesmerised me—but she is ready to meet any shock of opposition for the sake of what she believes the Truth.

In reply to your kind inquiries after Papa I am thankful to say he is well—wonderfully free from infirmities or failure of faculties and looking ten years younger than his real age—I gave him your message and was charged to offer his respects in return.

Let me say this word before I bid you good bye. Neither you nor Mr. Williams should ever think of apologizing to me for not writing however long an interval may elapse between your letters. I do like a friendly letter from Cornhill—I like it well and sincerely; but if a thought were to cross me that such letter were written at a sacrifice of the writer's convenience—my pleasure in it would turn to grief. You need not doubt that I can wait long and quite patiently without being in the least hurt by silence. Believe this and that I am

Yours sincerely
C Brontë

MS BPM SG 43.

1. In Thackeray's novel *Pendennis* the hero's friend Captain Shandon exploits the rivalry between the publishers Bacon and Bungay (satirical versions of Henry Colburn and Richard Bentley) to place Pendennis's first attempt at writing, a sentimental poem entitled 'The Church Porch'.

2. Thackeray's *The Kickleburys on the Rhine* had been advertised in the *Athenaeum* for 30 Nov. 1850 as ready on 16 Dec. He notoriously wrote with the 'printer's devil' in the hall, waiting for copy: but the story was eventually published in time for Christmas. It was favourably reviewed in the *Leader* and temperately praised as 'a lively *ephemeron*' in the *Athenaeum* on 21 Dec.

3. Thackeray was the son of Mrs Henry Carmichael-Smyth (née Anne Becher) by her first husband, Richmond Thackeray. Mrs Carmichael-Smyth helped to look after Thackeray's daughters, Anne Isabella (1837–1919) and Harriet Marian ('Minny', 1840–75) after their mother Isabella became incurably mentally ill following Minny's birth. Their current governess, Miss Trulock (misnamed by CB) remained with the family from early 1850 until autumn 1852.

4. John Ruskin's picturesque moral tale, *The King of the Golden River; or The Black Brothers, A Legend of Stiria*: his Christmas book for 1850, with what most people would consider apt and vigorous illustrations designed by Richard Doyle.

5. 'The glory is departed,' as in 1 Samuel 4: 21.

6. Thackeray's novel, now published in volume form. See Letter 105 n. 5.

7. Smith, Elder published Ruskin's *The Stones of Venice. Volume the First—The* FOUNDATIONS in Jan. 1851; vols. ii and iii followed in 1853. Ruskin aimed to show that the Gothic architecture of Venice, unlike that of the Renaissance, 'had arisen out of . . . a state of pure national faith, and of domestic virtue.' His finely detailed drawings illustrate his central theme, that the beauty of ornament depended on its copying the natural forms created by God.

8. Richard Henry (later Hengist) Horne (1802–84), known as 'Orion Horne' since his publication of his epic poem *Orion* (1843) at a farthing per copy 'to mark the public contempt into which epic poetry had fallen'. His *A New Spirit of the Age* (1844) was published by Smith, Elder. It included a pen portrait of Harriet Martineau, to which E. B. Browning had contributed some information. Martineau had been satisfied with the portrait.

9. Henry George Atkinson (?1815–84), with whom Harriet Martineau wrote *Letters on the Laws of Man's Nature and Development*. She believed that Atkinson, a devotee of mesmerism and phrenology, which he regarded as sciences, had perceived the 'sole and eternal basis of wisdom'. Dismissing both theologians and 'so-called scientific men, who consider themselves philosophers', as unenlightened, Atkinson put forward his own quite unscientific description of

the 'organic arrangement' of the cerebrum. The two authors' speculations on the nature of the universe led them to assert the unknowability and consequent irrelevance of a 'First Cause' to man's mind and behaviour.

122. To George Smith, 5 February 1851

[Haworth]

My dear Sir

Perhaps it is hardly necessary to trouble you with an answer to your last as I have already written to Mr. Williams and no doubt he will have told you that I have yielded with ignoble facility in the matter of "The Professor".[1] Still it may be proper to make some attempt towards dignifying that act of submission by averring that it was done "under protest".

"The Professor" has now had the honour of being rejected nine times by the "Tr—de".[2] (three rejections go to your own share; you may affirm that you accepted it this last time, but that cannot be admitted; if it were only for the sake of symmetry and effect, I must regard this martyrized M.S. as repulsed or at any rate—withdrawn for the ninth time! Few—I flatter myself—have earned an equal distinction, and of course my feelings towards it can only be paralleled by those of a doting parent towards an idiot child. Its merit—I plainly perceive—will never be owned by anybody but Mr. Williams and me; very particular and unique must be our penetration, and I think highly of us both accordingly. You may allege that that merit is not visible to the naked eye. Granted; but the smaller the commodity—the more inestimable its value.

You kindly propose to take "the Professor" into custody. Ah—No! His modest merit shrinks at the thought of going alone and unbefriended to a spirited Publisher. Perhaps with slips of him you might light an occasional cigar—or you might remember to lose him some day—and a Cornhill functionary would gather him up and consign him to the repositories of waste paper, and thus he would prematurely find his way to the "buttermen" and trunk-makers.[3] No—I have put him by and locked him up—not indeed in my desk, where I could not tolerate the monotony of his demure quaker countenance, but in a cupboard by himself.

Something you say about going to London—but the words are dreamy, and fortunately I am not obliged at present to hear or answer them. London and Summer are many months away; our moors are all white with snow just now and little redbreasts come every morning to the window for crumbs—one can lay no plans three or four months beforehand. Besides—I don't deserve to go to London; nobody merits a treat or a change less. I secretly think, on the contrary, I ought to be put in prison and kept on bread and water in solitary confinement without even a letter from Cornhill—till I had written a book. One of two things would certainly result from such a mode of treatment pursued for twelve months; either I should come out, at the end of that time, with a 3 vol. M.S. in my hand, or else with a condition of intellect that would exempt me ever after from literary efforts and expectations.

You touch upon invitations from baronets &c.[4] As you are well aware, a fondness for such invitations and an anxious desire to obtain them—is my weak point. Aristocratic notice is what I especially covet, cultivate and cling to. It does me so much good; it gives me such large, free and congenial enjoyment. How happy I am when counselled or commended by a baronet or noticed by a lord!

Those papers on the London Poor[5] are singularly interesting; to me they open a new and strange world—very dark—very dreary—very noisome in some of its recesses—a world that is fostering such a future as I scarcely dare imagine—it awakens thoughts not to be touched on in this foolish letter. The fidelity and simplicity of the letter-press details harmonize well with the daguerrotype illustrations.

You must thank your Mother and Sisters for their kind remembrance and offer mine in return, and you must believe me

[Signature cut off.]

MS BPM SG 45.

1. CB had hoped that Smith, Elder might publish *The Professor*, since she had no other novel ready for them.
2. The publishing trade. The novel had been offered with her sisters' *Wuthering Heights* and *Agnes Grey* to Aylott & Jones and five other firms who all refused it. It was then sent alone to Smith, Elder on 15 July 1847, and rejected by them. Offered to them a second time, with CB's suggestion that it might be recast as a 3-volume novel, they had refused it by 18 Dec. 1847.
3. Waste paper was used for lining butter-barrels and leather travelling trunks. The MS remained at Haworth until 23 July 1856, when Sir James Kay-Shuttleworth asked CB's widower, A. B. Nicholls, to entrust it to Mrs Gaskell, but carried it off himself. In the end it was edited by Mr Nicholls, and first published by Smith, Elder on 6 June 1857. The MS is now in the Pierpont Morgan Library, New York.
4. Sir James Kay-Shuttleworth had been pressing in his invitations to a reluctant CB to accompany him and his wife to London in the spring of 1850.
5. *London Labour and the London Poor*, by Henry Mayhew; 3 vols. (London, 1850–1), followed by a fourth vol. by Mayhew and John Binny, *The Criminal Prisons of London* (1862).

123. To James Taylor, 11 February 1851

[Haworth]

My dear Sir

Have you yet read Miss Martineau's and Mr. Atkinson's new work "Letters on the Nature and Development of Man?."[1] If you have not—it would be worth your while to do so.

Of the impression this book has made on me—I will not now say much. It is the first exposition of avowed Atheism and Materialism I have ever read; the first unequivocal declaration of disbelief in the existence of a God or a Future Life—I have ever seen. In judging of such exposition and declaration—one would wish entirely to put aside the sort of instinctive horror they awaken and to consider them in an impartial spirit and collected mood. This I find it difficult to do. The strangest thing is that we are called on to rejoice over this hopeless blank—to receive this bitter bereavement as great gain—to welcome this unutterable desolation as a state of pleasant freedom. Who <u>could</u> do this if he would? Who <u>would</u> do it if he could?

Sincerely—for my own part—do I wish to find and know the Truth—but if <u>this</u> be Truth—well may she guard herself with mysteries and cover herself with a veil. If this be Truth—Man or Woman who beholds her can but curse the day he or she was born. I said, however, I would not dwell on what <u>I</u> thought; I wish rather to hear what some other person thinks; some one whose feelings are unapt to bias his judgment. Read the book then in an unprejudiced spirit and candidly say what you think of it; I mean—of course—if you have time—<u>not otherwise.</u>

Thank you for your last letter; it seemed to me very good; with all you said about the "Leader" I entirely agree.[2]

> Believe me—my dear Sir
> Yours sincerely
> C Brontë

MS Texas.

1. See Letter 121 n. 9. Atkinson declares that all religions block up the path to knowledge, and that Christianity will soon be recognized as 'no better than an old wife's fable . . . the Bible will be a curious and charming book for those days, when men will be burning all rubbish of theologies' (*Letters on . . . Development* (London, 1851), 239–40.)
2. The first number of this radical weekly advocating Chartism, republicanism, freedom of expression, and religious tolerance, edited by George Henry Lewes and Thornton Hunt, had appeared on 30 Mar. 1850. For Thornton Hunt see Letter 105 n. 1.

124. *To Ellen Nussey, 4 and 5 April 1851*

[Haworth]
Friday Evening 6 o'clock

Dear Ellen

Mr. Taylor has been and is gone; things are just as they were. I only know in addition to the slight information I possessed before that this Indian undertaking[1] is necessary to the continued prosperity of the Firm of Smith Elder & Co. and that he—Taylor—alone was pronounced to possess the power and means to carry it out successfully—that mercantile honour combined with his own sense of duty obliged him to accept the post of honour and of danger to which he has been appointed—that he goes with great personal reluctance and that he contemplates an absence of five years.

He looked much thinner and older—I saw him very near and once through my glass—the resemblance to Branwell struck me forcibly—it is marked. He is not ugly—but very peculiar; the lines in his face shew an inflexibility and—I must add—a hardness of character which do not attract. As he stood near me—as he looked at me in his keen way, it was all I could do to stand my ground tranquilly and steadily and not to recoil as before. It is no use saying anything if I am not candid—I avow then that on this occasion—predisposed as I was to regard him very favourably—his manners and his personal presence scarcely pleased me more than at the first interview. He gave me a book at parting requesting in his brief way that I would keep it for his sake and adding hastily "I shall hope to hear from you in India—your letters <u>have</u> been and <u>will</u> be a greater refreshment than you can think or I can tell."

And so he is gone, and stern and abrupt little man as he is—too often jarring as are his manners—his absence and the exclusion of his idea² from my mind—leave me certainly with less support and in deeper solitude than before.

You see dear Nell—we are still precisely on the same level—<u>you</u> are not isolated.

I feel that there is a certain mystery about this transaction yet and whether it will ever be cleared up to me, I do not know; however my plain duty is to wean my mind from the subject and if possible to avoid pondering over it—In his conversation he seemed studiously to avoid reference to Mr. Smith individually—speaking always of the "House"—the "Firm". He seemed throughout quite as excited and nervous as when I first saw him. I feel that in his way he has a regard for me; a regard which I cannot bring myself entirely to reciprocate in kind—and yet its withdrawal leaves a painful blank.

Saturday Morning

I have got your note. I fear your journey home³ must have sadly fagged you—but I trust that in a day or two you will begin to feel the benefits of the change. What endless trouble that unlucky little Flossy⁴ gives you! How strange that in her trouble she should nestle into your bed and portmanteau,⁵ poor little vermin!

Above you have all the account of "my visitor"; I dare not aver that your kind wish that the visit would yield me more pleasure than pain has been fulfilled—something at my heart aches and gnaws drearily—but I must cultivate <resignation and> fortitude—Papa—I am thankful to say—is a little better—though he improves but slowly—he and Mr. T—got on very well together, much better than the first time.

Write to me again <u>very soon</u>—Yours faithfully

CB

MS BPM Gr. E 21.

1. Smith, Elder had been involved in transactions with India from about 1824. By late 1850 George Smith, having retrieved the firm from the financial crisis caused by the defalcations of Patrick Stewart, was about to expand the firm's Indian trade. He had appointed James Taylor to further this expansion, and to establish 'Smith, Taylor and Co.' in Bombay. Before he left England in May 1851, Taylor arranged to call at Haworth Parsonage on his way back from a farewell visit to his relatives in Scotland. See Biographical Notes, pp. xliii–xliv.
2. CB's idea or image of James Taylor: an objective genitive.
3. EN had been staying at Haworth since late March.
4. Ellen's King Charles spaniel, offspring of Anne Brontë's dog Flossy. 'Vermin' or 'varmint' was a dialect term for a troublesome animal or mischievous child.
5. A clothes-rack or an arrangement of hooks to hang clothes on.

125. *To George Smith, 12 May 1851*

[Haworth]

My dear Sir

I fear it cannot be denied that Mr. Thackeray has actually gone and written a poem.[1] The <u>whole</u> of the May-day Ode is not poetry—<u>that</u> I will maintain; it opens with decent prose—but at the fourth stanza "I felt a thrill of love and awe"—it begins to swell: towards the middle it waxes strong and rises high, takes a tone sustained and sweet, fills the ear with music, the heart with glow and expansion—becomes—in a word—Poetry.[2]

Shame and Sin that the man who <u>can</u> write thus—should write thus so seldom!

How dare he sit half his life holding distaffs for the Omphales of Belgravia?—indolent intellectual Hercules—that he is[3]—Great image of Nebuchadnezzar's dream—made up of iron and clay—half strength—half weakness.[4]

Different indeed is Mr. Ruskin. (I have read the Stones of Venice through.)[5] Thackeray has no love for his Art or his Work: he neglects it; he mocks at it; he trifles with it. Ruskin—for <u>his</u> Art and <u>his</u> Work—has a deep serious passion. We smile sometimes at Ruskin's intense earnestness of feeling towards things that <u>can</u> feel nothing for him in return—for instance—when he breaks out in an apostrophe to a sepulchre "O pure and lovely Monument—My most beloved in Italy—that land of Mourning!". Over Thackeray's criminal carelessness of great faculties—the gift of God—we are oftener disposed to weep—only nobody would be such a simpleton as to weep where tears would be worse than wasted.

I wondered to myself once or twice whether there would be any chance of hearing his lectures.[6] No doubt they will be blent throughout with sarcasm calculated to vex one to the heart—but still—just out of curiosity one would like to know what he will say.

I do not quite understand about the "Guild of Literature"[7] though I have seen it mentioned in the papers—you must be kind enough to explain it better when I see you.

Of course I am not in the least looking forwards to going to London—nor reckoning on it—nor allowing the matter to take any particular place in my thoughts: no: I am very sedulously cool and nonchalant. Moreover—I am not going to be glad to see anybody there: gladness is an exaggeration of sentiment one does not permit oneself: to be pleased is quite enough—and not too well pleased either—only with pleasure of a faint tepid kind—and to a stinted penurious amount. Perhaps—when I see your Mother and Mr. Williams again—I shall just be able to get up a weak flicker of gratification—but that will be all. From even this effort—I shall be exempt on seeing you. Authors and Publishers are never expected to meet with any other than hostile feelings and on shy and distant terms. They never ought to have to shake hands: they should just bow to each other and pass by on opposite sides—keeping several yards distance between them. And besides—if obliged to communicate by Post—they should limit what they have to say to concise notes of about 3 lines apiece—which reminds me that this is too long and that it is time I thanked you for sending the Dividend[8]—and begged with proper form to be permitted to subscribe myself

respectfully Yours
C Brontë

MS BPM SG 48/10B.

1. Thackeray's *May Day Ode*, published in *The Times* for 30 Apr. 1851, was written to celebrate the opening of the Great Exhibition in Joseph Paxton's masterpiece, the 'Crystal Palace' in Hyde Park, on 1 May. It begins ineptly enough with the lines 'But yesterday a naked sod, | The dandies sneered from Rotten Row, | And cantered o'er it to and fro; | And see, 'tis done!'.
2. 'I felt a thrill of love and awe | To mark the different garb of each, | The changing tongue, the various speech | Together blent. | A thrill, methinks, like His who saw | "All people dwelling upon earth | Praising our God with solemn mirth | And one consent." '
3. Omphale was the legendary Queen of Lydia to whom Hercules was bound a slave for three years. He fell in love with her, and, wearing a female garment while she wore his lion's skin, spent the time spinning wool at her behest. Thackeray enjoyed the company of the aristocratic ladies of London's fashionable West End.
4. See Daniel 2: 33.
5. Volume i only. See Letter 121 n. 7, and *The Stones of Venice* i, ch. xi, § 24.
6. On 17 Apr. CB had accepted an invitation from George Smith's mother to stay with the family in London. Her visit was to begin on 28 May, so that on the following day she could attend Thackeray's second lecture in his series on *The English Humourists of the Eighteenth Century*. She was able to attend four of the six lectures.
7. A scheme set up by Edward Bulwer Lytton, Charles Dickens, other writers, and artists 'to encourage life assurance and other provident habits among authors and artists', and to provide other assistance. To raise funds, Lytton's comedy, 'Not So Bad as we Seem', would be produced by Dickens and performed by an amateur cast 'in a theatre constructed for the purpose'. The first two performances, on 16 and 27 May, took place at Devonshire House, by permission of the 6th Duke of Devonshire. It is possible that CB attended a later performance, on 2 July, in the Hanover Square rooms.
8. At CB's request, George Smith had invested the money she had received for the copyright of *Shirley* and for the cheap edition of *Jane Eyre* in $3\frac{1}{4}$ per cent reduced bank annuities, and had arranged to send her the dividends.

126. *To Revd Patrick Brontë, 7 June 1851*

112. Gloucester Terrace
Hyde-Park.

Dear Papa

I was very glad to hear that you continued in pretty good health and that Mr. Cartman[1] came to help you on Sunday. I fear you will not have had a very comfortable week in the dining-room[2]—but by this time I suppose the parlour reformation will be nearly completed and you will soon be able to return to your old quarters.

The letter you sent me this morning was from Mary Taylor; she continues well and happy in New Zealand and her shop seems to answer well. The French Newspaper duly arrived.[3]

Yesterday I went for the second time to the Crystal Palace—we remained in it about three hours—and I must say I was more struck with it on this occasion tha[n] at my first visit. It is a wonderful place—vast—strange new and impossible to describe. Its grandeur does not consist in <u>one</u> thing but in the unique assemblage of <u>all</u> things—Whatever human industry has created—you find there—from the great compartments filled with Railway Engines and boilers, with Mill-machinery in full work—with splendid carriages of all kinds—with harness of every description—to the glass-covered and velvet spread stands loaded with the most gorgeous work of the goldsmith and silversmith—and the carefully guarded caskets full of real diamonds and pearls worth hundreds of thousands of pounds.[4] It may be called a Bazaar or a Fair—but it is such a Bazaar or Fair as eastern Genii might have created. It seems as if magic only could have gathered this mass of wealth from all the ends of the Earth—as if none but supernatural hands could have arranged it thus—with such a blaze and contrast of colours and marvellous power of effect. The multitude filling the great aisles seems ruled and subdued by some invisible influence—Amongst the thirty thousand souls that peopled it the day I was there, not one loud noise was to be heard—not one irregular movement seen—the living tide rolls on quietly—with a deep hum like the sea heard from a distance.

Mr. Thackeray is in high spirits about the success of his lectures—it is likely to add largely both to his fame and purse; he has however deferred this week's lecture[5] till next Thursday at the earnest petition of the Duchesses and Marchionesses—who on the day it should have been delivered were necessitated to go down with the Queen and Court to Ascot Races. I told him I thought he did wrong to put it off on their account—and I think so still.

The Amateur Performance of Bulwer's Play for the Guild of Literature has likewise been deferred[6] on account of the Races—

I hope dear Papa that you Mr. Nicholls and all at home continue well. Tell Martha to take her scrubbing and cleaning in moderation and not overwork herself.

with kind regards to her and Tabby
I am your affectionate daughter
C Brontë

MS Pierpont Morgan.

1. Revd Dr. William Cartman, DD, headmaster of Ermysted's Grammar School, Skipton, 1841–67. A good friend of Mr Brontë and A. B. Nicholls, he had taken a funeral service and possibly other services at Haworth on Sunday, 1 June.
2. The room to the left of the front door as one approaches the Parsonage. The parlour, on the other side of the hall, was Mr. Brontë's usual sanctum.
3. Sent to Haworth by Mary's brothers from their home in Hunsworth.
4. The gems included the Koh-i-noor diamond presented to Queen Victoria in 1850 by the East India Company.
5. The third lecture, on Richard Steele, should have been given on Thursday, 5 June.
6. From 3 June to 18 June.

127. *To Ellen Nussey, 24 June 1851*

112. Gloucester Terrace
[London]

Dear Ellen

Your letter would have been answered yesterday but that I was already gone out before Post-time and was out all day—Since Sir J. K. S[huttleworth] discovered that I was in London—I have had precious little time to myself—he brings other people who are all very kind—and perhaps I shall be glad of what I have seen afterwards—but it is often a little trying at the time. On Thursday[1] the Marquis of Westminster asked me to a great party—to which I was to go with Mrs. Davenport[2]—a beautiful and—(I think) a kind woman too—but this I resolutely declined—On Friday I dined at the Shuttleworths and met Mrs. Davenport & Mr. Monckton Milnes[3]—On Saturday I went to hear & see Rachel[4]—a wonderful sight—terrible as if the earth had cracked deep at your feet and revealed a glimpse of hell—I shall never forget it—she made me shudder to the marrow of my bones: in her some fiend has certainly taken up an incarnate home. She is not a woman—she is a snake—she is the—. On Sunday I went to the Spanish Ambassador's Chapel—where Cardinal Wiseman[5] in his Archiepiscopal robes and Mitre held a Confirmation—The whole scene was impiously theatrical. Yesterday Monday I was sent for at ten to breakfast with Mr. Rogers the patriarch poet[6]—Mrs Davenport and Lord Glenelg[7] were there—no one else—this certainly proved a most calm refined and intellectual treat. After breakfast—Sir David Brewster[8] came to take us to the Crystal

Palace—I had rather dreaded this, for Sir David is a man of the profoundest science and I feared it would be impossible to understand his explanations of the mechanisms &c. indeed I hardly knew how to ask him questions—I was spared all trouble—without being questioned—he gave information in the kindest and simplest manner—After two hours spent at the Exhibition and when, as you may suppose—I was very tired—we had to go to Lord Westminster's and spend two hours more in looking at the collection of pictures in his splendid Gallery—I cannot now leave London till Friday—To-morrow is Mr. Smith's only holiday—(Mr. T[aylor]'s departure leaves him loaded with work—more than once since I came he has been kept in the City till 3 in the morning) he wants to take us all to Richmond and I promised last week I would stay and go with him—his Mother & Sisters—On Thursday I am also engaged—and after putting off Mrs. Gaskell again and yet again it is quite settled that I shall go to her on Friday.[9]

Can I throw all these people overboard—derange all plans—break all promises? Would it be rational to do this—? would it be right? Could it be done? Reflect—dear Nell, and be reasonable and charitable—Did I not tell you six weeks ago—that it was not likely I should see the Gorhams[10] as they would be with you while I should be in London?

I well knew that—once in London—contingencies might arise, which I could not over-rule.

Believe me
Yours faithfully
C Brontë

MS HM 24482.

1. 19 June. Richard Grosvenor, 2nd Marquess of Westminster (1795–1869; Lord Lieutenant of Cheshire 1845–67), owner of a great collection of pictures at his London mansion, Grosvenor House in Upper Grosvenor Street.
2. Lady Kay-Shuttleworth's cousin, née Caroline Anne Hurt (d. 1897), widow of Edward Davies Davenport (1778–1847) of Capesthorne Hall near Macclesfield in Cheshire. On 11 Feb. 1852 she married her second husband, the first Lord Hatherton.
3. Richard Monckton Milnes (1809–85; created Baron Houghton in 1865). His Yorkshire home was at Fryston, near Pontefract. Widely travelled, cultivated, hospitable, and a bibliophile, he was active in various good causes. He later cooperated with Mrs Gaskell in seeking to provide A. B. Nicholls with a pension or with advancement in the church before his marriage to CB.
4. The famous actress, née Élisa Félix (1820–58); CB's model for 'Vashti' in *Villette*. Charlotte saw her in *Adrienne Lecouvreur* by Scribe and Legouvé at the St James's Theatre on 7 June and in Corneille's *Horace* (*Les Horaces*) on 21 June.
5. Nicholas Patrick Stephen Wiseman (1802–65), leader of the Catholic revival in England. The Pope had appointed him Archbishop of Westminster on 6 Aug. 1850, and on 29 Sep. 1850 had raised him to the Cardinalate. His first pastoral letter proclaimed his intention to restore England 'to its orbit in the ecclesiastical firmament'. The British Press had reacted hysterically to this 'Papal Aggression'. The Spanish Ambassador's Chapel in Spanish Place, Marylebone, had been built in 1792.

6. Samuel Rogers (1763–1855), poet, banker, conversationalist, connoisseur of art, and phil-
   anthropist. He entertained distinguished guests at his famous breakfasts at 22 St James's Place.
7. Charles Grant (1778–1866), statesman; created Lord Glenelg in 1831. As Colonial Secretary 1835–9
   he had introduced the bill abolishing West Indian slavery.
8. Sir David Brewster (1781–1868), Scottish physicist and Royal Medallist who had made important
   discoveries in optics, written many works, and collaborated with Sir John Herschel, whose
   Results of Astronomical Observations had been published by Smith, Elder in 1847.
9. 27 June. CB's departure had been postponed so that she could attend Thackeray's lecture on
   Hogarth, Smollett, and Fielding on 26 June.
10. Ellen's friend Mary Gorham, and perhaps her mother and brother John, had been staying with
    the Nusseys. Their home was at Cakeham, near Chichester in Sussex.

128. *To George Smith, 1 July 1851*

[Haworth]

My dear Sir

After a month's voyaging I have cast anchor once more—in a rocky and
lonely little cove, no doubt, but still—safe enough.[1]

The visit to Mrs. Gaskell on my way home—let me down easily—though
I only spent two days with her—they were very pleasant. She lives in a
large—cheerful airy house, quite out of the Manchester Smoke—a garden
surrounds it, and as in this hot weather, the windows were kept open—a
whispering of leaves and perfume of flowers always pervaded the rooms. Mrs.
Gaskell herself is a woman of whose conversation and company I should not soon
tire—She seems to me kind, clever, animated and unaffected—her husband is a
good and kind man too.[2]

I went to Church by myself on Sunday Morning (they are Unitarians). On
my return shortly before the family came home from Chapel—the servant said
there was a letter for me. I wondered from whom—not expecting my Father
to write and not having given the address elsewhere. Of course I was not at
all pleased when the small problem was solved by the letter being brought—I
never care for hearing from you the least in the world. Comment on the
purport of your note is unnecessary. I am glad—yet hardly dare permit myself
to congratulate till the M.S is fairly created and found to be worthy of the
hand—pen and mind whence it is to emanate.[3] His promise to go down into the
country is all very well—yet secretly I cannot but wish that a sort of 'Chamber
in the wall'[4] might be prepared at Cornhill—furnished (besides the bed, table,
stool and candlestick which the Shunamite "set" for Elisha) with a desk, pens,
ink and paper. Here the Prophet might be received and lodged; subjected to a
system kind (perhaps) yet firm; roused each morning at six punctually—by the
contrivance of that virtuous self-acting couch[5] which casts from it its too fondly
clinging inmate; served, on being duly arrayed, with a slight breakfast of tea
and toast: then—with the exception of a crust at one—no further gastronomic

interruption to be allowed till 7.p.m at which time—the greatest and most industrious of modern authors—should be summoned by the most spirited and vigilant of modern publishers to a meal comfortable and comforting—in short a good dinner—elegant, copious, convivial (in moderation) of which they should partake together in the finest spirit of geniality and fraternity—part at half-past nine—and at that salutary hour—withdraw each to recreating repose. Grand—would be the result of such a system pursued for six months.

Somehow I quite expect that you will let me see your "character"[6] though you did not promise that you would—Do not keep it back on account of any faults—Remember Thackeray seems to think our faults the best part of us. I will tell you faithfully whether it seems to me true or not—

In a day or two I expect to be quite settled at home—and think I shall manage to be quite philosophical &c. I was thankful to find my Father very well—he said that when I wrote I was to give you his best respects

I am sincerely Yours
C Brontë

MS BPM SG 49.

1. Charlotte had stayed with the Smiths in London from 28 May until 27 June, when she left to visit the Gaskells' home, Plymouth Grove in Manchester. She returned to Haworth on 30 June.
2. Revd William Gaskell (1805–84), assistant minister at Cross Street Unitarian Chapel, Manchester since 1828. CB also enjoyed the company of the Gaskells' youngest daughter, 5-year-old Julia, who had 'surreptitiously possessed herself of a minute fraction of' Charlotte's heart.
3. On 27 June 1851 Thackeray had signed a contract for his next novel, *Henry Esmond*, agreeing to submit to George Smith the completed manuscript for a 3-volume novel on 1 Dec. But during the summer of this year Thackeray was a 'soul in purgatory' after William Brookfield forbade his correspondence with his wife Jane. Then on 10 Nov. 1851 Thackeray began a lecture tour, confessing on 26 Dec. that he had not advanced five pages of *Esmond* while he was in Edinburgh. He did not complete the MS until 29 May 1852.
4. See 2 Kings 4: 8–10.
5. On display at the Great Exhibition which Charlotte had visited was 'a silent alarum bedstead to *turn* any one *out of bed* at a given hour', invented by 'Mr Jones of Lombard Street'.
6. George Smith recalled that he and CB had visited a phrenologist in June during her London visit. Dr J. P. Browne had produced a surprisingly apt analysis of Charlotte's disposition and skills, observing that she was sensitive, deeply thoughtful, and if not a poet 'her sentiments are poetical or at least embued with that enthusiastic glow which is characteristic of poetical feeling'. Browne's estimate of George Smith was on the whole less perceptive, but Charlotte commented, when she received it, that apart from 'the small vein of error' which flowed through it, it was 'like . . . as the very life itself'. See the 'Phrenological Estimates' in *CBL* ii. 657–62.

129. *To George Smith, 22 September 1851*

[Haworth]

My dear Sir

I am sure I am not low-spirited just now, but very happy and in this mood I will write to you.

That enclosed copy of a letter (ought I to return it?) gave me pleasure; it is comforting to be useful; it is pleasant to see a sprouting greenness where seed has been sown. I doubt not my well-intentioned preface-remarks[1] have ere this brought on you and Mr. Williams the annoyance of accumulated rubbish, and it would be hard indeed if amongst all the chaff should not now and then occur a few grains of wheat. I trust this may be the case in the present instance; I wish that from these grains may spring a promising crop.

Can I help wishing you well when I owe you directly or indirectly most of the good moments I now enjoy? Or can I avoid feeling grieved—mortified when the chance of aiding to give effect to my own wishes offers itself and—for want of strength—vitality—animal spirits—I know not what in me—passes by unimproved?[2] Oh that Serial! It is of no use telling you what a storm in a tea-cup the mention of it stirred in Currer Bell's mind—what a fight he had with himself about it. You do not know—you _cannot_ know how strongly his nature inclines him to adopt suggestions coming from so friendly a quarter; how he would like to take them up—cherish them—give them form—conduct them to a successful issue; and how sorrowfully he turns away feeling in his inmost heart that this work—this pleasure is not for him.

But though Currer Bell cannot do this—you are still to think him your friend—and you are still to be _his_ friend. You are to keep a fraction of yourself—if it be only the end of your little finger—for _him_, and that fraction he will neither let gentleman or lady—author or artist—not even Miss M'Crowdie[3] (the Scotch gentlewoman whose portrait you so graphically depict) take possession of—or so much as meddle with. He reduces his claim to a minute point—and that point he monopolizes.

I won't say I don't rather like Miss Girzy M'Crowdie. I believe one might get on with her pretty well. After all, depend on it—there would be a rude sort of worth in her.

What is it you say about my breaking the interval between this and Christmas by going from home for a week? No—if there were no other objection—(and there are many) there is the pain of that last bidding good-bye—that hopeless shaking hands—yet undulled—and unforgotten. I don't like it. I could not bear its frequent repetition. Do not recur to this plan. Going to London is a mere palliative and stimulant: reaction follows.

Meantime I really do get on very well: not always alike—and I have been at intervals despondent; but Providence is kind, and hitherto whenever depression passes a certain point—some incident transpires to turn the current—to lighten the load; a cheering sunrise has so far ever followed a night of peculiar vigil and fear. Hope indeed is not a plant to flourish very luxuriantly in this northern climate—but still it throws out fresh leaves and a blossom now and then—proving that it is far from dead—and as for Fortitude—Miss M'Crowdie herself will tell you what tenacious roots that shrub twines in a stony moorish soil.

Please to give my love to your Mother and Sisters and believe me

Yours sincerely and faithfully

C Brontë

MS BPM SG 57.

1. CB's dedication and preface to the 2nd edition of *JE* must have embarrassed her publishers as well as Thackeray, but her prefatory note to her 1850 edition of her sisters' works, praising her publishers' 'friendly and skilful' handling of *JE*, would prove useful to them.
2. CB was making slow progress with the writing of *Villette*, and she had rejected George Smith's suggestion that she might write a novel in the serial form. Even if she had the 'experience of a Thackeray or the animal spirits of a Dickens', she would 'publish no Serial of which the last number is not written before the first comes out' (to George Smith, 8 Sept. 1851).
3. Perhaps in 'Girzy M'Crowdie' George Smith had embodied his idea of the harsh duty of work, to which he had to devote so much of himself.

130. To James Taylor, 15 November 1851

Haworth

My dear Sir

Both your communications reached me safely, the note of the 17th. Septbr. and the letter of the 2nd. Octbr.[1] You do yourself less than justice when you stigmatise the latter as "ill-written." I found it quite legible, nor did I lose a word though the lines and letters were so close. I should have been sorry if such had not been the case, as it appeared to me throughout highly interesting. It is observable that the very same information which we have previously collected—perhaps with rather languid attention—from printed books—when placed before us in familiar manuscript and comprising the actual experience of a person with whom we are acquainted—acquires a new and vital interest: when we know the narrator—we seem to realize the tale.

The Bath-Scene amused me much. Your account of that operation tallies in every point with Mr. Thackeray's description in the "Journey from Cornhill to Grand Cairo".[2] The usage seems a little rough, and I cannot help thinking that equal benefit might be obtained through less violent means; but I suppose without the previous fatigue—the after-sensation would not be so enjoyable—and no doubt it is that indolent after-sensation which the self-indulgent Mahometans chiefly cultivate. I think you did right to disdain it.

It would seem to me a matter of great regret that the society at Bombay should be so deficient in all intellectual attraction. Perhaps however your occupations will so far absorb your thoughts as to prevent them from dwelling painfully on this circumstance. No doubt there will be moments when you will look back to London and Scotland and the friends you have left there—with some yearning—but I suppose business has its own excitement; the new country—the new scenes too—must have their interest—and as you will not lack books to fill your leisure—you will probably soon become reconciled to a change which—for some minds—would too closely resemble exile.

I fear the climate—such as you describe it—must be very trying to a European Constitution: in your first letter—you mentioned October as the month of danger: it is now over; whether you have passed its ordeal safely must yet for some weeks remain unknown to your friends in England. They can but <u>wish</u> that such may be the case.

You will not expect me to write a letter that shall form a parallel with your own either in quantity or quality; what I write must be brief—and what I communicate must be commonplace and of trivial interest.

I spent a few weeks in Town last Summer as you have heard—and was much interested by many things I heard and saw there. What now chiefly dwell in my memory are Mr. Thackeray's Lectures, Mademoiselle Rachel's Acting, D'Aubignés, Melville's and Maurice's Preaching[3] and—the Crystal Palace. Mr Thackeray's Lectures you will have seen mentioned and commented on in the Papers; they were very interesting. I could not always coincide with the sentiments expressed or the opinions broached—but I admired the gentlemanlike ease, the quiet humour, the taste, the talent the simplicity and the originality of the Lecturer.

Rachel's Acting transfixed me with wonder, enchained me with interest and thrilled me with horror.[4] The tremendous power with which she expresses the very worst passions in their strongest essence forms an exhibition as exciting as the bull-fights of Spain and the gladiatorial combats of old Rome—and (it seemed to me) not one whit more moral than these poisoned stimulants to popular ferocity. It is scarcely human nature that she shews you; it is something wilder and worse; the feelings and fury of a fiend. The great gift of Genius she undoubtedly has—but—I fear—she rather abuses than turns it to good account.

With all the three preachers I was greatly pleased. Melville seemed to me the most eloquent, Maurice—the most in earnest; had I the choice—it is Maurice whose ministry I should frequent.

On the Crystal Palace I need not comment: you must already have heard too much of it. It struck me at the first with only a vague sort of wonder and admiration, but having one day the privilege of going over it in company with an eminent countryman of yours—Sir David Brewster,[5] and hearing in his kindly Scotch accent his lucid explanation of many things that had been to me before a sealed book—I began a little better to comprehend it—or at least a small part of it. Whether its final results will equal expectation I know not.

My Father I am thankful to say continues in pretty good health. I read portions of your letter to him and he was interested in hearing them. He charged me when I wrote—to convey his very kind remembrances.

I had myself ceased to expect a letter from you. On taking leave at Haworth—you said something about writing from India—but I doubted at the time whether it was not one of those forms of speech which politeness dictates—and as time passed and I did not hear from you I became confirmed in this view of the subject. With every good wish for your welfare—

I am Yours sincerely

C Brontë

MS Pierpont Morgan, MA 2696.

1. James Taylor's letters had probably taken about 5 weeks to reach Haworth from Bombay.
2. Thackeray's amusing account of his Turkish bath in ch. 7 of *Notes of a Journey from Cornhill to Grand Cairo* (1846), when, 'dressed in three large cotton napkins' he had endured 'a soft boiling simmer', followed by a violent beating with a 'horse brush', a 'squirting fountain of warm water', and a drowning in lather.
3. On 1 June 1851 CB had heard the Swiss Professor of Church History, Jean Henri Merle D'Aubigné (1794–1872) preaching. He saw Catholicism as a growing threat to Protestantism in England, and advocated an international evangelical movement. Revd Henry Melvill (1798–1871), the evangelical Principal of Haileybury College, Hertford, preached regular Tuesday morning sermons at St Margaret's, Lothbury, where CB may have heard him. Revd Frederick Denison Maurice (1805–72), Christian Socialist and liberal theologian, had been a Professor at King's College, London, since 1840.
4. Cf. Letter 127.
5. See Letter 127 n. 8.

131. *To George Smith, 14 February 1852*

[Haworth]

My dear Sir

It has been a great delight to me to read Mr. Thackeray's Manuscript[1] and I so seldom now express any sense of kindness that for once you must permit me, without rebuke, to thank you for a pleasure so rare and special.

Yet I am not going to praise either Mr. Thackeray or his book. I have read, enjoyed—been interested and—after all feel full as much ire and sorrow as gratitude and admiration. And still—one can never lay down a book of his—without the last two feelings having their part—be the subject or treatment what it may.

In the first half of the work what chiefly struck me was the wonderful manner in which the author throws himself into the spirit and letter of the times whereof he treats; the allusions, the illustrations, the style all seem to me so masterly in their exact keeping, their harmonious consistency, their nice natural truth, their pure exemption from exaggeration. No second-rate imitator can write in this way; no coarse scene-painter can charm us with an illusion so delicate and perfect. But what bitter satire—what relentless dissection of diseased subjects! Well—and this too is right—or would be right if the savage surgeon did not seem so fiercely pleased with his work. Thackeray likes to discover an ulcer or an aneurism; he has pleasure in putting his cruel knife or probe into quivering, living flesh. Thackeray would not like all the world to be good; no great satirist would like Society to be perfect.

As usual—he is unjust to women—quite unjust: there is hardly any punishment he does not deserve for making Lady Castlewood peep through a key-hole, listen at a door and be jealous of a boy and a milkmaid.[2]

Many other things I noticed that—for my part—grieved and exasperated me as I read—but then again came passages so true—so deeply thought—so tenderly felt—one could not help forgiving and admiring.

I wish there was any one whose word he cared for to bid him good speed—to tell him to go on courageously with the book; he may yet make it the best thing he has ever written. But I wish he could be told not to care much for dwelling on the political or religious intrigues of the times. Thackeray, in his heart, does not value political or religious intrigue of any age or date; he likes to shew us human-Nature <u>at home</u>—as he himself—daily sees it; his wonderful observant faculty likes to be in action. In him—this faculty is a sort of Captain and Leader—and if ever any passage in his writings lacks interest—it is when this master faculty is for a time thrust into a subordinate position. I think such is the case in the former half of the present work; towards the middle he throws off restraint—becomes himself and is strong to the close. Everything now depends on the 2nd. & 3rd.vols. If in pith and interest they fall short of the first—a true success cannot ensue; if the continuation be an improvement upon the commencement—if the stream gather force as it rolls—Thackeray will triumph.

Some people have been in the habit of terming him the <u>second</u> writer of his day;[3] it just depends on himself whether or not these critics shall be justified in their award. He need not to be second. God made him second to no man. If I were he—I would shew myself as I am—not as critics report me; at any rate—I would do my best—but I believe Mr. Thackeray is easy and indolent and very seldom cares to do his best.[4]

Thank you once again, and believe me

Yours sincerely

C Brontë

MS BPM SG 68.

1. The first volume of the manuscript of Thackeray's novel, *Henry Esmond, Esq., A Colonel in the service of her Majesty Queen Anne | Written by himself | edited by W. M. Thackeray.* Thackeray's progress had been slow, but he managed to complete vols. ii and iii by 28 May 1852.
2. Lady Castlewood is angered by Esmond's visits to the milkmaid Nance Sievewright not only because he may have brought smallpox into the household, but because she is jealous of all pretty women. She watches and listens at a door when her husband plays cards with Lord Mohun in vol. i, ch.13.
3. Second to Dickens—a common judgement at the time.

4. In a letter of 25 Feb. 1852 to Mary Holmes, Thackeray admitted that he did not 'care a straw for
   a "triumph". Pooh!—nor for my art enough' (*The Letters and Private Papers of William Makepeace
   Thackeray*, ed. Gordon N. Ray, 4 vols. (1945), iii. 13.)

132. *To George Smith, 11 March 1852*

[Haworth]

My dear Sir

I am very glad to hear that Mr. Thackeray is "getting on" as he says—and it is
to be hoped the stimulus may prove more than temporary.[1] Is not the publication
of the Lectures "with no end of illustrations"—a most commendable idea?[2] I
should think everyone who heard them delivered will like to read them over
again at leisure: for my own part I can hardly imagine a greater treat, were it
only for the opportunity thereby afforded of fishing for faults and fallacies—and
of fuming, fretting and brooding at ease over the passages that excited one's
wrath. In listening to a lecture you have not time to be angry enough. Mr.
Thackeray's worship of his Baal—Bel—Beëlzebub (they are all one) his false
god of a Fielding—is a thing I greatly desire to consider deliberately.[3] In that red
book of yours (which I returned long ago) there was a portrait of the Author
of "Jonathan Wild"—in the cynical prominence of the under-jaw, one read the
man. It was the stamp of one who would never see his neighbours (especially
his women-neighbours) as they are—but as they might be under the worst
circumstances. In Mr. Thackeray's own nature is a small seasoning of this virtue
but it does not (I hope) prevail throughout his whole being.

I have read the "Paris Sketches"[4] slowly, and by regulated allowances of so
much per diem. I was so afraid of exhausting the precious provision too quickly.
What curious traces one finds (at least so it struck me) of a somewhat wild,
irregular and reckless life being led at that time by the Author! And yet how
good—how truthful and sagacious are many of the papers—such as touch on
politics for instance—and above all the critical articles—and then whatever
vinegar and gall—whatever idle froth a book of Thackeray's may contain it has
no dregs—you never go and wash your hands when you put it down—nor rinse
your mouth to take away the flavour of a degraded soul—Perverse he may be
and is—but—to do him justice—not degraded—no—never.

Is the 1st. no. of "Bleak House"[5] generally admired? I liked the Chancery
part—but where it passes into the autobiographic form and the young woman
who announces that she is not "bright" begins her history—it seems to me
too often weak and twaddling—an amiable nature is caricatured—not faithfully
rendered in Miss Esther Sum[m]erson.

Did I tell you that I had heard from Miss Martineau and that she has quite
thrown aside "Oliver Weld"[6] and calls it now "a foolish prank"—? For the

present she declines turning her attention to any other work of fiction; she says her time for writing fiction is past—this may be so.

Please to tell Mr. Williams that I mean (D.V.) to look over "Shirley" soon and to send him a list of errata[7]—but I marvel at your courage in contemplating a reprint; I cannot conceive a score of copies being sold.

Believe me

Yours sincerely

C Brontë

I return Mr. Thackeray's little illustrated note.[8] How excellent is Goldsmith issuing in full-blown complacency from Filby's Shop—with Dr. Johnson walking half-benignant—half-sarcastic by his side. Captain Steele too is very good. Surely if Mr. Thackeray undertook to furnish illustrations—he would not be troublesome and procrastinating about what he can dash off so easily and rapidly.

MS BPM SG 70. Postscript misplaced with MS SG 83.

1. George Smith had forwarded to CB a 'little illustrated note' from Thackeray, announcing that he was 'getting on' with the second volume of Henry Esmond.
2. Thackeray's Lectures on the English Humourists of the Eighteenth Century, with notes by James Hannay (1827–73), eventually published in Mar. 1853.
3. CB heard Thackeray lecture on Hogarth, Smollett, and Fielding on 26 June 1851. She deplored his failure to condemn Fielding's drinking the 'cup of pleasure' and getting into debt, owing to his taste for 'good wine, good clothes, and good company'. Fielding's Jonathan Wild was published in his 'Miscellanies' in 1743. See CB's letter to Smith of 26 Mar. 1853, and for Baal—Bel—Beëlzebub see Judges 2: 11–13, Jeremiah 51: 44, and Mark 3: 22.
4. Eighteen articles by Thackeray, written while he was studying drawing in Paris, 1832–3, most of them first published in magazines, and collected in one volume as The Paris Sketch-Book (July 1840).
5. The first of the twenty parts of Dickens's Bleak House was published on 28 Feb. 1852.
6. Harriet Martineau had wished to write a novel which would be published anonymously, and in July 1851 had sought CB's advice. Charlotte secured George Smith's interest in the matter, but in Dec. 1851 he rejected Oliver Weld as 'obnoxious in a business point of view'. Martineau attributed his refusal to her 'favourable representations and auguries on behalf of the Catholics'. See H. Martineau, Autobiography 3 vols., the third containing memorials by Maria Weston Chapman (London, 1877), ii. 381–3.
7. The second edition of Shirley, incorporating some minor corrections and revisions, was published in one volume in Nov. 1852.
8. Thackeray had sent three drawings, one of Richard Steele, one of Laurence Sterne ogling a shopgirl, and one of Johnson and Goldsmith walking in front of Filby's shop—from which Goldsmith ordered but did not pay for many splendid clothes. For the third drawing see Gordon N. Ray The Letters and Private Papers of William Makepeace Thackeray, ed. Gordon N. Ray (1945), iv. opp. 71, and 71 n. 10.

133. To Elizabeth Gaskell, 26 April 1852. [Fragments][1]

[Haworth]

... I lately got hold of a bound copy of Dickens's Houshold Words for 1851.[2] Therein I have as yet only read three articles to wit. Society at Cranford. Love at

Cranford. Memory at Cranford. Before reading them I had received a hint as to the authorship which hint gave them special zest. The best is the last—Memory; how good I thought it—I must not tell <u>you</u>.

The sketch you give of your work[3] (respecting which I am, of course, dumb) seems to me very noble; and its purpose may be as useful in practical result as it is high and just in theoretical tendency. Such a book may restore hope and energy to many who thought they had forfeited their right to both; and open a clear course for honourable effort to some who deemed that they and all honour had parted company in this world.

Yet—hear my protest!

Why should she die? Why are we to shut up the book weeping?

My heart fails me already at the thought of the pang it will have to undergo. And yet you must follow the impulse of your own inspiration. If <u>that</u> commands the slaying of the victim, no bystander has a right to put out his hand to stay the sacrificial knife: but I hold you a stern priestess in these matters.

MS untraced. Text: *CBL* iii. 42–3.

1. The original MS has not been located. The text in *CBL* is based on an early transcript by Alexander Symington, and quotations in Mrs Gaskell's *Life* of CB, ch. 24
2. Dickens's weekly magazine, *Household Words*, which appeared from 30 Mar. 1850 to 28 May 1859. CB had read the first, second, and third parts of Mrs Gaskell's *Cranford*. The first part only had appeared in 1851, the second on 3 Jan. 1852, and the third on 13 Mar. 1852.
3. *Ruth*, eventually published in Jan. 1853. The writing and reception of this story of a 'fallen woman' caused Mrs Gaskell much anxiety.

134. *To Ellen Nussey, 4 ?May 1852*

Haworth

Dear Ellen

The news of E[llen] Taylor's death came to me last week in a letter from Mary[1]—a long letter—which wrung my heart so—in its simple strong, truthful emotion—I have only ventured to read it once. It ripped up half-scarred wounds with terrible force—the death-bed was just the same—breath failing &c.

She fears she shall now in her dreary solitude become "a stern, harsh, selfish woman"—this fear struck home—again and again I have felt it for myself—and what is <u>my</u> position—to Mary's?

I should break out in energetic wishes that she would return to England—if Reason would permit me to believe that prosperity and happiness would there await her—but I see no such prospect. May God help her as God only can help!

I like to hear of your being cheerful—but I fear you impose on yourself too much fatigue with all this entertainment of visitors—Poor Emma Sherwood![2] Will she be at all provided for in case of her father's death—she will hardly like to turn governess. How are Mr. and Mrs. Clapham[3] & your Mother? You have not mentioned them lately. I continue better—and Papa is getting through the Spring admirably.

I am sure Miss Wooler would enjoy her visit to Brookroyd—as much as you, her company. Dear Nell—I thank you sincerely for your discreet and friendly silence on the point alluded to—I had feared it would be discussed between you two—and had an inexpressible shrinking at the thought—Now—less than ever—does it seem to me a matter open to discussion. I hear nothing.[4] And you must quite understand that if I feel any uneasiness—it is not the uneasiness of confirmed and fixed regard—but that anxiety which is inseparable from a state of absolute uncertainty about a somewhat momentous matter. I do not know—I am not sure myself tha[t] any other termination would be better than lasting estrangement and unbroken silence—yet a good deal of pain has been a[nd] must be gone through in that case. However to each—his burden.

I have not yet read the papers[5]—D.V. I will send them to-morrow.

Yours faithfully

C Brontë

Understand—that in whatever I have said above—I was not fishing for pity or sympathy—I hardly pity myself. Only I wish that in all matters in this world there was fair and open dealing—and no underhand work.

MS HM 24491.

1. Mary Taylor's cousin Ellen, who had been helping her in her shop in Wellington, New Zealand, had died of pulmonary tuberculosis on 27 Dec. 1851. CB, probably in error, dated the present letter 4 Mar. 1852, but it was not until 18 May that she sent on to EN 'Mary's letter announcing Ellen's death'.
2. Ellen Nussey's friend, daughter of Revd William Sherwood, MA, incumbent of St James's church, Bradford. He died on 4 May 1852 after a long period of ill-health.
3. Ellen Nussey's sister Ann and her husband Robert Clapham, whom she had married on 26 Sept. 1849.
4. From James Taylor in India. On 15 Nov. 1851 CB had replied to two letters from Taylor, dated 17 Sept. and 2 Oct., but had apparently not heard from him since then.
5. Probably the *Examiner* and the *Leader*, sent from London.

135. To Revd Patrick Brontë, 2 June 1852

Cliff House. Filey[1]

Dear Papa

Thank you for your letter which I was so glad to get that I think I must answer it by return of post. I had expected one yesterday and was perhaps a little unreasonably anxious when disappointed—but the weather has been so <u>very</u> cold that I feared either you were ill or Martha worse. I hope Martha will <u>take</u> care of herself—and cannot help feeling a little uneasy about her.

On the whole I get on very well here—but I have not bathed yet as I am told it is much too cold and too early in the season.

The Sea is very grand. Yesterday it was a somewhat unusually high tide—and I stood about an hour on the cliffs yesterday afternoon—watching the tumbling in of great tawny turbid waves—that made the whole shore white with foam and filled the air with a sound hollower and deeper than thunder. There are so very few visitors at Filey yet—that I and a few sea-birds and fishing-boats have often the whole expanse of sea, shore and cliff to ourselves—When the tide is out—the sands are wide—long and smooth and very pleasant to walk on. When the high tides are in—not a vestige of sand remains. I saw a great dog rush into the sea yesterday—and swim and bear up against the waves like a seal—I wonder what Flossy[2] would say to that.

On Sunday afternoon I went to a church[3] which I should like Mr. Nicholls[4] to see. It was certainly not more than thrice the length and breadth of our passage—floored with brick—the walls green with mould—the pews painted white but the paint almost all worn off with time and decay—at one end there is a little gallery for the singers—and when these personages stood up to perform—they all turned their backs upon the congregation—and the congregation turned their backs on the pulpit and parson—the effect of this manoeuvre was so ludicrous—I could hardly help laughing—had Mr. Nicholls been there—he certainly would have laughed out. Looking up at the gallery and seeing only the broad backs of the singers presented to their audience was excessively grotesque. There is a well-meaning but utterly inactive clergyman at Filey—and Methodists flourish.

I cannot help enjoying Mr. Butterfield's[5] defeat—and yet in one sense this is a bad state of things—calculated to make working-people both discontented and insubordinate. Give my kind regards—dear Papa—to Mr. Nicholls, Tabby and Martha—Charge Martha to beware of draughts and to get such help in her cleaning as she shall need. I hope you will continue well—Believe me

Your affectionate daughter
C Brontë

MS Pierpont Morgan.

1. Charlotte stayed in Filey, on the East Yorks. coast, c.27 May–24 June. Her depression had made a change of air desirable, and she needed to visit Scarborough to arrange for the re-lettering of Anne's gravestone in St Mary's churchyard. Five errors had to be corrected, but one still remains: Anne's age is given as 28 instead of 29.
2. The King Charles spaniel which had belonged to Anne Brontë.
3. Either the small Norman church at Speeton on the high cliffs between Filey and Flamborough, or St Oswald's church in Filey. Both churches were in poor condition. The negligent vicar of Filey was Revd Thomas Norfolk Jackson (?1808–91), vicar 1833–73.
4. Mr Brontë's curate and Charlotte's future husband, Arthur Bell Nicholls.
5. Richard Shackleton Butterfield JP (1806–69). Following the bankruptcy of James Greenwood (1793–1857) the wealthy Butterfield bought Greenwood's Bridgehouse mill and his house,

Woodlands, in Haworth. The weavers in his mill, paid at the lowest possible rate, and obliged to
work two looms simultaneously, walked out on 18 May. Eight were arrested when they refused
to return, of whom two were committed to two months' hard labour, but when a third man,
Robert Redman, declared that he could prove malpractices on Butterfield's part, Butterfield
admitted the truth. 'The bench . . . discharged all the prisoners and ordered him to pay them
3/6d. each for their day's wages.' See Juliet Barker, *The Brontës* (1994), 697–8.

136. *To Margaret Wooler, 23 June 1852*

Filey-Bay

My dear Miss Wooler

Your kind and welcome note reached me at this place where I have been
staying three weeks—quite <u>alone</u>. Change and sea-air had become necessary;
distance and other considerations forbade my accompanying Ellen Nussey to
the South—much as I should have liked it—had I felt quite free and unfettered;
Ellen told me some time ago that you were not likely to visit Scarbro' till the
Autumn—so I forthwith packed my trunk and betook myself here.

The first week or ten days—I greatly feared the sea-side would not suit
me—for I suffered almost constantly from head-ache and other harassing
ailments; the weather too was dark, stormy and excessively—<u>bitterly</u> cold; my
Solitude, under such circumstances, partook of the character of desolation; I
had some dreary evening-hours and night-vigils. However—that passed; I think
I am now better and stronger for the change, and in a day or two—hope to
return home.

E. Nussey told me that Mr. Wm. Wooler[1] said—people with my tendency to
congestion of the liver—should walk three or four hours every day; accordingly
I have walked as much as I could since I came here, and look almost as sunburnt
and weather-beaten as a fisherman or a bathing-woman[2] with being out in the
open air.

As to my work[3]—it has stood obstinately still for a long while: certainly a
torpid liver makes torpid brains: No Spirit moves me. If this state of things does
not entirely change—my chance of a holiday in the Autumn is not worth much.
Yet I should be very sorry not to be able to meet you for a little while at Scarbro'.

The duty to be discharged at Scarbro' was the chief motive that drew me to the
East Coast: I have been there—visited the Churchyard, seen the stone—there
were five errors—consequently I had to give directions for its being refaced and
re-lettered.

My dear Miss Wooler—I do most truly sympathise with you in the success
of your kind efforts to provide for your young kinsman[4]—I know what your
feelings would be under the circumstances. To me—the decision of his Uncles
seems <u>too</u> hard—<u>too</u> worldly, and I am glad that Providence saw fit to make you
the means of awarding him a milder doom. Poor youth! Such banishment might

have been justifiable in the case of a rough, reckless, unmanageable boy—but for one whose disadvantages had their source in over-timidity and weak nerves—it would have been really cruel. Very grateful must be his Mother's feelings towards you.

Give my kind regards to Mr. & Mrs. Carter—tell me about Ellen and Susan[5] when you write

[Signature lacking.]

MS Fitzwilliam.

1. Miss Wooler's brother, Dr William Moore Wooler of Dewsbury (1795–1873).
2. An attendant who helped a lady-bather to don the appropriate loose, enveloping garments within a bathing-machine, a small carriage which would be moved out into water deep enough for bathing.
3. The writing of *Villette*.
4. Not identified.
5. Revd Edward Nicholl Carter (1800–72), vicar of Heckmondwike, his wife Susanna (1800–72, a younger sister of Margaret Wooler), and their daughters Ellen (b. 1834) and Susan (b. 1837).

137. *To Ellen Nussey, 25 August 1852*

Haworth

Dear Ellen

I am thankful to say that Papa's convalescence seems now to be quite confirmed.[1] There is scarcely any remainder of the inflammation in his eyes and his general health progresses satisfactorily. He begins even to look forward to resuming his duty erelong[2]—but caution must be observed on that head. Martha has been very willing and helpful during Papa's illness—Poor Tabby is ill herself at present with English Cholera[3] which complaint together with influenza has lately been almost universally prevalent in this district; of the last—I have myself had a touch—but it went off very gently on the whole—affecting my chest and liver less than any cold has done for the last three years.

I trust, dear Ellen, you are well in health yourself—this visit to the South has not so far been productive of unmingled present pleasure—yet it may bring you future benefit in more ways than one.[4]

I write to you about yourself rather under constraint and in the dark—for your letters—dear Nell—are most remarkably oracular—dropping nothing but hints—which tie my tongue a good deal. What for instance can I say to your last postscript? It is quite Sybilline. I can hardly guess what checks you in writing to me—There is certainly no one in this house or elsewhere to whom I should shew your notes—and I do not imagine they are in any peril in passing through the Post-Offices.

Perhaps you think that as I generally write with some reserve—you ought to do the same. My reserve, however, has its foundation not in design, but in necessity—I am silent because I have literally nothing to say. I might indeed repeat over and over again that my life is a pale blank and often a very weary burden—and that the Future sometimes appals me—but what end could be answered by such repetition except to weary you and enervate myself?

The evils that now and then wring a groan from my heart—lie in position—not that I am a single woman and likely to remain a single woman—but because I am a lonely woman and likely to be lonely. But it cannot be helped and therefore imperatively must be borne—and borne too with as few words about it as may be.

I write all this just to prove to you that whatever you would freely say to me—you may just as freely write.

Understand—that I remain just as resolved as ever not to allow myself the holiday of a visit from you—till I have done my work. After labour—pleasure—but while work was lying at the wall undone—I never yet could enjoy recreation.[5]

Yours very faithfully
C Brontë

MS HM 24498.

1. In July Mr Brontë had been 'suddenly attacked with acute inflammation of the eye'. The Keighley surgeon William Ruddock had diagnosed symptoms of apoplexy, but 'active measures' succeeded in reducing the pulse rate. Mr Brontë was kept very quiet and his dangerous state was not revealed to him.
2. Mr Nicholls took all baptismal and burial services between 25 July and mid-Sept., and all marriage services 10 Aug. 1852–7 Feb. 1853.
3. Probably 'cholera nostras' or summer cholera, of which the symptoms were diarrhoea, vomiting, stomach-ache, and cramps. Unlike Asiatic cholera, it was rarely fatal to adults.
4. Ellen had acted as bridesmaid to her friend Mary Gorham (1826–1917) of Cakeham, near Chichester, at her marriage to Revd Thomas Swinton Hewitt (1817–?84) on 29 June 1852, and had stayed with them after their marriage.
5. After a long period in which she could not make progress with *Villette*, CB had resumed her writing in July, had perforce to stop during her father's illness, but by 3 Aug. was able to return to it. She had probably begun the third volume by late August. To lie at or by the wall means to remain idle or useless. CB's usage postdates the *Oxford English Dictionary*'s quotation from 1787.

138. *To George Smith, 30 October 1852*

[Haworth]

My dear Sir

You must notify honestly what you think of "Villette" when you have read it.[1] I can hardly tell you how much I hunger to have some opinion besides my own, and how I have sometimes desponded and almost despaired because there was no one to whom to read a line—or of whom to ask a counsel. "Jane Eyre" was not written under such circumstances, nor were two-thirds of "Shirley".[2] I got so miserable about it, I could bear no allusion to the book—it is not finished yet, but now—I hope.

As to the anonymous publication—I have this to say. If the witholding of the author's name should tend materially to injure the publisher's interest—to interfere with booksellers' orders &c. I would not press the point; but if no such detriment is contingent—I should be most thankful for the sheltering shadow of an incognito. I seem to dread the advertisements—the large lettered "Currer Bell's New Novel" or "New Work by the Author of 'Jane Eyre'".[3] These, however, I feel well enough are the transcendentalisms of a retired wretch—and must not be intruded in the way of solid considerations; so you must speak frankly.

The Bank Bill for my dividend arrived safely.[4]

I shall be glad to see Colonel Esmond.[5] My objection to the 2nd. Vol. lay here. I thought it decidedly too much History—too little Story.

You will see that "Villette" touches on no matter of public interest. I cannot write books handling the topics of the day—it is of no use trying. Nor can I write a book for its moral—Nor can I take up a philanthropic scheme though I honour Philanthropy—And voluntarily and sincerely veil my face before such a mighty subject as that handled in Mrs. Beecher Stowe's work—"Uncle Tom's Cabin".[6]

To manage these great matters rightly they must be long and practically studied—their bearings known intimately and their evils felt genuinely—they must not be taken up as a business-matter and a trading-speculation. I doubt not Mrs. Stowe had felt the iron of slavery enter into her heart from childhood upwards long before she ever thought of writing books. The feeling throughout her work is sincere and not got up.

Remember to be an honest critic of "Villette" and tell Mr. Williams to be unsparing—not that I am likely to alter anything—but I want to know his impressions and yours.

Believe me
Yours sincerely
C Brontë

MS BPM SG 74.

1. On 26 Oct. CB had sent to W. S. Williams the manuscript of the first two volumes of *Villette*, ending with ch. 27 (mistakenly numbered 28), 'The hotel Crécy'. In her accompanying note she had written, 'My wish is that the book should be published without Author's name.'
2. CB told Mrs Gaskell that the first chapter of *Shirley* that she wrote after her sister Anne's death was 'The Valley of the Shadow of Death'—the opening chapter of the third volume.
3. The title-page of the first edn. of *Villette*, vol. i., begins 'VILLETTE. | BY CURRER BELL., | AUTHOR OF "JANE EYRE," "SHIRLEY," ETC.'
4. George Smith had invested CB's literary earnings, on her behalf, in reduced bank annuities.
5. Thackeray had sent the final corrected proofs of *Henry Esmond* to Smith, Elder on 13 Oct. For CB's opinion of the novel, see Letter 131 and notes.
6. Harriet Beecher Stowe's *Uncle Tom's Cabin*, first published serially 1851–2, and then in book form on 20 Mar. 1852 in Boston, Mass. More than 200,000 copies were sold in seven months. In addition more than a million copies were sold in England in 1852.

139. *To George Smith, 3 November 1852*

[Haworth]

My dear Sir

I feel very grateful for your letter: it relieved me much for I was a good deal harassed by doubts as to how "Villette" might appear in other eyes than my own. I feel in some degree authorized to rely on your favourable impressions, because you are quite right where you hint disapprobation; you have exactly hit two points at least where I was conscious of defect: the discrepancy, the want of perfect harmony between Graham's boyhood and manhood; the angular abruptness of his change of sentiment towards Miss Fanshawe.[1] You must remember though that in secret he had for some time appreciated that young lady at a somewhat depressed standard—held her as a little lower than the angels,[2] but still—the reader ought to have been better made to feel this preparation towards a change of mood.

As for the publishing arrangements—I leave them to Cornhill. There is undoubtedly a certain force in what you say about the inexpediency of affecting a mystery which cannot be sustained—so you must act as you think is for the best. I submit also to the advertisements and large letters—but under protest, and with a kind of Ostrich-longing for concealment.

Most of the 3rd. Vol. is given to the development of the "crabbed Professor's"[3] character. Lucy must not marry Dr. John; he is far too youthful, handsome, bright-spirited and sweet-tempered; he is a "curled darling"[4] of Nature and of Fortune; he must draw a prize in Life's Lottery; his wife must be young, rich and pretty; he must be made very happy indeed. If Lucy marries anybody—it must be the Professor—a man in whom there is much to forgive—much to "put up with." But I am not leniently disposed towards Miss Frost[5]—from the beginning I never intended to appoint her lines in pleasant places.[6]

The conclusion of this 3rd. Vol. is still a matter of some anxiety. I can but do my best, however; it would speedily be finished—could I but ward off certain obnoxious headaches which—whenever I get into the spirit of my work, are apt to seize and prostrate me.

[Signature cut away.]

George Smith Esqr.

Colonel Henry Esmond is just arrived.[7] He looks very antique and distinguished in his Queen Anne's garb—the periwig, sword, lace and ruffles are very well represented by the old Spectator type.

MS BPM SG 75.

1. John Graham Bretton's boyhood and his early infatuation with Ginevra Fanshawe are largely imaginary creations. His adult appearance and more mature personality are recognizably based on George Smith, who recalled that his mother was the 'original' of Mrs Bretton. Ginevra is said

to have traits of two girls known to CB, Amelia Walker, a fellow-pupil at Roe Head school, and Maria Miller, a pupil at the Pensionnat Heger in 1843.

2. Cf. Psalm 8: 5.

3. Paul Emanuel, based on CB's Brussels teacher, Constantin Heger.

4. Cf. *Othello*, I. ii. 68. Desdemona's father could not believe that she would voluntarily seek Othello's 'sooty bosom' when she had shunned the 'wealthy curled darlings of our nation'.

5. The manuscript of *Villette* shows that Lucy's surname was first 'Snowe', then 'Frost', then 'Snowe' again.

6. Cf. Psalms 16: 6.

7. The three volumes of Thackeray's novel, printed by Bradbury & Evans and published by Smith, Elder, are handsomely set in old-face type, using long 's' and ligatures, and the imprint imitates eighteenth-century phrasing. CB's copy was inscribed 'Miss Bronte. | with W M Thackeray's grateful regards. | October 28. 1852.'

140. *To W. S. Williams, 6 November 1852*

[Haworth]

My dear Sir

I must not delay thanking you for your kind letter with its candid and able commentary on "Villette". With many of your strictures—I concur. The 3rd. Vol. may perhaps do away with some of the objections—others will remain in force. I do not think the interest of the story culminates anywhere to the degree you would wish. What climax there is—does not come on till near the conclusion—and even then—I doubt whether the regular novel-reader will consider "the agony piled sufficiently high"—(as the Americans say) or the colours dashed on to the Canvass[1] with the proper amount of daring. Still—I fear they must be satisfied with what is offered: my palette affords no brighter tints—were I to attempt to deepen the reds or burnish the yellows—I should but botch.

Unless I am mistaken—the emotion of the book will be found to be kept throughout in tolerable subjection.

As to the name of the heroine—I can hardly express what subtility of thought made me decide upon giving her a cold name; but—at first—I called her "Lucy Snowe" (spelt with an e) which "Snowe" I afterward changed to "Frost". Subsequently—I rather regretted the change and wished it "Snowe" again: if not too late—I should like the alteration to be made now throughout the M.S.[2] A <u>cold</u> name she must have—partly—perhaps—on the "lucus a non lucendo"[3]—principle—partly on that of the "fitness of things"—for she has about her an external coldness.

You say that she may be thought morbid and weak unless the history of her life be more fully given. I consider that she <u>is</u> both morbid and weak at times—the character sets up no pretensions to unmixed strength—and anybody living her life would necessarily become morbid. It was no impetus of healthy feeling which urged her to the confessional for instance[4]—it was the semi-delirium of solitary grief and sickness. If, however, the book does not express all this—there must be a great fault somewhere—

I might explain away a few other points but it would be too much like drawing a picture and then writing underneath the name of the object intended to be represented. We know what sort of a pencil[5] that is which needs an ally in the pen.

Thanking you again for the clearness and fulness with which you have responded to my request for a statement of impressions—I am, my dear Sir

Yours very sincerely
C Brontë

I trust the work will be seen in M.S. by no one except Mr. Smith and yourself.

MS BPM Gr. F11.

1. Thus in MS.
2. Lucy's surname is 'Frost' in the first two volumes of the fair copy MS, but in the early chapters of vol. iii CB altered 'Frost' to 'Snowe'. The printers were instructed to print 'Snowe' throughout.
3. An etymological contradiction, meaning literally 'a grove (called lucus) from not being light'.
4. See *Villette*, ch. 15. During a period of loneliness and depression while she was in Brussels, CB herself had made 'a real confession to see what it was like'. See Letter 24.
5. An allusion to the painter Orbaneja who, when they asked him what he was painting, used to answer, ' "Whatever it turns out." Sometimes he would paint a cock, . . . so unlike one that he had to write . . . beside it: *This is a cock*' (Cervantes, *Don Quixote*, pt. II, ch. 3).

141. *To Ellen Nussey, 15 December 1852*

[Haworth]

Dear Nell

I return Mrs. Upjohn's note.[1] It is highly characteristic, and not—I fear, of good omen for the comfort of your visit. There <u>must</u> be something wrong in herself as well as in her servants.

I enclose another note which—taken in conjunction with the incident immediately preceding it—and with a long series of indications whose meaning I scarce ventured hitherto to interpret to myself—much less hint to any other—has left on my mind a feeling of deep concern.

This note—you will see—is from Mr. Nicholls.[2] I know not whether you have ever observed him specially—when staying here—: your perception in these matters is generally quick enough—<u>too</u> quick—I have sometimes thought—yet as you never said anything—I restrained my own dim misgivings—which could not claim the sure guide of vision. What Papa has seen or guessed—I will not inquire—though I may conjecture. He has minutely noticed all Mr. Nicholl's low spirits—all his threats of expatriation—all his symptoms of impaired health—noticed them with little sympathy and much indirect sarcasm.

On Monday evening[3]—Mr. N—— was here to tea. I vaguely felt—without clearly seeing—as without seeing, I have felt for some time—the meaning of his constant looks—and strange, feverish restraint.

After tea—I withdrew to the dining-room as usual. As usual—Mr. N. sat with Papa till between eight & nine o'clock. I then heard him open the parlour door as if going. I expected the clash of the front-door—He stopped in the passage: he tapped: like lightning it flashed on me what was coming. He entered—he stood before me. What his words were—you can guess; his manner—you can hardly realize—nor can I forget it—Shaking from hea[d][4] to foot, looking deadly pale, speaking low, vehemently yet with difficulty—he made me for the first time feel what it costs a man to declare affection where he doubts response.

The spectacle of one ordinarily so statue-like—thus trembling, stirred, and overcome gave me a kind of strange shock. He spoke of sufferings he had borne for months—of sufferings he could endure no longer—and craved leave for some hope. I could only entreat him to leave me then and promise a reply on the morrow. I asked if he had spoken to Papa. He said—he dared not—I think I half-led, half put him out of the room. When he was gone I immediately went to Papa—and told him what had taken place. Agitation and Anger disproportionate to the occasion ensued—if I had <u>loved</u> Mr. N—— and had heard such epithets applied to him as were used—it would have transported me past my patience—as it was—my blood boiled with a sense of injustice—but Papa worked himself into a state not to be trifled with—the veins on his temples started up like whip-cord—and his eyes became suddenly blood-shot[5]—I made haste to promise that Mr. Nicholls should on the morrow have a distinct refusal.

I wrote yesterday and got this note. There is no need to add to this statement any comment—Papa's vehement antipathy to the bare thought of any one thinking of me as a wife—and Mr. Nicholls' distress—both give me pain. Attachment to Mr. N—— you are aware I never entertained—but the poignant pity inspired by his state on Monday evening—by the hurried revelation of his sufferings for many months—is something galling and irksome. That he cared something for me—and wanted me to care for him—I have long suspected—but I did not know the degree or strength of his feelings.

Dear Nell—good-bye

Yours faithfully
C Brontë

I have letters from Sir J. K. S.[6] & Miss Martineau, but I cannot talk of them now.

MS Berg.

1. In Oct. 1852 Ellen Nussey had received an invitation to visit Revd Francis Upjohn (1787–1874), the vicar of St Andrew's, Gorleston, Suffolk, and his wife Sarah, née Gorham (?1792–1881). If the visit were to prove mutually satisfactory, 'they would wish in a sense' to adopt Ellen, according to CB's reading of Mrs Upjohn's letter, 'with the prospect of leaving' her an indefinite amount of property. Charlotte considered the suggestion peculiar, and foresaw difficulties.
2. Arthur Bell Nicholls, Mr Brontë's curate. See the Biographical Notes, pp. xl–xli. His note has not been located.
3. 13 Dec.
4. CB wrote 'heat'.
5. The symptoms resembled those of Mr Brontë's dangerous apoplectic seizure in July 1852.
6. Sir James Kay-Shuttleworth.

142. *To Ellen Nussey, 18 December 1852*

Haworth

Dear Nell

You may well ask, how is it? for I am sure I don't know. This business would seem to me like a dream—did not my reason tell me it has been long brewing. It puzzles me to comprehend how and whence comes this turbulence of feeling.

You ask how Papa demeans himself to Mr. N[icholls]. I only wish you were here to see Papa in his present mood: you would know something of him. He just treats him with a hardness not to be bent—and a contempt not to be propitiated.

The two have had no interview as yet: all has been done by letter. Papa wrote—I must say—a most cruel note to Mr. Nicholls, on Wednesday. In his state of mind and health (for the poor man is horrifying his landlady—Martha's Mother[1]—by entirely rejecting his meals) I felt that the blow must be parried, and I thought it right to accompany the pitiless despatch by a line to the effect that—while Mr. N. must never expect me to reciprocate the feeling he had expressed—yet at the same time—I wished to disclaim participation in sentiments calculated to give him pain; and I exhorted him to maintain his courage and spirits.

On receiving the two letters, he set off from home.[2] Yesterday came the enclosed brief epistle.

You must understand that a good share of Papa's anger arises from the idea—not altogether groundless—that Mr. N. has behaved with disingenuousness in so long concealing his aims—forging that Irish fiction &c.[3] I am afraid also that Papa thinks a little too much about his want of money; he says the match would be a degradation—that I should be throwing myself away—that he expects me, if I marry at all—to do very differently; in short—his manner of viewing the subject—is—on the whole, far from being one in which I can sympathize—My own objections arise from sense of incongruity and uncongeniality in feelings, tastes—principles.

How are you getting on—dear Nell—and how are all at Brookroyd? Remember me kindly to everybody—Yours—wishing devoutly that Papa would resume his tranquillity—and Mr. Nicholls his beef and pudding.

C Brontë

I am glad to say that the incipient inflammation in Papa's eye is disappearing.

MS Berg.

1. Mrs John Brown, the sexton's wife.
2. Possibly Mr Nicholls stayed with his friend, Revd Joseph Brett Grant, at Oxenhope Vicarage, or with Revd Sutcliffe Sowden (1816–61), perpetual curate of St. James's, Mytholm, Yorks. 1841–52. vicar of Hebden Bridge 1853–61. He remained near enough to Haworth to baptize James Hartley on 16 Dec., and to officiate at the funeral of Susey Binns on 22 Dec. The enclosed 'epistle' has not been traced.
3. Unexplained.

143. *To Ellen Nussey, 2 January 1853*

[Haworth]

Dear Nell

I thought of you on New Year's night and hope you got well over your formidable tea-making: I trust that Tuesday & Wednesday will also pass pleasantly. I am busy too in my little way—preparing to go to London this week—a matter which necessitates some little application to the needle. I find it is quite necessary that I should go to superintend the press[1] as Mr. S[mith] seems quite determined not to let the printing get on till I come. I have actually only recd. 3 proof sheets since I was at Brookroyd. Papa wants me to go too—to be out of the way—I suppose—but I am sorry for one other person[2] whom nobody pities but me. Martha is bitter against him: John Brown says <u>he should like to shoot him</u>. They don't understand the nature of his feelings—but I see now what they are. Mr. N is one of those who attach themselves to very few, whose sensations are close and deep—like an underground stream, running strong but in a narrow channel. He continues restless and ill—he carefully performs the occasional duty—but does not come near the Church procuring a substitute every Sunday.

A few days since he wrote to Papa requesting permission to withdraw his resignation.[3] Papa answered that he should only do so on condition of giving his written promise never again to broach the obnoxious subject either to him or to me. This he has evaded doing, so the matter remains unsettled. I feel persuaded the termination will be—his departure for Australia.[4] Dear Nell—without loving him <yet I pity> I don't like to think of him, suffering in solitude, and wish him anywhere so that he were happier. He and Papa have never met or spoken yet.

I am very glad to hear that your Mother is pretty well—and also that <u>the</u> shirts are progressing. I hope you will not be called away to Norfolk[5] before I come home: I <u>should</u> like you to pay a visit to Haworth first. Write again soon.

Yours faithfully
C Brontë

MS Law-Dixon.

1. CB stayed in London with the Smiths at 112 Gloucester Terrace from 5 Jan., in order to read and correct the proof-sheets of *Villette*, published on 28 Jan. CB had sent the manuscript of the 3rd volume of the novel to George Smith on 20 Nov. He had been slow to acknowledge its receipt, and when he did so, had complained of the transfer of interest from the Brettons and Paulina to M. Emanuel and the pensionnat. On 8 Dec. CB had returned home after spending two weeks with the Nusseys at Brookroyd, only to find 'no proof-sheets—but a letter from Mr. S[mith] . . . something in the 3rd. vol. sticks confoundedly in his throat' (to Ellen Nussey, ?9 Dec. 1852).
2. A. B. Nicholls.
3. i.e. his resignation of his curacy at Haworth. The 'obnoxious subject' was of course his proposal of marriage to CB.
4. On 28 Jan., after a period of smouldering mutual resentment between himself and Mr Brontë, Mr Nicholls applied to the Society for the Propagation of the Gospel, offering himself as a missionary 'to the colonies of Sydney, Melbourne or Adelaide'.
5. To visit the Upjohns of Gorleston, on the border between Suffolk and Norfolk.

144. *To Ellen Nussey, 4 March 1853*

[Haworth]

Dear Ellen

I return Mrs. Upjohn's letter. She is really a most inconclusive person to have to do with: have you come to any decision yet?[1]

The Bishop has been and is gone.[2] He is certainly a most charming little Bishop—the most benignant little gentleman that ever put on lawn sleeves—yet stately too, and quite competent to check encroachments—His visit passed capitally well—and at its close, he expressed himself thoroughly gratified with all he had seen.

The inspector[3] has been also in the course of the past week—so that I have had a somewhat busy time of it—If you could have been at Haworth to share the pleasure of the company without being inconvenienced by the little bustle of preparation—I should have been <u>very</u> glad—but the house was a good deal put out of its way as you may suppose—All passed however orderly, quietly and well. Martha waited very nicely and I had a person to help her in the kitchen. Papa kept up too full as well as I expected—though I doubt whether he could have borne another day of it. My penalty came on in a strong headache and a bilious attack as soon as the Bishop was fairly gone. How thankful I was that it had politely waited his departure—I continue mighty stupid to-day—of course it is the reaction consequent on several days of extra exertion and excitement. It is very well to talk of receiving a Bishop without trouble, but you <u>must</u> prepare for him. We had the parsons[4] to supper as well as to tea. Mr. Nicholls demeaned himself not quite pleasantly—I thought he made no effort to struggle with his dejection but gave way to it in a manner to draw notice; the Bishop was obviously puzzled by it. Mr. N——also shewed temper once or twice in speaking to Papa. Martha was beginning to tell me of certain "flaysome"[5] looks also—but I desired not to hear of them. The fact is I shall be most thankful when he is well away—I pity him—but I don't like that dark gloom of his—He dogged me up the lane after the evening service in no pleasant manner—he stopped also in the passage after the Bishop and the other clergy were gone into the room—and it was because I drew away and went upstairs that he gave that look which filled Martha's soul with horror. She—it seems—meantime, was making it her business to watch him from the kitchen door—If Mr. N——be a good man at bottom—it is a sad thing that Nature has not given him the faculty to put goodness into a more attractive form—Into the bargain of all the rest he managed to get up a most pertinacious and needless dispute with the Inspector[6]—in listening to which all my old unfavourable impressions revived so strongly—I fear my countenance could not but shew them.

Dear Nell—I consider that on the whole it is a mercy you have been at home and not a[t] Norfolk during the late cold weather.

Love to all at Brookroyd
Yours faithfully
C Brontë

MS BPM Gr. E23.

1. See Letter 141 n. 1 and Letter 148.
2. Charles Thomas Longley (1794–1868), Bishop of Ripon 1836–56, Bishop of Durham 1856–60, Archbishop of York 1860–2, Archbishop of Canterbury 1862–8. At this period Haworth was in his diocese, and his visit would be pastoral, including meetings with the parochial clergy and an assessment of the church's provision for the parish.
3. All schools applying for school grants, such as the Church of England National Society School in Haworth, had to be inspected regularly by inspectors appointed by the Privy Council Committee on Education.
4. The local clergy would probably include J. B. Grant of Oxenhope and John Smith of Oakworth as well as Mr Nicholls. The Bishop detected the reason for Nicholls's disturbed state of mind and felt sympathy for him.
5. Fearsome, terrifying (dialect).
6. Mr Nicholls had some responsibility for the Haworth National School, and had greatly improved it; but he had written again to the Society for the Propagation of the Gospel on 23 Feb., and had been offered an interview in London. On 26 Feb. he wrote to say that he now had doubts about 'the desirableness of leaving the Country at present'.

145. *To George Smith, 26 March 1853*

Haworth.

My dear Sir

The "Mail" being now fairly gone out,[1] (at least I hope so) I venture to write to you.

I trust the negotiations to which you allude in your last, will be brought to an early and successful conclusion, and that their result will really be a division and consequent alleviation of labour.[2] That you had too much to do, too much to think about—nobody of course can know so well as yourself; therefore it might seem superfluous to dwell on the subject; and yet a looker-on could not but experience a painful prescience of ill sooner or later ensuing from such exertions if continued. That week of over-work which occurred when I was in London[3] was a thing not to be forgotten. Besides "cultivating the humanities"—be resolved to turn to account some part of your leisure in getting fresh air and exercise. When people think too much and sit too closely—the circulation loses its balance, forsakes the extremities and bears with too strong a current on the brain; I suppose exercise is the best means of counteracting such a state of things. Pardon me if I speak too much like a doctor.

You express surprise that Miss Martineau should apply to <u>you</u> for news of <u>me</u>. The fact is I have never written to her since a letter I received from her about eight weeks ago—just after she had read "Villette".[4] What is more—I do not know when I can bring myself to write again. The differences of feeling between Miss M. and myself are very strong and marked; very wide and irreconcilable. Besides I fear language does not convey to her apprehension the same meaning as to mine. In short she has hurt me a good deal, and at present it appears very plain to me that she and I had better not try to be close friends; my wish indeed is that she should quietly forget me. Sundry notions that she considers right and grand—strike me as entirely monstrous.[5] It is of no use telling her so: I don't want to quarrel with her, but I want to be let alone.

The sketch you enclose is indeed a gem; I suppose I may keep it? "Miss Eyre" is evidently trying to mesmerize "Pilot" by a stare of unique fixity, and, I fear I must add—stolidity. The embodiment of "Mr. Rochester" surpasses anticipation, and strikes panegyric dumb.

With regard to that momentous point—M. Paul's fate[6]—in case any one in future should request to be enlightened thereon—they may be told that it was designed that every reader should settle the catastrophe for himself, according to the quality of his disposition, the tender or remorseless impulse of his nature. Drowning and Matrimony are the fearful alternatives. The Merciful—like Miss Mulock, Mr. Williams, Lady Harriet St. Clair and Mr. Alexander Frazer[7]—will of course choose the former and milder doom—drown him to put him out of pain. The cruel-hearted will on the contrary pitilessly impale him on the second horn of the dilemma—marrying him without ruth or compunction to that—person—that—that—individual—"Lucy Snowe".

The "Lectures"[8] arrived safely; I have read them through twice. They must be studied to be appreciated. I thought well of them when I heard them delivered, but now I see their real power, and it is great.

The lecture on Swift[9] was new to me; I thought it almost matchless. Not that, by any means, I always agree with Mr. Thackeray's opinions, but his force, his penetration, his pithy simplicity, his eloquence—his manly sonorous eloquence command entire admiration. I deny, and must deny that Mr. Thackeray is very good or very amiable, but the Man is great.

Great but mistaken, full of errors—against his errors I protest—were it treason to do so.

I was present at the Fielding Lecture:[10] the hour spent in listening to it was a painful hour. That Thackeray was wrong in his way of treating Fielding's character and vices—my Conscience told me. After reading that lecture—I trebly feel that he was wrong—dangerously wrong. Had Thackeray owned a son grown or growing up:—a son brilliant but reckless—would he of [sic] spoken in that light way of courses that lead to disgrace and the grave?

He speaks of it all as if he theorized; as if he had never been called on in the course of his life to witness the actual consequences of such failings; as if he had never stood by and seen the issue—the final result of it all. I believe if only once the spectacle of a promising life blasted in the outset by wild ways—had passed close under his eyes—he never could have spoken with such levity of what led to its piteous destruction. Had I a brother yet living—I should tremble to let him read Thackeray's lecture on Fielding; I should hide it away from him. If, in spite of precaution, it fell into his hands—I should earnestly pray him not to be misled by the voice of the charmer—let him charm never so wisely.[11]

Not that for a moment—I would have had Thackeray to abuse Fielding, or Pharisaically to condemn his life; but I do most deeply grieve that it never entered into his heart sadly and nearly to feel the evil and the peril of such a career—that he might have dedicated some of his great strength to a potent warning against its adoption by any young man.

I believe temptation often assails the finest manly natures; as the pecking sparrow or destructive wasp attacks the sweetest and mellowest fruit—eschewing what is sour and crude. The true lover of his race ought to devote his vigour to guard and protect; he should sweep away every lure with a kind of rage at its treachery.

You will think this all far too serious I daresay; but the subject is serious, and one cannot help feeling upon it earnestly.

Believe me sincerely yours
C Brontë

MS BPM SG 81.

1. Smith, Elder provided postal facilities for mail to and from India, dispatching outward post to Marseilles, whence Thomas Waghorn organized its transport to Suez and then by the overland route to Bombay.

2. Smith was about to appoint a partner in the firm, Henry Samuel King (1817–78), formerly a bookseller in Brighton. The partnership lasted until the end of 1868.

3. CB had stayed with the Smiths in London from 5 Jan. until 2 Feb. 1853 in order to correct the proofs of *Villette*.

4. On 21 Jan. CB had written to Martineau, asking her to write frankly about her opinion of *Villette*. Martineau had praised some aspects of the novel, but had not liked 'the kind or the degree' of love, its prevalence in the book, or its effects on the action. CB was shocked and hurt; she had returned Martineau's letter, underlining her accusations and protesting against them, and she insisted that she understood the nature of true love: nobody should feel ashamed of an emotion which was essentially good and altruistic.

5. CB was especially disturbed by what she saw as atheism—the agnosticism expressed in Martineau's joint work with H. G. Atkinson, *Letters on the Laws of Man's Nature and Development* (London, 1851).

6. The fate of Paul Emanuel in *Villette*.

7. Dinah Maria Mulock, later Mrs. G. L. Craik, novelist (1826–87); William Smith Williams; Lady Harriet Elizabeth St Clair (d. 1867), daughter of the 3rd Earl of Rosslyn: both ladies had applied to Mr Williams 'for exact and authentic information' respecting the fate of M. Paul. (Referred to in a letter from CB to Williams of 23 Mar. 1853.) 'Alexander Fraser' was the name George Smith had used when he and CB, under the guise of 'Miss Fraser', had visited the phrenologist Dr J. P. Browne in late June 1851, and had received 'phrenological estimates' from him.

8. Thackeray's *Lectures on the English Humourists of the Eighteenth Century*, just published by Smith, Elder in one volume. CB had attended four of the lectures in London in 1851.

9. CB had missed this lecture on 22 May 1851. Thackeray admits that Swift is a great writer, but condemns him as a bully and coward who prostituted his talents for the sake of self-advancement. The moral of the 'Houyhnhnms' fable in *Gulliver's Travels* is damned as 'horrible, shameful, unmanly, blasphemous'.

10. A lecture on Hogarth, Smollett, and Fielding on 26 June 1851. Though Thackeray admits Fielding's weaknesses, his running into debt and readiness to borrow from friends, he has a genial tolerance for that liking for 'good wine . . . and good company' which led to the debts. CB's condemnation was fuelled by her agonizing recollection of the weaknesses and dissipation which contributed to Branwell's degradation and death.

11. A distortion of the psalmist's meaning in Psalm 58: 3–5.

146. *To Ellen Nussey, 6 April 1853*

Haworth.

Dear Ellen

I return Mrs. Upjohn's letter. She has indeed acted very strangely[1]—but it is evident to me that there is something very wrong either in herself, her husband, or her domestic arrangements or (what is perhaps most probable) in all three—and it may be that on the whole—provoking as this conclusion appears—it is the best for you that could well be arrived at. The grounds for expecting permanent good some time ago assumed a very unsubstantial appearance—the hope of present pleasure—I fear—would have turned out equally fallacious. Indeed I now feel little confidence in either comfort or credit ensuing from the connection in any shape.

My visit to Manchester[2] is for the present put off by Mr. Morgan[3] having written to say that since Papa will not go to Buckingham to see him he will come to Yorkshire to see Papa—when I don't yet know—and I trust in goodness he will not stay long—as Papa really cannot bear putting out of his way—I must wait however till the infliction is over.

You ask about Mr. N[icholls]. I hear he has got a curacy[4]—but do not yet know where—I trust the news is true. He & Papa never speak. He seems to pass a desolate life. He has allowed late circumstances so to act on him as to freeze up his manner and overcast his countenance not only to those immediately concerned but to everyone. He sits drearily in his rooms—If Mr. Cartman[5] or Mr. Grant or any other clergyman calls to see and as they think to cheer him—he scarcely speaks—I find he tells them nothing—seeks no confidant—rebuffs all attempts to penetrate his mind—I own I respect him for this—He still lets Flossy[6] go to his rooms and takes him to walk—He still goes over to see Mr. Sowden[7] sometimes—and poor fellow—that is all. He looks ill and miserable. I think and trust in Heaven he will be better as soon as he fairly gets away from Haworth. I pity him inexpressibly. We never meet nor speak—nor dare I look at him—silent pity is just all I can give him—and as he knows nothing about that—it does not comfort. He is now grown so gloomy and reserved—that nobody seems to like him—his fellow-curates shun trouble in that shape—the lower orders dislike it—Papa has a perfect antipathy to him—and he—I fear—to papa—Martha hates him—I think he might almost be <u>dying</u> and they would not speak a friendly word to or of him. How much of all this he deserves I can't tell—certainly he never was agreeable or amiable—and is less so now than ever—and alas! I do not know him well enough to be sure that there is truth and true affection—or only rancour and corroding disappointment at the bottom of his chagrin. In this state of things I must be and I am—<u>entirely passive</u>. <I know if I were near him> I may be losing the purest gem—and to me far the most precious—life can give—genuine attachment—or I may be escaping the yoke of a morose temper—In this doubt conscience will not suffer me to take one step in opposition to Papa's will—blended as that will is with the most bitter and unreasonable prejudices. So I just leave the matter where we must leave all important matters.

Remember me kindly to all at Brookroyd and believe me

Yours faithfully
C Brontë

MS BPM Gr. E24.

1. The arrangements for Ellen's visit to the Upjohns of Gorleston had been hampered by Mrs Upjohn's 'protractions and vacillations'. On 22 Mar. CB had written sympathetically to Ellen: 'It

is a trial of Job to be thus moved backward and forward by this most luckless of Mistresses and her tribe of reprobate servants.'

2. CB's visit to Mrs Gaskell's home, planned for March, did not take place until 21–8 Apr.
3. Mr Brontë's friend Revd William Morgan, BD, incumbent of Christ Church, Bradford 1815–51, who had moved to become the rector of Hulcott, Bucks. He admired CB's novels, and may have been the model for Revd Dr Thomas Boultby in *Shirley*.
4. At St Mary's church, Kirk Smeaton, six miles from Pontefract. The rector was Revd Thomas Cator (1790–1864).
5. Revd Dr. William Cartman of Skipton. See Letter 126 n. 1.
6. The spaniel which had formerly belonged to Anne Brontë.
7. Mr Nicholls's friend Revd Sutcliffe Sowden. See Letter 142 n. 2.

147. *To Ellen Nussey, 16 May 1853*

[Haworth]

Dear Ellen

Habituated by this time to Mrs. Upjohn's fluctuations—I received the news of this fresh put-off without the slightest Sentiment of wonder. Indeed I keep all my powers of surprise for the intelligence that you are safely arrived at Gorleston—and still more for the desired but very-moderately-expected tidings that you are happy there.

The east-winds about which you inquire have spared me wonderfully till to-day, when I feel somewhat sick physically, and not very blithe morally. I am not sure that the east winds are entirely to blame for this ailment—yesterday was a strange sort of day at church. It seems as if I were to be punished for my doubts about the nature and truth of poor Mr. N's regard. Having ventured on Whitsunday[1] to stay the sacrament—I got a lesson not to be repeated. He struggled—faltered—then lost command over himself—stood before my eyes and in the sight of all the communicants white, shaking, voiceless—Papa was not there—thank God! Joseph Redman[2] spoke some words to him—he made a great effort—but could only with difficulty whisper and falter through the service. I suppose he thought; this would be the last time; he goes either this week or the next. I heard the women sobbing round—and I could not quite check my own tears.

What had happened was reported to Papa either by Joseph Redman or John Brown[3]—it excited only anger—and such expressions as 'unmanly driveller'. Compassion or relenting is no more to be looked for than sap from firewood.

I never saw a battle more sternly fought with the feelings than Mr. N——fights with his—and when he yields momentarily—you are almost sickened by the sense of the strain upon him. However he is to go[4]—and I cannot speak to him or look at him or comfort him a whit—and I must submit. Providence is over all—that is the only consolation.

Yrs faithfully
C Brontë

MS Taylor Collection, Princeton.

1. 15 May.
2. Redman (?1796–1862) was appointed parish clerk by Mr Brontë in 1826. He was also the secretary to the local Board of Health from 1851.
3. The stonemason John Brown (1804–55) was the Haworth sexton.
4. Mr Nicholls left Haworth on 27 May to spend some time in the south of England before taking up his curacy in Kirk Smeaton.

148. *To Ellen Nussey, 27 May 1853*

Haworth

Dear Ellen

I was right glad to get your letter this morning and to find that you really were safely arrived at last. How strange it seems though that there should have been a sort of miscalculation up to the very last! I am afraid you would feel a little damped on your arrival to find Mrs. U[pjohn] from home.

However I <u>do</u> think it is well you are gone—the experiment was worth trying—and according to present appearances really promises very fairly. If tempers &c are only right—there seem to be many other appliances and means for enjoyment—I do not much like to hear of that supposed affection of the brain—if there <u>be</u> anything wrong there—it is to be feared that with time it will rather increase than diminish—however let us hope for the best. I trust Mr. U. may prove a pleasant well-informed companion.[1]

The biscuits came all right—but I believe you have sent about twice the quantity I ordered—you <u>must</u> tell me how much they cost dear Nell—or I shall never be able to ask you to render me a similar service again.[2]

I send by this post the Examiner and French paper. I suppose I had better suppress the Leader while you are at Gorleston. I don't think it would suit Mr. Upjohn.[3]

You will want to know about the leave-taking—the whole matter is but a painful subject but I must treat it briefly.

The testimonial[4] was presented in a public meeting. Mr. Fawcett[5] and Mr. Grant were there—Papa was not very well and I advised him to stay away which he did.

As to the last Sunday—it was a cruel struggle. Mr. N——ought not to have had to take any duty.[6]

He left Haworth this morning at 6 o'clock. Yesterday evening he called to render into Papa's hands the deeds of the National School—and to say good bye. They were busy cleaning—washing the paint &c. in the dining-room so he did not find me there. I would not go into the parlour to speak to him in Papa's presence. He went out thinking he was not to see me—And indeed till the very last moment—I thought it best not—But perceiving that he stayed long before going out at the gate—and remembering his long grief I took courage and went out trembling and miserable. I found him leaning again[st] the garden-door in a paroxysm of anguish—sobbing as women never sob. Of course I went straight to him. Very few words were interchanged—those few barely articulate: several things I should have liked to ask him were swept entirely from my memory. Poor fellow! but he wanted such hope and such encouragement as I <u>could</u> not give him. Still I trust he must know now tha[t] I am not cruelly blind and indifferent to his constancy and grief. For a few weeks he goes to the south of England—afterwards he takes a curacy somewhere in Yorkshire but I don't know where.

Papa has been far from strong lately—I dare not mention Mr. N's name to him—He speaks of him quietly and without opprobrium to others—but to me he is implacable on the matter.

However he is gone—gone—and there's an end of it. I see no chance of hearing a word about him in future—unless some stray shred of intelligence comes through Mr. Grant or some other second hand source. In all this it is not <u>I</u> who am to be pitied at all and of course nobody pities me—they all think in Haworth that I have disdainfully refu[sed] him &c.—if pity would do Mr. N——any good—he ought to have and I believe has it. They may abuse me, if they will—whether they do or not—I can't tell.

Write soon and say how your prospects proceed—I trust they will daily brighten—

Yrs. faithfully

C Brontë

MS BPM Gr. E 25.

1. Ellen reached Gorleston at some date between 19 and 26 May. For reasons which remain obscure, the situation in the Upjohns' household led to Ellen's leaving them less than a month after her arrival. From Gorleston she went to the home of her brother Revd Joshua Nussey (1798–1871), vicar of Oundle, Northants.
2. CB had asked Ellen to get '1lb of plain biscuits . . . and $\frac{1}{2}$ lb of invalid biscuits—and send them per rail' (to Ellen Nussey, 19 May 1853).
3. The *Examiner* (1808–81), originally a radical weekly, had reviewed *Jane Eyre* favourably on 27 Nov. 1847. CB never identifies the French papers lent to her by the Taylor family. The *Leader*, founded in Mar. 1850 by the radical freethinkers G. H. Lewes and Thornton Hunt, remained unconventional and outspoken in its criticism.
4. Mr Nicholls was presented with a handsome gold fob-watch, now in the BPM, with an inscription reading 'Presented to the Revd A. B. Nicholls B.A. by the teachers, scholars and congregation of St. Michael's Haworth Yorkshire May 25th 1853'.
5. Revd William Fawcett (1815–76), MA, vicar of Morton with Riddlesden, near Keighley, 1845–76, chaplain of St Mary, Warwick, 1875.
6. Mr Brontë's new assistant, Revd George Binks de Renzy, BA, did not take over Mr Nicholls's duties until 29 May. He was appointed stipendiary curate to the vicar of Bradford after he left Haworth in summer 1854.

149. *To Elizabeth Gaskell, 18 June 1853*

Haworth

My dear Mrs. Gaskell

I lay no flattering unction to my soul[1] that you <u>can</u> come, for I see most plainly that you <u>can't</u>.[2] It is best to face facts and make up one's mind to them; besides I would not have your visit to be breathless, hurried and wholly inconvenient to yourself; so I will suffer the prospect to recede; I will look forward to "purple Autumn".[3] You and the bright heath and ripe corn shall all be classed together in my expectations—nor am I entirely unhappy in the delay—it is only the protraction of a thought in which I find both a stay and a pleasure.

But neither—meantime—can <u>I</u> come to Manchester; my place is at home just now. I told you Papa had been indisposed—but I did not like to enter into particulars—the symptoms were such as—though not greatly affecting his general health—which is good—gave me heartfelt uneasiness—

One night—while I was ill[4]—I heard him pause on the staircase in coming up to bed—he delayed some time: I listened—he pronounced my name—I hastily rose—and threw something round me, I went to him—there he stood with his candle in his hand—strangely arrested—My dear Mrs. Gaskell—his sight had become suddenly extinct—he was in total darkness. Medical aid was immediately summoned—but nothing could be done—it was feared that a slight stroke of paralysis had occurred and had fallen on the optic nerve. I believed he would never see more; his own anguish was great.

Thank God! The light began to return to him next day—he said it seemed as if a thick curtain was gradually drawn up—he can now once more read a little and find his way, but the vision is impaired—his spirits often much depressed—and of course—you feel that I cannot leave him.

I shall now ask an old school-fellow to come and stay with me for a few days[5]—and I shall look forward with fond hope to you and Autumn. God bless you and yours and goodby'e

Yours affectionately,
C Brontë

MS untraced. Text: Horace Hird, *Bradford Remembrancer*, Bradford, 1972.

1. Cf. *Hamlet*, III. iv. 142.
2. Mrs Gaskell had originally planned to go to Haworth on 9 June. She eventually visited the Parsonage from 19 to 23 Sept. 1853.
3. Cf. James Thomson, *The Seasons*, 'Autumn', i. 674: 'Where Autumn basks, with fruit empurpled deep'.
4. From about 4 June CB had suffered from fever and a severe pain in the head which resisted all attempts to cure it until the middle of the month.
5. In a note of 23 June CB arranged for Ellen to arrive at Haworth on 30 June. The note is her last located letter to Ellen before their long estrangement. The length of Ellen's visit is not known, but

during it she discovered that Mr Nicholls's courtship was being taken seriously and not unkindly by CB. The friendship was not resumed until CB wrote to Ellen shortly before 21 Feb. 1854.

150. *To George Smith, 3 July 1853*

Haworth

My dear Sir

Nobody could read your last note without experiencing a sense of concern. Such a feeling indeed was inspired by a former letter of yours received in May;[1] but you then spoke of being better; the concluding lines were hopeful. Better—it seems—you are not; at least your spirits are not improved, and I write a line because whoever wishes you well can hardly rest satisfied without making some little effort to cheer you.[2]

Permit me to say that it is wise to anticipate better days with even sanguine confidence. I do not think your health is undermined; but your nerves have been so frequently overstrained with too much work that now they are relaxed, and both time and repose are absolutely necessary to the recovery of a healthy tone.

I suppose a very phlegmatic, heavy nature would never feel the evils from which you are now suffering; but where the nervous system is delicately constructed, and either from over-work or other causes has to undergo an amount of wear and tear beyond the average—the period of reaction necessarily arrives. What you now feel is always I believe felt at some time of life or other by those [who] have much to do or suffer—whose lot it is to bear heavy responsibilities, or undergo severe anxieties, and in whose moral constitution there is that degree of elaborateness which will result in sensitive feeling.

Notwithstanding your aged sensations—you are far too young to despair for a moment. You will be better: I know you will be better, but in care, in mental rest and moderate physical exercise lie the means of cure. Let no influence, let no exigency, if possible, impose on you the spur or the goad: I am sure you do not need these, nor ever did in your life; not even when you turn with distaste from the task of answering a friendly letter; and let me just say, though I say it not without pain, a correspondence which has not interest enough in itself to sustain life—ought to die.

Thank you for your kind inquiries about my Father: there is no change for the worse in his sight since I wrote last; rather—I think—a tendency to improvement. He says the sort of veil between him and the light appears thinner; his general health has however been lately a good deal affected—and desirable as it might appear in some points of view to adopt your suggestion with reference to seeking the best Medical advice—I fear that at present there would be a serious hazard in undertaking a long journey by rail. He must become stronger than he appears to be just now—less liable to sudden sickness and swimming in the head, before such a step could be thought of.

Your kind offer of attention in case he should ever come to Town merits and has my best acknowledgments. I know however that my Father's first and last thought would be to give trouble nowhere, and especially to infringe on no precious time. He would, of course take private lodgings.

As for me—I am and have been for some weeks—pretty much as usual again: That is to say—no object for solicitude whatever.

You do not mention whether your Mother and Sisters are well but I hope they are, and beg always to be kindly remembered to them. I hope too your partner—Mr. King[3]—will soon acquire a working faculty—and leave you some leisure and opportunity effectually to cultivate health.

Believe me
Sincerely yours
C Brontë

MS BPM SG 84.

1. A letter to which CB did not reply until 12 June, owing to her illness at that period.
2. Though Smith was depressed through overwork, he had found a hope of happiness in his personal life, for he first met his future wife, Elizabeth Blakeway (?1831–1914) at a ball at Clapham common 'on April 5th, 1853 . . . It was, with me, a clear case of "love at first sight"!' (quoted from Smith's 'Recollections' in Jenifer Glynn, *Prince of Publishers* (London, 1986), 77).
3. See Letter 145 n. 2.

151. *To Mrs. Elizabeth Smith, 21 November 1853*

Haworth.

My dear Mrs. Smith

I had not heard from your Son for a long time—and this Morning I had a note from him which though brief and not explicit seemed indicative of a good deal of uneasiness and disturbance of mind. The cover was edged and sealed with black but he does not say what relative he has lost. As it is not deep mourning I trust no harm has befallen any one very near to him, but I cannot resist writing to you for a word of explanation. What ails him? Do you feel uneasy about him, or do you think he will soon be better? If he is going to take any important step in life—as some of his expressions would seem to imply—is it one likely to conduce to his happiness and welfare?[1]

I hope your daughters and yourself are well. My Father's health was very infirm throughout the Summer, but I am thankful to say he is better now. Remember me kindly to your circle, and believe me

Sincerely yours
C Brontë

MS BPM SG 86.

1. A draft letter from Mrs Elizabeth Smith, George Smith's mother, responding to CB's questions, survives: the family were in mourning for her mother-in-law, who had died in September 'very old and sadly afflicted' so that the death was a merciful release. Mrs Smith hoped her son's health would continue to improve: 'He is quite well and very happy . . . he is thinking of taking a very important step in Life . . . with every prospect of happiness   I am very thankful and pleased about it—I am sure he will as soon as it is quite settled enter into all the particulars with you . . . He has been very much occupied till lately for his Partner at first rather increased than diminished his work. Now he is releiving [sic] him of the detail and George does not require to work so late.' In November George Smith proposed to Elizabeth Blakeway, whom he had first met in Apr. 1853. She gave no definite answer at first; but her father invited him to dine the following Sunday, and gave him permission to call every day. On the tenth day his proposal was accepted, and the marriage took place on 11 Feb. 1854.

152. To George Smith, 10 December 1853

[Haworth]

My dear Sir

In great happiness, as in great grief—words of sympathy should be few.[1] Accept my meed of congratulation—and believe me

Sincerely yours
C. Brontë

MS BPM SG 88.

1. George Smith recalled that he had written to inform CB of his engagement. He quoted this ungracious response, adding: 'She afterwards wrote more at length on the same subject when informing me of her engagement to Mr. Nicholls' ('Recollections', i. 118–19). See Letter 155.

153. To Ellen Nussey, 11 April 1854

Haworth.

My dear Ellen

Thank you for the collar—It is very pretty, and I <u>will</u> wear it for the sake of her who made and gave it.[1]

Mr. Nicholls came on Monday 3rd. and was here all last week.[2]

Matters have progressed thus since last July. He renewed his visit in Sept[embe]r—but then matters so fell out that I saw little of him. He continued to write. The correspondence pressed on my mind. I grew very miserable in keeping it from Papa. At last sheer pain made me gather courage to break it—I told all. It was very hard and rough work at the time—but the issue after a few days was that I obtained leave to continue the communication. Mr. N. came in Jan[uary] he was ten days in the neighbourhood. I saw much of him—I had stipulated with Papa for opportunity to become better acquainted—I had it and all I learnt inclined me to esteem and, if not love—at least affection—Still Papa was very—very hostile—bitterly unjust. I told Mr. Nicholls the great obstacles that lay in his way. He has persevered—The result of this his last visit is—that Papa's consent is gained—that his respect, I believe is won—for Mr. Nicholls has in all things proved himself disinterested and forbearing. He has shewn too that while his feelings are exquisitely keen—he can freely forgive. Certainly I must respect him—nor can I withold from him more than mere cool respect. In fact, dear Ellen, I am engaged.

Mr. Nicholls in the course of a few months will return to the curacy of Haworth. I stipulated that I would not leave Papa—and to Papa himself I proposed a plan of residence—which should maintain his seclusion and convenience uninvaded and in a pecuniary sense bring him gain instead of loss. What seemed at one time—impossible—is now arranged—and Papa begins really to take a pleasure in the prospect.

For myself—dear Ellen—while thankful to One who seems to have guided me through much difficulty, much and deep distress and perplexity of mind—I am still very calm—very—inexpectant. What I taste of happiness is of the soberest order. I trust to love my husband—I am grateful for his tender love to me—I believe him to be an affectionate—a conscientious—a high-principled man—and if with all this, I should yield to regrets—that fine talents, congenial tastes and thoughts are not added—it seems to me I should be most presumptuous and thankless.

Providence offers me this destiny. Doubtless then it is the best for me—Nor do I shrink from wishing those dear to me one not less happy.

It is possible that our marriage may take place in the course of the Summer. Mr. Nicholls wishes it to be in July. He spoke of you with great kindness and said he hoped you would be at our wedding. I said I thought of having no other bridesmaid. Did I say right? I mean the marriage to be literally as quiet as possible.[3]

Do not mention these things just yet. I mean to write to Miss Wooler shortly. Good-bye—There is a strange—half-sad feeling in making these announcements—The whole thing is something other than imagination paints it beforehand: cares—fears—come mixed inextricably with hopes. I trust yet to talk the matter over with you—

Often last week I wished for your presence and said so to Mr. Nicholls—Arthur—as I now call him—but he said it was the only time and place when he could not have wished to see you.

>   Good bye
>   Yours affectionately
>   C Brontë

MS Pforzheimer.

1. Margaret Wooler had acted as a peacemaker between CB and Ellen Nussey. Their estrangement since July 1853, caused by Ellen's hostility to the idea of Charlotte's possible marriage to Arthur Nicholls, had come to an end shortly before 21 Feb. 1854. By that date Ellen had received a letter from CB.
2. Mr Nicholls may have stayed with his friend J. B. Grant at Oxenhope vicarage.
3. As CB's marriage certificate shows, she and Arthur Nicholls were married in Haworth church on 29 June by licence, 'according to the Rites and Ceremonies of the Established church'. The marriage licence, dated 16 June 1854, permitted the marriage to take place 'without proclamation or publication of bans . . . provided there be no lets or impediment'. It was to be solemnized 'in the face of the Church between the hours of eight and twelve in the forenoon'.

154. To Ellen Nussey, 15 April 1854

[Haworth]
Saturday

My own dear Nell

I hope to see you somewhere about the 2nd. week in May.

The Manchester visit is still hanging over my head—I have deferred it and deferred it—but have finally promised to go about the beginning of next month—I shall only stay about 3 days then I spend 2 or 3 days at Hunsworth—then come to Brookroyd.^{1} The 3 visits must be compressed into the space of a fortnight if possible.

I suppose I shall have to go to Leeds.^{2} My purchases cannot be either expensive or extensive—You must just revolve in your head the bonnets and dresses—something that can be turned to decent use and worn after the wedding-day will be best—I think.

I wrote immediately to Miss Wooler and received a truly kind letter from her this morning. If you think she would like to come to the marriage I will not fail to ask her.

Papa's mind seems wholly changed about this matter; And he has said both to me and when I was not there—how much happier he feels since he allowed all to be settled. It is a wonderful relief for me to hear him treat the thing rationally—and quietly and amicably to talk over with him themes on which, once I dared not touch. He is rather anxious that things should get forward now—and takes quite an interest in the arrangement of preliminaries. His health improves daily, though this east-wind still keeps up a slight irritation in the throat and chest.

The feeling which had been disappointed in Papa—was <u>ambition</u>—paternal pride, ever a restless feeling—as we all know. Now that this unquiet spirit is exorcised—Justice, which was once quite forgotten—is once more listened to—and affection—I hope—resumes some power.

My hope is that in the end this arrangement will turn out more truly to Papa's advantage—than any other it was in my power to achieve. Mr. N. only in his last letter—refers touchingly to his earnest desire to prove his gratitude to Papa by offering support and consolation to his declining age. This will not be mere talk with him—he is no talker—no dealer in professions. Dear Nell—I will write no more at present. You can of course tell your Sister Ann & Mr. Clapham—the Healds[3] too if you judge proper—indeed I now leave the communication to you—I know you will not obtrude it where no interest would be taken.

Yours affectionately

C Brontë

MS BPM B.S. 95.2.

1. CB stayed with the Gaskells in Manchester 1–4 May, with Joseph and Amelia Taylor at Hunsworth 4–8 May, and with the Nusseys at Brookroyd, Birstall, 8–11 May.
2. CB may have done so; but she bought her wedding dress and some other garments for her trousseau in Halifax.
3. Revd William Margetson Heald (1803–75), vicar of Birstall, his wife Mary, née Carr, and his sister Harriet.

155. *To George Smith, 25 April 1854*

[Haworth]

My dear Sir

I thank you for your congratulations and good wishes; if these last are realized but in part—I shall be very thankful. It gave me also sincere pleasure to be assured of your own happiness[1]—though of that I never doubted—I have faith also in its permanent character—provided Mrs. George Smith is—what it pleases me to fancy her to be. You never told me any particulars about her—though I should have liked them much—but did not like to ask questions—knowing how much your mind and time would be engaged. What I have to say—is soon told.

The step in contemplation is no hasty one: on the gentleman's side, at least, it has been meditated for many years, and I hope that in at last acceding to it—I am acting right; it is what I earnestly wish to do. My future husband is a clergyman. He was for eight years my Father's curate. He left because the idea of this marriage was not entertained as he wished. His departure was regarded by the parish as a calamity—for he had devoted himself to his duties with no ordinary diligence. Various circumstances have led my Father to consent to his return, nor can I deny that my own feelings have been much impressed and changed by the nature and strength of the qualities brought out in the course of his long attachment. I fear I must accuse myself of having formerly done him less than justice. However he is to come back now. He has foregone many chances of preferment[2] to return to the obscure village of Haworth. I believe I do right

in marrying him. I mean to try to make him a good wife. There has been heavy anxiety—but I begin to hope all will end for the best.

My expectations, however, are very subdued—very different—I daresay—to what yours were before you were married. Care and Fear stand so close to Hope—I sometimes scarcely can see her for the Shadow they cast—And yet I am thankful too—and the doubtful Future must be left with Providence.

On one feature in the marriage I can dwell with unmingled satisfaction—with a certainty of being right. It takes nothing from the attention I owe to my Father. I am not to leave him—my future husband consents to come here—thus Papa secures by the step—a devoted and reliable assistant in his old age.

There can—of course—be no reason for witholding the intelligence from your Mother & Sisters; remember me kindly to them whenever you write.[3]

I hardly know in what form of greeting to include your wife's name—as I have never seen her—say to her whatever may seem to you most appropriate—and most expressive of good-will. I sometimes wonder how Mr. Williams is, and hope he is well. In the course of the year that is gone—Cornhill and London have receded a long way from me—the links of communication have waxed very frail and few. It must be so in this world. All things considered—I don't wish it otherwise.

Yours sincerely
C Brontë

MS BPM SG 90.

1. George Smith married Elizabeth Blakeway on 11 Feb. 1854. Beautiful and intelligent, she shared in Smith's plans, was a cheerful companion to him, and a gracious hostess to their guests.
2. Revd Dr. Walter Farquhar Hook of Leeds had enabled Monckton Milnes to offer Mr Nicholls a benefice in Lancashire or one in Scotland, but Nicholls refused both. In Nov. 1854 he also refused Sir James Kay-Shuttleworth's offer of the living of Habergham in Lancashire.
3. Perhaps Smith's mother and sisters were away on holiday, or had moved house. For four years after their marriage Smith and his wife lived at 112 Gloucester Terrace, London, the home he had shared with his mother and sisters,

156. To ?Elizabeth Gaskell,[1] ?early June 1854. [Fragment]

[Haworth]

... my conscience is satisfied—a sort of fawn-coloured silk—and a drab barège[2] with a little green spot in it—(I left them with the dress-maker at Halifax or you should have specimens—) Of the third—the wedding-dress—I wholly decline the responsibility. It must be charged upon a sort of friendly compulsion or over-persuasion. Nothing would satisfy some of my friends but white which I told you I would not wear. Accordingly they dressed me in white by way of trial—vowed away their consciences that nothing had ever suited me so well—and white I had to buy and did buy to my own amazement—but I took

23223223223232322323232

I got my dresses from Halifax[7] a day or two since—but have not had time yet to take the cord off the box—so I don't know what they are like. I had a most characteristic note from Amelia[8] lately. Has she written to you since she was at Tranby? Next time I write I hope to be able to give you clear information—and to tell you to come here without further delay. Good bye dear Nell.

Yours faithfully

C Brontë

I think 2 doz. Card envelopes will be sufficient. You had better order the same number of postage envelopes.

MS BPM Grolier E 28.

1. In Apr. 1853 Mr Nicholls had obtained a curacy at Kirk Smeaton, six miles south-east of Pontefract, Yorks., and had begun his duties there in Aug. 1853. See Letter 147 n. 4. He had previously complained of rheumatic pains.
2. Heavily deleted words follow in the manuscript. They may read in part 'He was very tiresome the last time—he was here— . . . would be the whole . . .'.
3. See Letter 153 n. 3. Mr Nicholls had wished the wedding to take place in July.
4. See Letter 148 n. 6.
5. CB had stayed with the Nusseys at Brookroyd 8–11 May.
6. Cards announcing the marriage and CB's married name, to be sent to friends and acquaintances who did not attend the ceremony. See Charlotte's wedding-card list (BPM Bon 126); CBL iii. 272–3.
7. See Letter 156, to ?Mrs Gaskell, early June 1854, fragment.
8. Amelia Taylor, née Ringrose. She had evidently revisited her former home at Tranby, near Hessle, Hull.

158. *To Margaret Wooler, 10 July 1854*

Banagher.[1]

My dear Miss Wooler

I know that in your kindness you will have thought of me some-times since we parted at Haworth—and I feel that it is time to give some account of myself.

We remained in Wales till Tuesday. If I had more leisure I would tell you my impressions of what I saw there—but I have at this moment six letters to answer and my friends are waiting for me to take a drive. I snatch a moment to devote to you and Ellen Nussey to whom you must kindly forward this note—as I long to let her know how I am getting on—and cannot write to her to-day or indeed this week.

Last Tuesday we crossed from Holyhead to Dublin—the weather was calm—the passage good. We spent two days in Dublin—drove over great part of the city—saw the College library, Museum, chapel &c.[2] and should have seen much more—had not my bad cold been a restraint upon us.

Three of Mr. Nicholls' relatives met us in Dublin—his brother and 2 cousins. The 1st (brother)[3] is manager of the Grand Canal from Dublin to Banagher—a sagacious well-informed and courteous man—his cousin[4] is a student of the University and has just gained 3 premiums. The other cousin was a pretty lady-like girl[5] with gentle English manners. They accompanied us last Friday down to Banagher—his Aunt—Mrs. Bell's[6] residence, where we now are.

I cannot help feeling singularly interested in all about the place. In this house Mr. Nicholls was brought up by his uncle Dr. Bell—It is very large and looks externally like a gentleman's country-seat—within most of the rooms are lofty and spacious and some—the drawing-room—dining-room &c. handsomely and commodiously furnished—The passages look desolate and bare—our bed-room, a great room on the ground-floor would have looked gloomy when we were shewn into it but for the turf-fire that was burning in the wide old chimney—. The male members of this family—such as I have seen seem thoroughly educated gentlemen. Mrs. Bell is like an English or Scotch Matron quiet, kind and well-bred—It seems she was brought up in London.

Both her daughters[7] are strikingly pretty in appearance—and their manners are very amiable and pleasing. I must say I like my new relations. My dear husband too appears in a new light here in his own country. More than once I have had deep pleasure in hearing his praises on all sides. Some of the old servants and followers of the family tell me I am a most fortunate person for that I have got one of the best gentlemen in the country. His Aunt too speaks of him with a mixture of affection and respect most gratifying to hear. I was not well when I came here—fatigue and excitement had nearly knocked me up—and my cough was become very bad—but Mrs. Bell has nursed me both with kindness and skill, and I am greatly better now.

I trust I feel thankful to God for having enabled me to make what seems a right choice—and I pray to be enabled to repay as I ought the affectionate devotion of a truthful, honourable, unboastful man.

Remember me kindly to all Mr. Carter's[8] family. When you write—tell me how you got home and how you are.

I received Ellen Nussey's last welcome letter—when she reads this she must write to me again. We go in a few days to Kilkee[9] a watering-place on the South-West Coast. The letters may be addressed—Mrs. Arthur Nicholls

Post-Office

Kilkee

County Clare

Ireland

Believe me my dear Miss Wooler

Always yours with affection & respect

C. B. Nicholls

MS Fitzwilliam.

1. Revd Sutcliffe Sowden of Hebden Bridge had officiated at CB's wedding on 29 June. Her bridesmaid was Ellen Nussey, and she was given away by Margaret Wooler, after Mr Brontë decided on the evening before the marriage that he would stop at home while the others went to church. The honeymoon began with a carriage-and-pair journey to Keighley station and a journey by train from there to North Wales, reaching the walled town of Conwy that evening. From there they travelled to Bangor, and, after an excursion through the splendid mountain scenery of Snowdonia, left Bangor on 4 July to cross Anglesey by rail to Holyhead. A smooth steamship passage to Dublin was followed by two days' sightseeing in the city, including a visit to Mr Nicholls's alma mater, Trinity College. A journey to Banagher, King's County (now Offaly), followed. They stayed at Cuba House, the home of Nicholls's aunt, Harriette Bell.

2. The library, completed in 1732, is a noble building in classical style. The ornate 'Venetian Gothic' museum was designed by Benjamin Woodward (1816–61). The chapel, designed by Sir William Chambers (1726–96) was completed in 1798.

3. Alan Nicholls (b. 1816). The Grand Canal links Dublin with Shannon Harbour, about two miles north of Banagher. It was an important means of transport, its vessels carrying passengers and heavy freight.

4. Joseph Samuel Bell, later LL.D. (1831–91), son of Dr Alan Bell and his wife Harriette; a brilliant student at Trinity College, Dublin. He eventually became rector of Kells and a canon of St Patrick's Cathedral, Dublin. He had won three prizes.

5. Mary Anna Bell (1830–1915), who had been known to Nicholls from her childhood, and who was to marry him on 26 Aug. 1864.

6. Mrs Bell, née Harriette Lucinda Adamson, widow of Revd Dr Alan Bell (1789–1839). He had been the headmaster of the Royal Free School at Cuba House, a substantial Georgian mansion, now demolished.

7. Mary Anna's sister was Harriet Lucinda (1833–1911), who later married her cousin John Evans Adamson (1821–69).

8. Revd Edward Nicholl Carter had married Margaret Wooler's sister Susan or Susanna, who had taught drawing at Roe Head school when CB was a pupil there.

9. MS reads 'Killkee'. See the next letter.

159. To Catherine Wooler,[1] 18 July 1854

Kilkee. Co. Clare, Ireland

My dear Miss Catherine

Your kind letter reached me in a wild and remote Spot—a little watering-place[2] on the South West Coast of Ireland.

Thank you for your kind wishes. I believe my dear husband to be a good man, and trust I have done right in marrying him. I hope too I shall be enabled always to feel grateful for the kindness and affection he shews me.

On the day of our marriage we went to Wales. The weather was not very favourable there—yet by making the most of opportunity we contrived to see some splendid Scenery—One drive indeed from Llanberis[3] to Beddgelert surpassed anything I remember of the English Lakes.

We afterwards took the packet[4] from Holyhead to Dublin. If I had time I would tell you what I saw in Dublin—but your kind letter reached me in a parcel with about a dozen more, and they are all to be answered—and my husband is just now sitting before me kindly stretching his patience to the utmost, but wishing me very much to have done writing, and put on my bonnet for a walk.

From Dublin we went to Banagher where Mr. Nicholls relations live—and spent a week amongst them. I was very much pleased—with all I saw—but I was also greatly surprised to find so much of English order and repose in the family habits and arrangements. I had heard a great deal about Irish negligence &c. I own that till I came to Kilkee—I saw little of it. Here at our Inn—splendidly designated "the West-End Hotel"—there is a good deal to carp at if one were in a carping humour—but we laugh instead of grumbling—for out of doors there is much indeed to compensate for any indoor short-comings; so magnificent an ocean—so bold and grand a coast—I never yet saw. My husband calls me—Give my love to all who care to have it and believe me dear Miss Catherine

Your old pupil
C.B. Nicholls.

MS Fitzwilliam.

1. Katherine Harriet Wooler (1796–1884), who is said to have taught French to Charlotte at her sister Margaret Wooler's school at Roe Head, Mirfield.
2. Kilkee is set picturesquely in a deeply curving bay on the Atlantic coast of County Clare. Charlotte and her husband stayed in the West End hotel at the southern end of the town.
3. The Llanberis Pass lies south of Bangor between the precipitous mountainsides of Snowdon and Glyder Vawr. The road to Beddgelert from the head of the Pass also follows a steep-sided river valley, passing lakes and dramatic waterfalls.
4. A paddle-steamer carrying mail as well as passengers.

160. *To Margaret Wooler, 22 August 1854*

Haworth.

My dear Miss Wooler

I found your letter with Many others awaiting me on my return home from Ireland. I thought to answer it immediately, but I reckoned without my host. Marriage certainly makes a difference in some things and amongst others the disposition and consumption of time. I really seem to have had scarcely a spare moment since that dim quiet June Morning when you, E. Nussey and myself all walked down to Haworth Church—. Not that I have been hurried or oppressed—but the fact is my time is not my own now; Somebody else wants a good portion of it—and says we must do so and so. We <u>do</u> 'so and so' accordingly, and it generally seems the right thing—only I sometimes wish that I could have written the letter as well as taken the walk.

We have had many callers too—from a distance—and latterly some little occupation in the way of preparing for a small village entertainment. Both Mr. Nicholls and myself wished much to make some response for the hearty welcome and general good-will shewn by the parishioners on his return; accordingly the Sunday and day-Scholars and Teachers—the church ringers, singers &c. to the number of 500 were asked to Tea and Supper in the school-room—. They seemed to enjoy it much, and it was very pleasant to see their happiness. One of the villagers in proposing my husband's health described him as "a consistent Christian and a kind gentleman." I own the words touched me—and I thought—(as I know you would have thought—had you been present)—that to merit and win such a character was better than to earn either Wealth or Fame or Power. I am disposed to echo that high but simple eulogium now. If I can do so with sincerity and conviction seven years—or even a year hence—I shall esteem myself a happy woman. Faultless my husband is not—faultless no human being is; but as you well know—I did not expect perfection.

My dear Father was not well when we returned from Ireland—I am however most thankful to say that he is better now—May God preserve him to us yet for some years! The wish for his continued life—together with a certain solicitude for his happiness and health seems—I scarcely know why—stronger in me now than before I was married. So far the understanding between Papa and Mr. Nicholls seems excellent—if it only continues thus I shall be truly grateful. Papa has taken no duty since we returned—and each time I see Mr. Nicholls put on gown or surplice—I feel comforted to think that this marriage has secured Papa good aid in his old age.

Are you at Richmond[1] alone my dear Miss Wooler? Are you well and enjoying some share of that happiness you so thoroughly deserve? I wonder when I shall see you again—now you are once at Richmond you will stay there a long time I fear. As I do not know your address I enclose this under cover to Mr. Carter,[2] answering his kind note at the same time. Yours always with true respect and warm affection

C. B. Nicholls.

MS Fitzwilliam.

1. Either the Surrey or the North Yorks. Richmond, both set in picturesque surroundings.
2. Miss Wooler's brother-in-law. Edward Nicholl Carter and his family had become Charlotte's friends when she was a governess with the Sidgwicks at Stonegappe in 1839. See Letter 7 n. 5.

161. To Ellen Nussey, [?20 October 1854]

[Haworth]
Friday Mor[nin]g.

Dear Nell

You would have been written to before now if I had not been very busy. Amelia, Joe, Tim & ?Anne[1] came on Tuesday Morning—Joe only stayed till the same evening—we had the others till yesterday. We got on with them better than I expected. Amelia seemed pleased and content and forgot her fancies for the time. She looked—not at all pretty—but stronger and in better health. Tim behaved capitally on the whole. She amused Papa very much—chattering away to him very funnily—his white hair took her fancy—She announced a decided preference for it over Arthur's black hair—and coolly advised the latter to "go to the barber, and get his whiskers cut off." Papa says she speaks as I did when I was a child—says the same odd unexpected things. Neither Arthur nor Papa liked A's look at first—but she improved on them—I think.

Arthur will go [to] the Consecration of Hep[tonst]all Church[2]—D.V. but I don't mean to accompany him—I hardly like coming in contact with all the Mrs. Parsons—if you were here I should go.

A[rthur] heard from Mr. Sowden[3] lately—an uninteresting letter—no remark on our vote of thanks &c. A brother of his is coming over. Arthur means to invite them both here for a night—I shall take stock of them and tell you what I think.

Arthur is impatient for his walk—I am obliged to scrawl hurriedly.

When I go to Brookroyd if I hear Mr. C—[4] or anybody else say anything to the disparagement of single women I shall go off like a bomb-shell—and as for you—but I won't prophecy,

Arthur has just been glancing over this note—He thinks I have written too freely about Amelia &c. Men don't seem to understand making letters a vehicle of communication—they always seem to think us incautious. I'm sure I don't think I have said anything rash—however you must <u>burn</u> it when read. Arthur says such letters as mine never ought to be kept—they are dangerous as lucifer matches—so be sure to follow a recommendation he has just given "fire them"—or "there will be no more." Such is his resolve. I can't help laughing—this seems to me so funny, Arthur however says he is quite "serious" and looks it, I assure you—he is bending over the desk with his eyes full of concern. I am now desired "to have done with it—" So with his kind regards and mine—Good-bye dear Ellen

Yours affectionately
CB: Nicholls

MS Pierpont Morgan, MA 2696.

1. Amelia and Joseph Taylor of Hunsworth with their 3-year-old daughter Emily Martha, affectionately named 'Tim'. Perhaps 'Anne' was a nursemaid.
2. The former church at Heptonstall, about nine miles south of Haworth, had been 'damaged beyond repair in a great gale in 1847. Bishop Longley of Ripon... was due to perform' the consecration ceremony of the new church on 26 Oct. See Margaret and Robert Cochrane, My Dear Boy: The Life of Arthur Bell Nicholls, B.A. (Beverley: Highgate Publications, 1999), 64–5.
3. Revd Sutcliffe Sowden, who had officiated at CB's wedding. His brother was Revd George Sowden (1822–99), curate of Houghton-le-Spring, Durham, 1853–61; vicar of Hebden Bridge,

Yorks., 1861–99. For his visit to Haworth Parsonage see George Sowden, *Recollections of the Brontës*, with supplementary material by Ian and Catherine Emberson (Todmorden: Angria Press, 2005).

4. Ellen Nussey's brother-in-law, Robert Clapham.

162. *To Ellen Nussey, 31 October 1854*

Haworth.

Dear Ellen

I wrote my last in a hurry, and as soon as I had sealed it—remembered that it contained no comment on what you had said about E. Cockhill's[1] illness—I was sorry—for the news had impressed me painfully and I wished much to know how she was getting on. Does the slight improvement continue? Her particular wish for champagne might imply a turn either for the better or the worse—I trust it was the former in her case—though I have known where such a caprice of the appetite has been of fatal augury. You will kindly remember to give me information respecting her when you write again.

The consecration of Heptonstall Church took place last Thursday—Arthur fully intended to go but a funeral kept him at home.[2] I regretted this as the day happened to be very fine. Mr. Grant went. He said there was a good attendance of the laity—but very few clergy—this was owing to the fact of invitations not having been sent.

I return Mrs. Hewitt's[3] letter—it bears that character of unassuming goodness and sense which marks all her letters—but I should fear her illness has perhaps been more serious than she allows. She is evidently not one to make much of her own ailments.

Dear Ellen—Arthur complains that you do not distinctly promise to burn my letters as you receive them. He says you must give him a plain pledge to that effect—or he will read every line I write and elect himself censor of our correspondence.

He says women are most rash in letter-writing—they think only of the trustworthiness of their immediate friend—and do not look to contingencies—a letter may fall into any hand. You must give the promise[4]—I believe—at least he says so, with his best regards—or else you will get such notes as he writes to Mr. Sowden—plain, brief statements of facts without the adornment of a single flourish—with no comment on the character or peculiarities of any human being—and if a phrase of sensibility or affection steals in—it seems to come on tiptoe—looking ashamed of itself—blushing 'pea-green' as he says—and holding both its shy hands before its face.

Write him out his promise on a separate slip of paper, in a legible hand—and
send it in your next. Papa I am glad to say continues pretty well—I hope your
Mother prospers—and that Ann is better—with love to all—Mr. C[lapham]
included—and Mercy if good—[5]

I am yours faithfully

C. B. Nicholls.

MS BPM B.S.96.5.

1. Thus in MS, for 'Cockill's'. Elizabeth Cockill (1813–54) was the daughter of Mrs Thomas Cockill,
   who was distantly related to the Nusseys. CB might have met Elizabeth at Oakwell Hall, Birstall,
   where the Cockill sisters and their mother ran a boarding-school. She died before 7 Nov. 1854.
2. Mr Nicholls had to take the burial service for Roger H. Greenwood, aged 1 year.
3. Ellen's friend Mary Hewitt, née Gorham, was pregnant. Her son Edward Swinton Hewitt was
   christened at East Marden, Sussex, on 31 Dec. 1854.
4. Ellen gave a conditional promise in response to this letter: 'My dear Mr Nicholls | As you seem
   to hold in great horror the ardentia verba [fervid words] of feminine epistles, I pledge myself to
   the destruction of Charlotte's epistles henceforth, if You, pledge yourself to no censorship in the
   matter communicated | Yours very truly | E. Nussey.'
5. The word is not clearly legible.

163. *To Ellen Nussey, 7 November 1854*

Haworth

Dear Ellen

The news of an acquaintance death always seems to come suddenly. I thought
ill of the previous accounts you had given of poor Elizabeth Cockhill—but still I
did not expect she would die so soon. And theirs is a family into which it is difficult
to realize the entrance of Death. They seemed so cheerful, active, sanguine. How
does Sarah[1] bear her loss? Will She not feel companionless—almost sisterless? I
should almost fear so—for a married Sister can hardly be to her like the other. I
should like to know too how Mrs. Cockhill is. Did she ever lose a child before?

Arthur thanks you for the promise.[2] He was out when I commenced this
letter, but he is just come in—on my asking him whether he would give the
pledge required in return—he says "yes we may now write any dangerous stuff
we please to each other—it is not "old friends" he mistrusts, but the chances of
war—the accidental passing of letters into hands and under eyes for which they
were never written."

All this seems mighty amusing to me: it is a man's mode of viewing correspondence—Men's letters are proverbially uninteresting and uncommunicative—I
never quite knew before why they made them so. They may be right in a sense.
Strange chances do fall out certainly. As to my own notes I never thought of
attaching importance to them, or considering their fate—till Arthur seemed to
reflect on both so seriously.

Mr. Sowden and his brother[3] were here yesterday—stayed all night and are but just gone. George Sowden is six or seven years the junior of Sutcliffe Sowden (the one you have seen) he looks very delicate and quiet—a good sincere man—I should think—Mr. S——asked after "Miss Nussey."

I will write again next week if all be well, to name a day for coming to see you—I am sure you want—or at least, ought to have a little rest before you are bothered with more company: but whenever I come—I suppose, dear Nell, under present circumstances—it will be a quiet visit and that I shall not need to bring more than a plain dress or two. Tell me this when you write.

Believe me
faithfully yours
C B Nicholls[4]

I intend to write to Miss Wooler shortly.

MS Pierpont Morgan, MA 2692.

1. Elizabeth's sister Sarah (1812–96). Another sister, Hannah (1810–93) was the wife of John Battye (1812–99), a local solicitor.
2. See the previous letter, n. 4. Clement Shorter's version of this sentence in *CB Circle* 494 and in his *The Brontës: Life and Letters* (1908), ii. 379, 'Arthur wishes you would burn my letters', was also used in Wise & Symington iv. 158. It was based on Ellen Nussey's deletion and revision of the text in surviving copies of the printed letters Horsfall Turner had produced for her. Ellen wished to conceal her own promise, and Nicholls's pledge in response to it.
3. Revd George Sowden. See Letter 161 n. 3. He recalled his 'extreme pleasure' in witnessing the 'complete happiness' of the Nichollses' married life. 'There was not a word of high-flown conversation. In fact, all was so simple.'
4. CB signed 'C Brontë', then corrected it to 'C B Nicholls'.

164. *To Ellen Nussey, 19 January 1855*

Haworth.

Dear Ellen

Since our return from Gawthorpe[1] we have had a Mr. Bell[2]—one of Arthur's cousins—staying with us—It was a great pleasure; I wish you could have seen him and made his acquaintance: a true gentleman by nature and cultivation is not after all an every-day thing.

As to the living of Habergham or Padiham—it appears the chance is doubtful at present for anybody—[3] The present incumbent[4] wishes to retract his resignation and declares his intention of appointing a curate for two years. I fear Mr. S[owden] hardly produced a favourable impression; a strong wish was again expressed that Arthur could come—but that is out of the question.

I very much wish to come to Brookroyd—and I hoped to be able to write with certainty and fix Wednesday the 31st. Jany. as the day—but the fact is I am not sure whether I shall be well enough to leave home. At present I should be a most tedious visitor. My health has been really very good ever since my return from Ireland till about ten days ago, when the stomach seemed quite suddenly to lose its tone—indigestion and continual faint sickness have been my portion ever since.[5] Don't conjecture—dear Nell—for it is too soon yet—though I certainly never before felt as I have done lately. But keep the matter wholly to yourself—for I can come to no decided opinion at present. I am rather mortified to lose my good looks and grow thin as I am doing—just when I thought of going to Brookroyd.

Poor Joe Taylor! I still hope he will get better[6]—but Amelia writes grievous though not always clear or consistent accounts.

Dear Ellen I want to see you and I hope I shall see you well.

My love to all   Yours faithfully
C B Nicholls

Thank Mr. Clapham for his hospitable wish—but it would be quite out of Arthur's power to stay more than one night or two—at the most.

MS BPM B.S. 99.

1. Sir James Kay-Shuttleworth had invited the Nichollses to stay with him at his home, Gawthorpe Hall, near Burnley, in Lancashire. They had planned to arrive on 9 Jan., and they stayed for two or three days. In her *Life* of CB, Mrs Gaskell wrote that Charlotte 'increased her lingering cold, by a long walk over damp ground in thin shoes'.
2. Revd James Adamson Bell (1826–91), second son of Mr Nicholls's uncle Dr Alan Bell; ordained 1852, MA Trinity College Dublin 1853. He had been the headmaster of the Royal Free School at Banagher since 1849, but was forced to leave it in Jan. 1867 following an enquiry by the Royal Commission on Endowed Schools into his retention of his stipend and rents despite his dismissal of all his pupils in 1865. See M. and R. Cochrane, *My Dear Boy*, 68, 116.
3. Sir James Kay-Shuttleworth had visited Haworth Parsonage on 11 Nov. 1854, and had made Mr Nicholls a formal offer of the living of Habergham, near Padiham, not far from Gawthorpe Hall. Nicholls had refused on the grounds that he was tied to Haworth during Mr Brontë's lifetime, and had suggested to Sutcliffe Sowden that he might wish to have the living.
4. Edward Arundel Verity, an eccentric and financially irresponsible clergyman.
5. The local doctor, Amos Ingham (1827–89) and the senior physician to the Bradford Infirmary, Dr William Macturk (1795–1872) were both called in to see CB, and in Mr Brontë's words, considered her illness 'symptomatic'—presumably of pregnancy.
6. Joseph Taylor suffered from a debilitating liver complaint and was frequently depressed. He died in Mar. 1857.

165. *To Laetitia Wheelwright,*[1] *15 February 1855*

[Haworth]

Dear Laetitia

A few lines of acknowledgment your letter <u>shall</u> have whether well or ill. At present I am confined to my bed with illness and have been so for 3 weeks. Up to this period since my marriage I have had excellent health—My Husband & I live at home with my Father—of course I could not leave <u>him</u>. He is pretty well—better than last summer. No kinder better husband than mine it seems to me can there be in the world. I do not want now for kind companionship in health and the tenderest nursing in sickness.

Deeply I sympathize in all you tell me about Dr. Wheelwright[2]—and in your excellent Mamma's anxiety—I trust he will not risk another operation. I cannot write more now for I am much reduced and very weak—

God bless you all!
Yours affectionately
C B Nicholls

MS King's School, Canterbury.

1. Laetitia Elizabeth Wheelwright (1828–1911), the daughter of Dr Thomas Wheelwright (1786–1861), who had moved from London to Brussels in July 1842. She and her sisters were day-boarders at the pensionnat Heger, where CB met them and began a friendship with Laetitia which continued when the family moved back to London. See Biographical Notes, p. xlv.
2. Dr Wheelwright had probably already had one operation for cataract.

166. To Ellen Nussey, c.21 February 1855

[Haworth]

My dear Ellen

I must write one line out of my weary bed. The news of Mercy's probable recovery came like a ray of joy to me. I am not going to talk about my sufferings[1] it would be useless and painful—I want to give you an assurance which I know will comfort you—and that is that I find in my husband the tenderest nurse, the kindest support—the best earthly comfort that ever woman had. His patience never fails and it is tried by sad days and broken nights. Write and tell me about Mrs. Hewitt's case, how long she was ill and in what way.[2]

Papa thank God! is better—Our poor old Tabby is <u>dead</u> and <u>buried</u>.[3] Give my truest love to Miss Wooler. May God comfort and help you.[4]

C B Nicholls

MS BPM B.S.101.

1. Mrs Gaskell was told that Charlotte's 'dreadful sickness increased and increased, till the very sight of food occasioned nausea. "A wren would have starved on what she ate during the last six weeks", says one. . . . Martha [Brown] tenderly waited on her mistress, and from time to time tried to cheer her with the thought of the baby that was coming. "I dare say I shall be glad sometime," she would say; "but I am so ill—so weary—" '. (Gaskell *Life*, ii ch. 13.)
2. A clear indication that Charlotte thought she was pregnant. Ellen's friend Mary Hewitt had been ill during her pregnancy in 1854, but had borne a son in or before December.
3. The Brontës' faithful servant Tabitha Aykroyd (b. ?1771) had died on 17 Feb. Mr. Nicholls took her burial service on 21 Feb.
4. Mercy Nussey recovered from her illness.

167. *To Amelia Taylor, née Ringrose, [?late February 1855][1]*

[Haworth]

Dear Amelia

Let me speak the plain truth—my sufferings are very great—my nights indescribable—sickness with scarce a reprieve—I strain until what I vomit is mixed with blood. Medicine I have quite discontinued—If you <u>can</u> send me anything that will do good—<u>do</u>.

As to my husband—my heart is knit to him[2]—he is so tender, so good, helpful, patient.

Poor Joe! long has he to suffer. May God soon send him, you, all of us health strength—comfort!

C. B. Nicholls

MS BPM B.S.103.

1. The letter is written in pencil, pitifully uneven and faint.
2. Cf. Colossians 2: 2, 'That their hearts might be comforted, being knit together in love.'

168. *To Ellen Nussey, [?early March 1855]*

[Haworth]

My dear Ellen

Thank you much for Mrs. Hewitt's sensible clear letter. Thank her too. In much her case was wonderfully like mine—but I am reduced to greater weakness—the skeleton emaciation is the same &c. &c. &c. I cannot talk—even to my dear patient constant Arthur I can say but few words at once.

These last two days I have been somewhat better—and have taken some beef-tea—spoonsful of wine & water—a mouthful of light pudding at different times—

Dear Ellen, I realize full well what you have gone through & will have to go through with poor Mercy—Oh may you continue to be supported and not sink! Sickness here has been terribly rife. Papa is well now. Kindest regards to Mr. & Mrs. C[lapham][1] your Mother, Mercy.

Write when you can.

Yours   C B Nicholls

MS BPM B.S.100.

1. The sudden death on 12 Mar. of Ellen's brother-in-law Robert Clapham shocked CB. Mr Nicholls wrote on 15 Mar. to assure Ellen and her family that they had 'all our sympathies in the awful & painful event'. He had broken the sad news to Charlotte 'as gently as I could but it was a great shock—She is much concerned both on your account, and that of poor Mrs. Clapham & also at the thought that she shall never see again one, whom she greatly respected.'

169. *The Revd A. B. Nicholls to Ellen Nussey, 31 March 1855*

Haworth

Dear Miss Nussey

Mr. Brontè's letter would prepare you for the sad intelligence I have to communicate[1]—Our dear Charlotte is no more—she died last night of Exhaustion.[2] For the last two or three weeks we had become very uneasy about her, but it was not until Sunday Evening that it became apparent that her sojourn with us was likely to be short—We intend to bury her on Wednesday morn[in]g—.

Believe me
Sincerely yours
A. B. Nicholls

MS BPM B.S. 247.2.

1. On 30 Mar. Mr Nicholls had been too distressed to write. Mr Brontë had written to tell Ellen that his 'Dear Daughter' was 'very ill and apparently on the verge of the grave— . . . the Doctors have no hope of her case, and fondly as we a long time, cherished hope, that hope is now gone.' CB died early in the morning of 31 Mar.
2. Dr Amos Ingham signed the death certificate, giving the cause of death as 'Phthisis'—wasting disease, a term most often used for the wasting accompanying tuberculosis, but in Charlotte's case probably caused by excessive sickness during pregnancy (hyperemesis gravidarum). The funeral service on 4 Apr. was taken by Mr Nicholls's friend, Revd Sutcliffe Sowden, and Charlotte was buried in the family vault within the church.

BIBLIOGRAPHY

Novels

Brontë, Anne, *Agnes Grey* (1847).
_____ *The Tenant of Wildfell Hall* (1848).
Brontë, Charlotte, *Jane Eyre* (1847).
_____ *Shirley* (1849).
_____ *Villette* (1853).
_____ *The Professor* (posthumously published, 1857).
Brontë, Emily, *Wuthering Heights* (1847).

All the above are published as World's Classics by Oxford University Press.

1. Poems

Brontë, Anne, *The Poems of Anne Brontë*, ed. Edward Chitham (London: Macmillan, 1979).
Brontë, Branwell, *The Poems of Patrick Branwell Brontë*, ed. Victor A. Neufeldt (New York: Garland, 1990).
Brontë, Charlotte, *The Poems of Charlotte Brontë*, ed. Victor A. Neufeldt (New York: Garland, 1985).
Brontë, Emily, *The Poems of Emily Brontë*, ed. Derek Roper with Edward Chitham (Oxford: Oxford University Press, 1995).

2. Early Writings

Brontë, Charlotte, *An Edition of the Early Writings of Charlotte Brontë*, ed. Christine Alexander, 3 vols. (Oxford: Basil Blackwell, 1987, 1991, 2004).

3. Biographies

Barker, Juliet, *The Brontës* (London: Weidenfeld & Nicolson, 1994).
Barnard, Robert, *Emily Brontë* (London: The British Library, 2000).
Gaskell, Elizabeth C., *The Life of Charlotte Brontë*, 1st edn. 2 vols. (London: Smith, Elder, 1857); ed. Angus Easson, World's Classics (Oxford: Oxford University Press, 1996).
Gérin, Winifred, *Anne Brontë: A Biography* (London: Allen Lane, 1959).
Lock, John, and Dixon, Canon W. T., *A Man of Sorrow: The Life, Letters and Times of the Revd. Patrick Brontë, 1777–1861* (London: Nelson, 1965).

4. *Letters*

Green, Dudley (ed.), *The Letters of the Reverend Patrick Brontë* (Stroud: Nonsuch, 2005)

Smith, Margaret (ed.), *The Letters of Charlotte Brontë, with a Selection of Letters by Family and Friends*, 3 vols. (Oxford: Clarendon Press, 1995, 2000, 2004).

Wise, T. J., and Symington, J. A. (eds.), *The Brontës: Their Lives, Friendships and Correspondence*, 4 vols. (Oxford: Basil Blackwell, 1932).

5. *Background and Context*

Alexander, Christine, and Smith, Margaret, *The Oxford Companion to the Brontës* (Oxford: Oxford University Press, 2003; paperback, 2006).

[Huxley, Leonard], *The House of Smith Elder* (London, printed for private circulation, 1923).

Ingham, Patricia, *The Brontës* (Oxford: Oxford University Press, 2006).

Miller, Lucasta, *The Brontë Myth* (London: Jonathan Cape, 2001).

INDEX

Selected Letters of Charlotte Brontë